PRAISE FOR T[...]

"What a masterpiece! Maslow 2.0—a must-r[...] what Maslow meant by self-transcendence. Part biography, part treatise, part how-to guide . . . I loved it!"

—Angela Duckworth, professor of psychology, University of Pennsylvania; CEO and founder of Character Lab; and *New York Times* bestselling author of *Grit*

"This is the book we've all been waiting for—nothing less than a breathtaking new psychology of humanity. Kaufman will show you how to live your life to the fullest, and in the service of others—all at the same time."

—Susan Cain, *New York Times* bestselling author of *Quiet*

"The concept of self-actualization and the transcendent values, which include justice, beauty, meaningfulness, and wholeness, provide a blueprint for a better world. This very well-written volume not only captures Maslow's work but infuses it with the spirit of inspiration. This book is a major advance in psychology."

—Aaron T. Beck, M.D., professor emeritus of psychiatry, University of Pennsylvania

"As a pioneer of humanistic psychology, Maslow is frequently referenced but rarely understood. Scott Barry Kaufman is here to change that. He does a first-rate job restoring the classic pyramid based on Maslow's own revisions and updating self-actualization in light of contemporary science."

—Adam Grant, *New York Times* bestselling author of *Originals* and *Give and Take*, and host of the *WorkLife* podcast

"In this book Kaufman studies the legacy of Abraham Maslow's life's work in humanistic psychology and expands on this with his own insights and studies. The book gives us a path to self-actualization, to becoming the best person we can possibly become. In the process we discover we do this connected to others and all reality."

—Sharon Salzberg, author of *Lovingkindness* and *Real Happiness*

"*Transcend* is rich, deep, and brilliant, a pleasure to read. Scott Barry Kaufman is the new generation's leading voice in humanistic psychology, a modern-day Abraham Maslow. Updating Maslow's hierarchy of needs with modern psychology research, *Transcend* will help readers embark upon a journey to the upper reaches of their potential."

—Emily Esfahani Smith, author of *The Power of Meaning*

"This splendid book is a twofer. It's a retelling of the life of Abraham Maslow woven through an insightful updating of Maslow's theory."

—Martin Seligman, director, Positive Psychology Center, University of Pennsylvania, and author of *The Hope Circuit*

"*Transcend* is a wonderful revival and update of a beloved classic psychological model, as well as a loving ode to its originator. A brilliant assemblage of our current understanding of psychological well-being."

—Mark Manson, *New York Times* bestselling author of *The Subtle Art of Not Giving a F*ck*

"Mastery in whatever field is an important goal to aspire to, but in these times, when people are experiencing depression and emptiness at an epidemic level, transcendence is an even more critical goal. Scott Barry Kaufman manages to integrate more than seventy-five years of research on the subject to show that the only way to fully self-actualize is, paradoxically, by getting outside of one's self. This is one of the best books on human potential I've ever read."

—Robert Greene, author of *The Laws of Human Nature*

"In this ambitious work, Scott Barry Kaufman not only excavates the unfinished elements of Maslow's famous hierarchy of needs, but updates and extends it with the latest science. *Transcend* is a compass for a life well lived."

—David Epstein, *New York Times* bestselling author of *Range*

"Scott Barry Kaufman is one of my favorite thinkers about the psychology of getting better and growing as a person."

—Ryan Holiday, *New York Times* bestselling author of *Stillness Is the Key*

"Both personal and universal, deep and engaging, easy to follow and mind-shifting, *Transcend* gives us a new understanding of Maslow's famous self-actualization model and shows us how we can all achieve the kind of life we aspire to."

—Lori Gottlieb, *New York Times* bestselling author of *Maybe You Should Talk to Someone*

"In an age focused on materialism and self-obsession, Kaufman boldly addresses the science of our deepest, most unanswered needs: connection, meaning, love, transcendence, and self-realization. A revolutionary book destined to become a classic."

—Emma Seppälä, Ph.D., author of *The Happiness Track*, and science director, Center for Compassion and Altruism Research and Education, Stanford University

"Many of the substantive issues humanistic psychology fought for in the middle part of the last century are now at the very core of modern psychology, regardless of your approach or orientation. It is especially timely to revisit the work of one of the greatest humanists of all time, Abraham Maslow, and to update his insights based on the half a century of data that have accumulated since his death. Scott Barry Kaufman has done just that in this wide-ranging and delightful book."

—Steven C. Hayes, codeveloper of acceptance and commitment therapy and author of *A Liberated Mind*

"In this wise, creative, surprising, and exceedingly humane book, Scott Barry Kaufman provides a hierarchy of needs for the modern world, blending the insights of humanistic psychology with the finding of cutting-edge science."

—Paul Bloom, Brooks and Suzanne Ragen Professor of Psychology, Yale University, and author of *Against Empathy*

"Scott Barry Kaufman revivifies the wisdom of humanistic psychology for a new millennium. He does it with evidence and discernment, without turning the world into a nail."

—Steven Pinker, professor of psychology, Harvard University, and
New York Times bestselling author of *Enlightenment Now*

"Synthesizing Maslow's wisdom with modern research, Scott Barry Kaufman takes our understanding of the good life to higher planes. Maslow would have been proud!"

—Tal Ben-Shahar, cofounder of the Happiness Studies Academy

"There are many books about happiness. There are fewer about living a good life—not a fixed state of being, but an ongoing process that encourages creativity, challenge, and meaning. *Transcend* is such a book: original, grounded in modern research, and thoroughly practical."

—Sean Carroll, author of *Something Deeply Hidden: Quantum Worlds
and the Emergence of Spacetime*

"Drawing on a vast range of source material, Kaufman has singlehandedly helped to reposition Maslow and humanistic psychology from the periphery to the center of mainstream psychological inquiry. A scientifically grounded, splendidly accessible road map for the spiritual and philosophical uplift of our field."

—Kirk Schneider, Ph.D., author of *The Spirituality of Awe*

"Reading *Transcend* would bring a broad smile to Maslow's face and maybe even a shout of 'Someone finally gets it.' Often he spoke in our seminars at Brandeis of his frustration that so few understood his work. Scott Barry Kaufman not only shows a rare and profound understanding of Maslow's ideas but, for the first time in fifty years, expands our knowledge of Maslow's core concepts. This book is worthy of being in every thinking person's library and being read more than once."

—L. Ari Kopolow, M.D., clinical assistant professor of psychiatry, George Washington University; president emeritus, Suburban Maryland Psychiatric Society; and former student of Abraham Maslow

"This is one of the most comprehensive books on what psychology has to say about the path to personal fulfillment. I walked away with a new, sophisticated lens for viewing the motivations behind my actions. I suspect readers will be equally enlightened."

—Todd B. Kashdan, Ph.D., professor of psychology, George Mason University, and author of *The Upside of Your Dark Side*

"With wisdom from many fields, and paths and principles to live, this book will enable you to rise to the greatest challenge of our times: to arrive at a new sense of ourselves that is kinder, more inclusive, and oriented to creating a better world. This is a profoundly important and timely book."

—Dacher Keltner, professor of psychology, University of California, Berkeley

TRANSCEND

THE NEW SCIENCE OF
SELF-ACTUALIZATION

Scott Barry Kaufman, Ph.D.

A TarcherPerigee Book

tarcherperigee

An imprint of Penguin Random House LLC
penguinrandomhouse.com

First trade paperback edition 2021

Sailboat illustrations by Andy Ogden.

Illustrations on pages 15 and 18 adapted from *Handbook of Personality*, third edition, Oliver P. John, Richard W. Robins, and Lawrence A. Pervin, editors. Copyright © 2010 The Guilford Press. Reprinted with permission of The Guilford Press.

Motivational Quality (MQ) Continuum adapted from C. Scott Rigby and Richard M. Ryan, "Self-Determination Theory in Human Resource Development: New Directions and Practical Considerations," *Advances in Developing Human Resources, 20*(2) (May 2018), 133–147, doi:10.1177/1523422318756954. Reprinted with permission of Sage Publications.

Ikigai adapted from Helgaknut | Dreamstime.com.

Unitary Continuum illustrated by Sacha D. Brown.

Abraham Maslow papers and "Axioms" from the Drs. Nicholas and Dorothy Cummings Center for the History of Psychology, The University of Akron.

The VIA Survey of Character Strengths (VIA Strengths & Their Opposites, Absences, Excesses), in Martin E. P. Seligman (2015), Chris Peterson's unfinished masterwork: The real mental illnesses, *The Journal of Positive Psychology, 10*: 3–6, is reprinted with permission of the publisher, Taylor & Francis Ltd., http://www.tandfonline.com, doi: 10.1080/17439760.2014.888582.

TarcherPerigee with tp colophon is a registered trademark of Penguin Random House LLC.

Library of Congress Cataloging-in-Publication Data

Names: Kaufman, Scott Barry, author.
Title: Transcend: the new science of self-actualization / Scott Barry Kaufman.
Description: New York: TarcherPerigee, 2020. | Includes bibliographical references and index.
Identifiers: LCCN 2019055447 (print) | LCCN 2019055448 (ebook) |
ISBN 9780143131205 (hardcover) | ISBN 9781524704988 (ebook)
Subjects: LCSH: Self-actualization (Psychology) | Self-esteem.
Classification: LCC BF637.S4 K395 2020 (print) | LCC BF637.S4 (ebook) | DDC 158/.9—dc23
LC record available at https://lccn.loc.gov/2019055447
LC ebook record available at https://lccn.loc.gov/2019055448

ISBN (paperback) 9780143131212

Printed in the United States of America
6th Printing

Book design by Renato Stanisic

This book is dedicated to Abraham Harold Maslow,
a dear friend I've never met.

Contents

A Note on Pronoun Usage xi

Preface xiii

Introduction: A New Hierarchy of Needs xxiii

PART I
Security

Prelude 3

Chapter 1
Safety 7

Chapter 2
Connection 35

Chapter 3
Self-Esteem 54

PART II
Growth

Prelude 83

Chapter 4
Exploration 91

Chapter 5

Love 118

Chapter 6

Purpose 149

PART III

Healthy Transcendence

Prelude 189

Chapter 7

Peak Experiences 193

Chapter 8

Theory Z: Toward the Farther Reaches of Human Nature 217

Live More in the B-Realm 245

Afterword: "Wonderful Possibilities and Inscrutable
Depths," Reprised 249

Acknowledgments 253

Appendix I: Seven Principles for Becoming a Whole Person 257

Appendix II: Growth Challenges 279

Notes 310

Index 380

A Note on Pronoun Usage

During the course of writing this book, I consulted a number of views on whether it would be appropriate to make all quotes gender-neutral throughout. My initial thinking about the matter was that since this is a book about our common humanity, the heavily gendered language of the founding humanistic psychologists seemed antithetical to that goal. However, upon further reflection, I decided to keep all quotes in their original form. For one, I wanted to maintain the integrity of the original writings and did not want to inadvertently change their intended meaning in unexpected ways. Also, I believe that hiding or whitewashing instances of sexism of the past isn't conducive to transcending sexism in the future. With that said, I believe the gendered quotes merely reflect the context and meaning of the word "man" in their time, which was universally understood as meaning all of humankind. Quotes aside, considering the strides we are making toward equality in this generation, I take responsibility for using more inclusive language whenever I can, and I hope this book reflects that intention. In essence, I hope everyone reading this book feels a sense of belonging, unconditional positive regard, and a sense of common humanity.

Preface

On June 8, 1970, a warm summer day in Menlo Park, California, Abraham Maslow was furiously writing in his notebook. His mind was full of so many theories and ideas about the higher reaches of human nature, including a theory he had been developing for the past few years: Theory Z. His wife, Bertha, lounged a few steps away by the pool at their home. Glancing at the time on his stopwatch, Maslow begrudgingly realized it was time to do his daily exercise. He was under strict doctor's orders to engage in light exercise to help rebuild his heart. Ever since a heart attack in December 1967, he had experienced frequent chest pains, constantly reminding him of his mortality. He canceled all speaking engagements and even declined to give a prestigious presidential address at the American Psychological Association.

Most people are familiar with Maslow's "hierarchy of needs," with self-actualization depicted at the top of a pyramid. Chances are, you learned about it in your introduction to psychology course in college or saw it diagrammed on Facebook.

As it's typically presented in psychology textbooks, humans are motivated by increasingly "higher" levels of needs. The basic needs—physical health, safety, belonging, and esteem—must be satisfied to a certain degree before we can fully self-actualize, becoming all that we are uniquely capable of becoming.

Some modern-day writers have interpreted Maslow's notion of self-actualization as individualistic and selfish.[1] However, a deeper look at Maslow's published and unpublished writings tells a very different story. In an unpublished essay from 1966 called "Critique of Self-Actualization

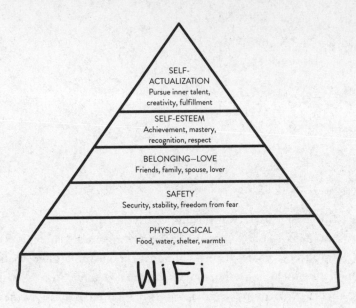

No, not *that* one.

Theory," Maslow wrote: "It must be stated that self-actualization is not enough. Personal salvation and what is good for the person alone cannot be really understood in isolation. . . . The good of other people must be invoked, as well as the good for oneself. . . . It is quite clear that a purely intrapsychic, individualistic psychology, without reference to other people and social conditions, is not adequate."[2]

During Maslow's later years, he became increasingly convinced that healthy self-realization is actually a *bridge* to transcendence. Many of the individuals he selected as self-actualizing people experienced frequent moments of transcendence in which awareness was expanded beyond the self, and many of them were motivated by higher values. At the same time, Maslow observed that these individuals had a deep sense of who they were and what they wanted to contribute to the world.

This created a deep paradox for Maslow: How could so many of his self-actualizing individuals simultaneously have such a strong identity and actualization of their potential, yet also be so *selfless*? In a 1961 paper, Maslow observed that self-actualization seems to be a "transitional goal, a rite of passage, a step along the path to the transcendence of identity. This is like saying its function is to erase itself."[3]

Maslow believed that striving toward self-actualization—by developing a strong sense of self and having one's basic needs met—was a crucial step along this path. As he wrote in his 1962 book *Toward a Psychology of Being*: "Self-actualization . . . paradoxically makes more possible the transcendence of self, and of self-consciousness and of selfishness."[4] Maslow observed that self-actualization makes it *easier* to merge as a part of a larger whole. Maslow's lectures, unpublished essays, and private personal journal entries make clear that he became preoccupied with this paradox of transcendence in the last few years of his life.

On September 14, 1967, Maslow delivered a riveting lecture at the San Francisco Unitarian Church titled "The Farther Reaches of Human Nature."[5] Those who were in attendance remarked that he looked frail and weak as he walked down the aisle to reach the podium at the front of the room. However, once he started speaking, he immediately lit up the room. "It is increasingly clear that a philosophical revolution is underway," he began. "A comprehensive system is swiftly developing like a fruit tree beginning to bear fruit on every branch. Every field of science and human endeavor is being affected."

Referring to the "Humanistic Revolution," Maslow explained that humanistic psychology is beginning to unearth the mysteries of "real human experiences, needs, goals, and values." This includes our "higher needs," which are also part of the human essence, and include the need for love, for friendship, for dignity, for self-respect, for individuality, and for self-fulfillment. After pausing for a moment, he took a bold next step:

> If, however, these needs are fulfilled, a different picture emerges. . . .
> The fully developed (and very fortunate) human being working under
> the best conditions tends to be motivated by values which transcend his
> self. They are not selfish anymore in the old sense of that term. Beauty
> is not within one's skin nor is justice or order. One can hardly class
> these desires as selfish in the sense that my desire for food might be. My
> satisfaction with achieving or allowing justice is not within my own

skin; it does not lie along my arteries. It is equally outside and inside: therefore, it has transcended the geographical limitations of the self.[6]

Maslow was working with great urgency on this idea. Just a few months after this speech, however, he suffered a coronary heart attack, revealing the source of his frailty during his lecture. He survived, but he said he suddenly felt less urgency. This confused him because it seemed to contradict his original theory, in which he argued that physical survival is the most important human need. In a journal entry dated March 28, 1970, he wrote:

> That's weird—that I should be enabled to perceive, accept, & *enjoy* the eternity & preciousness of the non-me world just because I became aware of my own mortality. The "being able to enjoy" is puzzling.[7]

Instead of falling all the way down to the bottom of his hierarchy, the awareness of his mortality actually *heightened* his own personal experience of transcendence. Noting a significant shift in values, Maslow observed: "The dominance hierarchy, the competitiveness and glory, certainly become foolish. There is certainly a shifting of values about what's basic and what's not basic, what's important and what's not important. I think if it were possible for us to die and be resurrected, it might then be possible for more people to have this post-mortem life."[8]

In his last major public seminar just a few months prior to his death, Maslow elaborated: "It's quite clear that we are always suffering from this cloud that hangs over us, the fear of death. If you can transcend the fear of death, which is possible—if I could now assure you of a dignified death instead of an undignified one, of a gracious, reconciled, philosophical death . . . your life today, at this moment, would change. And the rest of your life would change. Every moment would change. I think we can teach this transcending of the ego."[9]

During the last few years of his life, Maslow was working on a series of exercises to transcend the ego and live more regularly in the "B-realm"—the realm of "pure Being." He was also working on a comprehensive psychology and philosophy of human nature and society. In a journal entry dated December 26, 1967, just as he was leaving the hospital after his heart attack, Maslow wrote:

> New worries about the journals. What to do with them? The way I feel now, I just don't feel up to writing all the things I feel I ought to, the world needs, my duties. Wouldn't *mind* dying as a result, but I just don't have the stamina to *do* them. So the thought is save it all in little memos in these journals & the right person to come will know what I mean & why it *must* be done.[10]

On that warm, sunny day in Menlo Park, on June 8, 1970, Maslow put down his notepad, and with great frustration, he got up to do his daily exercise. He did not want to leave his work, even for a second. As he slowly started to jog, his wife, Bertha, wondered why he seemed to be moving in such an odd way.[11] Just as she was about to ask whether he was all right, Maslow collapsed. By the time she rushed to his side, Maslow was dead at the age of sixty-two, with so much of his work left unrealized.

ABOUT THIS BOOK

Maslow is destined, in my view, to be rediscovered many times before the richness of his thought is fully assimilated.

—Irvin D. Yalom, *Existential Psychotherapy* (1980)

The typical textbook version of Maslow's hierarchy of needs is seriously inaccurate as a reflection of Maslow's later formulation of theory. . . . The time has come to rewrite the textbooks.

—Mark E. Koltko-Rivera, "Rediscovering the Later Version of Maslow's Hierarchy of Needs" (2006)

When I discovered Maslow's later writings, sprinkled throughout a collection of unpublished essays, journal entries, personal correspondences, and lectures, I immediately felt a deep resonance with his thinking and vision, and deep admiration and affection for his life and work.

After listening to one particular lecture of Maslow's, I now even count him as a friend. One evening, while sitting on my bed listening to a series of public lectures he gave at the Esalen Institute in 1969, I was struck by his answer to a question from an audience member: "How do you define the word 'friendship'?"[12] Maslow began by defining a friend as someone who is truly "need-gratifying" and whose needs you want to gratify in return. He then defined the friendship of lovers as one where each other's needs melt into one, as the partner's needs become your needs.

But it's what Maslow said next that really got to me: "At a higher level . . . then something else happens that it's possible for me to feel very friendly, as I do, to count among my friends Abraham Lincoln, Socrates . . . Spinoza, I have great affection for Spinoza, great respect. At another level, corresponding to love or admiration or respect for the being of the other person. . . . It could be said that I have love for William James, which I do. I am very fond of William James. It happens sometimes, I talk about him in such an affectionate way, that people ask me, 'Did you know him?' [To which I reply,] 'Yes.' [Audience laughs.] 'Which [of course] I couldn't have.'"

My career as a psychologist—and my personal approach to life—has been profoundly shaped by Maslow's thinking and by the thinking of an entire generation of humanistic thinkers from the 1930s to the late 1960s, including Alfred Adler, Charlotte Bühler, Viktor Frankl, Erich Fromm, Karen Horney, Rollo May, and Carl Rogers. Their combined wisdom about essential human concerns—security, commitment, love, growth, meaning, authenticity, freedom, responsibility, justice, courage, creativity, and spirituality—is just as relevant today, if not more so. We live in times of increasing polarization, selfish concerns, and individualistic pursuits of power.[13]

Humanistic psychology sings to my own deepest being and resonates with my belief that to help people reach their full potential, we need to take into account the *whole person*. I have spent the past twenty years studying all kinds of minds,[14] from those who struggle with learning differences such as autism, dyslexia, ADHD, and generalized anxiety but who nonetheless have substantial talents, passions, and creativity; to prodigies with the normal social interests and playfulness of children but who also have an intense rage to master in a specific domain; to savants who have extraordinary dysfunction (e.g., have difficulty speaking) coupled with incredible skills (e.g., painting, playing the piano); to intellectually precocious youth who often feel isolated and awkward in school but who are ready and eager to master material many grade levels ahead of their peers; to adults with extremely high levels of narcissism who, though impeded by their intense self-absorption, have many other facets of themselves that want to be actualized.[15]

In my career it has become clear that the more we have limiting notions of potential that are dictated by others (schoolteachers, parents, managers, etc.), the more blind we become to the full potential of each and every unique individual and their own unique path to self-actualization and transcendence. My research has convinced me that we all have extraordinary creative, humanitarian, and spiritual possibilities but are often alienated from them because we are so focused on a very narrow slice of who we are. As a result, we aren't fulfilling our full potential. We spend so much time looking *outward* for validation that we don't develop the incredible strengths that already lie *within*, and we rarely take the time to fulfill our deepest needs in the most growth-oriented and integrated fashion.

Indeed, so many people today are striving for "transcendence" without a healthy integration of their other needs—to the detriment of their full potential. This ranges from people who expect a mindfulness retreat or yoga class to be a panacea for their traumas and deep insecurities, to spiritual "gurus" abusing their positions of power, to the many instances of vulnerable people (especially vulnerable young people) seeking unhealthy outlets for transcendence, such as violent extremism, cults, and gangs.

We also see this at play among the many divisions we see in the world today. While there is a yearning to be part of a larger political or religious ideology, the realization of this yearning is often built on hate and hostility for the "other," rather than on pride and deep commitment for a cause that can better humanity. In essence, there is a lot of pseudo-transcendence going on, resting on a "very shaky foundation."[16]

I have written this book to reinvigorate the wise, profound, and essentially human insights of humanistic psychology with the latest scientific findings from a wide range of fields—including positive psychology, social psychology, evolutionary psychology, clinical psychology, developmental psychology, personality psychology, organizational psychology, sociology, cybernetics, and neuroscience. The integration of a wide variety of perspectives is necessary for a more complete understanding of the full depths of human potential, as too much focus on a single perspective runs the risk of giving a distorted view of human nature. As Maslow said, "I suppose it is tempting, if the only tool you have is a hammer, to treat everything as if it were a nail."[17]

In this book, I will attempt to flesh out Maslow's outlines on the highest reaches of humanity, unravel the mysteries of his later writings, and integrate the corpus of ideas put forward in the humanistic psychology era with the wealth of scientific findings that have accumulated since then on the higher reaches of human nature, including my own research on intelligence, creativity, personality, and well-being. Throughout this book, I'll highlight the human potential for truth seeking, beauty, connection, exploration, love, flow, creativity, purpose, gratitude, awe, and other transcendent experiences that are deeply embedded in the fabric of human nature. I will also help you recognize and reflect on your most *unmet* needs, so that you can make concrete changes in your life to come closer to wholeness and transcendence in your daily life.

While this book is about our higher possibilities, I wholeheartedly believe that the best way to move toward greater growth and transcendence is not by ignoring the inevitability of human suffering but by *integrating everything that is within you*. This requires penetrating the depths of your being with piercing awareness with the intent of experiencing the full richness of human existence. This is very much in line with Maslow's call for a "Being-Psychology," which incorporates a full understanding of human needs that transcends the "psychopathology of the average" but also "incorporate[s] all its findings in a more inclusive and comprehensive structure which includes both the sick and the healthy, both deficiency, Becoming and Being."[18]

Too many people today are feeling deeply unfulfilled in our chaotic and divided world, which encourages the pursuit of money, power, greatness, even happiness, as the pinnacles of humanity. Yet despite climbing the status hierarchy and achieving monetary feelings of success, or even experiencing momentary feelings of happiness, we are still left feeling deeply unsatisfied, yearning for deeper connections with others and with our own fragmented selves. The social psychologist and humanistic philosopher Erich Fromm was quite right that there is an art of being.[19] But now there is also a *science* of being.

This book will present an update on Maslow's hierarchy of needs that is grounded in the latest science and provides a useful framework for making sense of your patterns of behavior and how your current way of being may be hindering your growth and transcendence. The aim is to help you boldly and honestly face who you are head on, so that you can become the person you really want to become. You'll find insights you can put into action in your own life. In the appendices I've presented even more practical exercises and ideas. And to deepen your quest further, go to *self actualizationtests.com* for online tests to help you gain deeper insight into your personality patterns so that you can help realize the best version of yourself.

Throughout the book, I hope to show you greater possibilities for yourself and the human species than you ever realized was possible. It turns out that self-actualization is only part of the journey; I'll help take you all the way.

Introduction:
A New Hierarchy of Needs

There is now emerging over the horizon a new conception of human sickness and of human health, a psychology that I find so thrilling and so full of wonderful possibilities.

—Abraham Maslow, *Toward a Psychology of Being* (1962)

Through his research on self-actualizing people, Maslow discovered that those who are reaching the full heights of their humanity tend to possess the characteristics most of us seek in life; they tend to be altruistic, creative, open, authentic, accepting, independent, and brave. However, Maslow did not prescribe that one *must* be this way. Instead, it was his belief that if society can create the conditions to satisfy one's basic needs— including the freedom to speak honestly and openly, to grow and develop one's unique capacities and passions, and to live in societies with fairness and justice—what naturally and organically emerges tends to be the characteristics that resemble the *best* in humanity.

Maslow viewed the role of the teacher, therapist, and parent as horticulturists, whose task is to "enable people to become healthy and effective *in their own style.*"[1] To Maslow, this meant that "we try to make a rose into a good rose, rather than seek to change roses into lilies. . . . It necessitates a pleasure in the self-actualization of a person who may be quite different from yourself. It even implies an ultimate respect and acknowledgement of the sacredness and uniqueness of each kind of person."

Maslow was passionate about the need for a "Being-Psychology"—a field that involves the systematic investigation of ends rather than means— *end-experiences* (such as wonder, laughter, and connection), *end-values* (such as beauty, truth, and justice), *end-cognitions* (such as efficient perception of reality and newness of appreciation), *end-goals* (such as having an ultimate concern or purpose), and with *treating people as ends unto themselves*, not means to an end (what Maslow referred to as "Being-Love," or "B-Love" for short). Maslow's call for a Being-Psychology—which he also sometimes referred to as "positive psychology"[2] or "orthopsychology"—was in response to a psychology focused more on "not-having rather than having," "striving rather than fulfillment," "frustration rather than gratification," "seeking joy rather than having attained joy," and "trying to get there rather than being there."[3]

Maslow was not alone. Between 1930 and 1970, a group of like-minded thinkers arose—including Alfred Adler, James Bugental, Charlotte Bühler, Arthur Combs, Viktor Frankl, Erich Fromm, Eugene Gendlin, Karen Horney, Sidney Jourard, Jim Klee, R. D. Laing, Rollo May, Clark Moustakas, Carl Rogers, Donald Snygg, and Anthony Sutich—who all saw the limitations of the experimental psychology, behaviorism, and Freudian psychoanalysis of the day. These disciplines, they felt, did not do justice to the individual as a whole; they left behind humanity's immense potential for creativity, spirituality, and humanitarianism. Referring to themselves as the Third Force, they attempted to integrate the insights of the more traditional perspectives while exploring "what it means to be fully experientially human and how that understanding illuminates the fulfilled or vital life."[4]

Eventually, the Third Force psychologists became known as the "humanistic psychologists," and the field was officially created when Maslow and Anthony Sutich launched *The Journal of Humanistic Psychology* in 1961. Today, there exist a number of psychotherapists and researchers explicitly working within the humanistic psychology tradition (many of them refer to themselves as "existential-humanistic" psychotherapists),[5] and there remains a strong emphasis on such humanistic themes as authenticity, awareness, compassionate social action, societal and ecological conditions most conducive to growth, spirituality, self-transcendence, integration, wholeness, and embracing the inherent struggles and paradoxes of human existence.[6] Within the humanistic psychology framework, the healthy personality is considered one that constantly moves toward freedom, responsibility, self-awareness, meaning, commitment, personal growth, maturity, integration, and change, rather than one that predominantly strives for status, achievement, or even happiness.[7]

In the late nineties, psychologist Martin Seligman galvanized the field of positive psychology in order to generate more rigorous scientific research on well-being and what "makes life worth living."[8] Today, humanistic psychologists and positive psychologists share a desire to understand and foster healthy motivation and healthy living.[9,10] The following thirteen sources of well-being have been rigorously studied over the past forty years, and each one can be reached in your own style:[11]

Sources of Well-Being

- *More positive emotions* (higher frequency and intensity of positive moods and emotions, such as contentment, laughter, and joy, in one's daily life)
- *Fewer negative emotions* (lower frequency and intensity of negative moods and emotions, such as sadness, anxiety, fear, and anger, in one's daily life)
- *Life satisfaction* (a positive subjective evaluation of one's life overall)
- *Vitality* (a positive subjective sense of physical health and energy)
- *Environmental mastery* (the ability to shape environments to suit one's needs and desires; to feel in control of one's life; to not feel overwhelmed by the demands and responsibilities of everyday life)
- *Positive relationships* (feeling loved, supported, and valued by others; having warm and trusting interpersonal relationships; being loving and generous to others)
- *Self-acceptance* (positive attitudes toward self; a sense of self-worth; liking and respecting oneself)
- *Mastery* (feelings of competence in accomplishing challenging tasks; a sense of effectiveness in accomplishing important goals one has set for oneself)

- *Autonomy* (feeling independent, free to make one's own choices in life, and able to resist social pressures)
- *Personal growth* (continually seeking development and improvement, rather than seeking achievement of a fixed state)
- *Engagement in life* (being absorbed, interested, and involved in one's daily activities and life)
- *Purpose and meaning in life* (a sense that one's life matters, is valuable, and is worth living; a clear sense of direction and meaning in one's efforts; a connection to something greater than oneself)
- *Transcendent experiences* (experiences of awe, flow, inspiration, and gratitude in daily life)

Note that many of these sources of well-being go beyond stereotypical notions of happiness. Becoming fully human is about living a full existence, not one that is continually happy. Being well is not always about feeling good; it also involves continually incorporating more meaning, engagement, and growth in one's life—key themes in humanistic psychology.

In this introduction, I will present a new hierarchy of human needs for the twenty-first century that is in line with the spirit of humanistic psychology but is also grounded in the latest science of personality, self-actualization, human development, and well-being. I believe the new hierarchy of needs can serve as a useful organizing framework for the field of psychology as well as a useful guide for your own personal journey of health, growth, and transcendence.

But first there are a number of common misconceptions about Maslow's hierarchy of needs that we must dispel at once.

LIFE IS NOT A VIDEO GAME

Maslow's theory of needs is often presented as a lockstep progression, as though once we satisfy one set of needs, we're done forever with concerning ourselves with the satisfaction of that need. As if life were a video game and once we complete one level—say, safety—some voice from above says, "Congrats, now you've unlocked belonging!," never to return to the prior need in the hierarchy. This is a gross misrepresentation of Maslow's theory, as well as the spirit of Maslow's overall body of work. While rarely acknowledged as one, Maslow was actually a developmental psychologist at heart.[12]

Maslow emphasized that we are always in a state of becoming and that one's "inner core" consists merely of "potentialities, not final actualizations" that are "weak, subtle, and delicate, very easily drowned out by learning, by cultural expectations, by fear, by disapproval, etc.," and which can all too easily become forgotten, neglected, unused, overlooked, unverbalized, or suppressed.[13] Maslow made it clear that human maturation is an ongoing process and that growth is "not a sudden, saltatory phenomenon" but is often two steps forward and one step back.[14]

An underdiscussed aspect of Maslow's theory is that his hierarchy of needs serves as an organizing framework for different states of mind—ways of looking at the world and at others. Maslow argued that, when deprived, each need is associated with its own distinctive world outlook, philosophy, and outlook on the future:

> Another peculiar characteristic of the human organism when it is dominated by a certain need is that the whole philosophy of the future tends also to change. For our chronically and extremely hungry man, Utopia can be defined simply as a place where there is plenty of food. He tends to think that, if only he is guaranteed food for the rest of his life, he will be perfectly happy and will never want anything more. Life itself tends to be defined in terms of eating. Anything else will be defined as unimportant. Freedom, love, community feeling, respect, philosophy, may all be waved aside as fripperies that are useless, since they fail to fill the stomach. Such a man may fairly be said to live by bread alone.[15]

While Maslow often relied on extreme examples such as these, he was also quick to point out that most people "are partially satisfied in all their basic needs and partially unsatisfied in all their basic needs at the same time."[16] He was insistent that "any behavior tends to be determined by several or *all* of the basic needs simultaneously rather than by only one of them," and that any one of us at any moment in time can return to a particular state of mind depending on the deprivation of the need.[17]

Another common misconception is that the needs are isolated from one another or don't depend on one another in any meaningful way. Again, this couldn't be further from what Maslow's theory *actually* stated: "[The human needs] are arranged in an integrated hierarchy rather than dichotomously, that is, they rest one upon another. . . . This means that the process of regression to lower needs remains always as a possibility, and in this context must be seen *not* only as pathological or sick, but as absolutely necessary to the integrity of the whole organism, and as prerequisite to the existence and functioning of the 'higher needs.'"[18]

The English humanistic psychotherapist John Rowan used the analogy of Russian nesting dolls to illustrate Maslow's notion of an integrated hierarchy: each larger doll includes all the smaller dolls but also transcends them.[19] Once we are working on our highest purpose, for instance, our needs for safety, connection, or self-esteem don't vanish; instead, they become *integrated* with our more transcendent purpose. When the whole person is well-integrated, all of their basic needs are not merely met but work together to facilitate growth toward realizing their highest goals and values.

Another implication here is that if you try to grow too soon without a healthy integration of your insecurities and deprivations, the growth is less likely to reach its full height. Listening to a meditation app for a few minutes once a week or doing the downward-facing dog yoga pose every morning won't magically give you a deep sense of self-worth and connection with others. Again, Maslow viewed development as often involving a two-steps-forward, one-step-back dynamic,[20] in which we are continually returning to our basic needs to draw strength, learn from our hardships, and work toward greater integration of our whole being.

Modern-day presentations of Maslow's theory often leave out this critical notion of an in-

Maslow never actually created a pyramid to represent his hierarchy of needs.

tegrated hierarchy and instead focus on the stage-like pyramid—even though in his published writings *Maslow never actually created a pyramid to represent his hierarchy of needs*.[21,22] Todd Bridgman and his colleagues examined in detail how the pyramid came to be and concluded that "Maslow's Pyramid" was actually created by a management consultant in the sixties. From there, it quickly became popular in the emerging field of organization behavior. Bridgman and his colleagues note that the pyramid resonated with the "prevailing [post-war] ideologies of individualism, nationalism and capitalism in America and justified a growing managerialism in bureaucratic (i.e., layered triangular) formats."[23]

Unfortunately, the continual reproduction of the pyramid in management textbooks had the unfortunate consequence of reducing Maslow's rich and nuanced intellectual contributions to a parody and has betrayed the actual spirit of Maslow's notion of self-actualization as realizing one's creative potential for humanitarian ends.[24] As Bridgman and his colleagues noted, "Inspiring the study of management and its relationship to creativity and the pursuit of the common good would be a much more empowering legacy to Maslow than a simplistic, 5-step, one-way pyramid."[25]

Finally, there is a common misconception that Maslow's theory didn't allow for cross-cultural variation or individual differences. However, Maslow acknowledged that not only can our basic needs ebb and flow in salience across a person's lifetime, but there can also be significant cultural and individual differences in the order in which people satisfy their basic needs.[26] For instance, a number of societies that lack important resources for security and health— such as a war-torn society where there is real

We can work on multiple needs simultaneously.

danger and fear on a regular basis—will certainly be focused more on the basic necessities of survival. Even so, such societies can supply, to a certain extent, a sense of community, respect, and the opportunities to develop skills and talents. As the consultant Susan Fowler notes, "People are 'self-actualizing' all over the place."[27] Addressing real structural inequalities around the world is absolutely *essential* to giving everyone opportunities to self-actualize and transcend, but this does not mean that people must wait to work toward a deeper sense of fulfillment until more security-related needs are met. We can work on multiple needs simultaneously.

Even *within a society*, people differ in what needs they are most motivated to pursue due to a combination of temperament and environmental experiences. For instance, some people are consistently more interested in forming deeper connections with others, whereas others are more consistently driven by accolades and the respect of others. And even *within individuals*, our needs are likely to change in importance as we mature and develop. Again, the key here is change and growth.

While the precise ordering of Maslow's hierarchy of needs has shown to vary by culture, from person to person, and even within a person's own lifetime, there is one core aspect of Maslow's hierarchy that *has* stood up remarkably well to modern scientific scrutiny. Let's take a look at that now.

DEFICIENCY VS. GROWTH

While most people focus on the triangular arrangement of the needs, Maslow actually emphasized a different feature of the hierarchy. Maslow argued that all the needs can be grouped into two main classes of needs, which must be integrated for wholeness: deficiency and growth.

Deficiency needs, which Maslow referred to as "D-needs," are motivated by a lack of satisfaction, whether it's the lack of food, safety, affection, belonging, or self-esteem. The "D-realm" of existence colors all of our perceptions and distorts reality, making demands on a person's whole being: "Feed me! Love me! Respect me!"[28] The greater the deficiency of these needs, the more we distort reality to fit our expectations and treat others in accordance with their usefulness in helping us satisfy our most deficient needs. In the D-realm, we are also more likely to use a variety of defense mechanisms to protect ourselves from the pain of having such deficiency in our lives. Our defenses are quite "wise" in the sense that they can help us to avoid unbearable pain that can feel like too much to bear at the moment.

Nevertheless, Maslow argued that the growth needs—such as self-actualization and transcendence—have a very different sort of wisdom associated with them. Distinguishing between "defensive-wisdom" and "growth-wisdom," Maslow argued that the Being-Realm of existence (or

B-realm, for short) is like replacing a clouded lens with a clear one. Instead of being driven by fears, anxieties, suspicions, and the constant need to make demands on reality, one is more accepting and loving of oneself and others. Seeing reality more clearly, growth-wisdom is more about "What choices will lead me to greater integration and wholeness?" rather than "How can I defend myself so that I can feel safe and secure?"[29]

From an evolutionary point of view, it makes sense that our safety and security concerns, as well as our desires for short-lived hedonic pleasures, would make greater demands on our attention than our desire to grow as a whole person. As the journalist and author Robert Wright put it in his book *Why Buddhism Is True,* "The human brain was designed—by natural selection—to mislead us, even enslave us."[30] All that our genes "care" about is getting propagated into the next generation, no matter the cost to the development of the whole person. If this involves narrowing our worldview and causing us to have outsize reactions to the world that aren't actually in line with reality, so be it.

However, such a narrowing of worldview runs the risk of inhibiting a fuller understanding of the world and ourselves. Despite the many challenges to growth, Maslow believed we are all capable of self-actualization, even if most of us do not self-actualize because we spend most of our lives motivated by deficiency. Maslow's emphasis on the dialectical nature of safety and growth is strikingly consistent with current research and theorizing in the fields of personality psychology, cybernetics, and artificial intelligence. There is a general consensus that optimal functioning of the whole system (whether humans, primates, or machines) requires both stability of goal pursuit in the face of distraction and disruption as well as the capacity for flexibility to adapt and explore the environment.[31]

Recognizing that security and growth are the two foundations necessary for becoming a whole person, including healthy transcendence, it's time for a *new* metaphor.

A NEW METAPHOR

The pyramid from the sixties told a story that Maslow never meant to tell; a story of achievement, of mastering level by level until you've "won" the game of life. But that is most definitely not the spirit of self-actualization that the humanistic psychologists emphasized. The human condition isn't a competition; it's an experience. Life isn't a trek up a summit but a journey to travel through—a vast blue ocean, full of new opportunities for meaning and discovery but also danger and uncertainty. In this choppy surf, a clunky pyramid is of little use. Instead, what is needed is something a bit more functional. We'll need a *sailboat*.

As we sail through the adventure of life, it's rarely clear sailing. The boat itself protects us from seas that are rarely as calm as we'd like. Each plank of the boat offers security from the waves. Without it, we'd surely spend all our energy trying to stay above water. While even one plank is better than nothing, the bigger the boat, the more waves you can endure. Likewise in life, while safety is an essential foundation for feeling secure, adding on strong connections with others and feelings of respect and worthiness will further allow you to weather the storms.

Having a secure boat is not enough for real movement, however. You also need a sail. Without a sail, you might be protected from water, but you wouldn't go anywhere. Each level of the sail allows you to capture more wind, helping you explore and adapt to your environment.

Note that you don't "climb" a sailboat like you'd climb a mountain or a pyramid. Instead, you *open* your sail, just like you'd drop your defenses once you felt secure enough. This is an ongoing dynamic: you can be open and spontaneous one minute but can feel threatened enough to prepare for the storm by closing yourself to the world the next minute. The more you continually open yourself to the world, however, the further your boat will go and the more you can benefit from the people and opportunities around you. And if you're truly fortunate, you can even enter ecstatic moments of peak experience. In these moments, not only have you temporarily forgotten your insecurities, but you are growing so much that you are helping to raise the tide for all the other sailboats simply by making your way through the ocean. In this way, the sailboat isn't a pinnacle but a whole *vehicle*, helping us to explore the world and people around us, growing and transcending as we do.

OPENING YOUR SAIL

Just what are the metaphorical components of the boat that ultimately provide the vehicle for transcendence? The needs that comprise the boat itself are safety, connection, and self-esteem. These three needs work as a whole dynamic system, and the severe thwarting of any aspect of the whole can have profound effects on the rest of the system. Under good conditions, the security needs work together to spiral upward toward greater security and stability, but under unfavorable conditions, they can lead to profound insecurity and instability—causing us to get stuck in our journey as we focus our attention on defending ourselves. Unfortunately, too many people get caught up in insecurity throughout their lives, and stay there, missing out on the immense beauty in the world that is still left to explore and the possibilities for their own self-actualization and, ultimately, transcendence. We miss the ocean for the waves.

What about the sail? The sail represents *growth*. While growth lies at the heart of self-actualization, one fair criticism of the term "self-actualization" is that it is a vague hodgepodge of characteristics and motives lumped together under a single umbrella.[32] Maslow recognized this, and in his later writings, he preferred the term "fully human" to capture what he was really trying to get at.

To help clarify this point, I have broken self-actualization—and therefore growth—into three specific needs for which there is strong contemporary scientific support: exploration, love, and purpose. I believe that these three needs capture the essence of how Maslow really conceptualized self-actualization. Further, I believe these three needs cannot be reduced to the security needs, or completely reduced to one another (although they can build on one another). These three needs work together synergistically to help us grow as a whole person. Under favorable conditions, the satisfaction of these needs helps us move toward greater health, wholeness, and transcendence. Under unfavorable conditions, we become preoccupied with safety and security and neglect our possibilities for growth.

At the base of growth is the spirit of *exploration*, the fundamental biological drive that is the springboard for growth. Exploration is the desire to seek out and make sense of novel, challenging, and uncertain events.[33] While security is primarily concerned with defense and protection, exploration is primarily motivated by curiosity, discovery, openness, expansion, understanding, and the creation of new opportunities for growth and development. The other needs that comprise growth—love and purpose—can build on the fundamental need for exploration to reach higher levels of integration within oneself and to contribute something meaningful to the world.

I believe the drive for exploration is the core motive underlying self-actualization and cannot be completely reduced to any of the other needs, including our evolved drives for affiliation, status, parenting, and mates. While I do agree with evolutionary psychologist Douglas Kenrick and colleagues that the hierarchy of needs can be built on an evolutionary foundation, I believe the need for exploration deserves a place at the evolutionary table all on its own.[34]

Finally, at the top of the new hierarchy of needs is the *need for transcendence*, which goes beyond individual growth (and even health and happiness) and allows for the highest levels of unity and harmony within oneself and with the world. Transcendence, which rests on a secure foundation of both security and growth, is a perspective in which we can view our whole being from a higher vantage point with acceptance, wisdom, and a sense of connectedness with the rest of humanity.

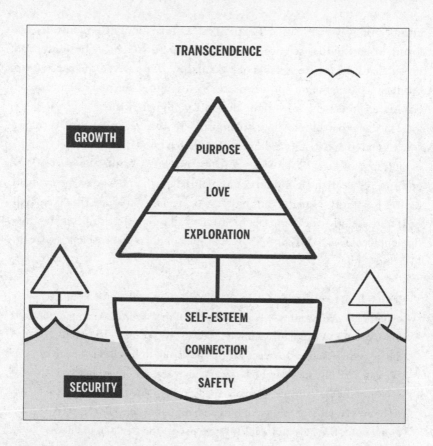

ALL AT SEA[35]

Life comes from physical survival; but the good life comes from what we care about.

—Rollo May, *Love & Will* (1969)

The new hierarchy of needs that I present in this book is fundamentally human. Yes, we are apes, but we are apes insatiably curious about personal identity, creative expression, meaning, and purpose. Humans have developed a capacity for growth unprecedented in the animal kingdom. We are truly unique in the long time scale of our goals and in the flexibility to choose which goals we most wish to prioritize, and therefore in the number of ways we can self-actualize. Think about the many diverse forms of art, music, science, invention, literature, dance, business, and sports that humans are capable of actualizing. We evolved the capacity to produce very elaborate and diverse cultures, and what makes cultures so elaborate is precisely our unique flexibility of goal pursuit.

The fact that humans are so unusual in this regard means that not every goal that satisfies a human being has any direct connection to evolutionary fitness. Take Skee-Ball, for instance. While the goal of becoming a Skee-Ball champion could be linked in some way to the evolved desires for status, esteem, and mastery, to *completely* reduce the Skee-Ball goal to these other needs in the hierarchy of human needs misses the fundamental *humanity* of Skee-Ball. As personality neuroscientist Colin DeYoung notes,

> It's hard not to realize that there is something more than the usual evolutionary constraints, when you think of the Skeeball Champion of the Universe. We don't have monkeys who are Skeeball champions. There is this freedom to select various goals and to invent new goals. We can certainly tie them back to certain evolved motives, but you can't just list the individual's evolved adaptations and from there be able to figure out what the range of human beings' possible behaviors is going to be. We have to be able to give people the freedom to choose from a very large menu of possible goals and pursuits and, even more than that, freedom to invent new ones.[36]

Of course, we do share many drives with other animals, and understanding the panoply of evolved psychological mechanisms is a very worthy goal.[37] However, it's notable that no other animal has existential crises quite to the extent that we do. In *The Sane Society,* Erich Fromm argued that the human condition involves the fundamental tension between our common nature with other animals and our uniquely developed capacities for self-awareness, reason, and imagination. As Fromm notes, "The problem of man's existence, then, is unique in the whole of nature; he has fallen out of nature, as it were, and is still in it; he is partly divine, partly animal; partly infinite, partly finite."[38]

To use the sailboat metaphor, while we each travel in our own direction, *we're all sailing the vast unknown of the sea.* Human existence comes with conditions that are sometimes hard to swallow and difficult to comprehend, but there

While we each travel in our own direction, we're all sailing the vast unknown of the sea.

is something comforting about the fact that we all exist together and have to confront the same existential dilemmas. As one patient told existential psychotherapist Irvin Yalom, "Even though you're alone in your boat, it's always comforting to see the lights of the other boats bobbing nearby."[39] Here are the four "givens of existence" that Yalom argues all humans must reconcile:

(1) Death: the inherent tension between wanting to continue to exist and self-actualize and the inevitability of perishing,

(2) Freedom: the inherent conflict between the seeming randomness of the universe and the heavy burden of responsibility that comes with the freedom to choose one's own destiny,

(3) Isolation: the inherent tension between, on the one hand, wanting to connect deeply and profoundly with other human beings and be part of a larger whole and, on the other hand, never fully being able to do so, always remaining existentially alone, and

(4) Meaninglessness: the tension between being thrown into an indifferent universe that often seems to have no inherent meaning and yet wanting to find some sort of purpose for our own individual existence in the incomprehensibly short time we live on the planet.[40]

Therefore, the new hierarchy of needs is not only a theory of human nature but is ultimately a theory of *human existence.* Unearthing the evolved tendencies and instincts of humans is very important, and I will do so throughout this book. But I'm ultimately interested in what makes human life valuable and significant to the individuals *who are actually living it.* This book is not only about the parts of our evolutionary heritage but also about how each and every one of us can *transcend* our parts—becoming something greater than the sum of our parts as we each deal with the givens of existence in our own style.

THE GOOD LIFE

I do not accept any absolute formulas for living. No preconceived code can see ahead to everything that can happen in a man's life. As we live, we grow and our beliefs change. They must change. So I think we should live with this constant discovery. We should be open to this adventure in heightened awareness of living. We should stake our whole existence on our willingness to explore and experience.

—Martin Buber, as quoted in Aubrey Hodes,
Martin Buber: An Intimate Portrait (1971)

"No one can build you the bridge on which you, and only you, must cross the river of life. There may be countless trails and bridges and demigods who would gladly carry you across; but only at the price of pawning and forgoing yourself. There is one path in the world that none can walk but you. Where does it lead? Don't ask, walk!" . . . It is . . . an agonizing, hazardous undertaking thus to dig into oneself, to climb down roughly and directly into the tunnels of one's being.

—Friedrich Nietzsche, *Schopenhauer as Educator* (1874)

The vision of the good life I present in this book isn't one that is typically touted these days. It's not one where the primary motivation is money, power, social status, or even happiness. Instead, the good life that I present, which is deeply grounded in the core principles of humanistic psychology and a realistic understanding of human needs, is about the healthy expression of needs in the service of discovering and expressing a self that works best for *you*.

The good life is not something you will ever achieve. It's a way of living. As Carl Rogers noted, "The good life is a *process,* not a state of being. It is a direction, not a destination."[41] This process won't always bring feelings of happiness, contentment, and bliss, and it may even sometimes cause pain and heartache. It's not for the "faint-hearted," as Rogers notes, as it requires continually stretching outside your comfort zone as you realize more and more of your potentialities and launch yourself "fully into the stream of life."[42] Just like it takes courage to open your sail on a sailboat and see where the winds will take you, it takes a lot of courage to become the best version of yourself.[43]

Nevertheless, if you stick with it, you are sure to live a richer life, one that is better characterized by adjectives such as "enriching," "exciting," "rewarding," "challenging," "creative," "meaningful," "intense," and "awe-inspiring." I believe in the fundamental capacity of humans for growth. No matter your current personality or circumstance, I believe that this book can help you grow in precisely the direction you truly want to grow, in your own style, and in such a way that allows you to show the universe that you really existed, and benefited others, while you were here.

Let's begin the process of becoming.

PART I

Security

SELF-ESTEEM

CONNECTION

SAFETY

Prelude

In 1927, nineteen-year-old City College of New York undergraduate Abe Maslow registered for a course called the Philosophy of Civilization. It turned out to be too difficult for him, and he dropped out. Still, his life would be forever changed, planting a major seed for his future development. The young Maslow experienced what developmental psychologist Howard Gardner refers to as a "crystallizing experience"—a memorable, dramatic moment in which we make contact with stimuli that just clicks and makes us think "Aha—that's me!"[1]

Maslow, reflecting on the experience thirty-five years later in an unpublished note, wrote: "This turned out to be one of the most important educational experiences of my life, because it introduced me to William Graham Sumner's *Folkways*, which changed my life. But this is exactly what our professor warned us about in his first lecture of the semester. 'If you really read this book you can never be the same again. You can never again be an innocent.'"[2]

Folkways inspired Maslow to have an appreciation for cultural influences on behavior. But it also inspired him to appreciate the potent driving force of human needs. Because the pattern of environmental contingencies differs from one society to another, different societies develop different folkways for meeting the same fundamental needs. As Sumner put it,

> Every moment brings necessities which must be satisfied at once. Need was the first experience, and it was followed at once by a blundering effort to satisfy it. . . . The method is that of trial and failure, which produces repeated pain, loss, and disappointments. Nevertheless, it is a

method of rude experience and selection. The earliest efforts of man were of this kind. Need was the impelling force.[3]

Almost instantly, Maslow was bitten by the anthropology bug. The following year, he would transfer to the University of Wisconsin, where he read voraciously from such seminal anthropological figures as Margaret Mead, Branisław Malinowski, Ruth Benedict, and Ralph Linton (whom his wife, Bertha, had as a professor). When he moved to New York City in 1935, he sat in on many anthropology classes and seminars with Ruth Benedict, Ralph Linton, Alexander Lesser, and George Herzog. In fact, he would form a close friendship with Ruth Benedict, drawn to her wit, brilliance, and kindness. Maslow also became a member of the American Anthropological Association and delivered talks at their conferences.[4]

In 1938, early in Maslow's professional career as a psychologist, Ruth Benedict helped him secure a grant-in-aid to spend (along with Lucien Hanks and Jane Richardson) an entire anthropological summer among the Northern Blackfoot Indians on the Siksika reserve in Alberta, Canada.[5] Maslow became very fond of the Blackfoot way of life. According to Martin Heavy Head, Maslow was so inspired by his visit that it "shook him to his knees."[6] Maslow was particularly impressed with the general lack of crime, violence, jealousy, and greed among the Blackfoot, along with their high levels of emotional security, firm yet caring child-rearing practices, community feeling, egalitarianism, and generous spirit. In fact, Maslow believed that the Blackfoot Indians scored so high on his tests of emotional security precisely because of their societal structure and community spirit.

According to Maslow's biographer Edward Hoffman, Maslow observed among the Blackfoot that "wealth was not important in terms of accumulating property and possessions: *giving it away* was what brought one the true status of prestige and security in the tribe."[7] In contrast, Maslow was shocked by the cruelty of the European-Americans who lived nearby: "Those Indians on the reservation were decent people; and the more I got to know the whites in the village, who were the worst bunch of creeps and bastards I've ever run across in my life, the more it got paradoxical."[8] It's clear from Maslow's visit that he learned quite a bit about the

First Nations perspective, including the importance of community, gratitude for what one has, and giving back to future generations.[9,10]

At the same time, the visit also had a deep influence on Maslow's thinking about an intrinsic human nature.[11] While he went into the visit with a strong belief in cultural relativism, he was struck by how much of a connection he felt with the Blackfoot Indians.[12] In a summary report a few weeks after his fieldwork, Maslow wrote:

> It would seem that every human being comes at birth into society not as a lump of clay to be molded by society, but rather as a structure which society may warp or suppress or build upon. My fundamental data supporting this feeling is that my Indians were first human beings and secondly Blackfoot Indians, and also that in their society I found almost the same range of personalities as I find in our society—with, however, very different modes in the distribution curves. . . . I am now struggling with a notion of a "fundamental" [or] "natural" personality structure.[13]

In an unpublished note in December of the same year, Maslow wrote: "My new notion of Fundamental or Natural Personality . . . Proposition: That human beings are at birth and today deep down, secure and with good self-esteem, to be analogized with the Blackfoot Indian or the chimpanzee or the baby or the secure adult. And then societies do something to this Natural Personality, twist it, shape it, repress it . . ."[14]

In his book, Sumner emphasized that cultural folkways should not be evaluated as universally "good" or "bad" but should be understood based on their adaptive value—their effectiveness in satisfying an impelling need. Likewise, Maslow believed that humans are basically good but that life's pressures and frustrations make them seem otherwise.[15] In another unpublished note from 1938, Maslow wrote: "People are all decent underneath. All that is necessary to prove this is to find out what the motives are for their superficial behavior—nasty, mean, or vicious though that behavior may be. Once these motives are understood, it is impossible to resent the behavior that follows."[16] Suffice it to say, this was a radical departure from the psychoanalytic view of the time that what people really are underneath is a cauldron of destructive impulses relating to either self-preservation or sex!

In the same unpublished note, Maslow then went on to ponder why people could be so cruel. He concluded that it's due to "the insecurity cycle—from this flows everything. . . . The person who behaves badly behaves so because of hurt, actual and expected, and lashes out in self-defense, as a cornered animal might. The fact is that people are good, if only their fundamental wishes are satisfied, their wishes for affection and security. Give people affection and security, and they will give affection and be secure in their feelings and behavior." Continuing his train of thought, Maslow argued that everything that is "nasty, mean, or vicious" is an overcompensatory attempt to satisfy the basic needs of security, affection, and self-esteem.

Many contemporary studies from a wide range of perspectives support Maslow's thinking on the behavioral manifestations of the "insecurity cycle." The common core of this cycle is *fear*. Whatever the particular form it takes, some sort of fear pervades the deprivation of each of the needs that comprise this cycle.

If you have too many psychological fears, this may be an indication that you may be too caught up in securing your boat, with potentially serious consequences to actually moving along the expansive ocean. This first section of the book is dedicated to helping you curb your insecurities, so that you can stand on as secure a foundation as possible and really focus on the things that give you the greatest meaning, growth, and creativity in your life.

Let's start with the most essential need that comprises security: safety.

CHAPTER 1

Safety

*The average child and, less obviously, the average adult in our society
generally prefers a safe, orderly, predictable, lawful, organized world, which
he can count on and in which unexpected, unmanageable, chaotic, or other
dangerous things do not happen, and in which, in any case, he has powerful
parents or protectors who shield him from harm.*

—Abraham Maslow, *Motivation and Personality* (1954)

While overall the world has dramatically improved in many ways—
people are living longer, healthier, freer, and more peacefully[1]—
many people around the world in the first quarter of the twenty-first
century still find themselves living in an unpredictable, chaotic world, and
for many, chaos invades their personal environment. In the United States
alone, around ten million Americans working full time are still living
below the official poverty line. Basic fundamental needs such as housing
and health care are in crisis for large swaths of Americans, despite the
striking growth in incomes of the top 1 percent. Indeed, over thirty-three
million Americans do not have health insurance, and over half of Americans do not even have $400 on hand to help deal with a catastrophe.[2]

As the author Ruth Whippman has pointed out, we have created a societal narrative around health and wellness that essentially inverts Maslow's
hierarchy of needs, placing self-actualization as a viable alternative to these
fundamentals, instead of something that is built on a strong foundation of
safety and security. In her article "Where Were We While the Pyramid
Was Collapsing? At a Yoga Class," Whippman writes, "We are focusing on
the tip of Maslow's pyramid at the clear expense of its base."[3]

While Maslow never actually created a pyramid to represent his theory (see Introduction), he repeatedly emphasized the need for the most fundamental needs to be met in order for one to even have the opportunity to realize their full potential. Maslow's own working-class upbringing as the eldest son of Russian Jewish immigrants, and being the target of constant anti-Semitic bullying as a child, influenced his lifelong focus on social change. One of his students who took his class in the 1960s noted that Maslow fiercely advocated for the reduced-price meals in schools as a way of reducing the roadblocks to the healthy growth and development of impoverished children.[4]

Modern-day science makes clear that unpredictability has far-reaching consequences for the lives we can envision and create for ourselves. The need for safety, and its accompanying needs for stability, certainty, predictability, coherence, continuity, and trust in the environment, is the base upon which all the others are fulfilled. The need for safety is tied to the struggle to make sense of experiences and a motivation to gain control over violated expectations. Having a safe base allows a person to take risks and explore new ideas and ways of being, while also allowing the opportunity to become who you truly want to become. In the absence of that base, people become overly dependent on the protection, love, affection, and esteem of others, which can compromise growth, development, and meaning in life.

The need for safety is tied to a particular form of meaning in life. Psychologists have identified three different forms of meaning: coherence, purpose, and mattering.[5] Purpose involves a motivation to realize future-oriented and valued life goals. Mattering consists of the extent to which people feel that their existence and actions in the world are significant, important, and valuable.

The need for coherence is the form of meaning that is most strongly tied to the need for safety. Does my immediate environment make sense? Is there any predictability and comprehensibility in my life? Coherence is necessary to even get a chance to pursue one's larger purpose or pursue various ways that one can matter in this world.[6] As the meaning researchers Frank Martela and Michael Steger put it, "We need something to anchor our values upon, and when our lives feel incomprehensible, finding the things that make our lives worth living might be hard if not impossible."[7]

There are constructive routes to coherence. For instance, researchers have found that coherence is associated with greater religiosity, spirituality, and the ability to grow from trauma, such as enduring cancer.[8] But there are also more destructive routes to coherence, and the need to regain a sense of safety can lead to aggression and antagonism. Too much chaos and unpredictability pitches us into a state that psychologists call "psychological entropy."[9]

PSYCHOLOGICAL ENTROPY

The human brain is a prediction machine.[10] We are constantly processing incoming information and assessing how it matches our expectations. Instructed (but not completely determined) by a blueprint from our genes, the brain attempts to help us satisfy our basic needs by directing our behaviors, thoughts, and emotions in ways that will reach its goals. Keep in mind that "goals" is used very broadly here, ranging from security goals, such as acquiring food, belonging, status, and mates, to more "purpose"-related goals, such as becoming a world-class athlete or helping poor people in developing countries. As noted earlier, humans are quite unique in their flexible repertoire of goals.

First applied to the operation of physical systems, entropy is a measure of disorder. But the very same principles of entropy that apply to physical thermodynamic systems, such as self-organization, apply to all information-processing systems, including the brain, nervous system, and psychological processes of humans.[11] All biological organisms—including humans—survive insofar as they are able to effectively manage internal entropy.[12]

In the state of psychological entropy, we experience uncomfortable feelings such as anxiety and distress. Stress systems in the body are activated and set off a cascade of hormones—including cortisol—that circulate throughout the body and prepare it to take some kind of action.[13] Additionally, particular brain areas associated with vigilance, emotion, memory, and learning are activated, as are genes that control inflammation and longevity at a cellular level.[14]

To be sure, there will always be a certain amount of psychological entropy in our lives: we never achieve full mastery over our environment, and things we thought we could predict are constantly changing. A certain amount of stress and unpredictability is healthy and normal. As the British philosopher Alan Watts put it, "There is a contradiction in wanting to be perfectly secure in a universe whose very nature is momentariness and fluidity."[15] Or as mathematician John Allen Paulos notes, "Uncertainty is the only certainty there is, and knowing how to live with insecurity is the only security."[16]

Some people—those with high levels of neuroticism, need for closure, and obsessive-compulsive disorder—find uncertainty *particularly* aversive. Neuroticism is a personality trait characterized by a pattern of negative affect, anxiety, fear, and rumination. When people high in neuroticism are exposed to uncertain feedback compared to negative feedback, the nervous system delivers an outsize emotion-laden response.[17] As psychologists Jacob Hirsh and Michael Inzlicht note, people scoring high in neuroticism "prefer the devil they know over the devil they do not know." The implications of neuroticism for mental health are tremendous, with some researchers going so far as to argue that neuroticism is the common core of all forms of psychopathology![18]

While some people are hypersensitive to cues of threat, most people feel at least some discomfort when facing the unknown. And there are some fears that everyone has to some degree, such as the fear of failure, fear of rejection, fear of losing control, fear of losing emotional connection, and fear of losing reputation.[19] The ability to reduce, manage, and even embrace uncertainty is important for everyone seeking to develop the whole person. It is critical not only to health and wellness but also to survival.

Persistent fear and anxiety can have serious consequences on learning, behavior, and health.[20] Repeated exposure to discrimination, violence, neglect, or abuse can have lifelong consequences; they alter connections in areas of the developing brain that are particularly sensitive to stress.

While many brain alterations are adaptive—they make sense in relation to detecting threat—they have costs to the organism as a whole. Indeed, our genes don't "care" about our happiness or even our mental health; if they could speak, they'd tell us that they care only about propagating themselves into the next generation. If that means obtaining biological goals at the expense of higher-order goals (such as your purpose), so be it. Even though you may deeply desire to put your full powers toward composing a new symphony or solving a complex mathematical proof, the system can't perform the work at full capacity—can't use all of its energy—when there is too much psychological entropy.

At various levels of biological functioning, our bodies are constantly attempting to minimize surprise—the experience of entropy and unpredictability—by adjusting the response to environmental input. If internal entropy levels become too great, we are forced to develop alternative strategies to minimize entropy and satisfy our basic needs. If nothing works, over time, the system fails to adapt and eventually deteriorates.

There are deep implications here not just for our physiological functioning but also for our psychology. We use a fair amount of physical energy to run our brains, which allows us to maintain a reasonable degree of predictability and coherence in order to determine what actions will move us closer toward our goals. The more uncertainty we perceive in our lives, the more metabolic resources we waste and the more stress we experience. When internal disorder becomes too great, we are at risk of resorting to strategies that are destructive to others, not to mention to our whole selves. Our sense of possibility shrinks, and we are dominated by an exquisitely narrow repertoire of emotions, thoughts, and behaviors, leaving us with diminished potential to become the person we truly want to become. If you've spent the entire previous night lying awake worrying about an ambiguous blood test result, it might be hard to compose a symphony the next day.

Research is clear that our psychological processes are deeply intertwined with our physiology. For that reason, I feel comfortable combining the physiological and safety needs that Maslow proposed. When safety needs are severely thwarted, people react in quite specific ways to restore balance, or homeostasis. Looking at human behavior through such a lens allows us to see maladaptive behavior nonjudgmentally yet gain a good understanding of our fellow humans.

Any person at any point in time could become dominated by safety needs and would likely act in a predictable fashion in accordance with fundamental principles of human nature. When safety needs are thwarted, we lose trust in others and regard people with suspicion. We can very easily turn to destructive routes in order to regain safety, such as involvement in gangs and organized crime. As Maslow put it, "There is a character difference between the man who feels safe and the one who lives his life out as if he were a spy in enemy territory."[21]

Let's begin with an example we can all relate to: hunger.

FEELING HUNGRY

We should never have the desire to compose music or create mathematical systems, or to adorn our homes, or to be well dressed if our stomachs were empty most of the time, or if we were continually dying of thirst, or if we were continually threatened by an always impending catastrophe, or if everyone hated us. . . . Obviously a good way to obscure the higher motivations, and to get a lopsided view of human capacities and human nature, is to make the organism extremely and chronically hungry or thirsty.

—Abraham Maslow, *Motivation and Personality* (1954)

"Hangry"—literally a combination of "hungry" and "angry"—has emerged as a cute little expression often used in a joking manner. But true hunger is no laughing matter for the billions of people around the world who experience food insecurity on a regular basis.

There are serious consequences of hunger for both humans and non-humans. Lack of a reliable source of food gives rise to food insecurity, which tends to produce a specific cluster of negative behaviors: increased impulsivity and hyperactivity, increased irritability and aggression, increased anxiety, and a propensity to use rewarding narcotics.[22] The evidence that food uncertainty begets this cluster of behaviors is striking and vast; it includes studies of induced food deprivation among insects, birds, and mammals (including humans); studies of people who are crash dieting and forced to undergo "therapeutic" starvation; and studies of people with clinical eating disorders.

The cluster of behaviors results specifically from extreme hunger, not from preexisting personality differences. In one classic study, researchers noted that patients began the experiment compliant, pleasant, and optimistic but became increasingly impulsive and angry—to the point of engaging in physical abuse—during therapeutic starvation.[23] In one instance, a "man asked for help after discharge because he was so angry when in traffic that he feared he would kill any aggravator by smashing his car into them."[24]

Hunger increases the motivation to work or pay for food, while it decreases motivation to work or pay for any kind of non-food reward.[25] The suite of behaviors associated with hunger is best viewed not as a system failure but as an adaptation, a response consisting of alternate strategies to improve the location, capture, and defense of food resources, even at the expense of achieving other goals.[26]

If the alternate strategies keep failing to achieve their aim, anxiety and hyperactivity may eventually give way to depression and lethargy. This point is really key: it is prolonged food uncertainty that produces this cluster of behaviors, not complete deprivation. Prolonged food uncertainty causes so much psychological entropy that a sense of helplessness eventually sets in and other systems start deteriorating. British psychologist Daniel Nettle contends that some behaviors commonly seen among the economically deprived—such as impulsivity, aggression, and anxiety—result more from regular hunger deprivation than from any preexisting differences among social classes.[27]

Most strikingly, many of the behaviors that arise from hunger significantly reverse upon refeeding.[28] We are hungry until we're not. And when we're not, we forget what it was like to feel hungry. Until the next time.

Now that we covered an example that all of us can resonate with, let's start to build up to more complex and psychological forms of insecurity, starting with our next example, attachment.

THE NEED FOR ATTACHMENT SECURITY

Life is best organized as a series of daring ventures from a secure base.

—John Bowlby

The human infant starts life as a totally helpless creature, completely dependent on a caregiver to get basic physiological needs met. Through the responsiveness and reliability of the caregiver, the infant develops a sense of security that needs will be met. At the same time, the infant develops an emotional attachment to the caregiver, and that bond provides a secure base and safe haven for the ever-growing infant to survive, deploy curiosity, and explore the environment.

Integrating Freudian theory with the emerging science of ethology (the study of animal behavior through an evolutionary lens), cybernetic theory, control systems theory, and developmental psychology, British psychologist John Bowlby proposed the existence of an "attachment behavioral system" designed over the eons of human history to motivate the desire to increase proximity between caregivers and vulnerable infants, children, or adults.[29] Proximity-seeking behaviors, according to Bowlby, serve the function of reducing feelings of fear and anxiety and are activated when the infant feels scared or vulnerable.

In outlining this sytem, Bowlby drew a lot on core principles of control theory, which rely on if/then procedures. Indeed, we have many unconscious drives that are encoded into our system in an if/then manner, and as we'll see later in the book, that insight is precisely what allows us to consciously override the system and take control of our automatic habits. However, as children we don't yet have the cognitive brakes of reflection that allow us to halt the attachment behavioral system.

Bowlby argued that the attachment system goes through a series of if/then questions, starting with "Is the caregiver near, attentive, and responsive?"[30] If the child perceives that the answer is "yes," she will feel loved, secure, and confident and be more likely to explore, play, and socialize with others. If the child perceives the answer to be "no," she will experience anxiety and be more likely to show a range of behaviors designed to bring a caregiver close, including heightened vigilance and vocalizations

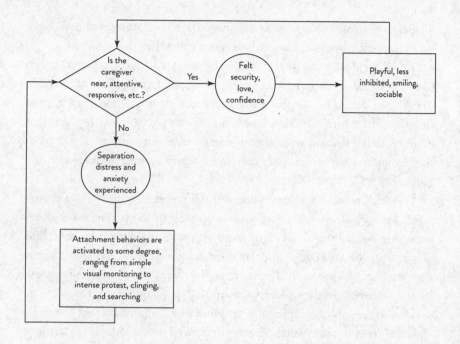

of distress (crying). Bowlby theorized that such behaviors would continue until the child is able to establish a comfortable level of proximity to the attachment figure. And if the attachment figure failed to respond, the child would completely withdraw, as so often happens with prolonged separation or loss.

Exquisitely attuned to how we are treated at times of stress, the attachment system keeps track of successes at obtaining proximity and comfort from attachment figures—beginning with parents but eventually expanding to friends and romantic partners. Bowlby argued that from the physical presence of the caregiver we gradually develop mental representations, or "internal working models," of others and of the self, which allow us to forecast the behaviors of others based on prior experiences. Through interactions with various attachment figures over the course of our lives, we develop models of the availability and sensitivity of others to our needs, as well as views of our own goodness and worthiness of love and support.

These internal working models influence the expectations and beliefs we often implicitly hold of relationships more generally.

Bowlby's ideas were put to the test by Mary Ainsworth, an American Canadian developmental psychologist, who found that infants predictably display one of several distinctive "attachment patterns."[31] In the "strange situation procedure" she developed, a nine- to twelve-month-old infant comes into the lab and after getting comfortable, is briefly separated from the parent and left alone with a stranger before being reunited with the parent.

Bowlby's prediction proved correct: the presence of the stranger provokes anxiety in infants, causing them to look to the parent for reassurance that everything is all right. And when the parent leaves the child alone with the stranger, children show additional distress: they appear distracted in playing with their toys or they vocalize distress. When the mother returns, most children (around 62 percent) crawl toward her, seeking to reestablish comforting proximity to the familiar caregiver.

That's *most* infants. What Ainsworth noticed is that some infants (about 15 percent) are extremely distressed by the separation, but when the caregiver returns, they crawl toward her yet resist contact—arching their back, flopping around, or otherwise signaling that they are definitely *not* OK with being abandoned.[32] Ainsworth saw this as an insecure form of attachment. The child is not able to completely regulate and restore emotional equilibrium after having been left unprotected. She labeled this "anxious-resistant attachment."

Ainsworth observed another form of insecure attachment, which she labeled "avoidant," among another 25 percent of the infants. These infants are clearly distressed by the separation, but when the mother returns, they behave as if they do not really need her comfort, contact, or support. It is as if they are saying, "Whatever, I don't need you anyway."

Ainsworth's pioneering work on infant attachment has been extended to the study of adult relationships.[33] Take a look at the four main attachment types that have been found among adults:

___ It is easy for me to become emotionally close to others. I am comfortable depending on them and having them depend on me. I don't worry about being alone or having others not accept me. (*Secure*)

___ I am uncomfortable getting close to others. I want emotionally close relationships, but I find it difficult to trust others completely or to depend on them. I worry that I will be hurt if I allow myself to become too close to others. (*Fearful, or Fearful-avoidant*)

___ I want to be completely emotionally intimate with others, but I often find that others are reluctant to get as close as I would like. I am uncomfortable being without close relationships, but I sometimes worry that others don't value me as much as I value them. (*Preoccupied*)

___ I am comfortable without close emotional relationships. It is very important to me to feel independent and self-sufficient, and I prefer not to depend on others or have others depend on me. (*Dismissing, or Dismissing-avoidant*)

Did you deeply resonate with any of these profiles? If so, great! You've begun a process of self-awareness that can be really helpful for your relationships. Most people, however, do *not* fit neatly into a single category or they identify with more than one category. It turns out that the typology of attachment patterns may be too simplistic and too static. R. Chris Fraley and his colleagues found that people actually differ from one another in a more continuous, rather than categorical, fashion.[34] We all lie *somewhere* on each of the attachment style dimensions—ranging from *not at all me* to *very much me,* with most people somewhere in between the extremes.

It turns out that the four adult categories of attachment style—secure, fearful, preoccupied, and dismissing—can be represented as a combination of just two dimensions: anxious and avoidant. The *anxious-attachment* dimension reflects a concern about being rejected and abandoned and is the product of beliefs about whether others will be there for you in times

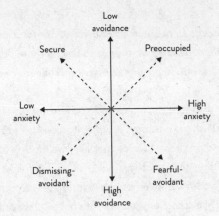

of need. The *avoidant-attachment* dimension has less to do with a sense of safety and more to do with how you regulate your emotions in response to stress—whether you use others as a secure base or pull away and withdraw from them.

Studies show that these two dimensions are only weakly correlated with each other, which creates the possibility that people can score high on both dimensions. A further implication is that "secure attachment" doesn't exist as a separate category; secure attachment is just the combination of low anxiety and low avoidance.* Modern research suggests that there is no such thing as a completely securely attached person (have you ever met one?); all of us are at least a little bit anxious and avoidant when stress rears its head in our relationships.

Nevertheless, your particular placement on the anxious- and

> **There is no such thing as a completely securely attached person; all of us are at least a little bit anxious and avoidant when stress rears its head in our relationships.**

---

* If you must know the other combinations: "fearful-avoidant attachment" is a combination of high anxiety and high avoidance, "preoccupied attachment" is a combination of high anxiety and low avoidance, and "dismissive attachment" is a combination of low anxiety and high avoidance.

avoidant-attachment dimensions has important implications. Those who score lower on these dimensions tend to report more constructive ways of coping and regulating their emotions, thoughts, and behavior, and they report higher levels of relationship satisfaction, psychological adjustment, healthy self-esteem, and even heightened altruism, volunteerism, empathy, and increased tolerance of people who are in a different social group than those who are more insecurely attached.[35] It's clear that secure attachment doesn't just set the stage for more satisfying relationships; it also sets the stage for many other aspects of growth.

On the flip side, attachment insecurity—particularly anxious attachment—has been linked to depression, anxiety, loneliness, neuroticism, impulsivity, personality disorders, perfectionism, obsessive-compulsive tendencies, substance abuse, post-traumatic stress disorder (PTSD), and a general tendency to doubt one's own ability to cope with stressful events and challenges.[36] In terms of physical health, insecure attachment has also been linked to cardiovascular disease, inflammation, poor immune functioning, and neuroendocrine activation of the stress response.[37] Since secure attachment is related to so many areas of life, let's take a closer look at just how those who are more securely attached interact with the world.

CHOOSE YOUR OWN ATTACHMENT

What is the way of being for securely attached people? In one seminal study, social psychologist Nancy Collins asked participants to describe how they would feel and behave in various scenarios designed to tap into basic attachment themes, including emotional availability when needed and reliance on a partner as a secure base.[38] Compared with securely attached adults, anxiously attached participants explained events in more negative ways and reported more emotional distress in response to situations such as "didn't respond when you tried to cuddle" and "wanted to spend an evening by himself/herself" that were more likely to lead to conflict.

In a clever variant of those studies, Amanda Vicary and R. Chris Fraley asked people to imagine themselves in a relationship and to "choose their own adventure" in a way that simulated the relationship across time.[39] Insecurely attached adults tended to make choices that were destructive to the relationship (e.g., not mentioning having lunch with an ex and allowing the partner to feel jealous), and the choices had a direct effect on their satisfaction in the relationship. Let's play along:

You spend the evening at your partner's house. At one point, your partner gets a call and goes into the other room to answer it. Twenty minutes later, your partner comes back and tells you it was his ex calling to say hello. You know that they are still friends and talk occasionally. Your partner asks if you're okay with the fact that he still talks to his ex.

Do you say:
(a) "Yeah, I'm glad to know you can still get along with people you've dated."
(b) "Not really, I'm a little worried something may still be going on between you two."

Your partner continues talking about his ex and you're starting to feel a little jealous. The week before, someone you used to be interested in called to ask you out, but you didn't tell your partner because it wasn't a big deal to you and you'd more or less forgotten about it. While your partner is talking about his ex, you suddenly remember the incident and figure he will probably be jealous if you tell him.

Do you:
(a) Not mention the incident to him, not wanting him to feel jealous.
(b) Casually bring up the incident, hoping he will feel a little jealous.

The following week, your partner comes over to your place. You are just hanging out and having a good time when you begin to get into a discussion about the relationship. Your partner says he feels that things are getting serious and that you should have a discussion about where things are going.

Do you say:

(a) "That's a good idea," figuring it can help the relationship if you're both on the same wavelength.

(b) "Maybe we should take a break," figuring he is having second thoughts about the relationship and you should end things before he does.

Note: If you're wondering, those who are more securely attached are more likely to choose option A of these scenarios.

Still, the insecurely attached weren't *hopeless*. Although they made destructive choices at the beginning of the stories, they gradually came to make better choices (although they did not improve as quickly as the more securely attached individuals). Critically, when they interacted with a warm, concerned partner, they made a greater number of beneficial relationship choices. The same was true of securely attached participants.

So yes, insecurely attached individuals tend to make choices in their relationships that bring out the negative outcomes they most fear and even *expect*. But these findings also suggest that the sensitivity of the partner really matters. A form of marital therapy called Emotionally Focused Therapy for Couples (EFT) shows promise in improving overall relationship satisfaction by fostering secure attachment bonds in intimate relationships.[40] Partners learn to see their relationship as a safe haven, secure base, and source of resiliency in times of stress and adversity.

Couples are encouraged to express deep-seated attachment fears and needs that lead them into destructive response patterns in the relationship. Making their attachment-related concerns explicit and discussing them with a sensitive, attentive partner can be immensely helpful for both partners, boosting intimacy and relationship satisfaction.

The vulnerabilities of highly avoidant and anxious individuals, troublesome as they may be, are activated only when such individuals encounter *specific* types of stressful circumstances.[41] According to Jeffry Simpson and W. Steven Rholes, highly avoidant individuals are activated by very particular types of stressful situations, such as feeling pressure to give or receive support, to become more emotionally intimate, or to share deep personal emotions. Likewise, highly anxious individuals are activated by situations that specifically threaten the stability or quality of their current relationships.[42]

While these responses to particular relationship triggers may be adaptive or "wise" in a narrow sense, defense responses to attachment crises are ultimately destructive to the relationship and to the whole person. Fortunately, Simpson and Rholes found that even in the face of triggering events, insecurely attached individuals have the power to depart from their insecure working models, especially when they are with more committed partners who are sensitive to their specific attachment-relevant needs and concerns.[43]

Too often, adult attachment patterns are seen as fixed, unchanging, and set forever by insensitive parenting. But the most comprehensive studies of the continuity of attachment styles suggest that there is only little continuity between early childhood attachment patterns and adult attachment patterns.[44] Working models can change over time in response to new experiences or events. Even a brief priming intervention in which participants received text messages designed to promote feelings of security had the effect of reducing anxiety levels![45]

Of course, sensitivity and responsiveness to needs in childhood do matter. Training parents to be sensitive to their child's needs leads to greater attachment security in the child.[46] And in some particularly reactive children, adequate parental sensitivity can make such a difference that the child develops high levels of curiosity and exploration rather than fear and anxiety.[47]

Children are particularly vulnerable to threats to wholeness and integration when they are given tasks they are incapable of mastering, or in instances in which parents force them to make important household decisions that are beyond their capabilities, such as taking care of their parents' needs. Sensitivity to a child's needs does not mean *overindulging* the child, however. The Viennese psychiatrist Alfred Adler argued that pampering children could severely undermine social and emotional growth.[48] Inspired by Adler, Maslow wrote, "Children need strong, firm, decisive, self-respecting, and autonomous parents—or else children become frightened. Youngsters need a world that is just, fair, orderly, and predictable. Only strong parents can supply these important qualities."[49]

Think of it this way: early childhood interactions with an attachment figure serve as a foundation upon which later experiences are built.[50] A working model that says that others can't be relied on and that you are unlovable influences the developing child's life and future interactions with others in both subtle and not-so-subtle ways. But early attachment patterns are far from destiny. As attachment expert R. Chris Fraley told me,

> Think of development as an architectural process, where you lay a foundation, and then you begin to build a scaffolding, you begin to build a framework. The way development works is that you start at that ground level, and that constrains what you can do from that point forward, but it doesn't determine how high the building will eventually be—that is a function of what you continue to do as you climb the scaffolding and continue to construct the structure.[51]

Our current attachment patterns are influenced by our entire history of relationships and social interactions. Early childhood experiences need not have a lasting effect; responses can change for the better over time. Our working models can evolve and change in response to our own personal growth, as well as the sensitivity and availability of our partners. And while particular relationship dynamics can activate long-established strategies of responding, we are not slaves to those patterns. The more a couple can become aware of the pull of old patterns and work together to be sensitive to each other's needs, the greater the likelihood that a relationship can flourish.

While attachment insecurity is certainly important for our understanding of growth, what about more severe and persistent forms of insecurity? What about the consequences of maltreatment, abuse, violence, and other regularly threatening environmental conditions? Let's turn to these now.

TRAUMA ON THE BRAIN

Ensuring that young children have safe, secure environments in which to grow, learn, and develop healthy brains and bodies not only is good for the children themselves but also builds a strong foundation for a prosperous, just, and sustainable society.

—Nathan Fox and Jack Shonkoff, "How Persistent Fear and Anxiety Can Affect Young Children's Learning, Behavior and Health" (2011)

While early childhood experiences of responsive care help create a safe, secure base for future exploration and for enriching social interactions and intimate relationships, emerging research indicates that not all insecure environments have the same long-term effects. Most parenting styles do not leave an indelible mark on the child's personality as an adult.[52] But there are persistent, long-term effects of certain harsh early life stressors.

Contrary to popular conceptions, Bowlby's theory was actually not meant to be restricted to helpless infants; it was based on a more general theory about human nature. Bowlby's theory of attachment grew out of his personal experiences with adolescents who had faced early adversity. Some were foster children, some of whom had been moved around multiple times; some had lost their parents; and some were juvenile delinquents.[53] But Bowlby noticed a common thread: most of the adolescents had a difficult time forming close emotional bonds with others.

Nearly half of children living in poverty in the United States today witness violence, more than 130 million children have witnessed intimate partner violence in the home, and over 200 million have suffered some form of sexual abuse.[54] Millions more experience emotional abuse daily, such as a parent intentionally inducing feelings of guilt, shame, or fear to serve their own emotional needs, or denigrating or destroying things the child values.

Neglect can be just as damaging as abuse—a parent being repeatedly unresponsive to a child's distress and social needs, expecting a child to manage situations that are unsafe or beyond what could possibly be expected based on their development, or neglecting to provide basic needs such as food, clean clothing, shelter, and dental and medical care.

By a variety of mechanisms, external treatment by caregivers and unreliable environments get wired into the young child's developing brain. According to the predictive-adaptive-response theory (PAR), early childhood adversity serves as a "weather forecast" of the conditions into which the individual will mature, and it is adaptive for an individual who suffered early adversity to develop behavioral strategies attuned to the anticipated environment.[55] Cognitive neuroscience research has demonstrated that the brain reconfigures itself in line with the predictions it has made about the future based on prior experiences.[56] Understanding how the brain reconfigures itself to cope with anticipated trauma is key to understanding the durable effects on cognition, emotional regulation, and social functioning seen in those who experience persistent anxiety, fear, and unpredictability in childhood.

Although the potential for recovery is not completely lost—the brain does leave itself open to the possibility for future revisions, meaning there is some neural plasticity—early life stressors do create *constraints* on development. They do so by activating genes that cause critical developmental periods to come to a close.[57] As Martin Teicher and colleagues explain, "Brain development is directed by genes but sculpted by experiences."

The areas of the brain that are particularly sensitive to early life stressors include the *hippocampus*, involved in the formation and retrieval of memories and imaginings; the *amygdala*, involved in vigilance and detection of emotional significance; the *anterior cingulate cortex*, involved in error detection, impulse control, and allocation of mental resources; the *corpus callosum*, which connects the brain's left and right hemispheres; and the *prefrontal cortex*, particularly the medial and orbital prefrontal cortices, which are involved in long-term decision-making, evaluating situations, and emotional self-regulation.[58] Each of the brain areas has a different sensitive period in which stress can do the most damage.

Early childhood adversity changes the brain in very specific ways to cope with abuse and neglect.[59] In particular, alterations occur first in sensory systems and pathways that act as the brain's first filters of information from the outside world. For instance, exposure to parental verbal abuse alters the auditory cortex and language pathways. Observing domestic violence alters connections between visual-related areas of the brain and areas associated with fear and intense emotions. Sexual abuse affects areas of the brain that represent genitalia and the recognition of faces. And exposure to emotional abuse alters brain regions associated with self-awareness and self-evaluation.

Additionally, children exposed to any form of maltreatment show an enhanced amygdala-based response to threatening faces and a reduction in the strength of the neural pathways associated with the conscious perception of threat and the activation of memories from the event. This overall pattern suggests that when experiencing abuse, the brain modifies itself in such a way as to cut off conscious perception of the abusive experience while simultaneously fostering avoidance of future situations that may pose similar threats. This is similar to what some psychiatrists call "splitting."

Adaptive, of course, doesn't necessarily mean socially desirable, healthy, or even conducive to happiness. Selfish, competitive, and aggressive traits may have evolved to help "solve life's adaptive problems in the face of an unpredictable and harsh world."[60] But the adaptations people make to maltreatment do not necessarily imply psychopathology either. When Martin Teicher began studying the neurology of abuse and neglect, he expected to find a clear distinction between resilient brains and maltreated brains. Instead, he was surprised by what he found. While many individuals who underwent persistent abuse and neglect had brains resembling the brains of people who had psychopathology, many of them didn't actually require any diagnosis of psychopathology.

In fact, maltreatment-associated brain changes have very distinct clinical, neurobiological, and genetic features that differentiate it from psychopathology.[61] One intriguing possibility to explain these results is that many individuals with maltreatment-related brain adaptations are highly resilient individuals and are able to recruit other psychological and environmental resources (e.g., perseverance, social support, or community resources) that allow them to be resilient in the face of stress.

Unfortunately, not all young children who are maltreated in harsh and unpredictable environments have additional resources to help them cope with the stress—a reality that has deep implications for the long-term consequences of early adversity. In general, when people experience persistent fear and anxiety, the amygdala and hippocampus work together to associate that fear with the context that elicited the fear response. In children or adults, the resulting "fear conditioning" can have lasting effects.

As a result of physical abuse, a child tends to become fearful of both the person and the context in which the abuse occurred. Over time, the cues to context can become generalized, and the fear response can be activated by people and places bearing only a small resemblance to the original context of the maltreatment.[62] The processes occur automatically, below the level of conscious awareness; the reflective mind does not participate in or even realize what is happening. As a result, early childhood perceptions that the world is a dangerous place can affect social interactions that occur later in life under far less threatening conditions.

Such fear responses are not automatically extinguished over time. Brain science suggests that fear learning is a very different process from fear unlearning. As child development psychologists Nathan Fox and Jack Shonkoff explain, "Fears are not just passively forgotten over time; they must be actively unlearned."[63] While fear can be learned relatively early in life, and is influenced by both the frequency and emotional intensity of the event, unlearning can occur only after particular areas of the prefrontal cortex have properly matured, when they have enough power to regulate the amygdala and other subcortical brain areas associated with the anticipation of reward.[64]

The concept of learned helplessness addresses a related phenomenon. In their classic studies beginning in the late 1960s, psychologists Steven Maier and Martin Seligman found that, given enough repeated shocks, dogs eventually stop trying to escape from their situation even when they eventually are given the opportunity to do so.[65] They just gave up, apparently believing that nothing they could do would matter. The researchers called the resulting state of defeat "learned helplessness" and came to see it as a major cause of depression.

In a recent review of the evidence that has accumulated in the fifty years since their groundbreaking studies—which have since been generalized to other animals, including rats and humans—Maier and Seligman concluded that they actually had it *completely backward*.[66] The latest research suggests that the passivity and feeling of lack of control is actually the default response in animals, an automatic, unlearned reaction to prolonged adversity. What must be learned is *hope*—the perception that one can control and harness the unpredictability in one's environment. The capacity for hope relies on development of the medial prefrontal cortex, which is not completed until early adulthood.

The lack of hope may be the true source of many of the behaviors associated with harsh and unpredictable conditions, particularly those related to extreme poverty. Young people who express feelings of hopelessness and feel as though they have no promising future tend to report more violent and aggressive behavior, substance use, and sexual risk-taking than those who don't express hopelessness—even though those very behaviors make it even more difficult to escape poverty.[67]

People who regularly experience conditions of harshness and unpredictability due to poverty tend to prioritize their most pressing needs at the expense of longer-term needs. Often there is little choice: living in harsh and unpredictable environments often brings with it a range of health and safety hazards, including pollution, noise, lead exposure, environmental tobacco smoke, violent crime, and unsafe housing. The lack of wealth and influence limits future outcomes and causes a shift in priorities to the basics: survival and reproduction.[68]

Perceptions of harshness and unpredictability have an important effect on health-related decisions, such as smoking. In a clever series of studies, Gillian Pepper and Daniel Nettle experimentally altered the perceived controllability of mortality risk. They found that simply making people think that the conditions of mortality in their environment were beyond their control caused people to choose an unhealthy food reward (chocolate) over a healthier food reward (fruit).[69]

A reflection of the reliability of environments, security is built on trust. In another study, Nettle and his colleagues transported student volunteers in Britain to an economically deprived neighborhood that had relatively high levels of crime.[70] The student volunteers walked around delivering questionnaires to houses. (There was a van waiting nearby anytime anyone wanted to bail.) In just under forty-five minutes, the volunteers circulating in the deprived neighborhood showed large increases in paranoia levels and plummeting social trust—approaching the average levels of the inhabitants themselves (which were relatively high).

If just "being there" for only a brief amount of time has such an effect, imagine the consequences of living under harsh and unpredictable conditions day in and day out. As the researchers note, "This may mean that differences in social attitudes between individuals and between populations might be more labile and more context-dependent than previously thought."[71] This point is really important to emphasize. Instead of viewing the "poor" as a separate class of human, we should recognize our common humanity and acknowledge that we would all most likely act in *very similar ways under very similar circumstances.*[72]

The possibilities for reversing hostility among people living in neighborhoods with extreme poverty and instability is often underestimated. In one remarkable natural experiment, researchers set out to assess changes in aggression over an eight-year period among a representative sample of children living in poverty (one quarter of them being Native American).[73] Halfway through the study, a gambling casino opened on the Indian reservation, and every man, woman, and child living on the reservation began receiving a percentage of the royalties.

The effects of moving out of poverty were clearly visible. Those who received the royalties experienced a reduction in psychiatric symptoms so marked that "by the fourth year the symptom levels were the same in children who moved out of poverty as in children who were never poor."[74] For those who were never poor, there was little change in psychiatric symptoms. Critically, the effect of moving out of poverty was strongest for behavioral symptoms such as aggression and hostility.

Although harsh and unpredictable early life experiences do have a lasting influence on our brain and behavior, the research suggests that we are still able to respond to our immediate adult circumstances, and in the long run, people are capable of turning their earlier adversities into opportunities for growth (see Chapter 4). Maslow noted that healthy growth and development involve not only gratification of our basic needs but also the ability to endure deprivation and grow as a result.[75]

Nevertheless, every child deserves to grow up with a sense of personal control over their environment and to see real hope for themselves and others in their community. One of the most important paths to upward social mobility and possibility in life is through education. Regardless of a child's home or neighborhood environment, it is possible to instill a sense of safety and predictability and hope in children who see very little of it in their lives.

HOPE THROUGH AN INTELLIGENT VIEW OF INTELLIGENCE

Children in extreme environments have hidden strengths that can be built upon. Psychologist Bruce Ellis and colleagues argue that individuals who have grossly unmet safety needs may prioritize skills and abilities that make sense in context even though such skills may make them less likely to do well on standardized tests of academic achievement.[76]

According to his Theory of Successful Intelligence, intelligence researcher Robert Sternberg emphasizes the importance of viewing intelligence in context.[77] The kinds of executive functioning skills (such as attention and impulse control) that support doing well in school may not be the same skills necessary for survival in one's local ecology. According to Sternberg:

> Successful intelligence is one's ability to choose and successfully work toward the attainment of one's goals in life, within one's cultural context or contexts. . . . What differs is the nature of the problems encountered in various ecological contexts. . . . For example, one child may focus during the day on how to solve an algebra problem, another on how to get past drug dealers on the way to school, another on how to ice-fish so that his family has something to eat for dinner. The mental processes may be similar or identical—what differs is the kinds of knowledge and skills to which they give rise.[78]

Unfortunately, much research on disadvantaged youth operates under a "deficit model," in which individuals are seen as broken and in need of fixing. But such an approach leaves out a lot of intelligence. As Ellis and his colleagues note, "Missing from this deficit approach is an attempt to leverage the unique strengths and abilities that develop in response to high-stress environments."[79] In fact, they go so far as to suggest that disadvantaged children and youth may be "cognitively gifted" for functioning in harsh, unpredictable environments.

Recent research conducted on birds, rodents, and humans suggests that exposure to high levels of harshness and unpredictability can actually improve forms of attention, perception, learning, memory, and problem-solving that are ecologically relevant under such harsh conditions.[80] Skills range from enhanced emotion recognition of angry or fearful faces and enhanced memory for negative, emotionally laden, or stressful events to an enhanced ability for learning things at an implicit, experiential level and an enhanced ability to flexibly switch attention. Attention-switching may help those in harsh environments track new information coming from the environment at a fast rate.

Other research shows that individuals of low socioeconomic status have an advantage in social-cognitive tasks involving contextual information, such as the ability to read others' affective states.[81] In one study, high school–educated university employees outperformed college-educated university employees on a standard test of empathic accuracy, correctly labeling the emotions displayed in a variety of posed facial expressions.[82] "Enhanced empathic accuracy may promote behavioral prediction and management of external social forces and help individuals exert control over their life," note Ellis and his colleagues.

Because such skills may promote survival in unsafe, hostile environments, Ellis and colleagues argue that educators need to work *with* them rather than *against* them. They propose that curricular content, delivery, and instructional practices be designed to leverage the unique strengths of "stress-adapted" children. Such a curriculum could incorporate concepts and problem-solving skills that are more relevant to the problems children regularly face in harsh and unpredictable environments as well as encourage more opportunities for moving around and doing independent projects on the computer and with others. Many children who are labeled as having attention-deficit/hyperactive disorder (ADHD), for instance, may be better adapted to a constantly changing environment and do their best under such conditions. Indeed, recent research suggests that children who display the characteristics of ADHD show many creative strengths that can be drawn upon.[83]

At the same time, their potential to learn and climb the educational ladder must be supported, as it is a true path to personal control and opportunity. Building on the strengths of stress-adapted children can also include showing them that they don't have to make a choice between street smarts or school smarts. When marginalized urban youth are treated as failures in school and their challenges are emphasized, they are forced to develop alternative strategies to succeed. As educational psychologist Beth Hatt notes,

> It is their own way of refiguring smartness and finding some sense of agency within the institutionalized figured world of smartness where schools overwhelmingly do not allow for students to be both street smart and book smart. Allowing for both would involve reinventing the idea of the "good" student, of what counts as legitimate knowledge, and broadening definitions of success within schools beyond grades and test scores.[84]

Many individuals growing up in harsh and unpredictable environments receive messages early on that they are not school smart. As a result, they begin to disengage from school, an adaptive response to the situation. That's why those whose safety needs are grossly unmet need a *real* reason to have hope.

An emerging field in education called "possibility development" focuses on helping adolescents imagine possibilities for a better world and a better place for themselves and others. Led by educational psychologist Michael Nakkula, possibility development targets various aspects of agency, including attitude toward learning, engagement, and giving students an "authentic voice," in which they feel as though they are making choices that have a real impact on their desired future.[85]

As with all students, those who experience harsh and chaotic environments need reminders that their success is largely a matter of their own effort and engagement in meaningful activities.[86] They may need a wide array of options in courses, majors, leadership opportunities, and civic engagement opportunities—and even the choice to leave school if it's best for their development (at least for a while).

For students starting out on an uneven playing field—with an extremely unsafe environment—the path to high academic achievement can be extremely nonlinear and nontraditional. As Michael Nakkula notes, students who take a nonlinear path to school achievement—the "Crooked-A's"—can look very different from stereotypical straight-A students.

There are a number of ways that "Crooked-A's" can be supported. Research highlights a focus on future possible selves. In one study, participants who wrote a letter to their imagined future selves were less likely to agree to hypothetical illegal actions.[87] In an additional study conducted by the same researchers, those who interacted with a digitally created version of their future self via virtual reality were less likely to cheat when the opportunity arose in a subsequent trivia quiz.

In another line of research, middle school students who were asked to identify their most important personal values and explain why they mattered achieved higher grades during the semester; they were also assigned to fewer remedial classes and more advanced math classes.[88] The effects were particularly strong among those students often considered the hardest to reach.

In other research, inner-city eighth graders were asked to imagine a future possible self, to list the obstacles they might encounter in realizing that self, and to describe strategies they would use to overcome the obstacles.[89] The students were 60 percent less likely to repeat eighth grade and showed greater academic initiative, had improved standardized test scores and school grades in the ninth grade, had fewer absences and instances of misbehavior in the classroom, and scored lower on measures of depression. The effects persisted over a two-year follow-up period and proved to be directly caused by changes in the students' view of their possible selves.

Of course, there is more to life than getting good grades, and many "Crooked-A's" have immense creativity and innovative ideas because they see the world differently. As organization psychologist Adam Grant notes, "Getting straight A's requires conformity. Having an influential career demands originality."[90] Colin Seale, founder of thinkLaw—an organization that helps educators leverage inquiry-based instructional strategies to close the critical thinking gap and ensure they reach all students regardless of race, zip code, or what side of the poverty line they were born on—was himself born to a single mother and incarcerated father and raised in Brooklyn. Seale passionately believes that today's disruptors can be to-morrow's innovators, and asks us to "imagine a world where instead of thinking of students who always get into some sort of trouble as 'bad,' we see their leadership potential and own up to the necessary, albeit challenging responsibility to help them fulfill this potential . . ."[91]

Regaining a sense of coherence and hope in one's immediate environment is immensely valuable to those whose safety needs are unmet. Yet safety is only one part of a secure foundation for growth. In order for us to fully open our sails and move full steam ahead, it's also essential to have belonging and affection in our lives. That's next.

CHAPTER 2

Connection

In the fall of 1930, twenty-four-year-old Harry Harlow stepped onto the University of Wisconsin, Madison, campus for his first day as an assistant professor. As he tried to find his way across the vast campus, he kept getting mistaken for a lost freshman. When he finally reached his office, he found a student sitting at his desk. "Hello, do you know where Dr. Harlow is?" asked Abraham Maslow, only three years younger than his new professor. Harry Harlow stared at his first doctoral student for a moment. "Yes," he replied.[1]

Maslow became not only Harlow's student but also his research assistant and dear friend. They clearly admired and valued each other. Maslow respected Harlow's wit, remarking that he was a "very brilliant man . . . I had dinner at his home, and so on. And we had chats and we could talk about things." In return, Harlow once fondly reminisced that "Abe never forgot his debt to monkeys, or perhaps we should say their debt to him."[2]

Maslow's experience with Harlow inspired his own seminal contributions to primate psychology. While working on "a million boring delayed-reaction" tasks with monkeys, Maslow quickly acquired great affection for them. "The fact was that I was fascinated with them," he later recalled. "I became fond of my individual monkeys in a way that was not possible with my rats."[3] Maslow's work on food preferences later led him to distinguish between the notions of "hunger" and "appetites" and influenced his thinking about power and esteem needs. His affectionate interactions with Harlow, as well as his observation of Harlow's groundbreaking research, also undoubtedly had a lasting influence on Maslow's belief in the need for affection.

In his 1958 presidential address to the American Psychological Association, Harlow admonished his peers: "Psychologists, at least psychologists who write textbooks, not only show no interest in the origin and development of love or affection, but they seem to be unaware of its very existence." For much of the history of psychology, love and affection were ignored as a subject suitable for scientific investigation. Those who did approach the topic came at it tangentially or treated it so technically, it was hardly recognizable. The behaviorist John Watson described love as "an innate emotion elicited by cutaneous stimulation of the erogenous zones." Freud reduced tenderness to "aim-inhibited sexuality." To Freud, love was a compromise, a side effect of getting what we really want, which is sex.*

Interested in the effects of maternal deprivation of love and affection, Harlow embarked on his now-famous experiments on infant rhesus monkeys. He placed the infants in a cage and presented them with two very different mothers. One mother was made of bare wire and could give milk through an attached bottle. The second was made of soft terrycloth and looked soft and cuddly but was not capable of providing milk.

The responses of the monkeys were quite striking. Whenever they experienced anxiety, they ran straight to the cloth monkey and clung to her for support. Not only did they calm down when near the cloth mother, they also became braver. In one set of studies, Harlow placed a menacing metal robot with flashing eyes and large teeth into the cage. After clinging to the cloth mother for support, the monkeys ventured forth to confront the scary robot!

The findings were highly influential and demonstrated the importance of physical touch and reassurance in social development. Harlow's further research—including thousands of carefully controlled experiments—were likewise revelatory about the effects of a repeated lack of affection. He found that while infant monkeys could technically survive without a real mother (as long as food was provided), they grew up missing fundamental social skills, such as not being able to get along with the other monkeys. They also experienced sexual difficulties once they grew into adulthood.

---

* Although that is undoubtedly true for *some* people!

The females displayed little affection toward their own offspring, rarely touching them or serving as a source of reassurance. Often they were abusive toward their children, hitting and biting them.

Harlow's research identified connection as essential to normal development. Maslow proposed that belonging and affection were fundamental needs in their own right—not reducible to safety or sex. This work set the stage for the scientific investigation of the importance of connection. Now, sixty years on, a wealth of research has firmly established that belonging and intimacy are not only essential to survival of the individual and of the species but it is also essential to full development of the whole person.

If both the physiological and the safety needs are fairly well gratified, there will emerge the love and affection and belongingness needs, and the whole cycle already described will repeat itself with this new center. . . . He will want to attain such a place more than anything else in the world and may even forget that once, when he was hungry, he sneered at love as unreal or unnecessary or important. . . . Now he will feel sharply the pangs of loneliness, of ostracism, of rejection, of friendlessness, of rootlessness.

—Abraham Maslow, *Motivation and Personality* (1954)

Sam had an extreme need to belong. When he walked down the street, he smiled at everyone who passed him on the street. When they didn't smile back, or especially if they looked at him funny, he would take it personally and feel like a loser for the rest of the day. He joined many clubs in college, even ones that he found boring. But he had to constantly feel a sense of belonging, even if sometimes the club or cause he was a part of went against what he felt in his gut to be true or important. It was only later in his life, once he finally experienced a meaningful, mutual relationship, that he realized that what he had really been seeking all those years was not many superficial connections but just a few deeper connections in which he felt that his whole self was being seen (not just the aspects of himself that were appreciated by the particular group he joined), and in which he could genuinely care about the whole being of another person.

The need for connection—to form and maintain at least a minimal number of positive, stable, intimate relationships—is a fundamental need that affects our whole being, permeating our entire suite of emotions, thoughts, and behaviors. While individuals differ in the strength of this need, connection is an irreducible, undeniable human need. The need for connection actually consists of two subneeds: (a) The need to belong, to be liked, to be accepted, and (b) The need for intimacy, for mutuality, for relatedness.

While these two subneeds are often treated synonymously in the psychological literature, I believe they are worth teasing apart, since they can diverge in important ways, with important implications for health and growth.

THE NEED FOR BELONGING

When one feels belonging, one feels accepted and seen, and when one is deprived of belonging, one feels rejected and invisible. These emotions stem from a deeply evolved "social protection system" that clearly had important survival and reproduction functions during the course of human evolution.[4] Strong affiliations among small-group tribe members throughout history offered greater resources, information, and cooperation to overcome stress and threat. Since we are intensely social animals, the need to seek at least a minimal amount of acceptance while avoiding complete rejection is vitally important for gaining social rewards in virtually all social situations—from social influence to social support to group membership to acquaintances to friendships to romantic relationships.[5]

It makes sense that evolution would endow us with an exquisitely sensitive social protection system that continually tracks our levels of belonging, detects threats to acceptance, and warns us (through incredibly painful emotions) whether the perceived threat is high and whether exclusion and ostracism are possible. It is perfectly normal for perceived signs of rejection to trigger uncomfortable emotions, such as hurt feelings, jealousy, and sadness, as well as increased attention and focus on solving the problem.[6]

The social pain that accompanies perceptions of low belonging has been shown to be indistinguishable from physical pain, with severe consequences on the functioning of the whole person. "For a social species, to be on the edge of the social perimeter is to be in a dangerous position," declares social psychologist John Cacioppo.*[7] "The brain goes into a self-preservation state that brings with it a lot of unwanted effects," from "micro-awakening" in the middle of the night as the brain remains on high alert for threats, to "social evasion" and depression, to various forms of narcissism (as we'll see in the next chapter), to even such catastrophic effects as suicide and mass shootings, two phenomena that are on the rise.[8] In the U.S., suicide rates have increased by 25 percent since 1999, with the rate among fifteen- to twenty-four-year olds rising steadily since 2007.[9] In the eleven years after 2005, there were more mass shooting incidents and deaths than in the previous twenty-three years combined. It is likely that belonging and acceptance are increasingly thwarted, leading to both trends.

In times of relative safety, the need for belonging may not be as essential as in times of increased perceived instability and danger in the environment, when the social protection system is most likely to become activated and exert its effects. For instance, under such circumstances, individuals increasingly identify with specific groups, often to the exclusion of other groups.

This was so clearly shown in the Robbers Cave study, in which researchers introduced a threat at a summer camp, motivating each boy to cling to his own group especially strongly.[10] Similar behavior occurs in terrorist organizations, where members become more connected under conditions of external threat (or perceived threat).[11] Lack of resources can also be a strong motivator of belonging: in a study that awarded one group a prize based solely on a coin flip, researchers observed greater cohesion within both the rewarded and non-rewarded groups.[12]

Group cohesion can be very difficult to change, even when the group membership is essentially meaningless. One recent study randomly

---

* While I was writing this book, John Cacioppo sadly passed away at the age of sixty-six: Roberts, S. (2018). John Cacioppo, who studied effects of loneliness, is dead at 66. *The New York Times*. Retrieved from https://www.nytimes.com/2018/03/26/obituaries/john-cacioppo-who-studied-effects-of-loneliness-is-dead-at-66.html.

assigned young children to unfamiliar groups and then provided information about the nature of the group. In one condition, they emphasized that groups were based on deep and internal aspects of the child, while in the other condition they emphasized that the groups were randomly assigned.[13]

The researchers found that even when the groups were arbitrary and presumably meaningless, the five- to eight-year-olds developed equally

> Our tribal impulses run deep and spring early.

strong in-group biases as children who were in more meaningful groups! Only when they went to extremes—such as actually flipping a coin to help the children understand randomness and actually switching the groups for children in order to emphasize that group assignment was arbitrary, unimportant, and very unlikely to be based on any meaningful aspects of the child—were they able to reduce bias to any significant extent on some of their measures. And even after going through such extremes, the researchers *still* found that children in both conditions were equally likely to give more stickers to their in-group. It's clear: our tribal impulses run deep and spring early.

Independent of societal conditions, however, people differ greatly from one another in their need for belonging, which—like every other need presented in this book—is a result of a multitude of individual genes intricately interacting with personal experiences.[14] As we saw in the previous chapter, above and beyond the effects of our genes, early childhood attachment insecurity influences the development of brain regions associated with avoidance and sensitivity to threat, which can lead to the development of an extreme need for belonging. As a result, some people get stuck on this need. You can gauge the extent of your own need for belonging by seeing how much you agree with the following statements:[15]

- I try hard not to do things that will make other people avoid or reject me.
- I need to feel that there are people I can turn to in times of need.
- I want other people to accept me.

- I do not like being alone.
- It bothers me a great deal when I am not included in other people's plans.
- My feelings are easily hurt when I feel that others do not accept me.
- I have a strong need to belong.

As with all the other needs, the critical metric is the distance between your need for belonging and just how unmet this need is in your daily life. Research shows that those who report the highest levels of loneliness are those who have the highest *unmet* need to belong. The greater the discrepancy between a person's need to belong and their satisfaction with their personal relationships, the higher the levels of loneliness and the lower the levels of life satisfaction in their daily lives.[16]

This finding applies both to those who are living alone as well as those who are living with others. Simply living with someone does not guarantee that connection needs are being met. It's the *quality* of the connections that matter for predicting loneliness, not the quantity of connections or even the proximity of the connections. Let's take a closer look at this other essential component of connection.

THE NEED FOR INTIMACY

While the social protection system has as its main goal the avoidance of rejection, the intimacy system is more about connecting to loved ones, caring and protecting them, reducing their suffering, and supporting their growth, happiness, and development. Here are some statements that you can use to gauge the strength of your need for intimacy.[17]

NEED FOR INTIMACY

- I have a close, intimate relationship with someone.
- I like to fully immerse myself in a relationship.
- I want to be able to share all the good and negative emotions in a relationship.
- I don't like being separated from the people I really care about.
- My thoughts often revolve around my loved ones.

- Sometimes I feel a deep connection and complete unity with another person.
- I don't keep any secrets from the people I love.

While a secure attachment style serves as a critical foundation for connection, it does not assure intimacy. The essence of intimacy is a *high-quality connection*. What is a high-quality connection? Jane Dutton and Emily Heaphy define a high-quality connection as a "dynamic, living tissue that exists between two people when there is some contact between them involving mutual awareness and social interaction."[18] A high-quality connection makes both people feel especially vital and alive. A low-quality connection, on the other hand, can be downright depleting. As one business manager put it, "Corrosive connections are like black holes: they absorb all of the light in the system and give back nothing in return."[19]

All high-quality connections share some common characteristics. First, they involve what Carl Rogers referred to as "unconditional positive regard."[20] Each person in the relationship feels seen and cared about and feels safe expressing a full range of experiences and thoughts. According to psychologist Lance Sandelands, high-quality connections create a feeling of "living presence, a state of pure being, in which isolating worries, vanities and desires vanish within a single vital organism."[21]

High-quality connections also include a sense of *mutuality*; both parties are engaged and participating. While positive regard is a momentary feeling of acceptance of the whole being of another person, mutuality "captures the feeling of potential movement in the connection . . . born from mutual vulnerability and mutual responsiveness."[22] The feeling of mutuality often has an air of buoyancy and spontaneity to it, which Dutton and Heaphy note creates "expansive emotional spaces that open possibilities for action and creativity."[23] High-quality connections that furnish opportunities for self-disclosure, emotional intimacy, trust, and openness have been shown to increase life satisfaction everywhere in the world.[24]

Finally, high-quality connections foster what social psychologist Sara Algoe refers to as "positive interpersonal processes," defined as "the good stuff that keeps us coming back for more in a friend or loved one."[25] This includes having fun together, sharing laughs, doing kind things for one another, celebrating good news together, admiring the other person's virtues, and expressing gratitude.

The importance of fostering high-quality relationships for health and growth should not be understated. In a study of the happiest 10 percent of college students, one characteristic stood out: *they all enjoyed a highly fulfilling social life.*[26] High-quality connections affect a variety of life domains, acting as a "rising tide" that enhances the effects of other sources of well-being, such as good physical health, self-esteem, optimism, constructive coping, and perceived control over the environment.[27]

THE BIOLOGY OF HIGH-QUALITY CONNECTIONS

The biology of the modern brain reflects the evolutionary heritage of this fundamental need. When we have a high-quality connection that gets us in tune with another human being—whether it's confiding a vulnerability to someone, gossiping about a common enemy, or sharing simple moments of laughter and joy—our "calm-and-connect" system comes alive. This system involves a suite of biological responses that work together to intensify a deep connection with another human being.[28]

In such moments of "positivity resonance"—as psychologist Barbara Fredrickson puts it—one person's brain literally syncs up with the other person's brain, a phenomenon sometimes referred to as "neural coupling." Partners experience an enhanced ability to anticipate the other's stream of thought and to feel the same emotions, sometimes even physically feeling their pain.[29] As Fredrickson notes, such "micro-moments of connection" are "tiny engines" that can set off upward spirals in your life, helping you to grow and become a better version of yourself.[30]

The brain's opioid system is a key player in increasing connection. While the opioid system is not specific to social connection—in fact, the opioid system is really the "pleasure system"—it just so happens that social connections provide the most important and dramatic experiences of pleasure in our lives most of the time.[31] During heightened social connection, the opioid system downregulates the HPA axis, dampening the body's response to stress. The opioid system is also involved in feelings of loss and grief when a social bond is lost.[32] The opioid system is so integral to the connection system that one prominent team of neuroscientists deemed strong social connections "in some fundamental neurochemical sense opioid addictions."[33]

Another key player in the connection system is the neuropeptide oxytocin. Oxytocin is produced in the hypothalamus and functions both as a hormone and as a neurotransmitter.[34] There is some evidence that oxytocin increases the willingness to trust and cooperate, while also enhancing the ability to discern cues of trust and goodness in others.[35,36] Oxytocin is also part of the calm-and-connect system; it dials down the sensitivity to threats in specific parts of the amygdala, downregulating feelings of distress and fear.[37]

While some researchers have referred to oxytocin as the "love hormone" or even the "cuddle hormone," more recent research suggests that the effects of oxytocin on social behaviors are highly dependent on context.[38] Oxytocin increases in-group favoritism, taking costly risks (including lying) to improve the welfare of your group, and conformity, trust, and cooperation for the in-group.[39] However, oxytocin's effect on trust is actually reduced when another person is perceived as untrustworthy, is unknown, or is a member of an out-group that has conflicting views and values from the in-group.[40] When the in-group and out-group have similar views and values, oxytocin doesn't seem to show this in-group bias.[41]

Therefore, while oxytocin does help strengthen connections with others and is a key player in the calm-and-connect system, it is becoming increasingly clear that oxytocin is not the "universal love hormone." It might be more accurate to think of oxytocin as the "in-group love hormone."[42] For this reason, in the new integrated hierarchy of needs I present in this book, I clearly distinguish between the need for connection and the need to give unconditional love that can operate independently of the connection you feel with someone (see Chapter 5).

Yet another key player in the connection system is the tenth cranial nerve, also known as the vagus nerve. The vagus nerve emerges from the brain stem deep within the skull and connects the brain to many organs, including the heart and lungs. The vagus nerve soothes a racing heart, encourages eye contact with another person, and synchronizes facial expressions. The strength of the vagus nerve—referred to as vagal tone—can be reliably measured; it is associated with physical, mental, and social flexibility and the ability to adapt to stress. Those with higher vagal tone experience greater connection with others in their daily lives, and in turn, this greater connection increases vagal tone, causing "upward spirals of the heart."[43]

Connection (and lack of connection) clearly have powerful effects on our brain and physiology, with deep implications for our mental and physical health. In fact, they can be matters of life and death.

LONELINESS KILLS

A recent survey suggests that 40 percent of adults say they are lonely, with approximately 42.6 million adults over the age of forty-five reporting chronic loneliness.[44] In his book *Loneliness: Human Nature and the Need for Social Connection,* social psychologist John Cacioppo reports that "social isolation has an impact on health comparable to the effect of high blood pressure, lack of exercise, obesity or smoking."[45]

Loneliness is proving a serious threat to public health.[46] Studies show that social isolation impairs immune functioning and increases inflammation, processes linked to a wide range of health issues, including heart disease and diabetes.[47] One study, from the University of York, found that people who are isolated or lonely have a 29 percent higher risk of coronary heart disease and a 32 percent higher risk for stroke compared to a control group of people having a strong social network.[48]

Loneliness is not making us just temporarily ill; it is *literally killing us.*[49] One study found that the feeling of loneliness, social isolation, or living alone increases the risk of death by 26 percent, 29 percent, and 32 percent, respectively.[50] Those with a subjective feeling of loneliness as well as an objective separation from others face the greatest risk of mortality. Loneliness poses a risk of mortality comparable to that of smoking and double that of obesity, and elderly individuals and those without adequate social interaction are twice as likely to die prematurely.[51]

No human being is exempt from the dire consequences of loneliness, and no other basic human need satisfaction can substitute for a deep connection—not money, not fame, not power, not popularity, not even belonging and acceptance—even though we often seek one or another of these other routes in the false hope that they will fully satisfy our need for connection. As Leo Braudy notes in his extensive review of the history of the quest for fame, the desire for fame is often based on a "dream of acceptance" that includes the notion that becoming famous will make the person feel loved, accepted, and sought after by others for the rest of their lives.[52]

As many people who have actually achieved fame can attest, though, the dream is often very illusory and even when achieved, fame remains deeply unsatisfying. While the two motives do seem to inhabit completely different ways of being, in a well-known 1962 essay called "Love and Power" in *Commentary* magazine, the political scientist Hans Morgenthau argues that love and power are actually united in a common motive: the striving to escape loneliness. According to Morgenthau, power and love offer very different strategies for achieving the same goal: "Love is reunion through spontaneous mutuality, power seeks to create union through unilateral imposition."

But as Morgenthau notes, power is a deeply unsatisfying substitute for intimacy: "Yet of what love can at least approximate and in a fleeting moment actually achieve, power can only give the illusion." The same also applies to the quest for fame. An implication, according to Morgenthau, is that the quest for power, in an attempt to make oneself whole, always inevitably makes one want even *more* power. One consequence is the deep irony that the most powerful people tend to be the loneliest. As Morgenthau notes, this helps explain the need for continuous demands to be referred to as "our beloved leader" among those with the greatest thirst for power (e.g., Stalin, Hitler).

Loneliness may be part of the cause of celebrity suicides. As Cacioppo notes, "Millionaires, billionaires, tend to feel lonely. A lot of athletes often feel lonely. Lots of people want to be their friend, but how would you feel if all the people who want to be your friend, you had the alternative interpretation that they want material or social benefits that you could give them."[53]

Take the wildly popular and openly gay novelist Stephen Fry, who attempted suicide after interviewing a Ugandan politician who sought to make homosexuality punishable by death.[54] Soon after the encounter, Fry "paced around trying to analyse what it was that had disappeared from me. It seemed as though the whole essence of me had disappeared. Everything that was me was no longer there. Just some feeling came over me that this was the end."

After consuming as many pills and as much vodka as he could round up, he was found unresponsive in his hotel room by his TV producer and the hotel staff, who had broken down the door to his room.[55] "How can someone so well-off, well-known and successful have depression?" he later wrote on his website.

> *Lonely?* I get invitation cards through the post almost every day. I shall
> be in the Royal Box at Wimbledon and I have serious and generous
> offers from friends asking me to join them in the South of France, Italy,
> Sicily, South Africa, British Columbia and America this summer. I have
> two months to start a book before I go off to Broadway for a run of
> *Twelfth Night* there.
>
> I can read back that last sentence and see that, bipolar or not, if I'm
> under treatment and not actually depressed, what the *fuck* right do I
> have to be lonely, unhappy or forlorn? I don't have the right. But there
> again I don't have the right *not* to have those feelings. Feelings are not
> something to which one does or does not have rights.
>
> In the end loneliness is the most terrible and contradictory of my
> problems.

What has gone so wrong in our society that loneliness is so rampant? For one, there is a stigma against admitting loneliness and a taboo against openly wanting to make new, close friends. But this is just one part of a larger picture. "We are doing things that are just so unnatural with regards to our need for social connection, and then we wonder why we're not

What has gone so wrong in our society that loneliness is so rampant?

feeling connected," observes Emma Seppälä, science director at the Center for Compassion and Altruism Research and Education at Stanford University.[56] Seppälä continues:

> The way we are prioritizing our life, and what we are prioritizing, often goes against our greatest need for belonging. Whether it's material goods or pleasures, financial advancement, or social advancement, we're missing the point completely. We're not seeing that our greatest happiness comes from connection, whether from family or religious or social community, something greater than yourself, something transcendental. We are so lost and there's a reason why so many people feel lost and anxious and depressed and lonely.[57]

Let's start with money.

MONEY, MONEY, MONEY

While it certainly takes a certain amount of money to meet our most fundamental safety needs and even get an opportunity for growth and development (see Chapter 1), money is no guarantee that any of the other needs of humanity will be satisfied in a healthy fashion. You can clearly see this all around the world: despite things getting better economically, a pervasive sense of anxiety, loneliness, and social isolation still pervades even those with financial security.

Many countries that are economically deprived nevertheless find ways of increasing social belonging among their inhabitants. Even studies conducted in the slums of Calcutta, India, show that the levels of life satisfaction among inhabitants are higher than those of the average American (although not as high as the richest people in India)![58] Also, there are plenty of examples of people who choose an "environmentally friendly" or "voluntarily simplistic" lifestyle, who also score high in life satisfaction despite their low income.[59]

In fact, research shows that, beyond a certain point, having more money can even be *detrimental* to growth and happiness. For one thing, more money tends to increase the materialistic drive, and materialism has been linked to decreases in happiness over time.[60] We adapt quickly to the rewarding feeling of getting more money—what's often referred to as the "hedonic treadmill"—leading to the constant feeling that no amount of money will ever be enough. As one team of researchers put it, "The cycle [of] . . . thrilling purchase, excitement fade, and subsequent desire for new material possessions . . . lends itself to materialism and decreased well-being."[61]

More money also gives us more choices, and research shows that not only can more choices be overwhelming and stressful—"the paradox of choice"—but those who earn more than $100,000 a year spend more of their time engaging in unenjoyable activities (e.g., grocery shopping, commuting) and less time engaging in leisure than those earning less than $20,000 a year.[62]

More money also tends to make people less egalitarian and less empathetic toward strangers.[63] Households that earn more than $100,000 a year donate a smaller percentage of their income to charity than those earning less than $25,000 a year.[64] Even participating in an experience that makes you feel that you occupy a higher relative social class makes you less likely to give to charities than if you feel you are from a lower social class.

Valuing money is equally detrimental to satisfaction. Those who value money as a source of happiness report being less satisfied with their lives, and when people work explicitly toward goals involving wealth, fame, or beauty, their well-being decreases.[65] Even the simple act of noticing small amounts of money while engaging in another enjoyable task (e.g., savoring a piece of chocolate) reduces enjoyment of that activity.[66]

The message is clear: beyond a certain income (enough to make you feel safe and secure), how you spend your money becomes more important than how much money you have.[67] One key distinction is between *material* purchases and *time-saving* purchases.[68] One large-scale study found that using money to delegate to others unwanted tasks such as cooking and cleaning is associated with higher life satisfaction, even after controlling for income.

Another key difference is between *material* purchases and *growth* purchases. Money that is used to foster personal growth—such as contributing to a charity, taking vacation and retreats with family and coworkers, or choosing housing that's closer to fostering a community or for engaging in opportunities to master a skill or hobby—is more associated with life satisfaction and well-being than spending money on material goods.[69] In fact, inducing people to think about having more time for meaningful social connections increases feelings of happiness, studies show, whereas priming people to think about money has no such effect.[70] Just how much is connection worth? In one study, researchers concluded that friends are worth more than a new Ferrari.[71]

An often-overlooked growth purchase is therapy. Research shows that psychotherapy can be highly cost-effective in satisfying people's need to be seen; it is at least thirty-two times more cost-effective in raising life satisfaction than merely gaining more income.[72]

Looking at all of this research, Rabbi Hyman Schachtel really seemed to be onto something when he said, "Happiness is not having what you want, but wanting what you have."

SOCIAL MEDIA

People will tear you apart and if you're not strong, it'll just rip through your soul. . . . [P]eople will be like . . . "You need to get your likes up." How about I try liking myself? That'll be actually a challenge.

—Social media influencer Brittany Furlan, *The American Meme* (2018)

Excessive social media use is often cited as another culprit of modern loneliness. Today there are many social media outlets to offer the allure of connection, including Facebook, Twitter, Instagram, Tumblr, and Snapchat. There are more ways to be popular to the masses, even if for just a moment, than at any other time in the history of the planet.

To be sure, for some, social media may be the only way to connect with others, and it has enormous potential for fulfilling the need for connection. Social media can be particularly essential for those with disabilities. As Asaka Park, an autistic teenager, put it, "Social media gives [disabled people] access to a social life and community involvement in an otherwise inaccessible world."[73] Having a healthy integration of Facebook and the Internet with the rest of one's life is possible and can be conducive to forming lasting friendships.[74]

The use of dating websites can also be beneficial to the growth of relationships: one study found that couples who met their spouse on a dating website that allows connection on a number of meaningful criteria reported greater satisfaction and experienced fewer divorces.[75] Nevertheless, this is not how most people use social media. The superficiality of Tinder and the push for ever more "friendships" on Facebook work against the deepening of any one connection.

> Social media simultaneously enlarges the possibility of forming loving relationships while also making it easier to avoid forming meaningful ones.

Consider this modern paradox: social media simultaneously enlarges the possibility of forming loving relationships while also making it easier to avoid forming meaningful ones. This is due, in part, to the allure of mass acceptance over individual connection, a powerful, evolutionarily deep-seated allure that is steering us away from wholeness. One recent study that tracked social media habits over a few weeks found that Facebook use was associated with lower feelings of happiness and life satisfaction.[76] Interacting online with people directly (not just through "likes" and viewing their page), however, did not produce these negative outcomes. "We've gone against our instincts, and we have fewer and fewer moments together," notes Emma Seppälä. "There is something we are doing here that is profoundly unnatural yet is going against what we really desperately need, which is connection."[77]

Maybe we can learn something from cultures that prioritize high-quality connections over belonging and acceptance.

BLUE ZONES OF CONNECTION

In cultures that foster face-to-face interactions, people tend to be highly satisfied and live long lives. Author and explorer Dan Buettner investigated groups around the world, including the people of Ikaria, a Greek island in the Aegean Sea.[78] Living to one hundred is common among the Ikarians. What's their secret?

Healthy diet and moderate exercise certainly play a role. But those factors are part of a larger web of mutually reinforcing strands that all add up to longer, healthier lives. Inhabitants report that they care little about money. "For many religious and cultural holidays, people pool their money and buy food and wine to be shared communally. If there is money left over, they give it to the poor. It's not a 'me place.' It's an 'us place,'" noted one of the island's few physicians, Dr. Ilias Leriadis.

The social structure is particularly important. Instead of high social media use, inhabitants enjoy frequent face-to-face interaction and social support. "Even if you're antisocial, you'll never be entirely alone," writes Buettner. "Your neighbors will cajole you out of your house for the village festival to eat your portion of goat meat." The Japanese notion of *ikigai* (the reason for which you wake up in the morning) is pervasive. "It gets centenarians out of bed and out of the easy chair to teach karate, or to guide the village spiritually, or to pass down traditions to children."[79]

The elderly in Ikaria are celebrated and kept engaged in the community; they live with their extended family until well into their one hundreds! As one 101-year-old Ikarian put it, "We just forget to die." Americans, by contrast, "shut the elderly away," says Seppälä.[80] Buettner's findings suggest that perhaps in addition to spending $30 billion a year on vitamins and supplements, $70 billion on dieting, and $20 billion on health-club memberships, Americans should also spend a bit more money on cultivating high-quality connections.

The science is clear: social connection is not a reflection merely of the expansiveness of your social networks, your popularity, or the number of people you know. The need for connection is most likely to be satisfied when we have secure, stable, and intimate connections with at least a few people in our lives. When we feel secure and satisfied in our relationships, we are much more likely to develop a stable sense of self-worth and mastery. However, when our need for connection is severely thwarted, we tend to display a much more insecure need for belonging and care much more about status and popularity.[81]

Since we are such a social species, it would make sense that the need for connection is not only concerned with intimacy and relationships but also has a tremendous impact on our self-esteem. Let's turn now to the final plank in the foundation of our sailboat, the need for a healthy, secure self-esteem that will allow us clearer sailing.

CHAPTER 3

Self-Esteem

Somewhere between 1932 and 1933, Maslow received a recommendation from his colleague Kimball Young at the University of Wisconsin to read *The Interpretation of Dreams* by Freud. Maslow immediately became fascinated by psychoanalysis and found that the book matched his own personal experiences like nothing else had before.[1] The book soon led Maslow to the work of Alfred Adler, founder of Individual Psychology, who had a very different take on human nature than Freud's.

Although one of the originators of the psychoanalytical movement, Adler eventually went his own path, arguing for the importance of an "aggressive instinct" distinct from the libidinal and self-preservation instincts Freud emphasized.* Adler also developed a concept he called "*Gemeinschaftsgefuhl,*" or "social interest," which he considered a fundamental human drive, alongside the aggressive instinct. Adler noted that we are social animals, with a basic striving for connection and community and an interest in making a positive impact on the world.

Maslow became even more captivated by Adler's writings, and one reason was Adler's focus on equality, mutual respect, and civic values. These concerns really spoke to Maslow's abiding ambition to help make the world more peaceful, especially given the moment in world history. There's no doubt that Adler's humanistic philosophy was a major inspiration for Maslow's eventual humanistic psychology.

---

* While Freud was originally dismissive of an aggressive instinct, to be fair to Freud, in his later book *Civilization and Its Discontents,* he referred to a "destructive instinct" and wrote, "I can no longer understand how we could have overlooked the universality of non-erotic aggression and destruction and could have omitted to give its due significance in our interpretation of life."

But Maslow was equally, if not more so, drawn to Adler's discussions of the power drive and its potential for destruction. Drawing on Nietzsche's idea of the "will to power," Adler argued that humans have a fundamental "striving for power," which he sometimes also referred to as a "striving for perfection," a "striving for superiority," a "striving for godlikeness," and a "striving for the enhancement of the personality." To Adler, too much striving for power and dominance over others and too little social interest can lead to what resembles evil, something he sensed was emerging in the world at the time, especially among the Nazis in Germany.

Inspired by Adler's ideas and eager to further study the push for power and its relationship to Freud's ideas about the libidinal drive, Maslow approached Harlow, now his doctoral advisor, eager to empirically test the seemingly competing ideas of Freud and Adler. Harlow was fine with this topic, although he required that any thesis he supervised be carried out with animals other than humans. Thus began Maslow's sophisticated research on sex and dominance among monkeys, a topic almost entirely unexplored until then.

One of Maslow's findings was that what appears to be sexually motivated behavior is often a reflection of power explainable by each monkey's status within a dominance hierarchy. Maslow found clear differences between sexually motivated and dominance-motivated "mounting," noting that "sexual behavior is used as an aggressive weapon often, instead of bullying or fighting, and is to a large extent interchangeable with these latter power weapons."[2]

Maslow also observed that the most dominant monkey was not always male. These early observations with dominant female monkeys, as well as his encounter with Adler's notion of "masculine protest"—in which women reject traditional feminine roles—surely influenced Maslow's later sexological research on dominance and sexuality among humans, particularly women. As Maslow wrote in a 1942 paper,

> Practically all the books on sexual and love technique make the stupid
> mistake of assuming that all women are alike in their love demands.
> And so we find that general instructions are given to apply to all

lovemaking as if one woman were equal to any other woman. . . . They are even more absurd when they speak as if the sexual act were merely a problem in mechanics, a purely physical act rather than an emotional, psychological act.[3]

These ideas were so radical at the time that in the early sixties, feminist author and activist Betty Friedan cited Maslow's sexological studies as support for her feminist approach to psychology distinct from Freudian psychoanalysis.[4] Friedan also drew on Maslow's writings on the importance of need fulfillment to argue that women in America are actively encouraged to evade their human growth and potential.

By 1935, Maslow wrapped up his doctoral studies on sex and dominance among monkeys and started preparing a proposal to present his findings at the American Psychological Association annual convention. He was delighted to have his work accepted as part of a research symposium led by the legendary Edward Thorndike. Fortuitously—especially considering he was concerned he wouldn't find a job after graduation— the young Maslow and his work so impressed Thorndike that he invited him to come to Columbia University in New York City to work as his postdoctoral fellow. Maslow happily accepted.[5]

The very same year that twenty-seven-year-old Maslow set foot in New York City was, coincidentally, the year that Adler, sensing danger in Europe, also permanently immigrated to New York City. Eager to tell Adler all about his doctoral research and how he had been testing his ideas on power, Maslow attended an open house that Adler hosted on Fridays at his suite in the Gramercy Park Hotel. To Maslow's surprise, only a few others showed up to the discussions, which gave him a chance to speak intimately with Adler.

Pleased with Maslow's work validating his own theories, Adler often met him for dinner, and over the course of eighteen months, the two formed a friendship and mentorship. But a few notable encounters were not so rosy. One night, as Maslow and Adler were dining at the Gramercy Park Hotel restaurant, Maslow casually asked Adler a question that implied that Adler was once a disciple of Freud. Adler became visibly angry and began talking so loudly as to make a scene.[6] Adler insisted he was never a disciple of any sort of Freud and had always been an independent physician and researcher. Nearly shouting, he stated that such a notion was a "lie and a swindle" concocted by Freud after their break. Shocked at Adler's outburst, Maslow was mortified to have upset his intellectual hero.[7]

Their last meeting was in early 1937, in Adler's suite. After a lecture and heated group discussion, Adler apparently thrust Maslow into a corner and, staring at him intently, asked, "Well, are you for me or against me?" Upset, Maslow never attended another gathering in Adler's suite. In May of that year, Adler had a heart attack and died while on a tour in Scotland; Maslow deeply regretted their last interaction and wished their mostly inspiring relationship could have ended on a less antagonistic note.[8]

Those few hairy moments aside, Adler clearly had a deep influence on Maslow's work, and his work continued to influence Maslow's evolving thinking about the self-esteem needs. In 1937, the year Adler died, Maslow published the first of his studies on "dominance-feeling" among humans, a term he soon changed to "self-esteem." Adler's influence is clearly visible in Maslow's paper, titled "Dominance-Feeling, Behavior, and Status."[9] In it, Maslow argued the importance of distinguishing between the feelings of dominance and dominance behavior. "Dominance-feeling," Maslow contended, includes feelings of self-confidence, high self-respect, and evaluation of self; a feeling of being able to handle other people; a feeling of mastery; a feeling that others do and ought to admire and respect one; a feeling of general capability; an absence of shyness, timidity, self-consciousness, or embarrassment; and a feeling of pride.

"Dominance-behavior," on the other hand, does not always match what the person is genuinely feeling and can often be a form of overcompensation. Maslow distinguished between "compensatory dominance" and healthy, or "natural," dominance (akin to what modern psychologists refer to as assertiveness). Maslow pointed out that people often exhibit dominance behavior in the absence of feeling secure and confident. He argued that these are instances of an overcompensation for the lack of dominance-feeling. As he explained in a footnote, in such cases the behavior is not so much dominant as domineering, "with antagonism to others, willfullness, impoliteness, selfishness, aggressiveness, tyrannizing, etc."

Maslow went on to note that such overcompensation is "apt to give the observer the impression of being strained and unnatural. It is more aggressive and louder than seems to be appropriate to the situation. It is, in some cases, apt to be even somewhat vulgar, and may sometimes also give the observer the impression of expressing defiance or a chip-on-the-shoulder attitude, rather than calm assurance. . . . In other instances, the compensatory behavior took the form of apparent snobbishness with haughty, cold, aloof behavior."[10]

Maslow's observations have a clear parallel in Adler's writings about overcompensation, in which Adler wrote about people turning their challenges and deficits into growth and strength. Having suffered from rickets in childhood, Adler personally knew how potent the feelings of adequacy or inferiority were and argued that overcoming or channeling such feelings in healthy directions was necessary for successful adaptation to life. Adler believed that one of the best paths for overcoming the seductive allure of power over others was cultivating the drive for social interest. In his later writings, Adler distinguished between striving for power and striving for mastery and overcoming obstacles. He argued that both offer ways of satisfying our "striving for perfection" but that the mastery drive is more about overcoming one's personal challenges than wielding power over others.

Maslow elaborated further distinctions in the self-esteem needs in his 1954 book, *Motivation and Personality,* in which he laid out his broader framework of human needs. Echoing his earlier 1937 paper, Maslow noted the distinction between a secure self-esteem, which he associated with real strength and earned confidence, and insecure self-esteem, which he associated with the power drive. Those with an insecure self-esteem, he said, are "interested not so much in helping weaker people as in dominating them and hurting them."[11]

In this chapter, I will show what modern science has revealed about the importance of having a healthy integration of the need for self-esteem. There are healthy ways of regulating and expressing this fundamental need and unhealthy, insecure ways of regulating the need for self-esteem that can thwart your growth and development as a whole person.

HEALTHY SELF-ESTEEM

All people in our society (with a few pathological exceptions) have a need or desire for a stable, firmly based, (usually) high evaluation of themselves, for self-respect, or self-esteem, and for the esteem of others.

—Abraham Maslow, *A Theory of Human Motivation* (1943)

The most important attitude we have may be the attitude we have toward ourselves. A basic sense of self-worth and confidence in the effectiveness of our actions provides a fundamental foundation for growth. Self-esteem is one of the strongest correlates of life satisfaction (although the strength of the correlation differs based on culture), and low self-esteem is one of the biggest risk factors for depression.[12]

Maslow and other humanistic psychologists, such as Carl Rogers, have been blamed for inspiring the self-esteem movement in the United States, which reached its apotheosis in the 1980s and 1990s, with a focus on feeling good about oneself as the answer to all of life's problems.[13] But a close reading of the psychological literature suggests that the problem isn't with self-esteem but the *pursuit* of self-esteem.[14]

The latest research suggests that a healthy self-esteem is an outcome of genuine accomplishment and intimate connection with others, and of a sense of growing and developing as a whole person. As psychologists Richard Ryan and Kirk Brown note, becoming too focused on improving one's self-esteem is an indication that something has gone awfully wrong in self-regulation and well-being.[15] And as Jeff Greenberg and his colleagues put it, "Difficulty maintaining self-esteem, and maladaptive efforts to do so, may be central to a variety of mental health problems."[16] Indeed, when self-esteem is too much of a concern relative to other needs, this is an indication that one's self-esteem has become unhealthy—highly insecure, unstable, and highly dependent on the validation of others.

So what is a healthy self-esteem? Modern research has identified two distinct faces of healthy self-esteem: self-worth and mastery.[17] You can get a sense of where you stand on these two components of self-esteem by seeing how much you agree with the following statements:[18]

SELF-WORTH
- I like myself.
- I am a worthwhile human being.
- I am very comfortable with myself.
- I am secure in my sense of self-worth.
- I have enough respect for myself.

MASTERY
- I am highly effective at the things I do.
- I am almost always able to accomplish what I try for.
- I perform very well at many things.
- I often fulfill my goals.
- I deal well with challenges in my life.

Regardless of where you currently stand, there is always room for growth. Let's take a look at each of these two aspects of healthy self-esteem more closely.

SELF-WORTH

Self-worth involves the evaluation of your overall sense of self: *Are you a fundamentally good person with social value in this world?* Feeling worthy of who you are as a person lays a healthy foundation for who you want to become.[19]

Maslow sometimes distinguished between the need for self-esteem and the need for esteem from others.[20] However, modern research shows that the evaluation of others is often linked to our self-esteem. Like it or not, we are a social animal, and the judgments we formulate of our self frequently incorporate the judgment of others. Social psychologist Mark Leary's research has shown that our feelings of self-worth strongly track our social value, or at least our perceptions of our social value. (Sometimes our perceptions are inaccurate.)[21]

Leary and his colleagues Katrina Jongman-Sereno and Kate Diebels distinguish two forms of social value we can have in this world: *relational social value* (the degree to which we regard our relationship with others as personally valuable and important) and *instrumental social value* (the degree to which others perceive us as possessing resources and/or personal characteristics that are important for the benefit of the collective good).[22] Those with a high sense of self-worth tend to like themselves, and view themselves as having high relational value.

This is why feelings of self-worth are so strongly linked to the need for belonging. The social protection system that underlies the need for belonging tries to prevent damage by regulating our behavior *before* we are actually rejected.[23] Research shows that being moderately rejected (or at least perceiving moderate rejection) tends to be just as anxiety-inducing and painful as being greatly rejected—an unmistakable signal to take corrective action. Conversely, being moderately accepted tends to increase feelings of self-esteem just about as much as being highly accepted. This finding suggests that the consequences of complete rejection in our ancestral past when we interacted in small-scale hunter-gatherer societies was catastrophic. Even though social rejection is rarely as catastrophic in modern times, we still have remnants of that mechanism of the mind.

Self-worth is often influenced by praise and acceptance from others, and this tendency never goes away entirely, no matter how secure one's sense of self-worth. As the researchers Romin Tafarodi and William B. Swann Jr. note, "At no point in development do we become numb to the moral judgment of those whom we take an interest in. As social animals, we cannot refrain from peering into the looking glass that others hold up to us, as much as we may distrust the images we see there."[24] Still, the more our judgment of self-worth becomes internalized, the less the power of others has to completely sway how we see ourselves.[25]

MASTERY

The second face of self-esteem—mastery—involves the evaluation of your overall sense of agency: *Are you an intentional being who can bring about your desired goals by exercising your will?*[26] As Tafarodi and Swann note, "Human development is characterized as much by the need to know 'who we are' as 'what we can do.'"[27] A global evaluation, mastery is generalized across many different domains of your life. Of course, you have greater mastery and expertise in some areas than others, but a healthy self-esteem involves not only liking yourself but also having an overall feeling that you are a competent human being.[28]

Your entire life history of successes and failures influence the attitude you have toward yourself as an intentional being capable of reaching your goals in life. The more successful you are at making progress toward your goals, the more confident you feel, and the two tend to spiral upward toward a stable sense of mastery. Vice versa, the more your goals are thwarted in life, the more you tend to spiral downward toward insecurity and feelings of incompetence. Since we are such a social species, mastery also tends to be linked to social value, but mastery tends to track instrumental social value more than relational social value. Those with high mastery tend to have traits that confer greater social status in their society due to their usefulness to others—not necessarily the characteristics that are valued in a friend, family member, or social group.

While both a healthy sense of self-worth and mastery are strongly related to each other—people tend to develop both forms of self-esteem in tandem—the two can come apart. It's possible to view yourself as a willful agent in the world, capable of accomplishing your goals, but not really like or respect yourself. And vice versa, it's possible to like yourself while not feeling very effective in reaching your goals. Tafarodi refers to these situations as "paradoxical self-esteem" and has shown that such variations have implications for how we process and remember social feedback from others.[29]

Now that we've outlined the two main components of a healthy self-esteem, it's time to clear up a common misconception: *high self-esteem is not the same as narcissism*. Unfortunately, the perpetuation of this stereotype cheapens the value of self-esteem, which truly is an important human need.

SELF-ESTEEM VS. NARCISSISM

Too often, psychologists and people in the media conflate a healthy self-esteem with narcissism. Contrary to many people's perceptions, narcissism and self-esteem have very different developmental pathways and outcomes in life.[30] Those with a high self-esteem believe they are worthy and competent and strive for intimate, meaningful connections with others, but they don't necessarily view themselves as *superior* to others.

Developmentally, both narcissism and healthy self-esteem start to develop around the age of seven. At this age, children draw heavily on social comparisons with others and start to evaluate themselves along the lines of "I am a loser," "I am worthy," and "I am special." Children come to view themselves as they perceive they are seen by others.[31] However, the development of narcissism and high self-esteem show the *mirror image* of each other throughout development: whereas self-esteem tends to be at its lowest in adolescence and slowly increases throughout life, narcissism tends to peak in adolescence and gradually declines throughout the life–span.[32]

The development of self-esteem and narcissism are also influenced by different parenting styles. Narcissism tends to develop in tandem with parental *overevaluation*: parents who raise children who exhibit high levels of narcissism tend to overclaim their child's knowledge, overestimate their child's IQ, overpraise their child's performance, and even tend to give their child a unique name to stand out from the crowd.*[33] In contrast, high self-esteem develops in tandem with parental warmth. Parents who raise children who exhibit high levels of self-esteem tend to treat their children with affection and appreciation. They treat their children as though they matter.

It's clear that the real concern in society should not be with fostering healthy self-esteem. If anything, more could be done to help all children feel valued, respected, and genuinely competent as human beings. Instead, more attention should be paid to the difference between healthy and unhealthy expressions of the common need for self-esteem. Let's take a closer look at the two main unhealthy attempts at regulating the need for self-esteem.

---

* Interestingly, giving inflated praise (e.g., "You made an incredibly beautiful drawing!") to children with low self-esteem tends to backfire, leading to such children *decreasing* their challenge seeking and avoiding crucial learning experiences that would be conducive to their growth. See: Brummelman, E., Thomaes, S., de Castro, B. O., Overbeek, G., & Bushman, B. J. (2014). "That's not just beautiful—that's incredibly beautiful!": The adverse impact of inflated praise on children with low self-esteem. *Psychological Science, 25*(3), 728–735.

THE TWO FACES OF NARCISSISM

In extremely insecure people, there are many ways in which this insecurity can express itself. . . . It may have the quality of seclusiveness and withdrawal . . . or it may have the quality of hostility, aggressiveness, and nastiness.

—Abraham Maslow, *Motivation and Personality* (1954)

Modern researchers have identified two unhealthy attempts at regulating the need for self-esteem: grandiose narcissism and vulnerable narcissism. When most of us think of the prototypical narcissist, we think of the grandiose narcissist: brash, boastful, noisy, and always demanding to be in the spotlight. However, psychologists have also identified a quieter manifestation of narcissism—vulnerable narcissism—characterized by extreme sensitivity to slights and a deep sense of shame over their grandiose desires that leads these individuals to despise the spotlight.[34]

Both faces of narcissism share a common set of features, including entitlement, exploitativeness, and grandiose fantasies. In fact, those displaying the features of vulnerable narcissism, paradoxically, surprise others with their grandiose fantasies of superiority.[35] Nevertheless, the source of hostility and antagonism differs for each form of narcissism.

Those who score high in grandiose narcissism tend to be antagonistic toward others for reasons relating to their desire to increase their social status and dominance (instrumental social value). Their entitlement is linked to their belief that they are special and superior and therefore deserving of greater resources and treatment. In contrast, those scoring higher in vulnerable narcissism feel hostility and distrust in reaction to their negative ideas about themselves and others, and their response is often rooted in traumatic childhood experiences. Their particular flavor of entitlement seems to be more linked to a belief that they deserve special attention because of their fragility, not their superior characteristics.

While there is much talk of "narcissists" these days, I take the perspective that *all of us have narcissistic tendencies to one degree or another*.

> All of us have narcissistic tendencies to one degree or another.

After all, to have narcissistic tendencies is to be human. Psychoanalysts such as Sigmund Freud, Annie Reich, Heinz Kohut, and Otto Kernberg saw the phenomenon of narcissism as "cathexis of the self," or an overinvestment in self—but they didn't view intense self-absorption as necessarily a bad thing.

Heinz Kohut believed it was better to take a patient's existing narcissistic tendencies and channel them into humor, creativity, empathy, and wisdom than attempt to eliminate narcissism entirely from their personality structure.[36,37] He referred to this as a "wholesome transformation."[38] In the same spirit, I will attempt to really get underneath the label "narcissism" so that we can see how wholesome transformation of our narcissistic tendencies can help us all become more secure, whole people.

Vulnerable Narcissism

Mary is a thirty-six-year-old woman whose parents divorced when she was fourteen. After the divorce, she lived mostly with her mother. However, due to her mother's addictions to various substances and erratic, often abusive behavior, Mary had to take on the responsibility of raising her younger brother, frequently ignoring her own needs. Now an adult with extreme uncertainty about herself and her career, she presents to the therapist with a mix of seemingly contradictory attributes, with features of grandiosity coexisting with intense self-absorption and constant feelings of inadequacy, shame, and vulnerability. Mary has an exaggerated sense of self-importance and appears to feel privileged and entitled. She expects preferential treatment and has fantasies of unlimited success, power, beauty, talent, and brilliance, while she also admits that she is constantly wondering whether she is fundamentally a good or a bad person. She seems unable or unwilling to understand or respond to others' real needs or feelings unless they coincide with her own or if it will make her feel better about herself. She also feels unhappy, depressed, and despondent and finds little pleasure or satisfaction in life's activities. Interpersonally, she constantly needs reassurance from others that she is a good person, gets upset and withdrawn at the slightest criticism, and is constantly on the lookout for signs of rejection. At the same time, she tends to be critical of others, angry, hostile, and oppositional or contrary. She tends to hold grudges and tends to have conflicts with authority figures. At the same time, Mary feels envious of others, tends to feel misunderstood, mistreated, or victimized, and tends to feel helpless and powerless.[39]

The characteristics associated with vulnerable narcissism illustrate the paradoxical features that tend to coexist when one's sense of self-worth is wildly in flux, fragile, and uncertain.[40] It turns out that there is really no such thing as low self-esteem. When people take self-esteem surveys, very few people report having *zero* social value. Instead, people who score low on self-esteem scales often score around the midpoint, suggesting they really have an *uncertain* self-esteem.[41]

The research on vulnerable narcissism suggests that high levels of uncertainty about one's worth as a human being often bring along with it hairpin triggers of shame and reactive hostility, avoidance of situations that may activate such triggers, grandiose fantasies of receiving validation and respect from others, a constant need for validation and attention from others (including feeling entitled to the attention of others and constant resentment for not being appreciated), a hiding of one's felt needs and perceived weaknesses, an excessive need to help others in order to feel good about oneself, and distrust and cynicism about people's true intentions. All of these characteristics tend to go together. Take a look at these statements and honestly assess the degree of your vulnerable narcissism in your daily life:[42]

VULNERABLE NARCISSISM SCALE

- I often feel as if I need compliments from others in order to be sure of myself.
- When I realize I have failed at something, I feel humiliated.
- When others get a glimpse of my needs, I feel anxious and ashamed.
- I often hide my needs for fear that others will see me as needy and dependent.
- I get angry when criticized.
- It irritates me when people don't notice how good a person I am.
- I like to have friends who rely on me because it makes me feel important.
- Sometimes I avoid people because I'm concerned that they'll disappoint me.

- Sometimes I avoid people because I'm concerned they won't acknowledge what I do for them.
- I often fantasize about being recognized for my accomplishments.
- When someone does something nice for me, I wonder what they want from me.

While these statements characterize "vulnerable narcissism," if we look beneath the label, we can see that all of these characteristics are simply ways of responding to others that add up to a really smart strategy for protecting oneself against the pain of being rejected. As we've seen, humans evolved a very powerful social protection system that keeps track of our current levels of belonging and acceptance in daily life. When rejection is perceived as imminent, we feel pain, and the system goes into hypervigilant mode to help protect us.

Unfortunately, our "inner social meter" can become woefully miscalibrated.[43] Traumatic early life experiences can cause us to perceive our social value and capacities in ways that are not accurate, and acting on these extremely miscalibrated beliefs can bring about the very outcomes we fear the most. Unfortunately, vulnerable narcissism has been linked to a history of traumatic experiences, including emotional, verbal, physical, and sexual abuse.[44,45]

To be sure, there is also a substantial genetic contribution to the development of vulnerable narcissism. Vulnerable narcissism develops through a complex process through which biological vulnerabilities (e.g., strong emotional sensitivity, impulsive antagonism, etc.) are amplified by family and school factors (e.g., invalidating parental behaviors, bullying by peers, etc.). Nevertheless, while genetic effects influence the sensitivity to particular environmental triggers, abusive parenting and other environmental conditions matter.[46]

Emotional abuse is a particularly crucial pathway to vulnerable narcissism, considering emotional abuse in childhood may be invisible to others and even to the child, who may not understand what constitutes abuse.[47] Emotional abuse can include having an extremely controlling, intrusive, or uncaring parent, or having a parent whose narcissistic needs are so great that they make the child feel guilty or ashamed for expressing their own needs or expressing their big dreams (which is a very normal childhood experience). In studies I've conducted with my colleagues Brandon Weiss, Joshua Miller, and W. Keith Campbell, we found that the following statement was significantly related to vulnerable narcissism: "As a child, I was often encouraged by my family to substitute my own needs for their own."*

While features of vulnerable narcissism may help in managing the overwhelmingly painful feelings of low self-worth and shame generated by rejection and early childhood abuse and can help minimize the chances that the abuse will ever happen again, vulnerable narcissism is linked to a host of beliefs, coping strategies, and attachment styles that ultimately inhibit health, growth, and integration. In our research, we found that vulnerable narcissism was associated with lower levels of life satisfaction, autonomy, authenticity, mastery, personal growth, positive social relationships, purpose, and self-acceptance in life, as well as a lack of trust in one's thoughts and feelings, and a profound lack of a sense of self.[48,49]

We also found an extremely strong relationship between vulnerable narcissism and reports of imposter syndrome. Those scoring high in vulnerable narcissism scored high on statements such as "I tend to feel like a phony," and "Sometimes I am afraid I will be discovered for who I really am." It's less likely that such individuals actually feel fraudulent and more likely that they engage a "self-presentation strategy" that serves as another way of protecting themselves against the potential pain of rejection. By adjusting the expectations of others, they won't feel as intensely ashamed if they do fail.[50]

We also found that those scoring high in vulnerable narcissism have

---

* There is an interesting link between adverse childhood experiences and entitlement that might help explain why neuroticism and antagonism are correlated in vulnerable narcissism. Research shows that ostracism and feeling wronged by society can increase feelings of entitlement, as demonstrated by even brief experiments in which making people feel like a victim makes it more likely they will behave selfishly. See: Poon, K-T., Chen, Z., & DeWall, C. N. (2013). Feeling entitled to more: Ostracism increases dishonest behavior. *Personality and Social Psychology Bulletin*, *39*(9), 1227–1239; Zitek, E. M., Jordan, A. H., Monin, B., & Leach, F. R. (2010). Victim entitlement to behave selfishly. *Journal of Personality and Social Psychology*, *98*(2), 245–255.

great difficulty reining in their strong impulses and taking constructive action on their own behalf. The defense mechanisms they tend to employ—harboring infantile and unrealistic fantasies, projecting responsibility onto others, being passive-aggressive in expressing their needs, apologizing for asserting their needs, experiencing somatic symptoms, isolating themselves from those who could offer support, suppressing emotions, reacting with anger when hurt or stressed, and engaging in impulsive behaviors such as eating to feel better and regain control—make sense for a vulnerable child trying to cope with intense pain and fear. But in adulthood, they prevent growth of the whole person.

From Vulnerability to Growth

Vulnerable narcissism need not be a barrier to growth. Any of us, regardless of our levels of these characteristics, can take charge of our lives and start to build a coherent and stable sense of self. A key way of overcoming severe self-esteem uncertainty is to shed the perfectionistic self-presentation. As one meta-analysis of the literature found, vulnerable narcissism is significantly linked to an obsessive concern over whether one is coming across as imperfect to others, as well as perceiving others as demanding perfection of oneself.[51]

Worrying less about what everyone thinks of you, taking more risks (even if they may make you look bad), and really testing whether everyone demands such a high level of perfection from you can stabilize self-esteem. People who actually test their self-beliefs are often shocked to discover just how accepting others are of their imperfections. In fact, they often find that being more vulnerable and authentic with others increases social connection. Since none of us is perfect, we tend to feel more comfortable with others who express our common humanity (including acknowledging human imperfections) rather than with those who always seem to have it all together.

Another step those scoring high on vulnerable narcissism can do to abet growth is to really understand the role of the social protection system. It evolved to detect threats to acceptance and belonging, *indiscriminate of the threat*. It overreacts. It is sometimes necessary to override the system. Do you really care what *everyone* thinks of you, or only what *particular* people think of you? Value the honest feedback of those who truly respect you and whom you respect.

Cognitive-behavioral therapy (CBT), dialectical behavioral therapy (DBT), and acceptance and commitment therapy (ACT) can be immensely helpful in learning to regulate the intense feelings of rejection and shame we often feel and the irrational, negative thoughts that are floating around constantly in our heads.[52] You really can "retrain your brain."[53] Steven Hayes, founder of the ACT approach to psychotherapy, has stated that an important outcome of ACT is "the ability to contact the present moment more fully as a conscious human being, and to change or persist in behavior when doing so serves valued ends."[54]

My colleagues and I found that vulnerable narcissism was correlated with statements such as "I'm afraid of my feelings" and "My thoughts and feelings get in the way of how I want to live my life."[55] This suggests that those who score high in vulnerable narcissism tend to avoid the very things that will give them the greatest happiness and growth in life. Once you actually test your fears of all the things that could happen, you find the reality often isn't nearly as bad as you thought it would be. In fact, once you embrace yourself and life, the reality is often positive. Since people tend to treat others the way they expect to be treated, changing your approach to the world often brings with it a change in how people approach you.

What's more, having dreams and ambitions is not something to be ashamed of. Those with vulnerable narcissism are likely to fear and avoid growth because they fundamentally don't feel worthy of it; instead, they concoct grandiose fantasies that they never reveal to others. This secrecy is unnecessary and counterproductive, as expressing ambition is healthy.

Maslow was deeply interested in how the suppression of healthy ambition can stunt self-actualization, and the tendency for people to fear growth. In an unpublished essay from 1966, Maslow noted that in our society we learn "to put on a chameleon-like cloak of false modesty or humility."[56]

Maslow argued that in order to avoid punishment from society, the person "becomes humble, ingratiating, appeasing, or even masochistic. In short, due to fear of punishment for being superior, she becomes inferior and throws away some of her possibilities for humanness. For the sake of safety and security, she cripples and stunts herself. . . . That is, she is evading the task for which her peculiarly idiosyncratic constitution fits her, the task for which she was born, so to speak. She is evading her destiny."[57] Maslow refers to this as the "Jonah Complex," a phenomenon described by the historian Frank Manuel. This phrase is based on the biblical tale of Jonah, who, out of fear, tries to run from God's prophecy, but he can find no place to hide. Finally, accepting his fate, he does what he was called to do.

So let me state this as clearly as possible: you may not be entitled to shine, but you have the *right* to shine, because you are a worthy human being. Changing your self-limiting narratives about your worthiness, asserting needs in a healthy way, overcoming your avoidance of fearful experiences, and taking responsibility for your behaviors—these actions strengthen

You have the *right* to shine.

and stabilize the vulnerable self. The great irony is that the less you focus on whether you are worthy and competent, and take that as a given, the greater the chances you will consistently accept your inherent worth.

I'll leave the last word in this section to Brené Brown, who has spent years studying shame, vulnerability, and the need for belonging:

> Stop walking through the world looking for confirmation that you don't belong. You will always find it because you've made that your mission. Stop scouring people's faces for evidence that you're not enough. You will always find it because you've made that your goal. True belonging and self-worth are not goods; we don't negotiate their value with the world. The truth about who we are lives in our hearts. Our call to courage is to protect our wild heart against constant evaluation, especially our own. No one belongs here more than you.[58]

Grandiose Narcissism

Jim is a fifty-eight-year-old man, currently separated, who is employed as a manager of a local retail store but dreams of one day doing great things, such as becoming a leader with high influence and social status and receiving many public accolades. As a child, his parents praised him for even the slightest accomplishments, constantly telling him and their friends that he was destined for greatness. Jim is psychologically insightful, tends to be energetic and outgoing, appears comfortable and at ease in social situations, is articulate, and has a good sense of humor. However, he also has an exaggerated sense of self-importance. He appears to feel privileged and entitled and expects preferential treatment, believing that conventional rules of conduct do not apply to him. He seeks to be the center of attention, expresses emotion in exaggerated and theatrical ways, and seems to treat others primarily as an audience to witness his own importance, brilliance, beauty, etc. He appears to believe that he should associate only with people who have high status or are otherwise "special." Jim is also highly self-critical; he sets unrealistically high standards for himself and is intolerant of his own imperfections. He also sets unrealistically high standards for others and tends to blame others for his difficulties, displaying intense anger when perceptions of his greatness and perfection are even a little bit threatened. Jim also tends to feel envious of and competitive with others, and he can be dismissive, haughty, and arrogant and show a striking lack of empathy.[59]

This profile illustrates the prototypical "grandiose narcissist" and the paradoxical features that arise when our need for agency and the esteem of others becomes so great that we protect a grandiose image of ourselves no matter the costs. Of course, simply having high ambitions and confidence is not the same as having *overconfidence*. In regulating our self-esteem in a healthy fashion, it's important to assess when our need for esteem has become so great that it is no longer in touch with reality or when it causes damage to others.

Whereas vulnerable narcissism reflects an array of coping behaviors that clearly stunt personal growth (such as depression and withdrawal), grandiose narcissism is more of a mixed bag. It comprises healthy traits such as assertiveness, a drive for leadership, and the ability to influence others, which can be conducive to reaching one's goals, having an impact on the world, and even feeling happy and satisfied in life. But it also encompasses characteristics that in the long run can hamper personal growth and achieving one's goals in life. Take a look at the following statements to gauge your own levels of grandiose narcissism.[60]

GRANDIOSE NARCISSISM SCALE

- I like being the most popular person at a party.
- I tend to take charge of most situations.
- When people judge me, I just don't care.
- I often fantasize about having lots of success and power.
- I aspire to greatness.
- I'm pretty good at manipulating people.
- I'm willing to exploit others to further my own goals.
- I deserve to receive special treatment.
- I don't worry about others' needs.
- Others say I brag too much, but everything I say is true.
- I will try almost anything to get my "thrills."

As these statements make clear, those scoring high in grandiose narcissism have a strong drive for instrumental social value, as well as the social status and public acclaim that tend to come along with it. At the same time, those who score high on this scale tend to care very little about their relational social value or if others think of them as a likable person. In fact, those scoring high in grandiose narcissism are often so preoccupied with their social standing that it often lowers their relational value in the eyes of others, and while they may think they are superior to others, they don't necessarily like themselves all that much as a whole person.

Instead, those who score high in grandiose narcissism are preoccupied with winning and view people as either winners or losers. A corollary is that those with high levels of grandiose narcissism often think very highly of the characteristics that are considered "special" or confer high social status in their society, but often don't think much of the quieter characteristics that often facilitate cooperation and being liked by others. In contemporary American culture, indicators of social status tend to be such things as money, power, intelligence, and overt indicators of success (awards, rankings, being pictured on the covers of magazines). Merely being a "nice" person doesn't tend to get your picture plastered around Times Square.

However, communal narcissism does exist. Communal narcissism is a particular manifestation of grandiose narcissism in which one is overconfident that they will be the *best* at helping others and are sure that *they alone* will bring peace and justice to the whole world—when in reality they aren't nearly as skilled or capable of bringing their communal ambitions as they lead others to believe, often leaving a lot of destruction in their wake.*[61]

While our research found that vulnerable narcissism was more clearly maladaptive across the board, the defense mechanisms of grandiose narcissism are much more of a mixed bag, at least in terms of harm to one's own self. In fact, we found that grandiose narcissism is related to reports of greater life satisfaction. But we found that this increased life satisfaction is likely to come with a cost—disconnection from one's own self.

We found that those scoring high in grandiose narcissism reported high levels of imposter syndrome, a weak sense of self, self-alienation, a greater likelihood of accepting external influence, and higher levels of experiential avoidance. Those scoring high in self-esteem showed the opposite pattern, suggesting that self-esteem is tied to a greater sense of connection with one's own self.

That's not surprising. Both forms of narcissism involve defense of a particular self-image. Vulnerable narcissists mount a vehement defense against being rejected and appearing unworthy of love and belonging. Grandiose narcissists fiercely defend a superior self-image. Both strategies can sometimes be helpful in achieving self-enhancing goals, but both incur the cost of others and a cost to one's capacity to connect deeply with one's most valued goals and desires.

We also found that while those with high levels of grandiose narcissism engage in a lot of projection, they tend to project their anger and frustration *outward*, being prone not just to reactive aggression when provoked but also to proactive aggression. For instance, those with high levels of grandiose narcissism strongly endorsed the statement "I pride myself on my ability to cut people down to size."[62] We also found that those scoring

---

* It's an open and interesting research question whether the communal flavor of grandiose narcissism is more common in communal societies (such as China) than in the United States. After all, the need for self-esteem is a fundamental need, and it has to manifest itself somehow.

high in grandiose narcissism tend to show a lot of denial, endorsing statements such as "People say I tend to ignore unpleasant facts as if they don't exist."

We found that grandiose narcissism is also related to a black-and-white view of others, seen in the endorsement of statements such as "As far as I'm concerned, people are either good or bad," as well as an extreme view of themselves, seeing themselves as fearless and bold. For example, we found a strong correlation between grandiose narcissism and the statement "I ignore danger as if I were Superman."

These overly inflated views of the self are linked to the high levels of perfectionism found among those who score high in grandiose narcissism.[63] One meta-analysis found that those scoring high in grandiose narcissism are more likely to impose harshly perfectionistic demands on others, showing perpetual dissatisfaction with their perceived flaws.[64] Grandiose narcissism was also correlated with perfectionistic self-promotion and fantasies of achieving perfection. However, those scoring high in grandiose narcissism don't tend to care much about the costs of behaving imperfectly themselves (most likely because they believe that no such imperfections exist).[65]

Note the contrast with vulnerable narcissism. Whereas those scoring high in vulnerable narcissism are more concerned about receiving approval and validation from others while avoiding the consequences of not appearing perfect, those scoring high in grandiose narcissism need constant acclaim to maintain an image of superiority at all times.[66]

Again, these can be effective strategies if you feel the need to constantly defend a superior sense of self. And sometimes it really does help to see yourself as being as fearless as Superman![67] The problem occurs when you really start to believe you *are* Superman, and act that way in all situations. The problem isn't with self-esteem but the *addiction* to self-esteem.

Addicted to Self-Esteem

While we each differ in our level of grandiose narcissism at any given moment in time, it's important to recognize that power can be intoxicating for any of us; it's a drive that comes along with being human. All of us, to some degree, enjoy the rush of power and the feeling of being highly respected by others. What seems to be particularly associated with grandiose narcissism is an addiction to the feeling of high self-esteem, not unlike other, more familiar addictions (such as cocaine or gambling) in which appetites are indulged to destructive extremes.[68]

When the addiction to esteem reaches a certain tipping point, it becomes particularly detrimental to growth: my colleague Emanuel Jauk and I found that in the upper range of grandiose narcissism, grandiose narcissism is associated with increases in vulnerable narcissism, antagonism, negative affect, and depression and is less associated with adaptive factors such as assertiveness and social potency.[69] This suggests that above a certain level of grandiose narcissism, there is a tendency toward a more rapid cycling between feelings of superiority and a sense of extremely low self-worth.

This may also help explain why, especially in clinical settings—in which symptoms have become so strong that a person seeks professional help—narcissism tends to come and go in cycles, and there is often a rapid cycling or even co-occurrence between vulnerability and grandiosity.[70]

When things are going well, and those scoring high in grandiose narcissism are ascending the social status hierarchy, they feel a rush of pride and excitement. However, as with most drugs, there is eventual tolerance, and the rush ceases to cause the same highs. When the highs fade, grandiose narcissists seek even greater glories (higher "doses"), looking for even more admiration and validation of their superiority anywhere they can get it, even from people and professions that don't genuinely interest them (e.g., running for a political office when you don't even really care for the politics).

As with any drug, however, the grandiosity isn't sustainable (eventually truth wins out over delusion), and those scoring extremely high in grandiose narcissism often end up in episodes of withdrawal, shame, or depression; their ability to maintain an unrealistic inflated self-evaluation fails, making them feel extremely vulnerable. But once the deep despair and feelings of unworthiness subside, the craving for that buzz of inflated self-esteem may revive receptiveness to admiration and positive feedback from others, kicking off the entire cycle all over again.

An addiction perspective on narcissism helps explain why those we label "narcissists" are so fascinating to everyone: those scoring high in grandiose narcissism indulge the strivings for esteem and power that we all have deep within us.[71] As social psychologists Roy Baumeister and Kathleen Vohs note:

> We think people are generally fascinated by others who do things that people themselves desire but do not indulge (either because of lack of opportunity or inner restraint). Sex, fame, money, power, and violence are perennial sources of fascination because people are curious to watch someone indulge the impulses that they themselves feel but cannot fully satisfy. Egotism may be another case.[72]

Truth is, any one of us, if given enough power (especially if we had little power previously), can become "addicted" to self-esteem, pursuing ever greater dosages of esteem from others to fuel the high it brings. This is why it's important to acknowledge that the altruistic tendencies that allow a person to achieve power in the first place can become compromised in the face of an abundance of power—and once its delights have been tasted, so to speak. Psychologist Dacher Keltner calls this the "power paradox"—the experience of power itself tends to destroy the skills that once earned us power.[73]

The excessive quest for power doesn't only apply at the individual level; it is also a source of a lot of narcissism seen at the collective level as well. In recent years, psychologists have been scientifically investigating "collective narcissism," a defensive form of in-group positivity.[74] People who score high on tests of collective narcissism believe that their in-group deserves special treatment and insist that their in-group gets the recognition it deserves. Just like individual narcissism, collective narcissism stems from the frustration that comes from the need for control and self-esteem and is an attempt to compensate for such insecurity.[75]

In contrast, self-esteem has been linked to healthy in-group positivity, which is more likely to foster both in-group and out-group love.[76] This is ultimately an uplifting message: just as it's possible to have healthy self-esteem, it's possible to have *healthy in-group love*—where it feels good to be a member of your in-group and in which you have great pride for the genuine accomplishments of your group without constantly experiencing hypersensitivity to intergroup threat and hostility.[77]

At the end of the day, I believe we shouldn't ignore the seduction of power or pretend that this pull is not a part of our common humanity. But striving for power does not necessarily have to lead to destruction. Almost all humans strive for mastery and to make a difference in the world, but as Adler noted, we also have a striving for social interest. We have *both* strivings within us. Therefore, the question remains: *How can we satisfy our self-esteem needs in the most authentic, healthy, and growth-fostering way?*

HEALTHY PRIDE

It seems to me that the [fully functioning] individual moves toward being, knowingly and acceptingly, the process which he inwardly and actually is. . . . He is not trying to be more than he is, with the attendant feelings of insecurity or bombastic defensiveness. He is not trying to be less than he is, with the attendant feelings of guilt or self-deprecation. He is increasingly listening to the deepest recesses of his physiological and emotional being, and finds himself increasingly willing to be, with greater accuracy and depth, that self which he most truly is.

—Carl Rogers, *On Becoming a Person: A Therapist's View of Psychotherapy* (1954)

The good news is that we can satisfy our self-esteem needs without the narcissistic self-presentation. The answer to cultivating a healthy self-esteem doesn't lie in hiding or suppressing the ego, as with vulnerable narcissism, or puffing up the ego so much that it engulfs the whole person, as with grandiose narcissism. Instead, the key to a healthy self-esteem is cultivating genuine relationships, skills, and competencies so that you can have healthy pride in your accomplishments.

While pride is often thought of as the "deadliest sin," modern research by Jessica Tracy and her colleagues suggests that some forms of pride can be an incredibly productive force in our lives. In fact, pride can be a great motivating force for reaching your personal goals and making a positive impact on the world. Instead, the issue is with how the power is obtained.

As Tracy's research has shown, there is a big difference between hubristic pride, which is paved with narcissism, self-aggrandizement, and antagonism at the expense of others, and healthy pride, which is paved with a healthy self-esteem and genuine accomplishments.* [78]

Those who regularly experience healthy pride tend to be friendly, social, agreeable, calm, resilient, creative, and popular. While both forms of pride are associated with higher social status, healthy pride is related to both higher social status and being genuinely respected, admired, and liked by others.[79] Clearly one does not have to make a choice between having higher social status or being admired and liked; it is possible to have *both*.

A recent study supports this point.[80] My colleague Reb Rebele and I gave people a list of things that affect one's quality of life and we asked them to indicate how much of each of the items they needed to feel satisfied with their lives. We found three clusters of motivations. The first cluster, which I refer to as the *status-driven life*, consisted of the drives for social status, money, power, high performance, achievement, impact on the world, and creativity. The second cluster, which I refer to as the *security-driven life*, primarily consisted of the needs for security, happiness, and close relationships. The third cluster, which I refer to as the *growth-driven life*, included the drives for high performance, achievement, creativity, and wanting to make an impact, but also included the drives for meaning, growth, close relationships, and the desire to make a positive impact on the world. We found that self-actualization was most strongly correlated with the growth-driven life and was unrelated to the status-driven life.

Note that wanting to make a positive impact on the world was correlated with a drive for meaning and growth. This is consistent with the idea, discussed frequently among the humanistic psychologists, that growth and humanitarian concerns tend to go together naturally. Note also that we found a difference between wanting to make an impact on the world more generally and wanting to make a positive impact on the world.

---

* Psychologist Jessica Tracy and her colleagues refer to healthy pride as "authentic pride." Given the ambiguity surrounding the word "authenticity," I prefer the term "healthy" (although there certainly exist ambiguities around that word as well).

The findings dovetail nicely with Keltner's definition of power as altering the states of others so as to make a difference in the world.[81] Using this broad definition of power, we can see that there are multiple ways to "make a difference in the world" and thus have power. Wanting to make the world a better place is primarily driven by the desire for growth—the cultivation of growth in one's self and others—not primarily the drive for money, status, and power.

So there you have it. If your primary goal in life is to have power, money, and status, that's fine, but you can probably stop reading this book right now. My advice would be to take close notes on the strategies of those who have an abundance of characteristics associated with grandiose narcissism. Individuals who have high levels of grandiose narcissism seem to find ways to get ahead and dominate, regardless of the costs to others.

If your primary goal in life is to be safe, secure, and happy, then you can probably stop reading this book right now as well. The chapters on security should offer you enough insight to have a more solid and secure foundation in your life.

However, if you truly wish to self-actualize—and even transcend—in your own style, driven by the desire for growth, exploration, purpose, creativity, and love for all of humanity, then keep reading. Because there's so much more sailing to go.

PART II

Growth

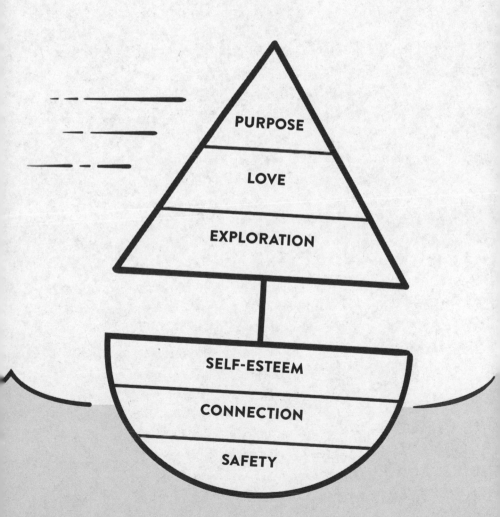

PURPOSE

LOVE

EXPLORATION

SELF-ESTEEM

CONNECTION

SAFETY

Prelude

As Maslow and his wife, Bertha, set foot in New York City in August of 1935, the world was very different from when Maslow was in graduate school. As fascism rose in Germany, Italy, Japan, and Spain, Maslow sensed a threat to humanity that greatly frustrated and saddened him.[1] Under a postdoctoral research assistantship with Edward Thorndike at Columbia University, Maslow continued some of his work on sex and dominance. However, his interests were becoming increasingly broad and humanitarian.

Due in part to the mass emigration of psychoanalysts from Europe, a truly unprecedented cultural renaissance was underway in New York City just as the Maslows were settling in. As Maslow described it, New York was the "center of the psychological universe . . . there has been nothing like it since Athens."[2] Within the span of about a decade (1935–45), Maslow learned from some of the most influential psychologists and anthropologists of his generation. And many became his friends.

Among them were New York's most prominent psychoanalytic practitioners and writers: Alfred Adler, Erich Fromm, Karen Horney, Bela Mittelmann, Emil Oberholzer, Abram Kardiner, David Levy, the Gestalt psychologists Max Wertheimer and Kurt Koffka, the neuropsychiatrist Kurt Goldstein, and Columbia University's prominent anthropologists Ruth Benedict and Margaret Mead.

Influential as all the mentors were, Maslow was particularly fond of Ruth Benedict and Max Wertheimer. He described his efforts to study self-actualization as an attempt to understand both of them, whom he "loved, adored, and admired and who were very, very wonderful people."[3] He admired them greatly, but he was also deeply curious about what made them so different from others. He took copious notes on their personality characteristics. In "one wonderous moment," he realized that their pattern of personality could be generalized, suggesting that he had discovered a kind of person. "There was wonderful excitement in that," he noted.[4]

One can see hints of Maslow's theory of self-actualization in a textbook on abnormal psychology that he co-authored with the psychoanalyst Bela Mittelmann in 1941.[5] This was no ordinary textbook on abnormal psychology. Right in the introduction, Maslow and Mittelmann stated that their concern was with understanding abnormal behaviors from the viewpoint of the person's "total personality" and in the context of their vital needs, aims in life, and "attempts at solving life's problems."[6] They argued that many apparently "conflicting" desires within an individual are often all reflections of the same goal—whether it's happiness, comfort, love, or self-respect. The only question is which is the best path to achieving those goals for the individual. "All human beings want the same things," they wrote. "The trouble is that there are many possible paths to these ultimate goals."[7]

Another unusual feature of this textbook on abnormal psychology is the inclusion of an entire chapter on the "normal personality." While acknowledging that there is no clear line between the normal and the abnormal personality, and emphasizing that normality is always relative to a particular culture, subculture, status, age, sex, and type of personality, Maslow and Mittelmann nevertheless outlined twelve "manifestations of normality." Many items on this list would closely resemble Maslow's list of the characteristics of self-actualizing people proposed a few years later, including adequate feelings of security and stable self-esteem; self-knowledge; the ability to accept love, affection and support; the freedom to express one's personality spontaneously and naturally; the ability to make efficient contact with reality; and an adequate integration and consistency of personality.

In one section of the chapter, the authors made clear that what they were describing was not necessarily the "ideal" personality—since the notion of the ideal personality involves values—but a "projection of the ideal of the particular individual who is carrying on the discussion." Nevertheless, they wrote that "it is hoped that science in its onward march will eventually take over the whole problem of values for study. . . . We see no reason to believe that this process will not eventually be extended so that most of our values, perhaps even all of them, will eventually come within the jurisdiction of science but until this is true, any discussion of the ideal personality must be postponed."[8]

Around the time of the publication of the abnormal psychology textbook, Maslow's research had shifted to something much more ambitious, comprehensive, and urgent—prompted, in part, by his encounter with many great intellects displaying a passionate concern for social change and world betterment, concerns that deeply resonated with him.

Maslow experienced a particularly transformative moment one afternoon shortly after the U.S. entered World War II, as recounted in an interview with *Psychology Today* toward the end of his life: "One day just after Pearl Harbor, I was driving home and my car was stopped by a poor, pathetic parade. . . . As I watched, the tears began to run down my face. I felt we didn't understand—not Hitler, nor the Germans, nor Stalin, nor the Communists. We didn't understand any of them. I felt that if we could understand, then we could make progress. I had a vision of a peace table, with people sitting around it, talking about human nature and hatred, war and peace, and brotherhood. I was too old to go into the army. It was at that moment that I realized that the rest of my life must be devoted to discovering a psychology for the peace table. That moment changed my whole life."[9]

Feeling as though his work as a psychologist could help "save the world and . . . prevent the horrible wars and the awful hatred and prejudice," Maslow began synthesizing an integrated theory of human motivation. You can clearly see how his theory represented an integration of all of his influences up to that point in his life.[10]

One particularly important influence on Maslow's theory of motivation was the writings of Kurt Goldstein, who the late neurologist Oliver Sacks described as "one of the most important, most contradictory, and now most forgotten figures in the history of neurology and psychiatry."[11]

Goldstein emigrated from Germany to the United States in 1935 at the height of his career, having lost everything he had built up over the course of fifty years in Europe, including the institute he founded. Through his treatment of young soldiers with traumatic brain injuries, Goldstein argued that the field of neurology needed a new "holistic approach" to fully understand the rehabilitation of patients, one that takes into account the "whole organism."

In his 1934 magnum opus *The Organism,* Goldstein observed that there is an innate "drive for self-preservation" among patients to "utilize the preserved capacities in the best possible way . . . We can say that an organism is governed by the tendency to actualize, as much as possible, its individual capacities, its 'nature,' in the world." Goldstein argued that this singular drive for "self-preservation" and "self-actualization" is "considered the basic law of life." Goldstein, like Maslow, was influenced by the Gestalt psychologists and their notion that the whole of the organism cannot be understood by looking only at isolated parts (such as particular brain deficiencies).

In 1943, Maslow brought all of these seemingly disparate threads together and seized upon the phrase "self-actualization" in his grand "Theory of Human Motivation." After discussing the basic needs for safety, security, belonging, affection, and esteem, Maslow went on to mention the existence of a higher need that is just as foundational as the basic needs:

> Even if all these [basic] needs are satisfied, we may still often (if not always) expect that a new discontent and restlessness will soon develop, unless the individual is doing what he, individually, is fitted for. A musician must make music, an artist must paint, a poet must write, if he is to be ultimately at peace with himself. What a man can be, he must be. He must be true to his own nature. This need we may call self-actualization. . . . It refers to man's desire for self-fulfillment, namely, to the tendency for him to become actualized in what he is potentially. This tendency might be phrased as the desire to become more and more what one idiosyncratically is, to become everything that one is capable of becoming.[12]

After Maslow published his 1943 paper, he felt an urgency to further socially relevant research.[13] On May 19, 1944, he drafted an introduction to a twenty-one-chapter magnum opus that he hoped would serve as a grand unifying vision of humanity.[14] By June, he had completed a detailed outline for this ambitious book but eventually decided to put the project on hold and instead focus more systematically on his investigation of self-actualizing people.

Maslow had been asking his Brooklyn College students to write essays on the "most self-actualized" person they knew, and he was considering the students' responses. He also was informally observing the characteristics of his friends, colleagues, and relatives. But he acknowledged that he wasn't being systematic enough. So on May 6, 1945, he started the "Good Human Being [GHB] Notebook" to organize all his findings in one place.[15] In his first entry, Maslow wrote:

> After fussing along for some years I have decided to dig into GHB research and do it more formally and rigidly. It's all very difficult, though. Lots of problems. As things stand now, I try to be as conscious as possible of insurmountable difficulties, and then I go ahead anyway.[16]

Maslow's work on self-actualization was really his search for the characteristics of the "good" human being. Maslow believed that human nature was basically good, and his work was an attempt to systematically show that this is the case by studying those who he considered most fully human. As he noted in an interview many years later, "I wanted to prove that humans are capable of something grander than war, prejudice, and hatred. I wanted to make science consider all the people: the best specimen of mankind I could find."[17]

Maslow continued his work on self-actualization due in part to his fervent belief that in self-actualizing people, "we find a different system of motivation, emotion, value, thinking, and perceiving." In an entry in his notebook in mid-January 1946, Maslow wrote:

> There seems to be no intrinsic reason why everyone shouldn't be this way [self-actualizing]. Apparently, every baby has possibilities for

self-actualization, but most all of them get it knocked out of them. . . . I think of the self-actualizing man not as an ordinary man with something added, but rather as the ordinary man with nothing taken away.[18]

"I think of the self-actualizing man not as an ordinary man with something added, but rather as the ordinary man with nothing taken away."

While there are certainly seeds in his notebook of some of the characteristics that eventually made his final list, there is a great leap from the GHB notebook to his published paper of 1950 entitled "Self-Actualization: A Study of Psychological Health."[19] Maslow kept his notebook off and on between 1945 and 1949, but he dropped off substantially in his entries after 1946 due to health problems (which later in life would be diagnosed as a heart attack). It is interesting to think about what went through his head in those years that allowed him to make such a big leap. As Richard Lowry notes, "One has the impression that somewhere along the way there has been a great deal of shaping, polishing, and setting."

In his paper, Maslow noted that in addition to studying personal acquaintances and friends, and screening three thousand college students, which yielded only one "immediately usable subject and a dozen or two possible future subjects," he also studied the characteristics of public and historical figures. Two "fairly sure" historical figures were Abraham Lincoln ("in his last years") and Thomas Jefferson. Seven "highly probable public and historical figures" included Albert Einstein, Eleanor Roosevelt, Jane Addams, William James, Albert Schweitzer, Aldous Huxley, and Baruch Spinoza.

Despite his so-called methods, however, Maslow admitted that his list of the characteristics of self-actualization were the result not of a systematic line of research but of a composite "global or holistic impression" based on a small number of sources.[20] Acknowledging the limitations of his methodology, he put forward the list in the hopes that it might serve as the basis for further study.

CHARACTERISTICS OF SELF-ACTUALIZATION

It's been about seventy years since Maslow published his list of the characteristics of self-actualizing people, but his paper provides a wealth of still-testable ideas. I was very curious just how many of his proposed characteristics of self-actualization would hold up if properly tested, so I converted his characteristics into a scale and formally administered them to a wide range of people. After a few iterations, I found that ten characteristics stand the test of scientific scrutiny and are all significantly related to one another (in other words, those who score high in one characteristic tend to also score high in the others as well). To take the self-actualization test, go to *selfactualizationtests.com*.

CHARACTERISTICS OF SELF-ACTUALIZATION

- *Truth Seeking* (e.g., "I am always trying to get at the real truth about people and nature.")
- *Acceptance* (e.g., "I accept all of my quirks and desires without shame or apology.")
- *Purpose* (e.g., "I feel a great responsibility and duty to accomplish a particular mission in life.")
- *Authenticity* (e.g., "I can maintain my dignity and integrity even in environments and situations that are undignified.")
- *Continued Freshness of Appreciation* (e.g., "I can appreciate again and again, freshly and naively, the basic goods of life, with awe, pleasure, wonder, and even ecstasy, however stale these experiences may have become to others.")
- *Peak Experiences* (e.g., "I often have experiences in which I feel new horizons and possibilities opening up for myself and others.")
- *Humanitarianism* (e.g., "I have a genuine desire to help the human race.")
- *Good Moral Intuition* (e.g., "I can tell deep down right away when I've done something wrong.")
- *Creative Spirit* (e.g., "I have a generally creative spirit that touches everything I do.")
- *Equanimity* (e.g., "I tend to take life's inevitable ups and downs with grace, acceptance, and equanimity.")

It's striking just how many of the characteristics of self-actualizing people that Maslow proposed almost seventy years ago can be reliably and validly measured. Nevertheless, Maslow was way off base about one important thing: the characteristics of self-actualization are not nearly as rare as he believed. I found no gender, race, or ethnicity differences in self-actualization, and there was no association with age (at least for those above the age of eighteen, since that was the age requirement of my study), which is interesting considering that Maslow believed that it was very rare for a college student to display the characteristics of self-actualization.

Do these characteristics matter? They sound nice, but does self-actualization *really* have any relevance anymore in this cutthroat, competitive world we live in? Turns out, the characteristics of self-actualization matter quite a bit. Just as Maslow predicted, those with higher self-actualization scores were much more motivated by growth, exploration, and love of humanity than the fulfillment of deficiencies in basic needs. Self-actualization scores were associated with multiple indicators of well-being, including greater life satisfaction, curiosity, self-acceptance, positive relationships, environmental mastery, personal growth, autonomy, and purpose in life. Self-actualization also predicted job performance, job satisfaction, and reports of greater talent, skill, and creative ability across a wide range of fields, from the arts and sciences to business and sports.

The characteristics of self-actualization can conceptually be grouped into four categories, which will form the remainder of this book: exploration, love, purpose, and transcendence. Together, the first three enable growth. At the base of growth is exploration, which all other growth needs draw on. Therefore, that's where our journey into growth naturally begins.

CHAPTER 4

Exploration

If I were to wish for anything, I should not wish for wealth or power, but for the passionate sense of the potential, for the eye which, ever young and ardent, sees the possible. Pleasure disappoints, possibility never. And what wine is so sparkling, what so fragrant, what so intoxicating, as possibility!

—Søren Kierkegaard, *Either/Or* (1843)

The need for exploration—the desire to seek out and make sense of novel, challenging, and uncertain information and experiences[1]—is an irreducible fundamental need. A central problem of existence is managing uncertainty and reducing the entropy and disorder in our lives, which is always increasing. While facing increasing uncertainty can be a source of great anxiety, as Maslow noted, the unknown also has its delights.[2] In fact, it's often necessary to leave the safety of familiarity, at least to some extent, in order to grow. It takes courage to grow.

> **It takes courage to grow.**

To Maslow, the key to helping people move toward growth is to make the growth choice more attractive to people and less threatening, and make the safety choice less attractive and more costly, so that a person can feel unthreatened, free, and spontaneous enough to "dare to choose the unknown."[3]

Shedding the defenses that have provided a sense of protection throughout one's life can be an incredible source of stress. Nevertheless, in the long run, we only grow when we at least move in the direction of growth. Maslow believed that if people are inwardly free, they will more often than not choose wisely, in a healthy and growth-oriented direction.[4] To Maslow, this is how the psychology of being and the psychology of becoming can be reconciled. Just by being yourself and shedding your defenses and fears and anxieties, you move forward and grow.

This process is clearly visible among young children. Infants and young children are naturally exploratory, curious, fascinated, and playful, wondering about their new world. However, they are also scared and find the unknown intensely frightening. Young children test the waters and look to their parents or others in their environment to know whether it's safe to explore. A child who feels too safe will become bored and seek to move on to "higher" exploratory delights. Too much safety holds kids back from real opportunities for learning and growth.

As a response to "helicopter parenting"—overly protective and intrusive parenting—Lenore Skenazy founded the Free-Range Kids movement, in which parents are encouraged to raise children to function independently with reasonable acceptance of the risks. Along with Daniel Shuchman, Peter Gray, and Jonathan Haidt, Skenazy also founded the nonprofit Let Grow, whose mission is to counter the "culture of overprotection" with the aim of future-proofing our kids and our country.[5]

Exploration is not just for kids, and it is unfortunate that the spirit of exploration and play often wanes in adulthood. However, those who seek out and actively engage with the unknown are in a better position to extract the possible delights of the unknown and to learn and grow as a whole person. Maslow predicted this would be the case when he wrote: "Our healthy subjects are generally unthreatened and unfrightened by the unknown. . . . They accept it, are comfortable with it, and, often are even more attracted by it than by the known." You can gauge your current levels of the need for exploration by taking a look at the following statements created by Todd Kashdan and his colleagues:[6]

EXPLORATION SCALE
- I view challenging situations as an opportunity to grow and learn.
- I am always looking for experiences that challenge how I think about myself and the world.

- I seek out situations where it is likely that I will have to think in depth about something.
- I enjoy learning about subjects that are unfamiliar to me.
- I find it fascinating to learn new information.

Exploration is not only conducive to growth but can also help quell our deepest anxieties and fears. As Maslow noted, one way of coping with anxiety is to render our deepest fears "familiar, predictable, manageable, controllable, i.e., unfrightening, and harmless . . . to know them and to understand them."[7] In this way, increasing knowledge doesn't only help us grow, it can also serve as an "anxiety-reducing function."

Indeed, Todd Kashdan and his colleagues found that the need for exploration was positively correlated with "stress tolerance"—the willingness to embrace the inherent anxiety of a new, unexpected, complex, mysterious, obscure event. Stress tolerance demonstrated the strongest correlations with every single dimension of well-being they measured, including happiness; meaning in life; satisfaction of the needs for mastery, autonomy, and relatedness; and the existence of a lot of positive emotions in daily life.

THE FUEL OF EXPLORATION

The potential for growth from disorder has been encoded deeply into our DNA. We didn't only evolve the capacity to regulate our defensive and destructive impulses (i.e., to become more secure), but we also evolved the capacity to make sense of the unknown. Engaging in exploration allows us to integrate novel or unexpected events with existing knowledge and experiences, a process necessary for growth.[8]

The general motivation for exploration is driven by dopamine.[9] Dopamine is often labeled the "feel-good molecule," but this is a gross mischaracterization of this neurotransmitter. Dopamine's primary role is to make us *want* things, not necessarily like things. We get the biggest rush of dopamine coursing through our brains at the possibility of reward, but this rush is no guarantee that we'll actually like or even enjoy the thing once we get it. Dopamine is a huge energizing force in our lives, driving our motivation to explore and facilitating the cognitive and behavioral processes that allow us to extract the most delights from the unknown.[10]

If dopamine is not all about feeling good, then why does this myth persist in the public imagination? I think it's because so much research on dopamine has been conducted in regard to its role in motivating exploration toward our more primal "appetitive" rewards, such as chocolate, social attention, social status, sexual partners, gambling, or drugs like cocaine. However, in recent years, other dopamine pathways in the brain have been proposed that are strongly linked to the reward value of *information*.[11]

People who score high in the general tendency toward exploration are not only driven to engage in behavioral forms of exploration but also tend to get energized through the possibility of discovering new information and extracting meaning and growth from their experiences. These "cognitive needs," as Maslow referred to them, are just as important as the other human needs for becoming a whole person.

In the rest of this chapter, I will briefly touch on five subneeds of exploration that cover both behavioral and cognitive forms of exploration: (1) social exploration, (2) adventure seeking, (3) posttraumatic growth, (4) openness to experience, and (5) intellect. It is my hope that this chapter helps get your explorative juices flowing and inspires you to embrace the delights of the unknown.

SOCIAL EXPLORATION

We humans are social animals, and engagement in social life is necessary for health and well-being. However, there is a clear difference between the form of social engagement that arises from insecurity and deprivation (e.g., the extreme need for belonging and attachment) and the sort of social engagement that is fueled by exploration and growth. In a set of revealing studies, Geneviève L. Lavigne and her colleagues found two clear orientations that relate to the need for belonging: a growth orientation, which is driven by curiosity, sincere interest in learning about others, and a desire to learn about oneself, and a deficit-reduction orientation, which is driven by an overly high need to feel accepted and to fill a deep void in one's life.[12]

The growth orientation to belonging was associated with a wide range of growth-oriented outcomes, including higher levels of secure attachment, past positive social interactions, resiliency, commitment toward an important relationship, and self-disclosure in relationships. In contrast, the deficit-reduction orientation was associated with various outcomes that stunt growth, including higher levels of social anxiety, social comparison, anxious-attachment style, a need for attention, and loneliness.

We can refer to the growth-oriented form of social engagement as social exploration, the drive to learn about people and engage in novel social experiences. The first aspect of social exploration is social curiosity, which involves a general interest in gathering information about how other people feel, think, and behave.[13] You can gauge your current levels of social curiosity with these five statements created by Todd Kashdan and his colleagues:[14]

SOCIAL CURIOSITY SCALE

- I like to learn about the habits of others.
- I like finding out why people behave the way they do.
- When other people are having a conversation, I like to find out what it's about.
- When around other people, I like listening to their conversations.
- When people quarrel, I like to know what's going on.

There are a number of reasons why social curiosity can be conducive to growth. For one, learning new information about other people and their behaviors gives us the possibility of learning from their mistakes, as well as becoming more aware of opportunities in life, without the need to personally undergo extensive trial and error. Learning information about others also enables us to effectively adapt to our social environment and facilitate relationships. After all, learning about people is extraordinarily complex and requires not only knowledge of their outward behaviors but also an understanding of their interior thoughts, feelings, and experiences.[15] It's no wonder why the drive to attain social information has been essential to the survival of our species.

Socially curious people make more effective use of social information, as they are more attentive to their social environment and use a wider range of cues for inferring the personality traits of others.[16] Research shows that socially curious people are indeed more accurate in assessing the personalities of people they've met for the first time, even after interacting only briefly with them.[17] This is particularly true for accurately perceiving the personality traits of extroversion and openness to experience, traits that are most visible within a short time span of getting to know someone. However, it is likely that the socially curious person who invests in deeper relationships with others has the greater capacity to gather a wealth of social information, as research shows that people who tend to invest more in close interpersonal relationships have the ability to make more accurate personality judgments over time.[18]

While social curiosity has been linked to a tendency to gossip, they are different drives.[19] Both social curiosity and the tendency to gossip involve an interest in social conversations, learning about others, and building relationships. However, gossip tends to be driven more by the desire for entertainment whereas social curiosity is driven more by the drive to learn and explore new information about people. Also, social curiosity, but not gossip, is associated with a curiosity for general knowledge and information, as well as a greater openness to experience.

Nevertheless, social curiosity and gossip probably co-evolved together as two different core drives of cultural learning. As Roy Baumeister has pointed out, humans evolved to participate and belong to a cultural society that allows individuals to share knowledge and rely on this knowledge rather than solely rely on their own experiences for learning. Social curiosity and gossip are essential for gathering and transmitting information about cultural norms and behaviors that are rewarded and punished and about who is worthy of trust and who should be treated with suspicion. Most gossip tends to be about the misadventures of others, which helps explain why 96 percent of gossiping evokes negative reactions, and people report that they learned useful lessons for their own lives in about two-thirds of the gossip they experienced.[20]

Therefore, it is likely that we evolved both an interest in those around us as well as an interest and pleasure in transmitting that information to others. Of course, the information that is acquired and transmitted is not always accurate, and people don't simply pass along information uncritically and unbiased by their own preconceptions. Group members like to validate one another's views and perspectives, and consensus building and validation of the dominant group's worldview often takes precedence over a search for truth. Those within a culture who express an unpopular opinion may be ignored or even oppressed, not because the view is necessarily incorrect but because it doesn't contribute to the construction of a shared mental reality. To help combat this bias and have a society that enjoys a shared reality that is also accurate requires different people, with their own interpretation of reality, debating and engaging with one another.[21]

Another important form of social exploration is the drive to actively engage in novel social and physical environments. This could include making a new friend, engaging in new discussions, volunteering for a new organization, or even trying out a new dance club.[22] Greater exposure to new social situations and with a greater range of different people and ideas provides a wealth of learning opportunities.[23]

Taken together, social curiosity and the drive to engage in novel social experiences comprise the need for social exploration, an important form of exploration for growth and learning among such a social species as human beings.

ADVENTURE SEEKING

Alex Honnold is self-described as a "professional adventure rock climber." Sometimes referred to by others as Alex "No Big Deal" Honnold, he has been free soloing—climbing without any ropes, harnesses, or protective equipment—some of America's biggest cliffs for the past twelve years, and on June 3, 2017, Honnold finally achieved his lifelong dream of free soloing the nearly three-thousand-foot El Capitan in Yosemite National Park. It took him three hours and fifty-six minutes to make it to the top all alone—with no support.

Why does he do it? What's driving him? Is it the adrenaline rush? When asked that question on the TV show *60 Minutes*, he said it's quite the opposite: "There is no adrenaline rush, you know? Like if I get a rush, it means that something has gone horribly wrong, you know? Because the whole thing should be pretty slow and controlled and like—I mean, it's mellow."[24] Instead, it seems to be all about the *exploration*. As he explained in another interview: "Maybe it is more complicated—trying to do things people haven't done before, to push my limits, to see what I'm capable of doing. In some way the drive is like curiosity, the explorer's heart, wanting to see what's around the corner."[25]

Honnold planned the El Capitan climb meticulously for a full year, visualizing and planning the climb in exquisite detail, memorizing the "choreography," and mastering the psychological head game. It's a tremendous amount of preparation for a brief amount of time, and with considerable risk. Honnold says he calculates risk just like anyone else, though, and deliberately decides whether it's worth it. "It's all a matter of choosing the amount of risk you're willing to accept, with open eyes," he notes. "I wonder if people that hate on risk-taking are as intentional in their choices as I am. How many people are choosing to live in a way that best suits their values and best fulfills them?"[26]

What seems to drive Honnold, and other adventure seekers like him, aren't the needs that comprise security, such as the needs for safety, connection, or self-esteem. Instead, Honnold seems much more driven by the desire to learn and grow and to master novel and complex challenges. Most climbers look at El Capitan and feel fear at the thought of climbing it. Honnold is able to master that fear through extensive preparation and thinking through every single potential consequence.

While Honnold likely has a genetic predisposition for adventure seeking—adventure seeking is correlated with genes that code for dopamine production[27]—he certainly wasn't born fearless. Honnold noted that when he first started free soloing, he faced great fear. After enough of these growth experiences, though, he trained himself to be fearless. As he put it in an interview, "My comfort zone is like a little bubble around me, and I've pushed it in different directions and made it bigger and bigger until these objectives that seemed totally crazy, eventually fall within the realm of the possible."[28] It appears that Honnold trained himself to have a high tolerance for stress so that he would be more capable of exploring the unknown, unimpeded by his own fears and anxieties.

This stress tolerance seems to have affected not just his climbing. Researchers placed Honnold in an fMRI machine and showed him a series of about two hundred images in rapid succession. Included were pictures of corpses with their facial features bloodily reorganized and a toilet full of feces. Most people would find the images extremely disturbing, and viewing them tends to activate the amygdala, a part of the brain critical for processing emotional significance. For Honnold, however, there was virtually no brain activity when viewing such images. The researchers propose that over many years he trained himself to manage fear and uncertainty, and while he was most certainly predisposed, this is a skill we can all learn.[29]

Scientists define "adventure seeking" as the willingness to risk physical, social, and financial safety for varied, novel, exciting, intense, and challenging sensations and experiences. Adventure seeking is part of a larger personality trait called "sensation seeking," which also includes things such as the drive to engage in new sensory experiences (e.g., taking psychedelics), susceptibility to boredom, and being extremely impulsive.[30] While adventure seeking can be distinguished from other forms of sensation seeking, what they all seem to have in common is extreme sensitivity to the possibility of reward and a hyperactive reward circuitry in the brain, particularly in the nucleus accumbens.[31] You can gauge your current levels of adventure seeking with these statements developed by Todd Kashdan and his colleagues:[32]

ADVENTURE-SEEKING SCALE
- The anxiety of doing something new makes me feel excited and alive.
- Risk-taking is exciting to me.
- When I have free time, I want to do things that are a little scary.
- Creating an adventure as I go is much more appealing than a planned adventure.
- I prefer friends who are excitingly unpredictable.

A wide variety of activities and professions can satisfy the need for excitement, novelty, challenge, and danger that adventure seekers crave.[33] Many are prosocial or neutral, such as having particular music and aesthetic preferences, having a high drive for creativity, or engaging in extreme sports, mountain climbing, civic engagement, volunteerism, firefighting, leadership, political participation, and military service.[34]

Adventure seeking is associated with more maladaptive outcomes as well, such as risky sex, antagonism, psychopathy, borderline personality disorder, risky driving behavior, gambling, and substance abuse.

What's the difference between the antisocial adventure seeker and the prosocial, aesthetic, or social adventure seeker? This is where a consideration of the whole person really matters. The manifestation of adventure seeking that is related to aggressive and dangerously risky outcomes is influenced by other traits arising from insecurity, such as emotional volatility, impulsivity, disinhibition, low premeditation, callousness, self-absorption, and antagonism.

This is why we must not be quick to judge a trait in isolation and why the path to becoming a whole person involves both security and growth. Exploration with great insecurity can lead to antisocial behaviors, but security without exploration can lead to frustration and boredom. One recent study among young children found that while high levels of exploration combined with low levels of self-control emerged as a liability for externalizing behavior—maladaptive behaviors directed outward to the environment—the reverse was also true: high levels of self-control combined with low levels of exploration was also a liability for externalizing behavior.[35] Too much of an imbalance of one over the other can lead to destructive outcomes.

Researchers have begun to look at the potential benefits of adventure seeking. Todd Kashdan and his colleagues found that people who rated themselves higher in adventure seeking tended to also report higher feelings of happiness, as well as the view that hedonism is a primary element of a life well lived. Adventure seeking wasn't all about hedonism, however; adventure seeking was also related to a desire for personal growth and to make a contribution to others, as well as less of a need for closure and less of a need to avoid fearful experiences.

Russell Ravert and his colleagues investigated the role of sensation seeking among a large sample of college students.[36] Arguing that exploration plays an important role in the transition to adulthood, they found that novelty seeking in particular was associated with reports of greater reaching toward one's best and full potential, as well as other markers of well-being. Some statements on their test of novelty seeking include "I would have enjoyed being one of the first explorers of an unknown land" and "If it were possible to visit another planet or the moon for free, I would be among the first in line to sign up."

In contrast, they found that intensity seeking was associated with lower levels of well-being and higher levels of risky behavior. Intensity seeking was measured through statements such as "I like the feeling of standing next to the edge of a high place and looking down." This dovetails nicely with what free-soloing climbers like Honnold find so rewarding, which is the exploration, not necessarily the adrenaline rush in the moment.*

Another recent study found that adventure seeking is associated with increased resilience (measured as increased positive emotions and life satisfaction) among those who had experienced trauma.[37] This association was partly explained through effective coping. High-adventure seekers are more likely to use a problem-focused coping strategy, which allows them to see stressors in their life as manageable. Those who employ a problem-focus coping style attempt to deal with stressful situations by changing the source of the stress. This includes problem-solving, seeking information or social support, and removing oneself entirely from the stressful situation.[38] This is typically contrasted from emotion-focused coping, in which one attempts to reduce the negative feelings associated with stress through strategies such as distraction, suppression, and drugs and alcohol.

Those who are higher in adventure seeking are more likely to use a problem-focused coping strategy because they are more motivated to face

> One does not have to be traumatized by trauma; one can *grow* from trauma.

---

* I also suspect that those scoring higher on the "dark triad" traits of narcissism, psychopathology, and Machiavellianism are more motivated by intensity seeking than the learning and growth that comes from novelty seeking.

unexpected and difficult issues head on and explore possible solutions than run away or hide from the problem indefinitely. In fact, this research points to a larger finding: one does not have to be traumatized by trauma; one can *grow* from trauma.

POST-TRAUMATIC GROWTH

Those who cope well with violent or life-threatening events are often viewed in terms of extreme heroism. However justified, this practice tends to reinforce the misperception that only rare individuals with "exceptional emotional strength" are capable of resilience.

—George Bonanno, "Loss, Trauma, and Human Resilience" (2004)

In some ways suffering ceases to be suffering at the moment it finds a meaning.

—Viktor Frankl, *Man's Search for Meaning* (1946)

In his seminal 2004 paper, clinical psychologist George Bonanno made waves for arguing for a broader conceptualization of stress responding.[39] Defining resilience as the ability of people who have experienced a highly life-threatening or traumatic event to maintain relatively stable, healthy levels of psychological and physical functioning, Bonanno reviewed a wealth of studies showing that resilience is actually common, that it is not the same as the simple absence of psychopathology, and that it can be attained through multiple, sometimes unexpected, routes. Considering that approximately 61 percent of men and 51 percent of women in the United States report at least one traumatic event in their lifetime, the human capacity for resilience is quite remarkable.[40]

In fact, many who experience trauma—such as being diagnosed with a chronic or terminal illness, losing a loved one, or experiencing sexual assault—not only show incredible resilience but actually thrive in the aftermath of the traumatic event. Studies show that the majority of trauma survivors do not develop PTSD, and a large number even report growth from their experience.[41] Richard Tedeschi and Lawrence Calhoun coined the term "posttraumatic growth" to capture this phenomenon, defining it as the positive psychological change that is experienced as a result of the struggle with highly challenging life circumstances.[42] These seven areas of growth have been reported to spring from adversity:

- Greater appreciation of life
- Greater appreciation and strengthening of close relationships
- Increased compassion and altruism
- The identification of new possibilities or a purpose in life
- Greater awareness and utilization of personal strengths
- Enhanced spiritual development
- Creative growth

To be sure, most people who experience posttraumatic growth would certainly prefer to have *not* had the trauma, and very few of these domains show more growth after trauma compared to encountering positive life experiences.[43] Nevertheless, most people who experience posttraumatic growth are often surprised by the growth that does occur, which often comes unexpectedly, as the result of an attempt at making sense of an unfathomable event.[44]

Rabbi Harold Kushner put it well as he reflected on the death of his son:

Growth and pain often coexist.[45]

> I am a more sensitive person, a more effective pastor, a more
> sympathetic counselor because of Aaron's life and death than I would
> ever have been without it. And I would give up all of those gains in a
> second if I could have my son back. If I could choose, I would forgo all
> of the spiritual growth and depth which has come my way because of
> our experiences. . . . But I cannot choose.[46]

Make no doubt: trauma shakes up our world and forces us to take another look at our cherished goals and dreams. Tedeschi and Calhoun use the metaphor of the seismic earthquake: we tend to rely on a particular set of beliefs and assumptions about the benevolence and controllability of the world, and traumatic events typically shatter that worldview as we become shaken from our ordinary perceptions and are left to rebuild ourselves and our worlds.

But what choice do we have? As Austrian psychiatrist Viktor Frankl put it, "When we are no longer able to change a situation, we are challenged to change ourselves." In recent years, psychologists have begun to understand the psychological processes that turn adversity into advantage, and what is becoming clear is that this "psychologically seismic" restructuring is actually necessary for growth to occur. It is precisely when the foundational structure of the self is shaken that we are in the best position to pursue new opportunities in our lives.

Similarly, the Polish psychiatrist Kazimierz Dabrowski argued that "positive disintegration" can be a growth-fostering experience. After studying a number of people with high psychological development, Dabrowski concluded that healthy personality development often requires the disintegration of the personality structure, which can temporarily lead to psychological tension, self-doubt, anxiety, and depression. However, Dabrowski believed this process can lead to a deeper examination of what one *could* be and ultimately higher levels of personality development.[47]

A key factor that allows us to turn adversity into advantage is the extent to which we fully explore our thoughts and feelings surrounding the event. *Cognitive exploration*—which can be defined as a general curiosity about information and a tendency toward complexity and flexibility in information processing—enables us to be curious about confusing situations, increasing the likelihood that we will find new meaning in the seemingly incomprehensible.[48] To be sure, many of the steps that lead to growth after trauma go against our natural inclinations to avoid extremely uncomfortable emotions and thoughts. However, it's only through shedding our natural defense mechanisms and approaching the discomfort head on, viewing everything as fodder for growth, that we can start to embrace the inevitable paradoxes of life and come to a more nuanced view of reality.

After a traumatic event, whether a serious illness or the loss of a loved one, it's natural to stew over the event, constantly thinking about what happened, replaying the thoughts and feelings over and over. Rumination is often a sign that you are working hard to make sense of what happened and are actively tearing down old belief systems and creating new structures of meaning and identity. While rumination typically begins as automatic, intrusive, and repetitive, over time such thinking becomes more organized, controlled, and deliberate.[49] This process of transformation can certainly be excruciating, but rumination, in conjunction with a strong social support system and other outlets for expression, can be very beneficial to growth and enable us to tap into deep reservoirs of strength and compassion we never knew existed within us.[50]

Likewise, emotions such as sadness, grief, anger, and anxiety are common responses to trauma.[51] Instead of trying everything we can to inhibit or "self-regulate" those emotions, experiential avoidance—avoiding feared thoughts, feelings, and sensations—paradoxically makes things worse, reinforcing our belief that the world is not safe and making it more difficult to pursue valued long-term goals.[52] Through experiential avoidance, we shut down our exploratory capacities, thereby missing out on many opportunities for generating positive experiences and meaning. This is a core theme of acceptance and commitment therapy (ACT), which helps people increase their "psychological flexibility."[53] By embracing psychological flexibility, we face the world with exploration and openness and are better able to react to events in the service of our chosen values.

Consider a study conducted by Todd Kashdan and Jennifer Kane, in which they assessed the role of experiential avoidance in posttraumatic growth in a sample of college students.[54] In this sample, the most frequently reported traumas included the sudden death of a loved one, motor vehicle accidents, witnessing violence in the home, and natural disaster. Kashdan and Kane found that the greater the distress, the greater the posttraumatic growth—but only in those with low levels of experiential avoidance. Those reporting greater distress and little reliance on experiential avoidance reported the highest levels of growth and meaning in life. The finding flipped for those resorting to experiential avoidance, and greater distress was associated with lower levels of posttraumatic growth and meaning in life. The study adds to a growing literature showing that people with low levels of anxiety coupled with low levels of experiential avoidance (i.e., high levels of psychological flexibility) report an enhanced quality of life.[55] But this study also suggests that there is increased meaning in life too.

The increased meaning can be great fodder for creative expression. The link between disadvantage and creativity has a long and distinguished history, but now scientists are starting to unravel the mysteries behind this link. Clinical psychologist Marie Forgeard asked people to report on the most stressful experiences of their lives and to indicate which ones had the biggest impact.[56] The list of adverse events included natural disaster, illness, accidents, and assault.

Forgeard found that the form of cognitive processing was critical in explaining growth after trauma. Intrusive forms of rumination caused a decline in multiple areas of growth, whereas deliberate rumination led to an increase in five domains of posttraumatic growth. Two of those domains—positive changes in relationships and increases in perceptions of new possibilities in one's life—were associated with increased perceptions of creative growth.

In her book *When Walls Become Doorways: Creativity and the Transforming Illness,* Tobi Zausner presented her analysis of the biographies of eminent painters who suffered from physical illnesses.[57] Zausner concluded that such illnesses led to the creation of new possibilities for their art by breaking old habits, provoking disequilibrium, and forcing the artists to generate alternative strategies to reach their creative goals.[58] Taken together, the research and anecdotes support the potentially immense benefit of engaging in art therapy or expressive writing to help facilitate the rebuilding process after trauma. Writing about a topic that triggers strong emotions for just fifteen to twenty minutes a day has been shown to help people create meaning from their stressful experiences and better express both their positive and negative emotions.

The willingness and desire to explore our full range of thoughts and feelings is important not only for posttraumatic growth but for growth in many other domains of life as well, including innovation and creativity. Let's take a deep dive into the realm of cognitive exploration and its fascinating manifestations, starting with one of the most central concepts in all of humanistic psychology: openness to experience.

OPENNESS TO EXPERIENCE

*I find [a fully functioning] person to be a human being in flow, in process,
rather than having achieved some state. Fluid change is central in the picture.
I find such a person to be sensitively open to all of his experience—sensitive
to what is going on in his environment, sensitive to other individuals with
whom he is in relationship, and sensitive perhaps most of all to the feelings,
reactions, and emergent meanings which he discovers in himself. The fear of
some aspects of his own experience continues to diminish, so that more and
more of his life is available to him. . . . Such a person is a creative person.*

> —Carl Rogers, "Toward Becoming a Fully Functioning Person" (1962)

*Creativity has its roots in the nonrational. . . . Science and education, being
too exclusively abstract, verbal and bookish, do not have enough place for
raw, concrete, esthetic experience, especially of the subjective happenings
inside oneself.*

> —Abraham Maslow, *Toward a Psychology of Being* (1962)

The concept of "openness to experience" played a central role in the
thinking of the founding humanistic psychologists. For both Carl Rogers
and Abraham Maslow, the height of self-actualization was creativity, and
one of the key drivers of creativity was openness to experience. Carl Rogers simply defined openness to experience as "the opposite of psychological defensiveness."[59] Rogers conceptualized openness to experience as a
mode of cognitive processing where one is open to all of one's personal
experiences, receiving conflicting information without forcing closure,
tolerating ambiguity, and seeing reality clearly without imposing predetermined categories onto the world.[60]

In the eighties, when personality psychologists started systematically
investigating the fundamental dimensions of personality, they found a
specific cluster of traits that people differ on which they labeled "openness
to experience." The array of characteristics that are part of openness to
experience—including imagination, aesthetic sensitivity, and intellectual
curiosity—are centrally human characteristics and help define and advance our species.

For the past decade, my colleagues and I have begun to unearth the specific motivational, cognitive, and neurobiological processes that drive this broad domain of personality, and a clear hierarchy has emerged.[61]

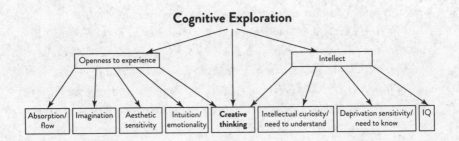

At the top of the hierarchy stands the general drive for *cognitive exploration*.[62] People who score high in cognitive exploration have both the desire and ability to explore the world cognitively through perception, sensation, imagination, and reasoning. Cognitive exploration is consistently related to measures of creativity, including creative thinking, creative achievement, creative professions, creative hobbies, and a creative personality, more generally.

Indeed, those scoring higher in cognitive exploration report spending more of their daily time on creative pursuits and say they would rather be making and creating things than merely observing the world.[63] Studies find that those scoring higher in cognitive exploration are in fact more likely to be doing something creative when sampled during a normal day.[64] For cognitive explorers, creativity is a way of being, expressed spontaneously and voluntarily, emanating from the core of their being.

Diving deeper into the hierarchy of cognitive exploration, we see cognitive exploration comprises two separate but related features: openness to experience and intellect. Whereas openness to experience reflects a drive for exploration of aesthetic, affective, and sensory information through imagination, perception, and artistic endeavor, intellect reflects a drive toward exploration of abstract and verbal intellectual information, primarily through reasoning. The following are a number of statements you can use to gauge your own level of openness to experience.[65]

OPENNESS TO EXPERIENCE SCALE

Absorption/Flow

- Sometimes I experience things as if they were doubly real.
- Sometimes I am so immersed in nature or in art that I feel as if my whole state of consciousness has somehow been temporarily changed.
- I often lose awareness of time and my physical surroundings.
- There is often a breakdown between myself and what I am creating—I am what I was writing/playing/painting.
- There is often a sense of "closeness" to what I am creating, a greater-than-normal emotional connection with it.

Imagination

- I enjoy imagining things vividly.
- I enjoy reading things that evoke visual images.
- I can clearly picture or remember some sculpture or natural object (not alive) that I think is very beautiful.
- I identify strongly with characters in movies I watch or books I read.
- I tend to describe things by using images, metaphors, or creative comparisons.

Aesthetic Sensitivity

- I have many artistic interests.
- I am fascinated by art, music, and/or literature.
- I have favorite poems and paintings that mean a lot to me.
- I see beauty in things that others might not notice.
- When I travel or drive anywhere, I always watch the landscape and scenery.

Intuition/Emotionality

- I like to rely on my intuitive impressions.
- I can often tell how people feel without them having to say anything.
- I enjoy learning by doing something, instead of figuring it out first.
- When I have a strong emotional experience, the effect stays with me for a long time.

• I'd rather be upset sometimes and happy sometimes than always feel calm.

In the brain, openness to experience is linked to the "default mode network," or as I like to refer to it, "the imagination network."[66] The processes that have been associated with this network of brain regions reflect the uniquely human capacities for self-reflection, identity, imagination, and meaning-making. Here's a list of some of the cognitive processes that have been linked to this network in recent years: daydreaming; mental simulation; remembering the past; thinking about the future; generating new ideas; improvisation and flow among jazz musicians, rappers, and poets; the comprehension of stories; reports of intense and personally moving aesthetic experiences; feeling inspiration for the virtue of others; and reflecting on mental and emotional states, both our own and those of others.[67]

The full suite of processes associated with the default network has been found to be critical for the healthy development of compassion, empathy, and the ability to understand ourselves, create meaning from our experiences, and construct a linear sense of self. Clearly the cognitive processes associated with the default network, and with openness to experience, form the very core of human experience.

Other research on openness to experience confirms what humanistic psychologists long suggested—that openness to experience is related to a lack of imposing predetermined conceptual categories onto the world. More technically, openness to experience has been linked to "latent inhibition," a preconscious, biologically based gating mechanism that we share with other animals and which is associated with dopamine production in the brain.[68] Latent inhibition helps us automatically precategorize stimuli as relevant or irrelevant to a current goal. As you can imagine, this is an immensely important mechanism, keeping us, as Søren Kierkegaard put it, from "drown[ing] in possibility."

But here's the kicker: those scoring higher in openness to experience tend to have a *reduced* latent inhibition, which results in immediate experience not being as shaped by prior experience. A reduced latent inhibition has been linked to both openness to experience and creativity.[69] As Barnaby Nelson and David Rawlings, who found a substantial link between openness to experience and the creative experience, put it,

> It is precisely this newness of appreciation, and the associated sense of exploration and discovery, that stimulates the deep immersion in the creative process, which itself may trigger a shift in quality of experience, generally in terms of an intensification or heightening of experience.[70]

This description is strikingly similar to Maslow's notion of "continued freshness of appreciation," which he believed was a central characteristic of self-actualization. According to Maslow, continued freshness of appreciation brings about an "acute richness of subjective experience." Maslow contrasted this with "staleness of experience," which he argued is often a result of "rubricizing or ticketing off a rich perception into one or another category or rubric as it proves to be no longer advantageous, or useful, or threatening or otherwise ego involved"[71]—for instance, automatically ignoring a beautiful sunset or disregarding a kind gesture from a friend because it has become so commonplace to you.

Having a reduced latent inhibition is essential not only for getting deeply absorbed in the creative experience but also for generating novel ideas and making unexpected connections. After all, how do you know whether an idea that seems irrelevant at first truly is irrelevant? Many of the greatest and most impactful ideas of all time seemed quite irrelevant, at least initially. As Edgar Allan Poe put it, "Yet experience has shown, and a true philosophy will always show, that a vast, perhaps the larger portion of the truth, arises from the seemingly irrelevant."[72] Swim in the sea of the irrelevant all the time, however, and you will eventually get lost.

INTELLECT: FINDING YOUR WAY BACK TO SHORE

Slipping into "craziness" is frightening only for those who are not fully confident of their sanity.

—Abraham Maslow, *Toward a Psychology of Being* (1962)

[Knowledge and understanding make] the person bigger, wiser, richer, stronger, more evolved, more mature. [They represent] the actualization of a human potentiality, the fulfillment of that human destiny foreshadowed by human possibilities.

—Abraham Maslow, *Toward a Psychology of Being* (1962)

While openness to experience is essential for entertaining the possibilities of creative potential, the human intellect is essential for finding your way back to shore. There are many aspects of the human intellect, but some of the most well-studied facets include IQ, intellectual curiosity, and the need to know solutions to problems. All of the facets of intellect can play an important role in truth seeking and reality monitoring and have been linked to the functioning of the "executive attention brain network."[73] This brain network is essential for helping us focus on the most immediate task, block out external distractions, suppress seemingly irrelevant information, flexibly switch our attention when necessary, deliberately plan future actions, and integrate multiple sources of information in working memory. Here is a scale measuring some of the characteristics of intellect (you can have your IQ assessed by a competent educational psychologist):

INTELLECT SCALE

Intellectual Curiosity/Need to Understand[74]
- I'm curious about many different things.
- I enjoy intellectual challenges.
- I actively seek out intellectual, philosophical discussions.
- I seek out situations that require thinking in depth about something.
- I don't like to know the answer without understanding the reasoning behind it.

Deprivation Sensitivity/Need to Know[75]
- Thinking about solutions to difficult conceptual problems can keep me awake at night.
- I can spend hours on a single problem because I just can't rest without knowing the answer.

- I feel frustrated if I can't figure out the solution to a problem, so I work even harder to solve it.
- I work relentlessly at problems that I feel must be solved.
- It frustrates me not having all the information I need.

Even though IQ, intellectual curiosity, and deprivation sensitivity are all significantly related to one another and rely heavily on the functioning of the executive attention brain network, there are also meaningful distinctions between the various manifestations of intellect. For one, intellectual curiosity (the need to understand) and deprivation sensitivity (the need to know) are only moderately correlated with each other, and compared to intellectual curiosity, deprivation sensitivity is less tied to well-being and the ability to cope with the stress of confronting new situations.[76]

This raises the interesting question of whether the need to understand is "higher" than the need to know. Put another way, is the need to know the more common and default response among humans to deprived information? Maslow raised this intriguing possibility almost seventy years ago when he noted that "once these desires [to know and understand] are accepted for discussion, we see that they too form themselves into a small hierarchy in which the desire to know is prepotent over the desire to understand."[77] Research suggests that intellectual curiosity may indeed be "higher" than the need to know the solution.

Another meaningful difference within the intellect domain is that between IQ and intellectual curiosity. In my doctoral research, I found only a moderate relationship between IQ and intellectual curiosity: there were plenty of people with sky-high IQ scores but little intellectual curiosity, and plenty of people with a lot of intellectual curiosity but with lower IQ scores.[78] Long-term studies have found that even though IQ is a strong predictor of academic achievement, intellectual curiosity is also a significant predictor of academic success, independent of IQ.[79] And when it comes to real-life creative achievement, intellectual curiosity predicts the creative achievement of inventions and scientific discovery even better than IQ.[80] So while IQ, intellectual curiosity, and the need to know often go together, they can also come apart in important ways.

Openness to experience and openness to intellect are only moderately correlated with each other, so it's possible for someone to be high in openness to experience but not to intellect, and vice versa. Openness to experience is more strongly related to achievement in the arts (particularly visual arts, music, creative writing, and theater/film), whereas intellect is more strongly related to achievement in the sciences (particularly inventions and scientific discovery).[81] Nevertheless, both openness to experience and intellect make important contributions to creative thinking, and self-actualized people are able to transcend the seemingly contradictory nature of these two ways of being.

THE CREATIVITY PARADOX

The road to creativity passes so close to the madhouse and often detours or ends there.

—Ernest Becker

There is only one difference between a madman and me. I am not mad.

—Salvador Dalí

How can two seemingly opposed sets of processes—on the one hand, processes associated with deep absorption, imagination, and a loose filter, and on the other hand, processes associated with deliberate reflection, evaluation, and a strong filter—both be tied to the very same outcome: creativity? How can this be?

Well, like most things relating to self-actualization, this is only an *apparent* paradox. Creativity is typically defined as the generation of ideas or products that are both novel and meaningful. Both aspects are important for creativity. As the philosopher Immanuel Kant once observed, "There can be original nonsense."[82] Adding meaning to the definition of creativity allows us to distinguish creative thought and behavior from merely eccentric or odd thought and behavior.[83] Meaning can cover a wide gamut, however, from practical inventions and innovative business models, to aesthetic experiences that evoke strong emotions, to intellectual ideas that stimulate and generate thought.

Since creativity requires both novelty and meaningfulness, it depends on both the generation of ideas or products and the selection of ideas to be explored, developed, or expressed. The more one generates new ideas and entertains unexpected connections, the more likely some of them will be new, and the more effectively one selects and develops particular ideas, the more likely that some of them will be meaningful. As Nobel Prize–winning chemist Linus Pauling put it, "The way to get good ideas is to get lots of ideas and throw the bad ones away." This often requires the ability to flexibly switch between seemingly contradictory modes of thought.

This is precisely what we see when we look at the creative brain. From 2014 to 2017, I was scientific director of the Imagination Institute *(imagination-institute.org)*, where, along with Martin Seligman, we hosted a series of imagination retreats—discussions with some of the most imaginative and productive people within their respective fields, ranging from psychology to physics to education to leadership to futurism to engineering to comedy to spirituality. In another endeavor, we funded sixteen research projects to advance our understanding of the measurement and development of imagination across all sectors of society.

One thing that was quite evident from the imagination retreats is that creative, self-actualized individuals are *very* human. Despite their high levels of self-actualization, they clearly still wrestled with many of the same problems of human existence that we all do. Nevertheless, they were very passionate about their work, and in solving problems within their domain, they often drew on their intuition and imagination just as much as, if not more than, their rationality and deliberate reasoning. This was just as true for the comedians as it was for the physicists.

The neuroscience research we funded supported this observation. One of our grantees was Roger Beaty, who has been on the front line of advancing our knowledge of the cognitive neuroscience of creative thinking. Beaty and his colleagues developed a map of the creative brain that allowed them to predict with a surprisingly high degree of accuracy the quality of creative thought.*[84]

---

* The quality of creative thought was assessed by a panel of raters who rated the quality on a five-point scale based on the following three criteria: Uncommonness (how uncommon the creative ideas were), Remoteness (how much the creative ideas strayed from obvious ideas), and Cleverness

Creative, self-actualized individuals are very human.

The map of the creative brain consisted of strong communication between the two brain networks discussed earlier that in most people work in opposition: the default network (associated with mental simulation, perspective taking, aesthetic experience, meaning-making, and construction of the self) and the executive attention network (associated with concentration, working memory, and inhibiting potentially distracting information). Beaty and his colleagues found strong communication between these two networks and the salience network. The salience network serves a similar function as latent inhibition, preconsciously tagging information generated from the default network as either relevant or irrelevant to the current task and then passing that information on to the executive attention network for further conscious reflection.

In another study conducted in the United States and China, Beaty and his colleagues found strong connectivity among the very same set of brain networks among those scoring high in cognitive exploration—including both openness to experience and intellect—while they were just sitting idly in the brain scanning machine.[85] It's as though these individuals were ready to activate any of the three brain networks at a moment's notice. Put another way, their *whole* self was on call.*

I believe these findings enrich our notions of human intelligence and expand our understanding of the depths of our cognitive capacities. I believe that many tests of "intellectual potential" (such as an IQ test) miss out on some core aspects of cognition that reflect the fundamental experience of being human, such as the individual's personal goals, dreams, and aspirations.[86] This is why I am very hesitant to prejudge a person's ultimate level of self-actualization based solely on the results of a single test, administered at a single point in time—even if it's my own test of self-actualization! In my research, I've seen over and over again the power of

---

(how much the creative ideas struck people as insightful, ironic, humorous, fitting, or smart). Note that this metric of the quality of creativity was strongly positively correlated with measures of creative behavior and achievement.

* It appears the cognitively flexible brain is also the neurologically flexible brain!

human intelligence when it is completely absorbed in a personally meaningful activity that matches one's own unique potentialities and engages both our rational facilities as well as the depths of our experience.

In his 1979 book *Psychology and the Human Dilemma,* the humanistic psychotherapist Rollo May noted that it's possible to think with the whole of one's being, and that self-awareness has an intellectual aspect, but it is not the *whole* of it:

> When you commit yourself to love, for example, or to some other form of passion or to a fight or to an ideal, you ought to be, if you are to be successful in your love or fight, related to yourself on many different levels at once. True, conscious awareness is present in your commitment; but you also experience subconscious and even unconscious powers in yourself. This self-relatedness is present in self-chosen abandon; it means acting as a whole; it is the experience of "I throw myself into this."[87]

So there you have it. Creative self-actualizers are capable of transcending the ordinary dichotomy between the intelligence of the mind and the wisdom of the heart. They are able to throw their whole selves into their work, flexibly switching between seemingly contradictory modes of being—the rational and the irrational, the emotional and the logical, the deliberate and the intuitive, and the imaginative and the abstract—without prejudging the value of any of these processes. Creative self-actualizers are true cognitive explorers.

CHAPTER 5

Love

We must understand love; we must be able to teach it, to create it, to predict it, or else the world is lost to hostility and to suspicion.

—Abraham Maslow, *Motivation and Personality* (1954)

Love is the only sane and satisfactory answer to the problem of human existence.

—Erich Fromm, *The Art of Loving* (1956)

At one particular advertising agency, a general air of competitiveness pervades the atmosphere. Meetings frequently consist of discussing how the company can achieve more and "dominate" the competition. However, Luisa, a quietly radiant person who attends all the meetings, stands out for a different reason than everyone else. Everyone loves Luisa. Whenever you are in the presence of Luisa, you can't help but feel uplifted. She seems to bring out the best in everyone, due in large part to her own ability to spot the best in others. Everyone wants Luisa on their team, not only because of her abundance of love but also because she is extremely thoughtful and dependable. While Luisa emits so much light, she doesn't sacrifice her own needs and is able to take care of herself when she must and she speaks her mind in a way that makes others *want* to listen to her viewpoint. Luisa tends to see the greater humanity in nearly every situation and discussion and tries her best to see some merit in all the different perspectives on the table.

Luisa's way of being is extremely undervalued in the world today. Since so many people focus on achievement, they will often strategically act more altruistic *in order to* achieve greater personal success. Unfortunately, society has deeply underestimated those who, just by *being who they are*, bring joy and light to everyone they meet. While this doesn't necessarily translate into publicly recognized success, the impact is immeasurable, and added up over a life, it can be even more impactful than awards and accolades. While you certainly don't have to be a Luisa to become self-actualized, there is a lot we can learn from the Luisas of the world about the value of striving for higher forms of love in order to reach a deeper sense of wholeness, integration, and transcendence in our lives.

In his book *Spiritual Evolution,* the psychiatrist George Vaillant writes that "successful human development involves, first, absorbing love, next, reciprocally sharing love, and finally, giving love unselfishly away."[1] Humans not only have a need for belonging and connection, but also have a need to feel as though they are having a positive impact in the lives of other people. To have the capacity to give love to those whom we don't even have direct contact with, or feel a personal connection to, is a major pathway to a life of greater health, vitality, meaning, and growth as a whole person, not to mention a way of feeling more secure.[2] As Claire Nuer, a Holocaust survivor, terminal cancer survivor, and pioneer in the field of Personal Mastery, put it, "The only way to create love, safety, and acceptance is by giving them."[3]

Herein lies a paradox: if belonging and connection really are security needs, then those who are engaged in high-quality connections should be love-gratified, no longer needing love in their lives—being love-satiated, they shouldn't be driven to experience or express any further love. Instead, Maslow observed that the *opposite* is often the case: "Clinical study of healthier people, who have been love-need–satisfied, shows that although they need less to receive love, they are more able to give love. In this sense they are more loving people."[4]

Maslow noted that when love is discussed in research papers and textbooks, the topic often focuses on love as a deficiency: "The love need as ordinarily studied . . . is a deficit need. It is a hole which has to be filled, an emptiness into which love is poured. . . . Intermediate states of pathology and health follow upon intermediate states of thwarting or satiation."[5] But he recognized that beyond a certain point of love fulfillment, we become more capable of turning our love outward.

Maslow explicitly distinguished "needing love" from "unneeding love" and referred to the former as D-love (deficiency love) and the latter as B-love ("love for the being of another person").[6] As Maslow noted, whereas D-love can be gratified, the entire concept of gratification hardly applies to B-love. Those who love from a place of B-love do not need to receive love except in "steady, small maintenance doses and they may even do without these for periods of time."[7]

Instead of *needing*, B-love is *admiring*, and instead of *striving* for satiation, B-love usually *grows* rather than disappears. As a result, B-love is typically a more enjoyable experience, as it is intrinsically valuable (not valuable as a means to some other end). Maslow wrote: "B-love is, beyond the shadow of a doubt, a richer, 'higher,' more valuable and subjective experience than D-love (which all B-lovers have also previously experienced)."[8]

The notion of B-love is similar to Buddhist meditation teacher Sharon Salzberg's notion of "real love," which she defines as the innate capacity we each have to love—in everyday life.[9] According to Salzberg, love is a freely given gift and we all have deep reservoirs of love within us that we can tap into anytime to generate even more love in our lives.

Similarly, in his book *The Art of Loving,* Erich Fromm argues that mature love is an active, not a passive, process; an attitude, not a feeling.[10] The beauty of viewing love as an attitude, or an orientation toward others, is that you don't need to wait until you have "positivity resonance" with another person before acting lovingly toward them.[11] This is why I find it necessary to distinguish B-love from the need for connection (see Chapter 2). As a person matures, and the needs of others become just as important as the needs of one's self, a person gradually transforms the idea of love from "being loved" into "loving," from a state of dependency in which one is rewarded by being loved to a loving orientation in which one is capable of loving the world at large. Fromm writes, "Infantile love follows the principle: '*I love because I am loved.*' Mature love follows the principle '*I am loved because I love.*' Immature love says, '*I love you because I need you.*' Mature love says, '*I need you because I love you.*'"[12]

As the existential psychotherapist Irvin Yalom observes, a mature framing of love as "need-free love" has extraordinary implications on a person's health and growth. In psychotherapy, people often complain of loneliness, which they often attribute to being "unloved" and "unlovable." But Yalom notes that the most productive personal development is often done in the opposite realm: *one's inability to be loving.* As Yalom points out, "Love is not a specific encounter but an attitude. A problem of not-being-loved is more often than not a problem of not loving."[13]

In this chapter, I will review my own passionate quest to scientifically study B-love and the profound implications of having a loving orientation toward others for health, growth, and healthy authenticity. My quest to scientifically study B-love, however, started out with its opposite, resting on the assumption that we can best define the light by peering as deeply as possible into the darkness.

THE LIGHT VS. DARK TRIAD

In spite of everything, I still believe that people are truly good at heart.
—Anne Frank, *The Diary of a Young Girl* (1947)

What's one less person on the face of the earth, anyway?
—Ted Bundy, quoted in Elliott Leyton, *Hunting Humans* (2003)

Why are dark triad people so seductive? I asked my colleague David Yaden in his office.[14] Immediately his ears pricked up, and he asked me to send him papers on the dark triad—thus proving my point. *They get all the research attention!* I complained. *Is there anything interesting at all about people who aren't assholes?* When I went back to my office, I emailed some papers to David and my colleague Elizabeth Hyde. In a quick email response, David simply wrote back, "Light triad?" Now my ears pricked up. *Is there such a thing? Has it been studied?*

The *dark* triad has already been well studied. First discovered by

Delroy Paulhus and Kevin Williams in 2002, the dark triad of personality consists of grandiose narcissism (entitled self-importance), Machiavellianism (strategic exploitation and deceit), and psychopathy (callousness, cynicism, and impulsivity).[15] Since that initial paper, hundreds of studies have been conducted linking the dark triad characteristics to a wide range of socially aversive outcomes, including higher levels of aggression and violence; instrumental sex; extremely strong motives for power, money, and social status; and even a higher likelihood of committing all seven "deadly sins."[16]

While other "dark traits" have been added to the dark triad in recent years (e.g., sadism, spitefulness), and each of these dark traits have multiple dimensions and unique properties (for instance, see Chapter 3 for a deep dive into narcissism), there does appear to be a "dark core" that is in common among all of them.[17] Research suggests that the dark core consists of a mix of callousness and dishonesty/manipulation.[18] This particular combination of characteristics seems to be key. In fact, just lacking empathy is only *weakly* related to the presence of aggression.[19] According to Aurelio Figueredo and W. Jake Jacobs, the dark core of the dark triad is best characterized by its "antagonistic social strategies": seeing others as objects to be exploited or rivals to be defeated.[20] Take a look at the following statements to gauge your current levels of dark core characteristics:[21]

DARK CORE SCALE (ANTAGONISTIC ORIENTATION TOWARD OTHERS)

- I can talk my way into and out of anything.
- I'm willing to exploit others to further my own goals.
- I deserve to receive special treatment.
- I don't get upset by the suffering of others.
- I do not waste my time hanging out with people who are beneath me.
- I hate being criticized so much that I can't control my temper when it happens.
- When someone does something nice for me, I wonder what they want from me.
- I will try almost anything to get my "thrills."

While antagonistic people certainly exist, what about *everyday saints*, those who consistently have a loving and beneficent orientation toward others? I'm not talking about the person who publicly does a lot of giving and receives many public accolades and awards for their giving. I'm talking about the person who, *just by their being*, shines their light in every direction. The person who isn't constantly strategic about their giving but who emits unconditional positive regard naturally and spontaneously because that's just who they are, or as Maslow put it, "as a rose emits perfume."[22]

This is what we set out to find. Through email exchanges and personal meetings, David, Elizabeth, and I looked at existing tests of the dark triad and brainstormed a variety of items relating to the opposite characteristics of each member of the dark triad. Our initial pool of items related to forgiveness, trust, honesty, caring, acceptance, seeing the best in people, and getting intrinsic enjoyment from making connections with others instead of using people as a means to an end. In other words: *B-love*.

We identified three clear members of the light triad: Kantianism, Humanism, and Faith in Humanity. Kantianism was our counterpart to Machiavellianism and was inspired by the philosopher Immanuel Kant's formula of humanity: "Act in such a way that you treat humanity, whether in your own person or in the person of any other, never merely as a means to an end, but always at the same time as an end."[23]

After further testing and collaboration with Eli Tsukayama, we found that the following statements do a good job of capturing a B-loving and beneficent orientation toward others:[24] (You can find your dark vs. light triad balance at *selfactualizationtests.com*.)

Kantianism
Treating people as ends unto themselves,
not as mere means.

The Light Triad

Humanism
Valuing the dignity and worth
of each individual.

Faith in Humanity
Believing in the fundamental
goodness of humans.

THE LIGHT TRIAD SCALE (B-LOVING, BENEFICENT ORIENTATION TOWARD OTHERS)

- I don't feel comfortable overtly manipulating people to do something I want.
- I prefer honesty over charm.
- When I talk to people, I am rarely thinking about what I want from them.
- I would like to be authentic even if it may damage my reputation.
- I tend to treat others as valuable.
- I tend to admire others.
- I tend to applaud the successes of other people.
- I enjoy listening to people from all walks of life.
- I tend to see the best in people.
- I think people are mostly good.
- I'm quick to forgive people who have hurt me.
- I tend to trust that other people will deal fairly with me.

We have now administered the Light Triad Scale (LTS) to thousands of people of different ages and gender, and the results are far-reaching.[25] First, it is clear that the light triad is not merely the opposite of the dark triad. While the two are negatively related to each other, the relationship is only moderate in size, suggesting *there is at least a little light triad and dark triad in each of us.* In my view, it's best to view those who score extremely high on the dark core of personality not as a separate species of human but as magnified and unleashed versions of potentialities that lie within all of us.

With that said, Anne Frank's words ring true. We found that the average person was tipped more toward the light triad relative to the dark triad in their everyday patterns of thoughts, behaviors, and emotions. In fact, extreme malevolence was extremely rare in the samples we studied. (Of course, it only takes a few people with extreme malevolence to cause massive damage to the rest of the world.)

We also confirmed Maslow's notion that those with a strong loving orientation are less likely to actually *need* love. Those scoring high on the

Light Triad Scale reported growing up with less chaos and unpredictability in their environment and reported "feeling a sense of contact with people who care for me," "feeling close and connected to other people," and "feeling a strong sense of intimacy with people." At the same time, they were less likely to report dissatisfaction with their relationships, scoring low on items such as "I was lonely," "I felt underappreciated by one or more important people," and "I had disagreements or conflicts with people."

In contrast, those scoring high on the dark triad showed the reverse pattern, reporting greater discord and unpredictability in their childhoods and both less satisfaction in their relationships and greater dissatisfaction in them. The findings suggest that those with a callous and manipulative orientation toward others are motivated more by deficiency than by growth in their interactions with other people.

We also found that the light triad correlated with a wide range of well-being and growth measures. Rather than laboriously go through all the correlations one by one, for the remainder of this chapter I will paint an overall portrait of the B-loving person. Note that this is an ideal, an aspirational portrait based on the composite of a large number of correlations. Nevertheless, the correlations do show what is possible among humanity.

PORTRAIT OF A B-LOVING PERSON

Self-actualizers have no serious deficiencies to make up and must now be looked upon as freed for growth, maturation, development, in a word, for the fulfillment and actualization of their highest individual and species nature. What such people do emanates from growth and expresses it without striving. They love because they are loving persons, in the same way that they are kind, honest, natural, i.e., because it is their nature to be so spontaneously . . . as a rose emits perfume, as a cat is graceful, or as a child is childish.

—Abraham Maslow, *Motivation and Personality* (1954)

Self-Transcendent Values

B-loving people are high in *universal concern* (commitment to equal opportunity, justice, and protection for all people), *universal tolerance* (acceptance and understanding of those who are different from oneself, and promoting harmony and peace among diverse groups), *trustworthiness and dependability for close loved ones*, and *benevolence and caring toward close friends and family.*[26] The greatest character strengths of B-loving people are kindness, love, zest for life, gratitude, perspective, forgiveness, social intelligence, appreciation, teamwork, hope, fairness, curiosity, judgment, humility, love of learning, humor, and spirituality.[27] B-loving people also score high on some agency-related traits, such as grit, industriousness, productiveness, organization, and responsibility.

Therefore, B-loving people show that agency and communion need not be at odds with each other. In his 1966 book *The Duality of Human Existence,* the psychologist David Bakan emphasized the importance of integrating two essential modes of human existence: *agency and communion.*[28] According to Bakan, agency involves self-protection, self-assertion, separation, and isolation, whereas communion involves participation, contact, openness, unity, and "non-contractual co-operation." Bakan argued that optimal mental health requires a state in which "there is a coalescence between charity and self-interest, between communion and agency."

Modern research has found striking support for this contention. Both agency and communion have distinct, positive implications for social functioning, health, and well-being.[29] Those with higher agency in life show greater independence, assertiveness, and constructive use of anger; display less emotional distress and anxious attachment; and are embedded in more supportive social networks.[30] Complementarily, those with higher communion are more comfortable with social relationships, are unlikely to experience problems when in relationships, and are more likely to have support available when in distress. It's clear that both of these dimensions of human existence can be in great harmony with each other, leading to greater growth and wholeness.

Those who are B-loving harmoniously integrate these two modes of human existence. In fact, the only value that is truly at odds with the values of B-loving people is the self-enhancing power motive that characterizes those scoring high on the dark triad. B-loving people also show us that compassion for one's in-group (benevolence and caring toward friends and family) need not be incompatible with self-transcendent values. Those who are B-loving value trustworthiness and dependability among close loved ones, while they are also open and accepting of diverse perspectives and walks of life. They transcend the false dichotomy between in-group love and unconditional love.

Healthy Compassion

B-loving people tend to enjoy caring for others and believe it's important to help alleviate the suffering of people from all walks of life. What's more, their motives are genuine: they are likely to endorse growth-fostering motives for helping others, such as "I like helping others because it genuinely makes me feel good to help others grow," "A main reason why I help others is a desire for personal growth," and "A main motivation why I give to others is to increase my openness to new experiences." B-loving people also tend to have grown up in environments in which helping others was highly valued (but their own personal needs were also valued).

Developmental psychologist Paul Bloom has pointed out the potential pitfalls of empathy, biasing us toward only helping people with whom we have a shared emotional experience.[31] Indeed, some of the greatest atrocities in human history have occurred in the name of empathy.[32] B-loving people tend to have a healthy form of compassion that is motivated by universal concern and integrates both cognitive *and* affective empathy.

Cognitive empathy reflects the ability to appreciate and understand another's feelings—a perspective-taking, "theory-of-mind" ability— whereas affective empathy reflects the capacity to share another person's emotional experience and to really feel what they are feeling.[33] Interestingly, many people who score high on the dark triad score high in cognitive empathy but not affective empathy, using their cognitive empathy skills to exploit the weaknesses of others, rather than identifying with their suffering.[34] To assess your placement on both dimensions, look at the following statements and see how much you are in agreement with them:[35]

COGNITIVE-AFFECTIVE EMPATHY SCALE

Cognitive Empathy

- When two people argue, I can see both points of view.
- I can tell when someone is feeling guilty.
- I can tell from their face and how they behave when someone is ashamed.
- I know when someone is unhappy even before they say why.
- When someone is disappointed, I can tell by how they look.

Affective Empathy

- I would feel bad for a friend left out of a fun activity.
- Seeing a thin, starving child would make me feel upset.
- If I saw a crying baby, I would feel sorry for it.
- I would feel angry if I saw a man hitting a defenseless woman.
- Seeing a man pointing a gun at an unarmed person would make me feel frightened.

While B-loving people tend to score high in affective empathy, they tend to score low in pathological altruism—the tendency to place another's needs above one's own in a way that may cause harm.[36] They have the capacity to accurately assess the *real* needs of others but not get swept away by their empathy in a way that is unhealthy or even damaging to themselves and others. This ability is due, in part, to their cognitive empathy as well as their healthy coping mechanisms.

Healthy Coping Mechanisms

A major concern for those in the helping professions—such as doctors, nurses, teachers, therapists, or chaplains—or those who tend to have extremely high levels of affective empathy, is "empathy burnout" (otherwise known as "compassion fatigue" or "generosity burnout").[37] It can be exhausting to constantly be loving to others. Loving people have many healthy coping mechanisms that can help protect them against burnout and can foster health and growth.

In George Vaillant's massive seventy-five-year Harvard study, he found that five mature coping mechanisms were associated with greater growth, positive mental health, warm human relationships, and successful careers (i.e., healthy adaptation to life).[38] B-loving people tend to focus on each of the following strategies when they feel that burnout is near:

- *Anticipation*: Realistic anticipation of or planning for future inner discomfort. According to Vaillant, "Anticipation permits the person to become aware of an event before it happens and thus attenuate associated anxiety and depression."[39] Examples include: "When I have to face a difficult situation I try to imagine what it will be like and plan ways to cope with it" and "If I can predict that I'm going to be sad ahead of time, I can cope better."[40]
- *Suppression*: Intentionally avoiding thinking about disturbing problems, desires, feelings, or experiences until a later time when they can more maturely be processed and integrated. Valliant found this was the coping mechanism that was most closely associated with successful adaptation—but was also the one most at risk for overuse. According to Vaillant, suppression doesn't mean complete repression or denial: "Suppression alters the world the least and best accepts the terms life offers. When used effectively, suppression is analogous to a well-trimmed sail. Every restriction is precisely calculated to exploit, not hide, the ultimate effects of the wind's passions."[41] Examples include: "I'm able to keep a problem out of my mind until I have time to deal with it" and "I can keep a lid on my feelings if letting them out would interfere with what I'm doing."[42]
- *Humor*: The use of humor to allow one to cope and yet still focus on the job that needs to get done. Mature coping (B-humor) is not self-derogatory and doesn't involve distraction or displacement away from the issue at hand. Valliant describes humor as "one of the truly elegant defenses in the human repertoire. . . . The capacity for humor, like hope, is one of man's most potent antidotes for the woes of Pandora's box."[43] Freud also believed that "humor can be regarded

as the highest of these defensive processes," placing it even above wit in terms of maturity. Indeed, I found a positive relationship between humor ability and the characteristics of self-actualization.[44] Along with anticipation and suppression, humor allows both the idea and the emotion to coexist in consciousness. For example: "I'm able to laugh at myself pretty easily" and "I'm usually able to see the funny side of an otherwise painful predicament."[45]

- *Sublimation*: Expression of aggression through pleasurable games, sports, hobbies, romance, and creative expression. For example: "I work out my anxiety through doing something constructive and creative like painting or woodwork" and "Sticking to the task at hand keeps me from feeling depressed or anxious."[46]

- *Altruism*: Getting pleasure from giving to others what you yourself would like to receive. For example: "I get satisfaction from helping others, and if this were taken away from me, I would get depressed" and "If I were in a crisis, I would seek out another person who had the same problem."[47] Altruism differs from the defense mechanism of projection in that it responds to the real needs of others, not projected needs.

The healthy coping strategies that B-loving people employ affect not only their relations with others—they also display healthy coping in relation to *themselves*.

Healthy Self-Love

"Modern culture is pervaded by a taboo on selfishness," wrote Erich Fromm in his 1939 essay "Selfishness and Self-Love."[48] Fromm notes that this cultural taboo has had the unfortunate consequence of making people feel guilty for showing themselves healthy self-love and has even caused people to become ashamed of experiencing pleasure, health, and personal growth.

B-loving people transcend the dichotomy between care to others and care to self, however. While there are surely narcissistic, unhealthy forms of self-love (see Chapter 3), *not all forms of self-love are unhealthy*. Inspired by

Fromm's essay, Maslow wrote that "we must not assume that selfish or unselfish behavior is either good or bad until we actually determine where the truth exists. At certain times, selfish behavior is good, and at other times, it is bad. It also may be that unselfish behavior is sometimes good and at other times bad."[49]

Maslow argued the need to distinguish between healthy selfishness, which is rooted in psychological abundance and the motivation to become a unique person and to learn, grow, and be happy, and unhealthy selfishness, which is rooted in psychological poverty, neuroticism, and greed. As Fromm put it, "Greed is a bottomless pit which exhausts the person in an endless effort to satisfy the need without ever reaching satisfaction."[50]

Both Maslow and Fromm held that healthy selfishness requires *healthy self-love*: a healthy respect for oneself and one's boundaries, and affirmation of the importance of one's own health, growth, happiness, joy, and freedom. B-loving people have healthy boundaries, self-care, and the capacity to enjoy themselves, even if it isn't necessarily helping anyone else. You can gauge your current levels of healthy selfishness by taking a look at the following statements. (And you can take the healthy selfishness scale online at *selfactualizationtests.com*.)

HEALTHY SELFISHNESS SCALE
- I have healthy boundaries.
- I have a lot of self-care.
- I have a healthy dose of self-respect and don't let people take advantage of me.
- I balance my own needs with the needs of others.
- I advocate for my own needs.
- I have a healthy form of selfishness (e.g., meditation, eating healthy, exercising, etc.) that does not hurt others.
- Even though I give a lot to others, I know when to recharge.
- I give myself permission to enjoy myself, even if it doesn't necessarily help others.
- I take good care of myself.
- I prioritize my own personal projects over the demands of others.

In my research I found that healthy selfishness was positively related to the light triad, as well as a number of other indicators of growth, including healthy self-esteem, life satisfaction, and authentic pride in one's work. It may seem paradoxical, but I also found that people who scored higher in healthy selfishness were more likely to care about others and report more growth-oriented motivations for helping others (e.g., "A main motivation why I give to others is to increase my openness to new experiences," "A main reason why I help others is a desire for personal growth," "I like helping others because it genuinely makes me feel good to help others grow").[51]

Healthy selfishness was negatively associated with vulnerable narcissism, depression, pathological selfishness ("I go out of my way to exploit situations for my own advantage"), and even pathological altruism. It's clear that healthy self-love can be distinguished from pathological self-love and even pathological self-sacrifice.

Individuals with high levels of healthy self-love also tend to show themselves self-compassion. We are often so cold to ourselves. As Fromm put it, "People are their own slave drivers; instead of being the slaves of a master outside of themselves, they have put the master within."[52] Self-compassion offers a valuable tool to help *free ourselves from ourselves*.

Psychologist Kristin Neff defines self-compassion as "seeing one's own experience in light of the common human experience, acknowledging that suffering, failure, and inadequacies are part of the human condition, and that all people—oneself included—are worthy of self-compassion."[53] Self-compassion is not only important for treating yourself as kindly as you'd treat a friend but is also critical for treating yourself with greater compassion than even *others* may treat you.

While the concept of self-compassion can be found in older Buddhist literature, modern research shows that self-compassion is associated with psychological health and emotional resilience, low anxiety, depression and stress, and greater happiness and optimism.[54,55] These six statements can give you a rough assessment of your current levels of self-compassion:[56]

SELF-COMPASSION SCALE

* When something painful happens, I try to take a balanced view of the situation.
* I try to see my failings as part of the human condition.
* When I'm going through a very hard time, I give myself the caring and tenderness I need.
* When something upsets me, I try to keep my emotions in balance.
* When I feel inadequate in some way, I try to remind myself that feelings of inadequacy are shared by most people.
* I try to be understanding and patient toward those aspects of my personality I don't like.

It's clear: those having a loving and beneficent orientation toward others tend to shine that very same light within. This flexibility in shining the spotlight of love is made possible, in large part, by the capacity to quiet the ego.

Quiet Ego[57]

The self can be our greatest resource, but it can also be our darkest enemy.[58] On the one hand, the fundamentally human capacities for self-awareness, self-reflection, and self-control are essential for reaching our goals. On the other hand, the self has a perpetual desire to been seen in a positive light. The self will do anything to disavow responsibility for any negative outcome associated with it. As one researcher put it, the self engenders "a self-zoo of self-defense mechanisms."[59] The defensive strategies to see the self in a positive light can be collectively summed up as the "ego."

A noisy ego spends so much time defending the self as if it were a real thing, and then doing whatever it takes to assert itself, that it often inhibits the very goals it is most striving for. In recent years, social psychologist Heidi Wayment and her colleagues have been developing a "quiet ego" research program grounded in Buddhist philosophy and humanistic psychology ideals, and backed by empirical research in the field of positive psychology.[60] The quiet-ego approach focuses on balancing interests of the self and of others and cultivating growth of the self and of others over time, based on self-awareness, interdependent identity, and compassionate experience.[61] Paradoxically, it turns out, quieting the ego is so much more effective in cultivating well-being, growth, health, productivity, and a healthy self-esteem than focusing exclusively on self-enhancement.[62]

B-loving people are much more likely to express the following four deeply interconnected facets of the quiet ego, which any of us can cultivate in ourselves:

- *Detached Awareness.* Those with a quiet ego have an engaged, nondefensive form of attention to the present moment. They are aware of both the positives and negatives of a situation, and their attention is detached from more ego-driven evaluations of the present moment. Rather, they attempt to see reality as clearly as possible. This requires openness and acceptance to whatever one might discover about the self or others in the present moment while letting the moment unfold as naturally as possible—an important component of mindfulness. It also involves the ability to revisit thoughts and feelings that have already occurred, examine them more objectively than perhaps one was able to in the moment, and make the appropriate adjustments that will lead to further growth.
- *Inclusive Identity.* People whose egos are turned down in volume have a balanced or more integrative interpretation of the self and others. They understand other perspectives in a way that allows them to identify with the experience of others, break down barriers, and come to a deeper understanding of common humanity. If your identity is inclusive, you're likely to be cooperative and compassionate toward others rather than working to help only yourself. Especially during moments of conflict, when your core values are challenged, you are capable of nevertheless listening to the other perspective and learning something from the person. Even if all you learned is how much you still believe in your own viewpoint, you still treated the person as human first.
- *Perspective-Taking.* By reflecting on other viewpoints, the quiet ego brings attention outside the self, increasing empathy and compassion. Perspective-taking and inclusive identity are intertwined, as either one can trigger the other. For instance, realizing what you have in

common with others can stimulate a greater understanding of their perspective.

- *Growth-Mindedness.* Turning down the dial on one's ego also allows for a mindset of personal growth. An interest in changing oneself over time increases the likelihood of prosocial behaviors because it causes one to question the long-term impact of their actions in the moment and to view the present moment as part of an ongoing life journey instead of a threat to one's self and existence.

A quiet ego is definitely not the same thing as a *silent* ego. Squashing the ego so much that it loses its identity does no one any favors. Instead, the quiet ego perspective emphasizes balance *and* integration. As Wayment and her colleagues put it, "The volume of the ego is turned down so that it might listen to others as well as the self in an effort to approach life more humanely and compassionately."[63] The goal of the quiet ego approach is to arrive at a less defensive and more integrative stance toward the self and others, not lose your sense of self or deny your self-esteem needs. It is entirely possible to cultivate an authentic identity that incorporates others without losing the self or feeling the need for narcissistic displays of superiority. A quiet ego is an indication of a healthy self-esteem, one that acknowledges one's own limitations, doesn't need to resort to defensiveness whenever the ego is threatened, and yet has a firm sense of self-worth and mastery.[64]

> A quiet ego is definitely not the same thing as a *silent* ego.

Healthy Authenticity

B-loving people are authentic, but in a healthy fashion. I believe it's critical to distinguish between unhealthy authenticity (D-authenticity) and healthy authenticity (B-authenticity). As Adam Grant points out, "Nobody wants to hear everything that's in your head."[65]

Indeed, healthy authenticity does not mean walking around all the time spontaneously telling everyone whatever you're feeling and thinking (that's just foolish). Healthy authenticity does not mean incessantly talking about yourself and your greatest accomplishments (that's just narcissism).

Healthy authenticity does not mean spontaneously giving in to your darkest impulses (that's just dark triad). Healthy authenticity does not mean fiercely protecting your values like you're defending a fort (that's just stubborn and inflexible). These are all common misconceptions of what healthy authenticity entails. In line with the sailboat metaphor for growth, organizational psychologist Herminia Ibarra notes that "when we're looking to *change* our game, a too rigid self-concept becomes an anchor that keeps us from sailing forth."[66]

Instead, healthy authenticity, of the sort that helps you become a whole person (B-authenticity), involves *understanding, accepting, and taking responsibility for your whole self as a route to personal growth and meaningful relationships.*[67] Healthy authenticity is an ongoing process of discovery, self-consciousness, and responsibility taking and is built on a secure foundation of a personality structure not dominated by the needs for safety, connection, and self-esteem. Springing from exploration and love, healthy authenticity allows you to truly face the unknown deep within yourself, accept the totality of your being, and become better at trusting that "alive, unique, personal center of ourselves," as the German psychoanalyst Karen Horney put it.[68,69]

The main components of healthy authenticity are self-awareness, self-honesty, integrity, and authentic relationships.[70] Here are some statements you can use to assess your placement on the core facets of healthy authenticity:

HEALTHY AUTHENTICITY SCALE

Self-Awareness
- For better or for worse, I am aware of who I truly am.
- I have a very good understanding of why I do the things I do.
- I understand why I believe the things I do about myself.
- I actively attempt to understand myself as well as possible.
- I am in touch with my motives and desires.

Self-Honesty
(These items are all reverse-coded, which means that the less you endorse these items, the more self-honest you are.)

- I'd rather feel good about myself than objectively assess my personal limitations and shortcomings.
- I tend to have difficulty accepting my personal faults, so I try to cast them in a more positive way.
- I try to block out any unpleasant feelings I might have about myself.
- I prefer to ignore my darkest thoughts and feelings.
- If someone points out or focuses on one of my shortcomings, I quickly try to block it out of my mind and forget it.

Integrity
- I try to act in a manner that is consistent with my personally held values, even if others criticize or reject me for doing so.
- I am true to myself in most situations.
- I am willing to endure negative consequences by expressing my true beliefs about things.
- I find that my behavior typically expresses my values.
- I live in accordance with my values and beliefs.

Authentic Relationships
- I want close others to understand the real me rather than just my public persona or image.
- In general, I place a good deal of importance on people I am close to understanding who I truly am.
- I make it a point to express to close others how much I truly care for them.
- I want people with whom I am close to understand my weaknesses.
- My openness and honesty in close relationships are extremely important to me.

The healthy authenticity of B-loving people contributes to their higher reports of satisfaction with their relationships, including their romantic relationships as well as their sexual experiences. In other words, B-loving people are more likely to experience *whole* love.

WHOLE LOVE

Mature love is union under the condition of preserving one's integrity, one's individuality. . . . In love the paradox occurs that two beings become one and yet remain two.

—Erich Fromm, *The Art of Loving* (1956)

B-Love, in a profound but testable sense, creates the partner. It gives him a self-image, it gives him self-acceptance, a feeling of love-worthiness and respect-worthiness, all of which permit him to grow. It is a real question whether the full development of the human being is possible without it.

—Abraham Maslow, *Toward a Psychology of Being* (1962)

The philosopher Alain de Botton once noted that "choosing whom to commit ourselves to is merely a case of identifying which particular variety of suffering we would most like to sacrifice ourselves for."[71] There is surely a grain of truth here. Due to the narratives and unrealistic expectations our society holds about romantic love, we often enter relationships with ideas that are destined to lead to disappointment and resentment. Many of us believe there is one right person out there for us, and we expect that partner to be our *everything*—we expect them to satiate our insatiable sex drive, satisfy our need for belonging, and quell our deepest existential feelings of despair. De Botton is quite right that romantic love doesn't have to be perfect. By forgiving our own foibles as well as accommodating those of our partner, we connect with our common humanity and foster growth in ourselves and our partner.

Surely, though, we strive for more than merely choosing how we would most like to suffer in our loving relationships! We strive toward a richer, deeper, more meaningful, and more transcendent experience of love. There may be no better example of how this apparent dichotomy is resolved than in the case of *self-actualizing love*, where two self-actualizing lovers maintain their strong individuality yet also transcend themselves, allowing for a more complete and transcendent love experience.

According to the self-expansion theory of love put forward by psychologists Arthur and Elaine Aron, a fundamental motivation in humans

is self-expansion, and one way (out of many ways) we fulfill this fundamental motivation is through romantic relationships, in which each partner incorporates aspects of the loved one's self into one's own self.[72] In
Motivation and Personality, Maslow has a chapter titled "Love in Self-
Actualizing People," in which he notes that "self-actualizing love shows
many of the characteristics of self-actualization in general."[73] I refer to
self-actualizing love as *whole love,* an enduring loving relationship that is
continually and reciprocally in a state of health, growth, and transcendence. Whole love may never be attainable, but we can all strive *toward* it,
the relationship getting closer and closer to becoming whole.

One key aspect of whole love is the healthy integration of the need for
individuality and the need for connectedness. In discussing self-actualizing
love, Maslow points out that "self-actualizing people maintain a degree of
individuality, of detachment, and autonomy that seems at first glance to
be incompatible with the kind of identification and love that I have been
describing."[74] Indeed, most of us fear that by becoming too close to another person, we will lose our individuality and sense of self, and there is
an entire literature on the potential for "role engulfment" when entering
a relationship, in which a person's identity becomes based on the role as a
good relationship partner, causing detachment from other roles, goals, and
priorities in life ("role abandonment").[75]

But this fear is transcended in whole love. For one, role engulfment is
most likely to exist among those who are obsessively passionate about
their relationship. For those who are harmoniously passionate about their
relationship—where their relationship feels freely chosen, makes them
feel good about who they are as a person, and is in harmony with the rest
of the activities in their life—their relationships show greater personal
growth, and they are more likely to maintain friendships, interests, and
activities outside the romantic relationship.[76]

A key to maintaining such a harmonious relationship is exercising a
certain degree of healthy selfishness in the relationship, which Maslow
describes as "a great self-respect, a disinclination to make sacrifices without good reason."[77] Maslow notes that self-actualizing lovers demonstrate
"a fusion of great ability to love and at the same time great respect for the

other and great respect for oneself."[78] Becoming a whole person requires setting appropriate boundaries and balancing one's own needs with the needs of others.

But perhaps the clearest way this paradox is resolved in whole love is by acknowledging that both partners can be interested in helping each other grow *in their own direction*. As Maslow notes, this requires not *needing* each other: "They can be extremely close together and yet go apart when necessary without collapsing. They do not cling to each other or have hooks or anchors of any kind. . . . Throughout the most intense and ecstatic love affairs, these people remain themselves and remain ultimately masters of themselves as well, living by their own standards even though enjoying each other intensely."[79]

Anxiously attached individuals have a desperate need to merge completely with the other person, whereas avoidant individuals have a desperate need to maintain their complete individuality. Both tendencies are not conducive to whole love, as whole requires an *openness* to love. The self-actualizing lover does not cling or push away, but witnesses, admires, and helps the other person grow. There is nothing incompatible between that and keeping your own sense of self.

Maslow's notion of B-love has hints of the Buddhist notion of nonattachment. At first blush, it may seem as though nonattachment is at odds with attachment theory. However, as psychologists Baljinder Sahdra and Phillip Shaver point out, both attachment theory and Buddhist psychology "highlight the importance of giving and receiving love and of minimizing anxious clinging or avoidant aloofness and suppression of unwanted mental experiences."[80]

The researchers developed a scale to measure Buddhist notions of nonattachment, which included statements such as "I can accept the flow of events in my life without hanging on to them or pushing them away," "I [don't] have a hard time appreciating others' successes when they outperform me," and "I can enjoy pleasant experiences without needing them to last forever."[81] They found that nonattachment was associated with lower levels of both anxious and avoidant attachment (the negative association with anxious attachment was particularly pronounced).

While the Buddhist notion of nonattachment is not the same as secure attachment (nonattachment in the Buddhist sense is broader than secure attachment to a caregiver), they are clearly related. The more we can be present in our relationships and not try to make the moment meet our prior expectations, the more we can help our partner grow as an individual. As Maslow notes,

> To be fully aware—as close to complete awareness as possible—means to focus wholly on the experience: to concentrate utterly, to pour one's whole self into it, and to be unaware of everything else in the entire world and in all of time. This state necessarily includes a nonawareness of one's own ego. Just as one knows that one has really listened to music because self-awareness disappeared (which also occurs during true creating and absorbed reading), so also is complete love marked by forgetting the self.[82]

Again, temporarily forgetting the self does not mean that we lose our individuality. On the contrary, as Maslow notes: "We have customarily defined [falling in love] in terms of a complete merging of egos and a loss of separateness, a giving up of individuality rather than a strengthening of it. While this is true, the fact appears to be at this moment that the individuality is strengthened, that the ego is in one sense merged with another, but yet in another sense remains separate and strong as always. The two tendencies, to transcend individuality and to sharpen and strengthen it, must be seen as partners and not as contradictories. Furthermore, it is implied that the best way to transcend the ego is via having a strong identity."[83]

Another core aspect of self-actualizing love is having a renewed sense of awe and wonder for your partner.[84] In this way, the normal choice between either security *or* exploration in a relationship is resolved. When it comes to romantic love, we often think of passion and excitement as being at odds with security and comfort. Indeed, for most people, when it comes to romantic relationships, the human drive for exploration does often conflict with our drive for stability and security.

In her insightful book *Mating in Captivity,* psychotherapist Esther Perel notes, "We seek a steady, reliable anchor in our partner. Yet at the same time we expect love to offer a transcendent experience that will allow us to soar beyond our ordinary lives. The challenge for modern couples lies in reconciling the need for what's safe and predictable with the wish to pursue what's exciting, mysterious, and awe-inspiring."[85]

While this is a common given dilemma of not only romantic relationships but *existence itself,* Maslow argues that "in self-actualizing people the quality of the love satisfactions and the sex satisfactions may both improve with the length of the relationship." How do self-actualizing lovers maintain the excitement, mystery, and unpredictability of the relationship while still maintaining great affection and closeness? Research shows that couples can overcome boredom and stagnancy of passion in relationships by engaging in joint participation of self-expanding activities that are novel, arousing, and exciting, and that provides new information and experiences.[86]

For further insight, I asked Sharon Salzberg, renowned Buddhist meditation teacher and author of *Real Love,* what she thought about this paradox, and she told me the following: "Obviously, romantic relationships are extremely complex, but from a meditative point of view, it's also interesting just to look at the simple role of attention. How often do we stop paying attention to our partner? You know, any amount of complacency, or taking someone for granted. Mystery doesn't necessarily only come from that sense of excitement. It doesn't only come from the unknown, it also comes from discovery, sometimes, as we discover each other."[87]

I love this answer, and it reminds me of the important distinction in the psychological literature between wanting and liking.[88] As Oscar Wilde once wrote, "In this world there are only two tragedies. One is not getting what one wants, and the other is getting it." Can we ever want what we already have? However, as Esther Perel points out, the entire question is part of the problem.[89] We can too easily operate under the false illusion that we ever actually have our partner, as if they are a possession of ours in the sense that we own a new smartphone or shiny new car. With material possessions, we often obsess over a product and all the possibilities of how we will use it, only to find ourselves not caring or wanting it anymore after we finally purchase the item.

However, this reasoning makes no sense when it comes to *human beings*, who are constantly growing and developing. The moment we take our partner for granted, and assume that we have them forever, is the moment we stop discovering and admiring the depths of their full humanity. The sustainability of passion in a relationship is limited only by the imagination of the partners and a commitment to the safe exploration and growth of each other's needs.[90] This not only helps to maintain passion in the relationship but also applies to the depths of enjoyment of the sexual experience.

B-Sex

Sex and love can be and most often are more perfectly fused with each other in [self-actualizing] people.

—Abraham Maslow, *Motivation and Personality* (1954)

While I was writing this book, a number of people asked me whether sex is a need. Of course, in the strict evolutionary sense, sex is a need, being a main mechanism for propagating the genes into the next generation. However, precisely because sex is such a powerful propagator of our species, there are many different motives for why humans have sex. You can bet that evolution would make us driven to have sex for as many reasons as possible.

As a result, sex can be used to fulfill a *variety* of psychological needs.* As self-help writer Mark Manson insightfully puts it, "Sex is a strategy we use to meet our psychological needs and not a need itself."[91] Clinical psychologist Cindy Meston and evolutionary psychologist David Buss identified *237 distinct reasons* why humans have sex, from the drive for simple stress reduction and increase in pleasure, to the motivation to increase power and social status, to the drive to increase self-esteem, to the drive for obtaining secure resources, to exacting revenge, to the exploratory drive of seeking varied experiences, to the expression of love and commitment.[92] These reasons can be roughly mapped onto each of the needs included in this book.

---

* Maslow considered sex a "purely physiological need." But I think that's incorrect. While physical pleasure may be *one* reason why we have sex, it's only one out of many. Humans are too psychological.

But here's the thing: *not all sexual motives are equally conducive to sexual satisfaction and growth as a whole person.* Our sexual activities seem to form their own hierarchy, ranging from D-sex (sex used as a way of temporarily fulfilling a deficiency in one's basic needs) to B-sex (sex used for the purposes of growth and deeper fulfillment). Again, one important variable that helps determine one's placement on this hierarchy is the functioning of the attachment system. Those who are most securely attached in their relationships (i.e., those with the lowest levels of attachment anxiety and attachment avoidance) tend to report the highest levels of sexual satisfaction.[93]

Attachment dynamics may also predict the degree to which people are comfortable with their own sexual exploration, or "sexploration."[94] Kinsey Institute social psychologists Amanda Gesselman and Amy Moors define sexploration as "the degree to which individuals are able to effectively explore multifaceted dimensions of sexuality (e.g., behaviors, identity) as a function of secure attachment dynamics."

Why would attachment dynamics be so tied to sexual satisfaction and sexploration? It has to do with the *motives* for having sex. Research shows that those high in attachment avoidance tend to have sex for reasons that are tied to the D-realm of existence, such as to avoid negative relational consequences or to increase one's status and prestige among friends—for instance, by impressing them with dramatic sexual exploits.[95] In turn, these motives for having sex, along with lower sensitivity to their partner's needs in times of distress, are associated with lower sexual satisfaction.

Those high in attachment anxiety also tend to be motivated by insecurity concerns, including having sex in order to please their partner and reduce uncomfortable feelings of relationship insecurity. While those high in attachment anxiety tend to report that they are more sensitive to their partner's needs, in actuality they tend to show *less* sensitivity toward their partner's real needs, are more controlling of the direction of the relationship, and are less likely to use sexuality as a way to value their partner. These behaviors, in turn, are associated with lower levels of sexual satisfaction. As one team of researchers put it,

> These [anxiously attached] individuals appear to be lacking in their
> ability to recognize the actual needs and cues of distress in their

partners, possibly because of being preoccupied with their own self-
centered worries and internal self-doubts. Such chronic worries would
tax their internal resources and prevent them from fully and genuinely
attending to their partner's own emotional experiences and needs . . .
and this would perhaps explain their lower tendency to use sex to value
their partner.[96]

Along these lines, research shows that people with elevated levels of
social anxiety report less satisfying sexual experiences; they report experiencing less pleasure and feelings of connectedness when sexually intimate compared to those who are not socially anxious.[97] When you are
preoccupied by self-evaluation or relationship insecurity, it's difficult to
fully enjoy the sexual moment.

Another important variable that affects one's sexual satisfaction is the
extent to which one has a healthy integration of one's sexual passions into
the rest of one's identity and life. Sexuality does not require a single partner (e.g., polyamory) or even a partner at all. What's important for health
and growth is that all of one's most passionate sexual activities are integrated and harmonious with one another, creating minimal conflict with
other activities (sexual and nonsexual) in one's life.

Research conducted by Frederick Phillippe and his colleagues have
found that higher levels of *harmonious sexual passion*—an inclination that
one's passionate sexual activities are freely chosen and are not in conflict
with other activities in one's life—have been linked to higher arousal
states, harmonious romantic passion, relationship quality, flow, sexual satisfaction, and less anxiety and intrusive sexual thoughts.[98]

In contrast, those with higher levels of *obsessive sexual passion*—an inclination that one's passionate sexual activities are out of control and are
not well integrated with the rest of one's passions in life—tend to report
lower rates of sexual satisfaction, as well as with higher rates of intrusive
sexual thoughts, difficulty in controlling their attention to alternative
partners when engaged in a relationship, conflict between sex and other
aspects of their life, overperception of sexual intentions in those they find
attractive, and even violent and aggressive actions when facing relationship threats, such as situations in which jealousy is triggered.

Finally, another factor that influences sexual satisfaction and sexploration is romantic passion, or eros. A critical distinction, made many times throughout human history, is between eros and sexuality. While the mere physical act of sexual intercourse can be driven by many potential needs, eros has a very specific function: *to grow and express the depths of one's love.* Sexuality is about stimulation and release, whereas eros is about imagination and possibility. As Rollo May notes in *Love & Will,* "The essence of eros is that it draws us from ahead, whereas sex pushes us from behind."[99] Similarly, Maslow noted that sexuality among self-actualizing lovers is "used as a foundation stone upon which higher things are built."[100]

Since eros involves a focus on growth rather than outcome, it is better suited for actually *enjoying* the experience. Clinical psychologist Anik Debrot and her colleagues found across multiple studies that affection explained the link between sex and well-being.[101] Tender moments during sex included "moments of love and security" and "affectionate or thoughtful signs from my partner." The more of these moments during sexual intercourse, the greater the levels of life satisfaction and positive emotions during the day, even having effects on the person's positive mood the *next* morning. What's more, drawing positive emotions from sexual intercourse was a protective factor for relationship decline, leading to greater relationship satisfaction over time. Consistent with Maslow's notion of the importance of the "pooling of needs" in a relationship, the greater one partner's positive emotions from sex, the greater the *other* partner's relationship satisfaction over time.

In a related study, Todd Kashdan and his colleagues found that higher reported sexual pleasure and intimacy lead not only to boosts in positive mood but also to increases in a sense of meaning in life.[102] These findings held regardless of one's relationship status. Just as being married doesn't necessarily indicate a lack of loneliness, being in a relationship doesn't necessarily mean one is having great sex. That said, Kashdan and his colleagues found that people who reported greater closeness within their relationship and greater sexual intimacy on a given day were more likely to report greater positive mood and meaning in life the next day. The reverse was not the case, however: increases in happiness and meaning did not lead to next-day sexual activity, pleasure, or intimacy.

The data is clear: regardless of one's erotic appetites or consensual sexual arrangements, pleasurable sex can be a great source of happiness, meaning, and growth. The more that one's sexual relationship(s) can afford time, focus, imagination, love, security, caring, and trust, the more satisfying the experience is likely to become. As Rollo May notes, "The untamed eros fights against all concept and confines of time. . . . Love grows in depth by virtue of the lovers experiencing encounter with each other, conflict and growth, all over a period of time."[103] Just like life, growth often takes time, and the fusing of B-love with B-sex can be an especially important path to growth as a whole person.

Is Love All You Need?

The science of B-love suggests that being loving is a powerful force, linked to healthy balance, growth, compassion, coping, self-love, authenticity, and even more satisfying sex. Which raises the question: Is love all you need? Interestingly, in my analysis of all the needs in this book, love was most strongly correlated with growth. Love is extremely important, if not most important, for becoming a whole person. Still, there's good reason to believe that love is not *all* we humans need.

For one, those who are B-loving may forfeit some of their healthy assertiveness and highest ambitions out of guilt for outshining those who are less fortunate. While this form of guilt springs from love and care for others, it nevertheless may hinder the full self-actualization of B-loving people.

Similarly, B-loving people can become easy targets for exploitation by more malevolent personalities. It's not that those who are B-loving aren't effective—we found they do tend to be more productive and hardworking—but extremely dark triad people may attempt to exploit their compassion and hard work to achieve their own self-enhancing goals.

Therefore, it's important to cultivate a healthy integration of agency and communion and recognize that both unmitigated agency (overdominance and control over others) and unmitigated communion (overinvolvement in the problems and suffering of others) are linked with poor health, anger, and relationship problems.[104]

Which brings us naturally to the next need in the integrated hierarchy. Throughout this book, as we've moved upward in the hierarchy toward wholeness and transcendence, we've built each new need very carefully upon one another. Now, with a secure foundation of safety, connection, and healthy self-esteem, and motivated by exploration and love, we are finally ready to strive toward a higher purpose that simultaneously benefits one's own self *and* the world.

CHAPTER 6

Purpose

Self-actualizing people are, without one single exception, involved in a cause outside their own skin, in something outside of themselves. They are devoted, working at something, something which is very precious to them— some calling or vocation in the old sense. They are working at something which fate has called them to somehow and which they work at and which they love, so that the work-joy dichotomy in them disappears.

—Abraham Maslow, *The Farther Reaches of Human Nature* (1971)

If one does not know to which port one is sailing, no wind is favorable.

—Seneca

The year was 1954, and it was the last day of classes at Brandeis University. Maslow was delivering one of his riveting lectures, and his students were completely transfixed. In his soft-spoken but intense manner, Maslow encouraged his students to be aware of the totality of their being, including their own unique talents and vast potentialities. He spoke of responsibility and how it was ultimately up to each of them to become all they could become in life. The students were moved, and many reported feeling an "almost palpable spirit of inspiration in the room."[1]

One young woman raised her hand. Maslow looked at her thoughtfully and acknowledged her. "I'm wondering about the final exam," she said. "Could you give us some idea about the questions on it?" Every head in the room turned toward this student with a mix of astonishment, shock, and disgust. For the first time in the course, Maslow appeared visibly angry. With a reddened face and vehemence in his voice, he replied,

"If you can ask a question like that at this moment, then I'm concerned about how much you've really understood here this semester."[2]

Ever since Maslow left Brooklyn College to start the Brandeis psychology department in 1951, he found that his relationships with students were not as congenial as they had been in the past. At Brooklyn College, the students hung on his every word, and he often admired the students more than the faculty. However, at Brandeis he felt the students lacked drive, ambition, and direction. As Maslow's biographer Edward Hoffman notes, "He was not content merely to see them learn the subject matter well. He wanted to uplift them morally as well as intellectually, to see them visibly mature on the path to self-actualization."[3] Some students perceived this as paternalistic and condescending.

Maslow's relationship with the faculty at Brandeis was also strained. For one, much of the department consisted of rigorous experimental psychologists, and Maslow's work at that point was primarily philosophical and theoretical. Also, as Ken Feigenbaum, an associate professor at Brandeis from 1962 to 1965, noted, Maslow was warm and friendly but blunt and honest to a fault.[4] Feigenbaum also observed that Maslow feared dying young, and his desire to get in all that he wanted to say before he died often left his students without the support they needed. In a journal entry dated January 22, 1961, Maslow wrote, "I guess one big factor underlying everything is the feeling that I have so much to give the world—the Great Message—and that this is the big thing. Anything else that cuts it or gets in the way is 'bad.' Before I die, I must say it all."[*][5]

Soon after that journal entry, Maslow received a welcome invitation that would give him just the freedom he desperately desired. The engineer and entrepreneur Andrew Kay, who founded Non-Linear Systems, invited Maslow to spend the summer of 1962 observing the managerial operations of his digital instrumentation manufacturing plant, visiting one afternoon a week and engaging in discussions with Kay. He offered a generous consulting fee, and Kay promised Maslow that he would find the visit interesting. Maslow readily accepted, thinking that even if the con-

---

[*] Funnily enough, he later inserted into this entry a note that says: "*Was a little tipsy.*" So perhaps he recognized how dramatic he was sounding!

sulting didn't work out well, he would have time to refine his ideas about Being-Psychology and his emerging interests in the psychology of science and religion without the pressures of teaching, grading exams, academic bureaucracy, or demanding students.

But Maslow was so impressed by the way Kay managed the plant that he forgot about the extensive books, papers, and file cards of ideas he had brought with him. Kay set out to increase the well-being and productivity of his employees by drawing heavily on the principles Maslow had put forward in *Motivation and Personality,* as well as on other seminal texts by management experts such as Peter Drucker and Douglas McGregor. Kay made radical changes to the operation of his plant so that each worker felt a sense of pride and ownership over the finished product. Maslow noted that the workers indeed looked happy and interested in their work.

Deeply immersed in his discussions with Kay and his observations of the workers and the management trainings that summer, Maslow decided to capture his thoughts. After he dictated his thoughts into a tape recorder, a number of secretaries transcribed his comments. All through the summer he consumed existing management literature, starting with Drucker's *The Practice of Management* and moving on to McGregor's *The Human Side of Enterprise.*

Maslow was particularly taken with McGregor's contrast between Theory X and Theory Y. According to McGregor, managers who subscribe to Theory X have an authoritarian style of management, believing that employees have little intrinsic motivation for their work and therefore must be controlled and given external rewards to reach their goals. In contrast, managers who subscribe to Theory Y have a more collaborative, trust-based style of management, centered on the belief that employees have the potential for self-motivation, enjoy taking ownership of their work, seek responsibility, and are capable of solving problems creatively.

This was Maslow's first exposure to industrial or managerial psychology, although both Drucker and McGregor were already deeply influenced by Maslow's theory of human motivation. From his close-up observations, Maslow realized the immense potential of the workplace for testing his ideas about self-actualization and world betterment. The experience "opened up to me a body of theory and research which was entirely new to me and which set me to thinking and theorizing." Before it, Maslow had deemed education the best means of improving the human species, but "only recently has it dawned on me that as important as education perhaps even more important is the work life of the individual since everybody works. . . . The industrial situation may serve as the new laboratory for the study of psychodynamics, of higher human development, of ideal ecology for the human being."[6]

At the end of his visit, Maslow compiled his many musings into a collection, "Summer Notes on Social Psychology of Industry and Management," which, to Maslow's delight, Kay offered to publish as a book. In October 1965, *Eupsychian Management: A Journal* was published, in virtually unaltered form from his dictations.[7] As Maslow wrote in the preface, "I've made no effort to correct mistakes, to second guess anything, to cover up my prejudices, or to appear wiser or more knowledgeable than I was in the summer of 1962."[8]

While not widely read by the general public, the book was read among many in the management field. The journal is a trove of new ideas, ranging from the need for enlightened management policies and the psychology of enlightened salespeople to employee motivation and healthy self-esteem in the workplace, from creativity to customer loyalty and enlightened leadership to methods of social improvement.*

One major thread was the idea of "synergy," which fascinated Maslow. It was a term he first learned from his friend and mentor, anthropologist Ruth Benedict, one of the main inspirations for his work on self-actualization (because he viewed her as so self-actualizing). Only a handful of people who had known Benedict personally (such as Margaret Mead) were aware of her idea of synergy, but it clearly left an imprint on Maslow, and he saw the relevance to enlightened management and self-actualization in the workplace.[9]

Benedict referred to synergistic cultures as those that are holistically

---

* Some musings are half-baked and rambling, and some are quite controversial, such as his reflections on how society should properly deal with resentment toward those who are naturally more talented or those who are natural leaders (the "aggridants"). Nevertheless, some ideas are extremely prescient, such as Maslow's prediction of the eventual downfall of the Soviet Union and of the emergence of technology creating an increasing need for meaning among employees.

structured and function for mutual benefit of the individual and the larger society.[10] Placing this notion within an organizational context, Maslow argued that in an enlightened or "eupsychian" workplace—meaning an environment conducive to self-actualization—that which is good for personal development is *also* good for the company. "[Self-actualizing] work transcends the self without trying to," Maslow dictated into his tape recorder.[11] "[Self-actualizing] work is simultaneously a seeking and fulfilling of the self and also an achieving of the selflessness which is the ultimate expression of *real* self."

In this way, according to Maslow, the ordinary dichotomy between selfish and unselfish is resolved because people who pursue their selfish gratifications are *automatically* helping others. Vice versa, when they are being altruistic, they are *automatically* rewarded and gratified because what pleases them the most is using their wealth and competence to benefit all the other members of the culture (such as was the case among the Blackfoot Indians he visited in the summer of 1938). In such cultures, Maslow pointed out, "virtue pays."[12]

The ordinary dichotomy between inner and outer is also resolved, according to Maslow, because the cause for which one works is "introjected" and becomes part of the self so that "the inner and the outer world fuse and become one and the same."[13] Maslow argued that such synergy is most likely to occur under ideal conditions, such as the case with McGregor's Theory Y, in which workers have an abundance of autonomy, cooperation, support, and trust.

In his summer notes, Maslow also noted his disdain for those "youngsters" who believed that self-actualization is all about impulsivity and doesn't require hard work. "They all seem to want to wait passively for it to happen without any effort on their part," he noted.[14] "Self-actualization is hard work. . . . It involves a calling to service from the external, day-to-day world, not only a yearning from within."[15]

In particular, Maslow argued for the path to self-actualization featured in the classic Japanese movie *Ikiru*: "Hard work and total commitment to doing well the job that fate or destiny calls you to do, or any important job that 'calls for' doing."[16] To Maslow, those who were most self-actualized pursued their calling, not happiness. Nevertheless, he pointed out that happiness often comes as a result anyway: "Happiness is an epi-phenomenon, a by-product, something not to be sought directly but an indirect reward for virtue. . . . The only happy people I know are the ones who are working well at something they consider important."[17]

In the many years since Maslow dictated those words to his tape recorder in the summer of 1962, psychologists have amassed a wealth of scientific findings suggesting that purpose is a crucial human need, as well as a major source of meaning and significance in our lives.

THE NEED FOR PURPOSE

Man's search for meaning is a primary force in his life. . . . There are some authors who contend that meanings and values are "nothing but defense mechanisms, reaction formations and sublimations." But as for myself, I would not be willing to live merely for the sake of my "defense mechanisms," nor would I be ready to die merely for the sake of my "reaction formations." Man, however, is able to live and even to die for the sake of his ideals and values!

—Viktor Frankl, *Man's Search for Meaning* (1959)

Before I started school striking I had no energy, no friends, and I didn't speak to anyone. I just sat alone at home, with an eating disorder. All of that is gone now, since I have found a meaning, in a world that sometimes seems shallow and meaningless to so many people.

Greta Thunberg, seventeen-year-old autistic climate change activist[18]

In the 2010 documentary *Cave of Forgotten Dreams*, filmmaker Werner Herzog and his camera crew take the viewer on a remarkable tour of the Chauvet Cave in southern France. Named for one of its 1994 discoverers, Jean-Marie Chauvet, the Chauvet Cave contains some of the best-preserved paintings ever unearthed, dating to 32,000 years ago. As Herzog puts it, the cave is like a "frozen flash of a moment in time." Among the hundreds of paintings of animals—including horses, mammoths, and bears—are a few panels of red ochre handprints. It's not hard to see the handprints and feel an instant connection with the strivings of our distant ancestors. Even as much as 32,000 years ago, our ancestors were driven to leave their mark (literally), to make it known that they were there and that they mattered.

There is something uniquely human about this instinct. Note that it wasn't the bears that drew beautifully expressive paintings or deliberately left fingerprints (although they inadvertently left their paw prints). It was *us*. Philosopher and novelist Rebecca Goldstein calls it the "mattering instinct."[19] There are many different paths to mattering, but one potentially strong route is through having a purpose.

The need for purpose can be defined as the need for an overarching aspiration that energizes one's efforts and provides a central source of meaning and significance in one's life. Having a purpose often causes a fundamental reordering of the most central motives associated with the self. Things that once preoccupied you suddenly cause you little concern and may even seem trivial.[20]

The existential-humanistic psychotherapist James Bugental noted how patients all tended to express similar concerns and preoccupations early in the therapy process—wanting to know whether they were basically "good" or "bad," reporting guilt for violating certain social codes, striving against feelings of impotency. "The neurotic is often so threatened by his restricted, covert concern that he is unable to allow himself investment in that which is truly important to him," Bugental wrote in his book *The Search for Authenticity*. But further into therapy, patients take on "authentic concerns," such as a willingness to be much more selective in their commitments and to let things matter. Their earlier concerns fall into perspective. Bugental also observed among his patients a shift in happiness as a goal. "The actualizing person is busy with the concerns to which he has chosen to commit his living and seldom stops to assess his happiness," says Bugental. "It seems only the neurotic and the unhappy that expend their concern explicitly and directly on their happiness. . . . Happiness is a state that is pushed away by the hand that would grasp it but that tends to accompany the person who is alive to his own being."[21]

In an unpublished essay from 1964 called "The Psychology of Happiness," Maslow argued for the need to redefine, and enrich, the entire concept of happiness. Contending that we must learn to give up happiness as the goal of life, he argued that it is a privilege of existence to have "worthwhile pain"—childbirth, loving someone very much even though you suffer their troubles as well, being tortured over your craft. Good living and happiness, Maslow contended, must be redefined to include such instances of "miserable privileges": "Perhaps we can define happiness as experiencing real emotions over real problems and real tasks."[22]

Another key aspect of purpose is that it is energizing. Having a purpose fuels perseverance despite obstacles because perseverance is seen as worth the effort. As Nietzsche said: "He who has a why to live for can bear almost any how." This was the motto of Viktor Frankl, whose experiences in the Nazi death camps led him to start a new form of psychotherapy called logotherapy, grounded in his notion that humans don't singularly have a "will to pleasure" (Freud) or a "will to power" (Adler) but also have a "will to meaning."[23] Frankl noted that "man is originally pushed by drives but pulled by meaning. . . . Man's primary concern is his will to meaning!"[24] When the primary will to meaning is frustrated, according to Frankl, our energies are projected into the will to power, and if that need is frustrated, energy is projected into the will to pleasure.

Frankl believed not only that the will to meaning is the most important existential concern in our lives but crucially that it is *irreducible* to the other needs. When Frankl was fourteen years old, his teacher taught him that a human being was nothing more than a process of combustion, and upon hearing this he sprang out of his chair and spontaneously asked, "What meaning does human life have then?"[25]

At sixteen, Frankl was already holding lectures in a philosophical circle in Vienna about the meaning of life, arguing that the purpose of life is not based on asking questions about life but *answering* the questions, or calls, that come from life. Later, in his classic book *Man's Search for Meaning,* Frankl wrote poignantly about how he witnessed that the ones who were most likely to survive in the concentration camps were those who believed there was a task waiting for them to fulfill. He argued that those who see a greater meaning in their lives are able to "transform a personal tragedy into a triumph, to turn one's predicament into a human achievement."[26,27]

Maslow often wrote about purpose as akin to having a calling. While the notion of a calling has religious connotations, many people report feeling "called into the future" regardless of their religiosity.[28] Science confirms that seeing one's work as a calling is related to satisfaction in life. Read the following three paragraphs and indicate which one most resonates with you:

JOB

Mr. A works primarily to earn enough money to support his life outside of his job. If he were financially secure, he would no longer continue with his current line of work; he would really rather do something else instead. Mr. A's job is basically a necessity of life, a lot like breathing or sleeping. He often wishes the time would pass more quickly at work. He greatly anticipates weekends and vacations. If Mr. A had his life to live again, he probably would not go into the same line of work. He would not encourage his friends and children to enter his line of work. Mr. A is very eager to retire.

CAREER

Mr. B basically enjoys his work but does not expect to be in his current job five years from now. Instead, he plans to move on to a better, higher-level job. He has several goals for his future pertaining to the positions he would eventually like to hold. Sometimes his work seems like a waste of time, but he knows that he must do sufficiently well in his current position in order to move on. Mr. B can't wait to get a promotion. For him, a promotion means recognition of his good work and is a sign of his success in competition with his coworkers.

CALLING

Mr. C's work is one of the most important parts of his life. He is very pleased that he is in his line of work. Because what he does for a living is a vital part of who he is, it is one of the first things he tells people about himself. He tends to take his work home with him and on vacations too. The majority of his friends are from his place of employment, and he belongs to several organizations and clubs relating to his work. Mr. C feels good about his work because he loves it and because he thinks it makes the world a better place. He would encourage his friends and children to enter his line of work. Mr. C would be pretty upset if he were forced to stop working, and he is not particularly looking forward to retirement.

Organizational psychologist Amy Wrzesniewski and her colleagues found that it's easy for most people to assign themselves to one of these dimensions (in fact, the researchers were surprised just how easily people were able to do so!).[29] They found that people who viewed their job as a calling reported greater levels of life satisfaction and job satisfaction and missed fewer days at work compared to those who viewed their job as just a job or as a career. The findings hold even when you control for income, education, and occupation, suggesting that satisfaction with life and with work may depend more on how you see your work than on income or occupational prestige. In fact, the following statement was strongly correlated with viewing your job as a calling: "If I was financially secure, I would continue with my current line of work even if I was no longer paid."

Finally, having a purpose involves responsibility. By committing to a higher aspiration, you are accepting responsibility for the consequences of your actions as you embark on the journey to fulfill your purpose. While taking personal responsibility for your actions doesn't necessarily involve moral responsibility, a common characteristic of those who make a positive impact on the world is that they do take "ultimate responsibility" for their actions, making the morally right choice in the service of a higher purpose.[30]

William Damon, who has extensively studied the path to purpose, uses the example of the highly successful businessman Max De Pree, founder of the Herman Miller office furniture company. While a lot of his competitors engaged in shady business dealings, such as bribing officials in order to get an edge, De Pree refused, making a commitment to being successful the right way, and in a way that he never had to be embarrassed about. He wanted to be able to look at himself in the mirror and be proud of who he saw.[31] Taking ultimate responsibility didn't keep De Pree from success as a businessman and as a bestselling author.

Indeed, the hallmark characteristic of the self-actualizing person may be the ability to strive for a purpose that will make one *unpopular* with the neighboring environment, particularly if the environment is unhealthy, hostile, or dangerous.[32] As Erich Fromm noted, to be sane in an *insane society* is in itself a marker of insanity! Maslow echoed this sentiment in the introduction to *Toward a Psychology of Being*:

> Does sickness mean having symptoms? I maintain now that sickness might consist of not having symptoms when you should. Does health mean being symptom-free? I deny it. Which of the Nazis at Auschwitz or Dachau were healthy? Those with stricken conscience or those with a nice, clear, happy conscience? Was it possible for a profoundly human person not to feel conflict, suffering, depression, rage, etc.?[33]

Maslow argued for getting in touch with your "intrinsic conscience," one based upon the accurate perception of your own nature, destiny, capacities, and calling in life. But what if you don't feel you have a calling? Or what if you have the *wrong* calling, one that is actually thwarting your growth, making you unhealthy, and not a good fit with your best selves? Or what if you do have the ideal calling, but you can't seem to be able to reach your goals? These are all important sources of frustration and insecurity, sure to impede growth. For the rest of the chapter, I will review the latest science on how to strive wisely and pursue wisely.

STRIVING WISELY

What is not worth doing is not worth doing well.

—Abraham Maslow, *Eupsychian Management* (1965)

Merely having a purpose is not enough for growth. There are many overarching strivings that we can consciously set for ourselves that don't actually help us grow as a whole person and, in many cases, can be downright detrimental to our self-realization. Research suggests that it's crucial to choose the right goals *for you*.

The What of Purpose

In the 1980s, Robert Emmons initiated a research program on personal strivings using an innovative method: he had people list their strivings.[34] This might not sound particularly innovative, but much of the prior research on the topic had asked people to identify their goals by choosing from a list preselected by the experimenter. Emmons utilized another innovation—pioneered by the flow and creativity researcher Mihaly Csikszentmihalyi—called "experiential sampling."[35] In this method, participants reported their moods and thoughts at regular intervals over a three-week period.

Emmons found a clear relationship between strivings and mood: the more people valued their striving and the more effort they put into succeeding in their striving, the more they reported feeling "happy," "joyful," and "pleased" over the course of three weeks. On the other hand, those who reported feeling "unhappy," "depressed," and "frustrated" reported a lower perceived probability of success, greater ambivalence about their striving, and greater conflict between strivings. Although the mere presence of personal strivings was related to higher life satisfaction, those who scored the highest in life satisfaction were those who perceived their strivings as important, valued, and not likely to produce conflict with their other strivings.

This early research into personal strivings was significant for showing the importance of having at least something to strive toward in life. Over the past twenty-five years, Emmons's graduate student Kennon Sheldon has been extending the research in a number of important directions.[36] One thing that Sheldon and his colleagues has shown is that while selecting and progressing toward one's personal strivings is conducive to well-being, the content of one's strivings also matters. Goals that are conducive to growth—mastery, self-improvement, creativity, connection, contribution to society—are likely to lead to greater well-being than goals concerned with status and driven by insecurity—attaining power, money, self-esteem, appearance, or popularity.

Of course, since we have many needs, we also have multiple strivings in life. When people are asked to list their strivings in psychology experiments, they tend to list a variety of strivings. However, most people's strivings aren't well integrated, and for some people, they may be down-right fragmented, leading to a sense of incoherence and lack of meaning in life. Research suggests that optimal psychological health requires not only the right goal content but also integration among our various strivings.

Ideally, our strivings would be organized in such a way that they are supportive of our "ultimate concern" and help us become a better whole person.[37] Self-regulation researchers emphasize that goal-directed behavior is hierarchically organized, from concrete, short-term, actionable goals on up to the most abstract, longer-term, overarching life goals.[38] Our highest-level strivings—for instance, "I want to become a great health coach"—are more likely to be conscious and self-defining than our lower-level strivings ("I want to eat that piece of pizza"), which tend to relate to activities that are more automatic and habitual.

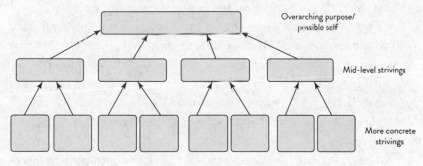

Goal Hierarchy of Personal Strivings

Even though many (perhaps most!) of our behaviors are influenced by automatic habits, and consciousness typically arrives late to the party, consciousness still has at least some capacity to select among behavioral possibilities, "throwing its weight behind one option or another."[39] It's hotly debated whether we literally have free will.[40] I won't settle the debate here, but I believe our most self-defining strivings or callings do give us free will in the sense that they allow us to intentionally cross the Rubicon from deliberation to commitment.[41] If we've chosen our purpose wisely, we can intentionally shift our priorities and reorganize our strivings so that they help serve a common purpose, enabling us to transcend our current selves and move toward our best possible selves.[42]

The importance of having a clear image of our possible self cannot be overstated. In the 1950s, creativity researcher E. Paul Torrance initiated a long-term study among a group of elementary school students with the aim of defining the most important characteristics of creativity throughout one's life-span. At the twenty-five-year follow-up, one of the most important predictors of creativity was the extent to which the participants "fell in love with a future image of themselves" in their youth.[43] This single variable outpredicted every single measure of school performance Torrance and his colleagues included in their study. In his paper "The Importance of Falling in Love with 'Something,'" Torrance wrote that "life's most energizing and exciting moments occur in those split seconds when our struggling and searching are suddenly transformed into the dazzling aura of the profoundly new, an image of the future."[44]

Therefore, the wisest path in life is to deliberately commit to a goal that is expressed in your vision of your future self and is highly integrated with your other strivings. You may have to consciously change habits that no longer serve the broader vision of who you could become. Indeed, your goal hierarchy doesn't have to consist solely of things on your to-do list; equally important is your *not*-to-do list. This may include something like "gracefully say no to opportunities that don't resonate with me at a deeper level."

Disintegrated hierarchies exist as well. Consider a person whose overarching striving is to "become a world-class musician":

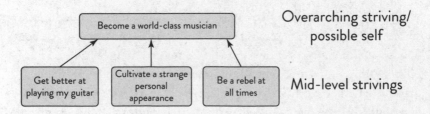

This person's more day-to-day strivings are a mixed bag of status-related and growth-oriented strivings. Not all of these strivings are equally conducive to their overarching aim of becoming a world-class musician, and this aspiring musician would be more likely to actually live their purpose if they swapped some of their mid-level goals with strivings more specifically actionable as well as more directly related to growth and mastery of craft—for example, seek out more mentors, work on promotional abilities relating to musicianship, go to more concerts and make more connections with those in the industry.

It's also possible to have a well-integrated goal hierarchy in service to an overarching striving that is just not worth striving for. For instance, you may have "get more social media followers" as your highest striving, but it's unlikely that the realization of this goal in and of itself will be conducive to growth as a whole person. Some people may even have a more general striving to simply "become famous." Here is an example of a well-integrated hierarchy with a goal that isn't directly related to growth:

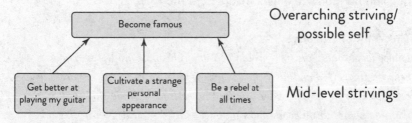

Sure, each of those lower-level goals may increase the likelihood of becoming famous, but is that overarching goal really worth striving for? If you have *multiple* higher-level strivings (it's possible to have more than one), then it's important to make sure there is even further integration among your striving hierarchies, so that one life project is likely to foster growth of the others. See page 164 for an example of a goal hierarchy that is likely to foster growth in many other areas of life.

Whatever your hierarchy, make sure that your various strivings and goals are organized to bring you closer to realizing your best possible self and help you to avoid the many (often seductive) distractions and external demands that are likely to keep you from your more overarching goals. In support of this, having growth-conducive strivings and a harmonious integration among them, researchers Sheldon and Tim Kasser found, are

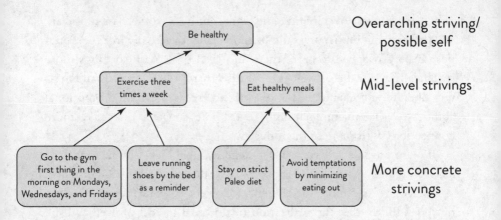

related to a variety of healthy outcomes, including greater daily mood, life satisfaction, self-actualization, vitality, engagement in meaningful activities, and harmony among one's different life roles.[45]

The Why of Purpose

Under ideal conditions there would be isomorphism, a mutual selection between the person and his [self-actualizing] work (his cause, responsibility, call, vocation, task, and so forth). That is, each task would "call for" just that one person in the world most uniquely suited to deal with it, like a key and a lock, and that one person would then feel the call most strongly and would reverberate to it, be tuned to its wave length, and so be responsive to its call. There is an interaction, a mutual suitability, like a good marriage or like a good friendship, like being designed for each other.

—Abraham Maslow, *Eupsychian Management* (1965)

It's important to not only choose goals that are highly conducive to growth, but to choose them for the right reasons—so that they resonate with you at a very deep level. It's entirely possible to adopt a growth goal but still not feel that it's *really* you.

Sheldon found that we can gain insight into the motivations underlying our strivings by consciously reflecting on the reasons *why* we chose certain goals. To see how this works, it's important to understand a central tenet of self-determination theory.[46] According to self-determination theory, people differ in the extent to which they feel ownership over their life. People differ dramatically in the extent to which they feel as though their choices reflect something deeper about themselves vs. being controlled by external forces or by internal insecurity and guilt. These various motivations lie on a continuum of "motivational quality," which is similar to Carl Rogers' notion of a "gradient of autonomy."[47]

Your motivational quality can range from total amotivation (just feeling like you're going through the motions) to external pressure, to internal pressure, to personal value, to intrinsic motivation, in which you find inherent satisfaction and enjoyment in your work. Those who have the highest quality motivation are those who highly value what they are doing and get inherent satisfaction from doing it.

Motivational quality (MQ) continuum

AMOTIVATION	EXTERNAL PRESSURE	INTERNAL PRESSURE	PERSONAL VALUE	INTRINSIC
• I feel as though I'm just going through the motions.	I'm controlled by: • Rewards/empty praise • Punishment/threats • Pressure by others	I'm controlled by: • Guilt/shame • Self-pressure • Ego involvement	I endorse and value the goals of my tasks and work (even if my work isn't directly enjoyable).	I find inherent satisfaction in my work. My work is implicitly enjoyable.
ASSOCIATED WITH: Lower productivity Lower creativity Less learning Less satisfaction with compensation Decreased commitment to values and policies Less loyalty and trust		LOWER MQ	HIGHER MQ	ASSOCIATED WITH: Stronger performance More innovation Deeper learning Greater job and compensation satisfaction Greater commitment to values and policies Greater loyalty and trust

Sheldon's major innovation was applying this powerful motivational framework to research on personal strivings. To his surprise, he found that just because someone listed a striving didn't mean they felt ownership over it. Some people's goals felt *non*-self-determined, as though it wasn't really coming from their deepest interests, values, talents, needs, or motives.[48]

What separated those with self-determined strivings from those who felt controlled? His early studies suggested that those who felt the greatest autonomy in their strivings were those who were more open to experiences and more mindful of their inner experience. They also scored higher on a test of self-actualization. Further studies found that the strivings that most accurately represent an individual are "self-concordant goals." A large body of research suggests that choosing self-concordant goals has important implications not only for setting off an upward spiral of growth, fulfillment, and well-being but also for the amount of effort you are willing to put into the striving—and the likelihood that you will eventually *attain* the goal.[49]

There are many reasons why you may be striving toward something that doesn't really suit you. For one, Sheldon found those who reported less self-concordance in their strivings—i.e., less of a fit with their intrinsic interests and values—were more reliant on external influence. Indeed, there are many societal pressures (e.g., parents, friends, social media, etc.) that can strongly influence your commitments and strivings. As a result, you can end up in situations or jobs that you may consciously value, or think you "should" value, but you don't *actually* value at a deep level. Many social pressures are well-meaning, like the pressure to do something for a prosocial purpose. However, as Adam Grant's research has shown, if you have a prosocial motivation but lack the intrinsic joy for the activity, that mismatch can have a detrimental effect on your persistence, performance, and productivity.[50]

We often operate so much at the level of our "rational self" (who we "should" be) that we lose touch with our "experiential self" (who we *actually* are).[51] But the experiential self often has considerable wisdom about who we are and, more importantly, who we *could* become. We shouldn't be ashamed of these signals; we should embrace them with full acceptance and understanding.

In trying to figure out the deeper aspects of yourself that are the *best* within you (i.e., your best selves), it might be helpful to assess your "signature strengths," or the particular aspects of your personality that you yearn to use, that enable authentic expression, and that energize you and give you a sense of vitality.[52] These include your various talents and your "character strengths"—those aspects of your personality that specifically contribute to the good life for yourself and for others.[53]

MORAL PURPOSE

When I talk about the need for purpose, someone inevitably asks, "What about Hitler? He seemed like he had a pretty strong sense of purpose." Here's the thing: I fully acknowledge that there are many instances throughout history of people fulfilling their need for purpose through destructive means. That's why I repeatedly emphasize an *integrated* hierarchy of needs. There are hazards in skipping right to purpose without working on other areas of growth. Modern research suggests that underlying violent extremism is the dominant need for personal significance—the desire to matter, to "be someone," and to have meaning in one's life.[54] Merely having a purpose is not always healthy. It is entirely possible to choose a striving that brings out the worst in yourself and others because it is motivated by a desperate, never-ending quest to fill a deficiency in one of the security needs, whether it's safety, belonging, or self-esteem.

While Hitler was probably fulfilling his need for purpose, was he doing so in the most growth-fostering way? (I'll leave that as a rhetorical question.) There is a reason why I place the need for purpose so high up in the integrated hierarchy. According to research, the most growth-fostering purpose is one that is built on a strong foundation of a secure environ-

> **Merely having a purpose is not always healthy.**

ment, belonging, connection, and a healthy self-esteem, and is driven by exploration and love. It requires a deep integration of many needs.

Psychologist Jeremy Frimer and his colleagues conducted an extensive analysis of influential moral figures throughout the past half century.[55] They based their selection on the criteria set forth by Anne Colby and William Damon in their book *Some Do Care*.[56] According to Colby and Damon, "moral exemplars" are:

- *Principled/virtuous*: They show "a sustained commitment to moral ideals or principles that include a generalized respect for humanity; or a sustained evidence of moral virtue."
- *Consistent*: They have "a disposition to act in accord with one's moral ideals or principles, implying also a consistency between one's actions and intentions and between the means and the ends of one's actions."

- *Brave*: They show "a willingness to risk one's self-interest for the sake of one's moral values."
- *Inspiring*: They have "a tendency to be inspiring to others and thereby to move them to moral action."
- *Humble*: They demonstrate "a sense of realistic humility about one's own importance relative to the world at large, implying a relative lack of concern for one's own ego."

Based on expert ratings of influential figures using these criteria, Frimer and his colleagues identified moral exemplars. The list of moral exemplars included Rosa Parks, Shirin Ebadi, Nelson Mandela, Mohandas Gandhi, Aung San Suu Kyi, the Dalai Lama, Martin Luther King Jr., Andrei Sakharov, Emmeline Pankhurst, and Eleanor Roosevelt. These individuals scored high on all five criteria as put forward by Colby and Damon.

In contrast were highly influential figures ranging from "tyrants" such as Adolf Hitler and Mao Zedong, who scored low on the principled/virtuous and humble dimensions but neutral on the remainder; to "sectarians" such as Vladmir Putin, Kim Jong Il, Eliot Spitzer, Donald Rumsfeld, and Mel Gibson, who scored low on all five moral dimensions; to "achievers" such as Marilyn Monroe, Bill Belichick, David Beckham, Condoleezza Rice, Hu Jintao, and Arnold Schwarzenegger, who scored close to the neutral point on all moral dimensions. While you may personally disagree with any of the classifications, the list is not divided on political grounds. At least on the topic of what makes a good person, liberals and conservatives actually draw on a strikingly similar moral foundation—including care, fairness, and purity—when making moral judgments about influential people.[57]

So what did they find? In one sense, all of the influential figures were cut from a similar cloth: they were all highly agentic in their goal pursuits. Indeed, psychologist Andrea Kuszewski has pointed out that the common thread between heroes and villains is their capacity for toughness, bravery, risk-taking, and rebelliousness.[58] She even has a name to describe such fearless heroes: X-Altruists.

That said, the two groups differed on key variables. The moral exemplars were much more balanced in their agency vs. communion needs, whereas all other influential figures demonstrated much stronger unmitigated agency. In particular, the moral exemplars demonstrated "enlightened self-interest," showing an integration of the agency and communion drives in such a way that advancing their own interests necessarily involved helping others.[59] This is strikingly similar to Maslow's conceptualization of synergy.

The influential figures were also extremely diverse in their ultimate purpose. For the moral exemplars, agency was always in the service of communion. Agency was just the tool used to accomplish their humanitarian striving. For instance, here's part of a speech delivered by Emmeline Pankhurst, a British suffragette, on October 21, 1913, in New York City:

> And so we are glad we have had the fighting experience, and we are glad to do all the fighting for all the women all over the world. All that we ask of you is to back us up. We ask you to show that although, perhaps, you may not mean to fight as we do, yet you understand the meaning of our fight; that you realize we are women fighting for a great idea; that we wish the betterment of the human race, and that we believe this betterment is coming through the emancipation and uplifting of women.[60]

In this speech, instrumental agency (fighting for rights) is in the service of communion (betterment of the human race). For the rest of the influential figures who were not moral exemplars, agency was in the service of agency. Either there was a complete absence of any clear prosocial goal or there was a call for some unspecified improvement (e.g., "greatness"), or there was an explicit expression of the desire for more power, money, status, or control over others. Frimer and his colleagues argue that while agency and communion are for most people psychologically separate (one is often active at any given time), those who are moral exemplars show an exceptional integration in these dualities of human existence.[61]

Now, we can't all be (nor do we all strive to be) a Mohandas Gandhi or Eleanor Roosevelt, but for most of us, the greatest source of growth, energy, and wholeness comes about when our agentic drive to realize the deepest part of us is harmoniously integrated with our drive to have a positive effect on others—whether it's through mastering a craft, giving birth to an artistic creation, inspiring leadership, or being involved in a humanitarian organization. We tend to be most happy, persistent, productive, and high-performing when we both feel self-determined and are motivated to make a positive impact.[62] As Sheldon put it, "The happiest person is the person doing good stuff for good reasons."[63]

Such a high level of integration is not easy and requires considerable self-development, but it's an essential part of becoming a whole person. As psychologists William Nasby and Nancy Read put it, "Agentic heroes separate to fight the dragon; only heroes on the higher, mythological level, integrating agency and communion . . . raise their swords to battle the real dragon within."[64]

Bringing it all together, striving wisely involves choosing overarching strivings that (a) really fit your deepest growth impulses, (b) feel enjoyable and are freely chosen, (c) help you move toward a future self that will continue to grow and contribute to society, and (d) are well integrated with your other strivings in life as well as your other basic needs.

But striving wisely is just the first step. In order to experience the fully transformative benefits of satisfying the need for purpose, it's crucial to *live* your purpose. Wisely.

PURSUING WISELY

If you deliberately plan on being less than you are capable of being, then I warn you that you'll be deeply unhappy for the rest of your life. You will be evading your own capacities, your own possibilities.

—Abraham Maslow, *The Farther Reaches of Human Nature* (1971)

Having a calling that really suits you is one thing; living your calling is quite another. Strivings are a crucial energizing force on your path to purpose. But striving is not enough. Living your calling involves pursuing wisely. The following characteristics are essential for living your purpose in the way that will lead to optimal health, growth, and well-being:

- SMART Goals
- Grit and equanimity
- Harmonious passion
- Exercising your signature strengths
- Hope
- Being supported
- Knowing when to move on

SMART Goals

In order to achieve the goals we set out for ourselves, it is extremely paramount that we set realistic, meaningful goals to set ourselves up for success. Therefore, we rely on the acronym SMART to reflect what goals should be: 1) specific, 2) measurable, 3) achievable, 4) relevant, and 5) time-specific.[65] By setting SMART goals, we can improve our self-efficacy by breaking down large global goals into smaller, more achievable tasks. We delve into each letter in the SMART acronym to provide further clarification.[66]

GLOBAL GOAL: I WANT TO EXERCISE MORE
Making it SMART

SPECIFIC: Objective should be as specific as possible. You must explicitly state what, where, when, and for whom you want something to happen. There are lots of ways to improve your well-being as a medical student, but home in on one domain and get specific:
e.g., "I want to exercise in the gym for at least 150 minutes per week (30 minutes 5×/week)"

MEASURABLE: Objective should be measurable, meaning that there should be current or baseline value and a level of change that is expected.
e.g., "I currently work out ~90 minutes/week, and I want to increase this to 150 minutes of exercise/week for the next month."

ACHIEVABLE: Objective must be realistic; if you overreach for unachievable goals, you can become disgruntled or lose your motivation.

Therefore, make sure that goals are within reach by creating a realistic time plan to achieve your goal.

e.g., "This is an achievable goal because I can definitely get this done in the mornings before class on Mondays, Thursdays, and Fridays and in the evenings on Wednesdays and Fridays." (If you know that you're not a morning person, it might be better to schedule your workouts in the afternoons.)

RELEVANT: Objective should be in line with overarching goals. Check in with yourself regularly to ensure that your short-term goals are aligned with your global goals.

e.g., "I want to exercise more because it always invigorates me and I feel better after I do it. Exercise improves my mood, cognition, ability to sleep, and overall vitality."

TIME-SPECIFIC: Objective should have a concrete time period so that you 1) can measure whether you have succeeded and 2) can modify goals proactively before a ton of time has passed.

e.g., "I want to exercise for 150 minutes/week for the next month; after each week, I will make sure that this is feasible and proceed accordingly."

Grit and Equanimity

Compared with what we ought to be, we are only half awake. Our fires are damped, our drafts are checked. We are making use of only a small part of our possible mental resources. . . . Men the world over possess amounts of resource, which only exceptional individuals push to their extremes of use.

—William James, *The Energies of Man* (1907)

Even a happy life cannot be without a measure of darkness, and the word "happy" would lose its meaning if it were not balanced by sadness. It is far better to take things as they come along with patience and equanimity.

—Carl Jung, *The Art of Living* (1960)

To live your purpose, it's important to recognize that your deepest passions develop and grow over time. Living your purpose consists of an ongoing, cyclical process of passion and perseverance.[67] One recent study found that the more one's calling grew over a two-year period, the more it was likely to be lived during the third year.[68]

Once a calling is engaged and you begin to make strides toward it, you will become more passionate about the endeavor, which will spur you to put in more effort, in an upward cycle of growth and development.[69] This is why it's so important to not view your passion and interests as already fully formed and simply in need of being discovered. People who believe that interests are relatively fixed are more likely to lose interest when things get difficult and are therefore more likely to give up too soon.[70] Just because you are striving wisely does not mean that it's going to be easy to *live* your highest strivings.

In recent years, the research of Angela Duckworth has popularized the concept of "grit"—passion and perseverance for long-term valued goals. Indeed, grit is absolutely *essential* for living your purpose.[71] As Duckworth puts it, "Grit is holding steadfast to that [long-term] goal. Even when you fall down. Even when you screw up. Even when progress toward that goal is halting or slow."[72] Grit is about *consistency* of your most deeply valued commitments and not giving up too soon just because the road becomes difficult. Grit, Duckworth notes, is "living life like it's a marathon, not a sprint."[73]

Unfortunately, misconceptions about grit abound.[74] One of the biggest misconceptions is that grit always means putting your head down and single-mindedly pursuing one particular goal no matter the consequences to yourself or to others. My colleague Reb Rebele and I were interested in testing this assumption, believing it is important to distinguish between having a *diversity* of interests (e.g., "A wide range of topics and projects excite me") and being *inconsistent* in your interests (e.g., "I feel as though my interests are very unstable, constantly changing like the wind").[75]

We found a *zero* correlation between having a diversity of interests and being inconsistent in your interests—but a significant *positive* correlation between having diverse interests and persevering in the face of adversity. In other words, having a number of projects on the go that you are excited about doesn't mean that you will be any more likely to give up on them. Having a diversity of interests was strongly related to the exploration drive, as well as higher levels of health, life satisfaction, self-acceptance, purpose in life, personal growth, feelings of wholeness, positive relationships, autonomy, stress tolerance, psychological flexibility, work satisfaction, work performance, creativity, and a drive to make a positive impact on the world. Inconsistency of interests was *negatively* related to many of these outcomes. Our research clearly shows that you can have a diversity of interests and yet still remain extremely consistent in your most deeply valued interests.[76] In fact, grit in combination with exploration and love (including healthy self-love) make it *more* likely that you will have the drive to persevere among setbacks.

The Buddhist concept of equanimity singularly encompasses the flavor of grit that I believe is most conducive to growth. Far from an obsessive pursuit of one's long-terms goals no matter the consequences, an important component of equanimity is radiating warmth and openness as you encounter the inevitable stressors of life. The Buddha characterized the person with equanimity as "abundant, exalted, immeasurable, without hostility and without ill-will."[77]

Equanimity also consists of a cultivation of mindfulness and observation, of not pursuing one's purpose with blinders on but constantly being open to new information, constantly seeking wisdom and honest awareness of reality, and constantly monitoring your progress and impact on your own personal growth as well as the impact on others.

A third aspect of equanimity is balance, stability, and centeredness. Equanimity draws on inner strength, grounded in healthy authenticity and the most alive center of your being. The more secure you are in who you are, the more likely you will be to withstand the inevitable roadblocks on your journey to pursue who you most wish to become.

In support of this, psychologists Mia Vainio and Daiva Daukantaite found that grit was correlated with a number of markers of well-being, including autonomy, environmental mastery, self-acceptance, personal growth, purpose in life, and positive relationships with others. However, this relationship *depended* on a person's reported level of authenticity (which included reports of greater integrity, self-connection, and resistance to external influence) and sense of coherence (the extent to which the world feels comprehensible, manageable, and meaningful).[78] It's clear: grit flavored with equanimity is most conducive to well-being and growth.

Now, you may wonder: *Just how tough can someone be who radiates warmth, acceptance, and nonjudgmental open awareness amid the inevitable harshness of life? Doesn't living your purpose sometimes require taking harsh action against someone?* Remember, equanimity is just one part of an integrated hierarchy of needs. Maslow himself observed that the characteristics of self-actualization can sometimes seem incompatible with action, especially when action really is necessary. "The demands of self-actualization may necessitate killing the tiger, even though B-cognition of the tiger is against killing the tiger," Maslow noted.[79] Indeed, sometimes it is necessary to take decisive action to protect your Being, or the Being of others. The key to living your purpose and becoming a whole person, then, is to have equanimity as your *default* but to retain the *capacity* for defense, fighting, and taking a forceful stand.

Nevertheless, for most people most of the time, equanimity is what is needed to weather the storms gracefully and stay focused amid troubles and dramas, which, if engaged, can too frequently keep you from doing what you were really meant to do in this world.

Harmonious Passion

As you live your purpose, there may be times when you get caught up in insecurity. Unfortunately, this can defeat the entire purpose of your purpose. Striving wisely requires assessing why you have committed to a particular purpose, an assessment that must be ongoing.

In the phrasing of passion researcher Robert Vallerand, are you more "harmoniously passionate" about your purpose-related activities, or has your passion for the activities become mostly obsessive? Vallerand and his colleagues define passion as a "strong inclination toward a self-defining activity that one likes (or even loves), finds important, and in which one invests considerable time and energy."[80] When you are passionate about something, it becomes a part of who you are ("I am a writer"), instead of just some activity you happen to enjoy participating in. Note that *both* harmonious and obsessive forms of passion are still forms of passion—they both involve engagement in activities that one loves and are self-defining. Nevertheless, these two forms of passion differ in how they've been integrated into your identity and life, with different impacts on your growth and development.[81]

As you live your purpose, ask yourself: *Am I pursuing these activities because they emanate from my best selves—so that I experience joy and freedom when engaging in them—or do I feel controlled and forced to pursue these purpose-related activities, either through external pressures or internal compulsions and feelings of guilt and anxiety?* It's also important to take stock of whether you have become so driven in pursuit of your purpose that it has eclipsed other sides of yourself or pushed aside other activities that aren't directly related to your purpose but also bring you a sense of growth and wholeness.

Of course, it's possible to have a mix of both obsessive and harmonious passion for your purpose-related activities, and obsessive passion can fuel your more immediate performance (especially when your ego is threatened).[82] Nevertheless, in the long run, having more pure levels of harmonious passion is much more conducive to physical health, well-being, mastery, performance, and creativity.[83] In fact, harmonious pursuit of your purpose can drive out obsessive ruminations and trivial insecurities.[84] And it fosters approaching your purpose-related activities with exploration and love, making it more likely that you will actually live your purpose.

Harmonious passion is growth-fostering also because it offers protection against the downsides of excess obsessive passion.[85] Obsessive passion encourages pursuit without regard for self-care and to the exclusion of other aspects of life—rest, enjoying a beautiful sunset, engaging in positive relationships, mastering a new hobby—that can be highly energizing. As you live your purpose, it's worth periodically reflecting on whether your passionate activities relating to your purpose have become too obsessive in a way that is impeding your growth as a whole person.

Exercising Your Signature Strengths

As you live your purpose, make sure that you are continually using your greatest personality strengths in new and different ways.[86] Multiple studies suggest that the more you can find new and different ways to use your signature strengths in your daily life, the greater your well-being and the lower the likelihood of experiencing anxiety and depression.[87] The more authentic you feel as you are pursuing your purpose, the more likely you will be to stand up straight in the face of hard knocks because you are driven by a solid core deep within.

Hope

There may be some character strengths that we'd all benefit from cultivating.[88] Two that are universally worth cultivating on the path to purpose have already been discussed: exploration and love. Another is hope. The hope I am referring to is not optimism, which is limited to the expectation of a positive future.[89] Instead, it consists of both the will and ways to get to your goal. The late hope researchers Charles Snyder and Shane Lopez have found that the more energized you are by your goal and the more you can imagine possible roadblocks and devise strategies to overcome obstacles, the more hope you will have and the less likely that roadblocks will stunt your growth.[90]

A hope mindset fosters belief that multiple paths are possible to get where you want to go and helps you remain flexible when any one pathway seems blocked. Hopeful people are more likely to interpret failures as opportunities for growth, attribute setbacks to a poor strategy rather than a character flaw, summon multiple resources and strategies for handling setbacks, and recognize the potential barriers to goal attainment.[91]

It was hope that got me through my childhood. As a young child, I had some auditory processing and anxiety challenges and was placed in special education. After a teacher in ninth grade questioned why I was still in special education, I became inspired to take myself out of special education. But test anxiety remained, making it difficult for me to take the classes I wanted to take and to get into the schools I wanted to get into for college. At every barrier, however, I tried to figure out alternative pathways. After getting rejected from the psychology department at Carnegie Mellon University, I auditioned for and was accepted into the opera department. Then I snuck into the psychology department through the back door! I was determined and energized to reach my goals despite the obstacles.

So I can personally attest to the power of hope, particularly as conceptualized by Snyder and Lopez. You can gauge your current levels of hope by taking their Hope Scale (or as they prefer to refer to it, the "Future Scale"):

HOPE SCALE

Goal-Directed Energy

- I energetically pursue my goals.
- My past experiences have prepared me well for my future.
- I've been pretty successful in life.
- I meet the goals that I set for myself.

Pathways

- I can think of many ways to get out of a jam.
- There are lots of ways around any problem.
- I can think of many ways to get the things in life that are important to me.
- Even when others get discouraged, I know I can find a way to solve the problem.

Research suggests that hope is related to a number of positive outcomes in life, including physical health, mental health, academic achievement, creativity, and athletic performance.[92] Hope can also help buffer against the negative effects of experiencing negative life events (such as developing depression), and can increase resiliency in the faces of loss and adversity.[93] In one recent study, which tracked a number of personality strengths over the course of a year, hope emerged as the only strength that uniquely buffered against the negative impact of traumatic life events on well-being.[94] Therefore, hope appears to be *particularly* important in promoting resiliency and equanimity, and thus it's an important tool for pursuing your purpose wisely.

Being Supported

Even the most explorative, loving, and purposeful individual will have difficulty fully self-actualizing in an unsupportive environment. While the psychological factors mentioned in this chapter—for example, hope and grit—are important, it's crucial that we don't immediately blame the lack of success among those who are severely disadvantaged or in harsh and unsupportive environments as merely lacking hope or grit. The *environment matters.*

Environmental support involves two components that work together to help bring out the best in people: enlightened leadership and enlightened culture. Although they are of value in all human endeavors and aspects of society, my focus here is on the organizational workplace, since so many people work and will be able to apply these lessons to their lives.

First, enlightened leadership. When leaders exhibit a distinct set of characteristics, employees are more likely to find their work fulfilling, intrinsically enjoyable, and important, and they report higher levels of organizational commitment, purpose, and creativity.[95] In the spirit of Maslow, I will refer to these characteristics as "enlightened leadership," although terms such as "transformational leadership" and "empowering leadership" have become popular in recent years. Enlightened leaders exhibit the following characteristics:

- Enlightened leaders lead by example. They set high standards for performance, work as hard as anyone else in the organization, and articulate clearly, with genuine enthusiasm, a compelling purpose or vision of the future for the organization.
- Enlightened leaders are good at informing employees. They make explicit links between the tasks of the job and the broader purpose and vision of the organization, make clear their expectations, and give honest and fair answers in response to their employees' concerns.
- Enlightened leaders trust employees, explicitly stating their confidence and belief that the employees will meet their high expectations.
- Enlightened leaders engage in participative decision-making, downplaying power hierarchies, encouraging and giving all employees an opportunity to voice opinions, and using feedback to make decisions in the workplace.
- Enlightened leaders are good at coaching employees, providing help when necessary, teaching employees how to solve problems on their

own, telling employees when they are performing well, helping them stay on task, and sometimes seeing greater possibilities for them than they may even see in themselves.

- Enlightened leaders show that they care about their employees, finding the time to chat with individual employees and get their feedback, figuring out ways of increasing well-being and meaning in the workplace, and assigning tasks that are challenging and will continually help their employees grow, develop, and feel a sense of authentic pride.

Another crucial aspect of being supported is the culture in which one works. An enlightened culture is *autonomy-supportive*.[96] Those who are in autonomy-supportive environments feel as though their decisions are freely chosen and that their most committed goals and highest strivings are self-endorsed, rather than a result of external rewards or obligations to follow the orders of a manager. Of course, some tasks are assigned by managers, but the key factor is that the person is provided with clear and meaningful explanations for *why* they are doing something, rather than feeling controlled or pressured to engage in a task, and employees feel some choice in how they manage their task. Recent research suggests that the more people feel psychologically free (autonomy), the more they take personal responsibility for their actions and the more likely they are to accept blame for their failures.[97] As Eleanor Roosevelt put it, "Freedom makes a huge requirement of every human being. With freedom comes responsibility." It seems responsibility is a burden that people are glad to bear—as long as they feel self-determined and autonomous in their decisions.

Autonomy-supportive organizations are open, forward-thinking, and growth-oriented. Employees feel safe to undertake risky, exploratory, and even failure-prone activities that may be crucial to creativity.[98] Employees also feel free not only in their self-expression; they also feel free to leave the organization if they find the job untenable. Modern organizations also discourage authoritarianism, so that if a senior person makes a serious mistake, they are allowed to be challenged. Everyone feels as though they are able to voice their opinions and will be able to engage in respectful, reasonable discussions with those who disagree.

Also, in autonomy-supportive organizations, the core values of the workplace are those that are endorsed by most of the employees and involve self-transcendent values that transcend particular group interests. As previously mentioned, most employees don't only want to perform well; they also want to feel that they are benefitting a greater good.[99] Employees are more likely to be motivated by growth when they feel as though the company cares about the broader community and all stakeholders, not just company owners.[100]

An autonomy-supportive environment also involves coworker support: coworkers or peers are interested in one another's growth and freedom and share expertise and knowledge, even helping someone who falls behind schedule or is having difficulty reaching their most deeply cherished strivings.[101] Research suggests that coworker support can enhance growth motivation, which provides the optimal fuel for living your purpose.[102] Such a culture also displays minimal cynicism. Everyone gives everyone else the benefit of the doubt and is continually trying to see the best in others. People aren't interacting with others only to get something from them, but they truly admire others and care for their growth, development, and freedom.

Finally, autonomy-supportive organizational cultures allow for a certain degree of job-crafting, whereby employees have some say in designing their job to allow growth, engagement, job satisfaction, resilience, purpose, and well-being.[103] Job crafters can redesign how they perform tasks, increasing social connection while engaging in their task, and reframe their task as something more meaningful and beneficial to society. The restaurant chef can become an artist. The nurse can become a therapist. Even the most seemingly limited jobs can afford opportunities for job crafting. As Justin Berg, Jane Dutton, and Amy Wrzesniewski note, "A machine operator who works on an assembly line may craft her job by forging enjoyable social relationships with coworkers or taking on additional tasks in order to use her talents, such as building a shelving system to organize important equipment."[104]

Job-crafting also has the potential to satisfy one's *unanswered* callings.

Job-crafting also has the potential to satisfy one's *unanswered* callings, or a longing and passion for an occupation other than the one they are currently working in.[105] The person may invest more time and energy into tasks that relate to one's passion, such as the librarian with a passion for helping others at a personal level who takes the time to talk with students and parents. Or they may *expand* their current task repertoire to include additional tasks related to their unanswered calling, such as the junior employee with a passion for writing and communication who becomes the go-to person for higher-level executives on matters of nuanced word choice and how to message things. Or they may *reframe* the purpose of work to better integrate the unanswered calling, such as the teacher with unanswered callings for music and painting who reframes his job as a performer and rock musician, incorporating unconventional methods into the classroom like jumping on top of tables and telling jokes to the students ("whatever it takes to engage them") or the teacher who views her role as a therapist, helping the whole of the student and other faculty members live more joyfully and creatively and with better love in their lives.

Of course, being exposed to one's unanswered calling—either vicariously or by incorporating relevant activities into one's current job—can potentially induce feelings of deep regret, anxiety, and stress for what *could have been*. However, Berg and his colleagues found long-lasting regret more likely occurs when a person with unanswered callings doesn't view their current occupation as a calling (what the researchers refer to as a "missed calling"). When employees viewed their current occupation as a calling, their "additional callings" were much less likely to be a source of negative emotions. I believe this is one reason why having a diversity of interests is associated with so many growth-related outcomes in life.

At the end of the day, if you find yourself in a culture that is too inhibiting of your growth and freedom, and in which you feel as though you have little opportunity to live your purpose or strike a healthy balance of other passions in your life, it might truly be time to move on. Indeed, knowing when an occupation or purpose is no longer serving your growth is also an essential part of becoming a whole person.

Knowing When to Move On

Purpose, of course, is not isolated from the other elements of growth. Exploration, love, and purpose—each is part of the sail, and an essential part of growth is flexibility in goal pursuits and strivings. It's possible to get stuck while trying to grow, and one indicator is the failure of purpose to serve your health, growth, and development. Sometimes it makes the most sense to change direction.

Of course, it's important not to move on too soon. Living your calling takes time, for developing both your calling and your strength to persevere and maintain equanimity in the face of hard knocks. Still, sometimes one's calling or highest-level striving turns out to be unattainable, and no amount of job-crafting or healthy environment will allow it to thrive. There are many reasons why—a truly out-of-reach goal ("make the NBA"), impairment by an accident, unemployment, or just plain growing older—although none of them deter growth altogether.

Facing the psychological challenges of trying to live one's purpose can often be a strong route to increased growth. As Maslow asks, "Is growth and self-fulfillment possible at all without pain and grief and sorrow and turmoil?"[106] Uncomfortable experiences are not necessarily bad, and protecting people from them shows a lack of respect for the integrity, nature, and future development of the person. Life, after all, is an ever-evolving process of discovery. There is something to be learned from *any* experience, no matter how unrelated it may seem to other areas of your life, including your future callings.

In fact, being able to disengage from goals that are thwarting growth and reengage with healthier goals tends to improve people's physical health and well-being.[107] Psychologist Carsten Wrosch and his colleagues propose that those who confront an unattainable goal can thrive by disengaging from the unattainable goal, withdrawing effort completely from pursuing the goal, and stopping to even think about the goal. In other words, sometimes the best thing for your growth and development is really just *letting go*. Far from quitting, it is the smart move because it frees up our limited resources to be applied to alternative choices that foster new purpose and promote future development.[108]

Change and development are features of life itself: people who thrive after goal disengagement pick themselves up again and identify, commit, and put effort toward more promising, higher-level strivings as quickly as possible.[109] Ideally, the new goal is energizing and self-organizing and provides a central source of meaning and significance.

While this takes us to the end of the need for purpose, purpose is actually just a bridge to even higher ceilings of human nature, something Maslow realized that summer during a seemingly chance encounter.

TOWARD HIGHER CEILINGS OF HUMAN NATURE

It was June of 1962, and Abe and his wife, Bertha, were driving down Highway 1 near Big Sur, California, looking for a place to stay. It had been a long day, they were growing tired, and they decided to search for an inn to spend the night. Lodging, or anything else, was sparse on the winding road. Driving in complete darkness, with the ocean pounding furiously against the cliffs, they noticed a light.[110]

Cautiously, the Maslows drove onto the grounds of Big Sur Hot Springs. As Maslow later noted, the scene reminded him of the Bates Motel from the movie *Psycho,* a spooky place at the end of nowhere.[111] At the check-in counter, a gruff Chinese man named Gia-Fu Feng unceremoniously asked, "What do you want?"[112] Maslow described Feng's manner as haughty and supercilious.[113] Feng offered a pen and curtly asked them to sign the register. Bertha was so put off by this cold welcome that she wanted to leave immediately, but Abe was too exhausted.

As Feng looked down at the register, his entire demeanor transformed. "Maslow?" Feng asked with new excitement. "*The* Abraham Maslow?" Bowing deeply, and in disbelief, the innkeeper chanted, "Maslow! Maslow! Maslow!" Richard Price, the co-founder of Esalen, rushed in, telling the new guests that Maslow's book *Toward a Psychology of Being* was required reading for the staff and that their entire mission (which was still in the planning stages) was to host workshops taught by leading writers, thinkers, and therapists interested in humanistic psychology.[114] Some of their earliest speakers included Maslow's friends and colleagues: Carl Rogers, Rollo May, Aldous Huxley, Frank Barron, Gardner Murphy, and Arnold Toynbee.

Maslow was, of course, flattered, and excited to see another real-world laboratory dedicated to his ideas. As the psychotherapist and author Jessica Grogan puts it, "At Esalen, he found kindred souls, people who really listened to his thoughts (unlike his peers at Brandeis)."[115] Michael Murphy (Esalen's other co-founder) was away that evening, but the two began a correspondence that fall and met in person in September 1964 in Los Angeles at an Association for Humanistic Psychology (AHP) meeting. A founding sponsor of AHP, Maslow addressed the room as a keynote speaker by holding up the Big Sur Hot Springs catalog and declaring, "I offer you this. The operative word is *hot*. This place is hot."[116] "From day one then we were like best friends," Murphy told me. According to Murphy, Maslow described Murphy to his daughters as "the son I never had," and Murphy thought of Maslow as a "second father."[117]

The summer of 1962 was quite the summer for Maslow. He not only witnessed his ideas being applied in the workplace but saw them becoming part of a growing spiritual movement. While he would soon have some reservations about how exactly his ideas were being applied by the counterculture, his encounters at Esalen definitely took his ideas about peak experiences in new directions. Ultimately, Maslow came to believe that self-actualization was not, in fact, the pinnacle of the hierarchy of human needs. He realized there is a human longing for something even higher. . . .

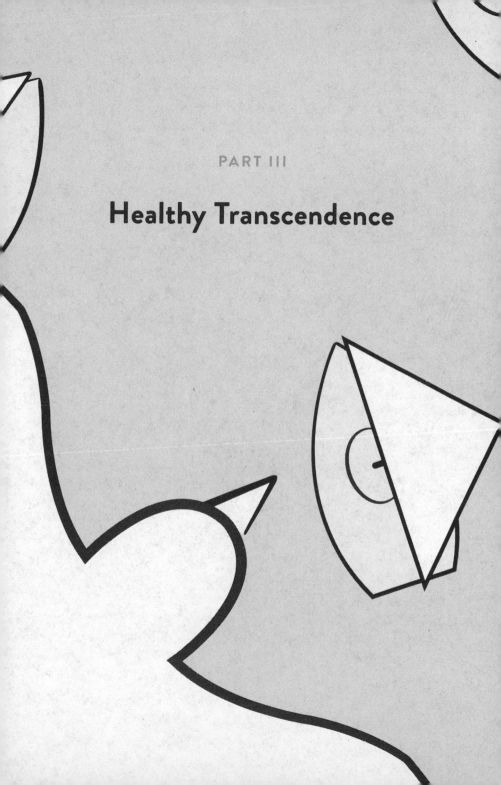

PART III

Healthy Transcendence

Prelude

On October 23, 1928, a twenty-year-old Abe Maslow submitted a handwritten undergraduate philosophy paper to his professor. It was a response to Ralph Waldo Emerson's acclaimed essay "The Over-Soul," considered by many to be one of Emerson's greatest writings. Not so for the young Abe. His essay began:

> I abhor, with all the vehemence that is in me, Emerson and his like. . . .
> Emerson, I say, is a wordy preacher, a superstitious mystic, a shoddy
> thinker (if I can dignify him by even calling him thinker), and finally as
> bad a philosopher as it is possible for a man to be. He rises calmly above
> all logic and rules of thought by which all other poor mortals are
> constrained. He is but a poet (a poor one to be sure) masquerading as a
> deep thinker . . .[1]

Talk about chutzpah! But Abe was just warming up. He went on for a few pages, harshly criticizing Emerson's "flowery" style of writing and contradictory logic: "What shall we say to all this confusion, these muddling sentences, these conflicting ideas?" wrote the young Abe. "Is this philosophy? It is not. What is it? It is rhetorical stupidity! It is bosh!"[2] Based on a reading of the large majority of his essay, I too would probably have reacted just as his professor, the noted philosopher Max Otto, did:

You write with vigor, and there is something appealing about that. At the same time, I cannot say much for your air of finality when you allow yourself to make quite unfounded statements. Why go on with your paper? I hope you can keep the directness and force of your criticism and associate it with more accurate knowledge.[3]

But there is more to the essay. Here is the final paragraph of an otherwise undistinguished undergraduate philosophy essay:

As for his proof of the existence of the Over-Soul by the mystic experience, I have but this to say. I have myself had the mystic experience . . . [in which] I experienced a blind groping for something, an overwhelming sense of unsatisfied desire, a helplessness which was so intense that it left me almost weeping. At the moment of the mystic experience, we see wonderful possibilities and inscrutable depths in mankind. . . . Why not ascribe [the wonders of the experience] to man himself? Instead of deducing from the mystic experience the essential helplessness and smallness of man . . . can we not round out a larger, more wonderful conception of the greatness of the human species and the wonderful vistas of progress just faintly glimpsed against the future?[4]

Now, if I read *this* paragraph by any one of my undergraduate students, I probably would have taken pause. Clearly here was a student triggered by something deep within him—which, yes, brought out great "vehemence." But here too was clearly a student with extraordinary vision and foresight into the human condition.

This undergraduate essay contains many seeds of Maslow's later development as a thinker, researcher, and writer. For one, much of Maslow's general style is captured here. Whatever else can be said of Maslow, when he wrote, he wrote with vigor. As his former colleague Richard Lowry notes, "[Maslow's] style, for better or worse, was the style of a man who felt he had a great deal of truth to impart to the world and who, perceiving that life is short, could scarcely take time out for the conventional amenities."[5] This essay also clearly demonstrates Maslow's penchant for speaking his mind honestly and directly. Maslow would repeatedly, in his lectures, writing, and personal journals, rail against "phoniness."[6]

Still, to me, what is most extraordinary about Maslow's essay on Emerson is how it contains all the seeds of his life's work.* Not only would Maslow end up spending the rest of his life actualizing this ennobling vision of humanity that he clearly saw from a young age, but it also shows that he had long been wrestling with a deep inner spiritual conflict that would only reach some semblance of a mature integration at the very end of his life. It's time to integrate not only Maslow's fractured self but also the entire hierarchy of needs that I've been presenting throughout this book. It's time for transcendence.

---

* Within "The Over-Soul" is a poem—which Emerson later published separately with the title "Unity"—that focuses on the inherent dualities of nature and the need for opposite extremes, such as "east and west," "sod and stone," and "night and day" to coexist for there to be wholeness. What the young Maslow may not have consciously realized is that these notions of integration, unity, and wholeness—the very themes of Emerson's essay—would resonate so deeply within his (dare I say) soul, they would soon form the bedrock of his new theory of human motivation and eventually set off revolutionary new waves in psychology.

CHAPTER 7

Peak Experiences

Heaven, so to speak, lies waiting for us through life, ready to step into for a time and to enjoy before we have to come back to our ordinary life of striving. And once we have been in it, we can remember it forever, and feed ourselves on this memory and be sustained in times of stress.

—Abraham Maslow, *Toward a Psychology of Being* (1962)

After completing *Motivation and Personality* in 1954, Maslow turned his attention to a particular characteristic of self-actualizing people that long fascinated him. Many of the self-actualizing people he studied tended to sound like traditional mystics, describing unusual moments of heightened joy, serenity, beauty, or wonder.[1] He was surprised, having begun his research under the impression that mystical experiences were rare, something that perhaps "happened to one saint every century."[2]

Instead, Maslow observed that peak experiences occurred in a wide range of people and seemed to have many triggers—whether an excellent athletic or music performance, creative experience, aesthetic perception, the love experience, sexual experience, childbirth, moments of insight and understanding, religious or mystical experience, or overcoming a profound challenge—"any experience that comes close to perfection."[3] What's more, it seemed that the greater a person's psychological health, the greater the frequency of such experiences, the higher their height, and the greater the intensity and the illumination. Such observations inspired Maslow to generalize the experience and "strip it of its traditionally religious meaning." In 1954, he was finally ready to take a deep dive into understanding these fascinating human experiences.*

It wasn't an easy path of inquiry. A lifelong atheist, Maslow associated organized religion with dogma and superstition. And although William James treated mystic experiences as a positive experience in his epic 1902 book *The Varieties of Religious Experience,* James discussed such experiences largely in a religious context.[†][4] When Maslow announced his intentions to formally study such experiences, he was greeted with skepticism by many of his colleagues. However, as Edward Hoffman put it, "Braving their good-natured sneers, [Maslow] ventured into this territory alone."[5]

Maslow read widely—from Eastern religious thought, including *The First and Last Freedom* by Indian philosopher J. Krishnamurti and *The Wisdom of Insecurity* by Alan Watts, to the literatures of mysticism, religion, art, creativity, and romantic love. He looked at descriptions of the yogic estatic state known as samadhi. He also plumbed Carl Jung's writings on religion, just then appearing in English translation. Maslow brainstormed examples of the mystic experience under the heading "timelessness" in his unpublished notes from the summer of 1954.[6] He noted examples of the mystic state, hypnotic trance, aesthetic absorption, and transcendent sex.

Ready to formally study the topic, Maslow designed a phenomenological approach. He gave the following prompt to 190 college students:

> I would like you to think of the most wonderful experience or
> experiences in your life; happiest moments, ecstatic moments, moments
> of rapture, perhaps from being in love, or from listening to music or
> suddenly "being hit" by a book or a painting, or from some great

---

* Among other reasons for his delay in diving deep into this topic, Maslow suffered from a mysterious illness in 1947, which was most likely his first heart attack.

† Psychological writings on the topic after James kept the religious undertones but viewed the mystical experience much less favorably. In 1927, the Nobel Prize winner Romain Rolland wrote Freud a letter requesting that he do an analysis of "spontaneous religious sentiment, which is . . . the simple and direct fact of the feeling of the 'eternal' . . . oceanic . . ." Freud's response? Such "oceanic experiences of oneness" are just a manifestation of infantile narcissism, a neurotic regression to the womb. There you go, sorted!

creative moment. First list these. And then try to tell me how you feel in such acute moments, how you feel differently from the way you feel at other times, how you are at the moment a different person in some ways.

Maslow also received reports from self-actualizing people whom he knew as well as unsolicited letters from people who had learned of his new research. Soon, he had accumulated more subjective reports on the mystical experience than any other major psychologist since William James. Just as he had done with his self-actualization research, he used the reports and his wide reading of the literature to create "an impressionistic, ideal, 'composite photograph'" of the "peak experience"—a term he settled on as less religious and more generalizable to the population at large.

By the spring of 1956, Maslow was so excited by his preliminary findings that he decided to share them with his colleagues. To his shock, the paper was rejected by one top journal after another: *Psychological Review, American Psychologist, Psychiatry*. He was suddenly aware of how far his research and thinking had gone from mainstream psychology. Undefeated, Maslow offered the article as his address at the 1956 convention of the APA, which had just elected him president of its prestigious Society for Personality and Social Psychology. As the keynote speaker, he was given the freedom to present on whatever topic he wanted.

Presented on September 1, 1956, Maslow's lecture was called "Cognition of Being in the Peak Experiences."[7] He began: "Self-actualizing people, those who have come to a high level of maturation, health, and self-fulfillment, have so much to teach us that sometimes they seem almost like a different breed of human beings. But because it is so new, the exploration of the highest reaches of human nature and of its ultimate possibilities and aspirations is a difficult and tortuous task."[8]

What was cognition like in the throes of the peak experience, these "transient states of absolute Being"? Maslow outlined seventeen characteristics, including:

- Complete absorption
- Richer perception

- Disorientation in physical time and space
- Intrinsic reward of the experience
- Ego transcendence
- Dichotomy transcendence
- Momentary loss of fears, anxieties, and inhibitions
- Greater acceptance and forgiveness of oneself and others
- Heightened aestheticism, wonder, awe, and surrender
- Fusion of the person and the world

Maslow noticed that for people in their highest moments, the true, the good, and the beautiful "are so highly correlated that for all practical purposes they are said to fuse into a unity."[9] Maslow believed that if this turned out to be correct, then it would be in direct contradiction to the common assumption in science that the more objective perception becomes, the more detached it becomes from values. "Fact and value have almost always (by intellectuals) been considered to be antonyms and mutually exclusive," Maslow wrote. "But perhaps the opposite is true, for when we examine the most ego-detached, objective, motivationless, passive cognition, we find that it claims to perceive values directly, that values cannot be shorn away from reality and that the most profound perceptions of 'facts' are tinged with wonder, admiration, awe and approval, i.e., with value."*

Maslow believed that peak experiences offer the opportunity to see more of the *whole truth*, unimpeded by the many cognitive distortions evolved to protect us from psychic pain. In his address, Maslow pointed out an implication: "If self-actualizing people can and do perceive reality more efficiently, fully, and with less motivational contamination than others do, then we may possibly use them as biological assays. Through their greater sensitivity and perception, we may get a better report of what reality is like . . . just as canaries can be used to detect gas in mines before less sensitive creatures can."[10]

To be sure, Maslow didn't believe that peak experiences *necessarily* lead

---

* This is an intriguing proposition, and one that, in my view, ought to be discussed and investigated more fully among modern-day psychologists.

to a more accurate perception of reality, and he pointed out that further reality testing is necessary.[11] Nevertheless, Maslow noted that peak experiences are often profound and transformative for the person experiencing them. Maslow cited two reports, one from a psychologist and one from an anthropologist, of experiences so intense "as to remove certain neurotic symptoms forever after."[12] Maslow commented that "the person is more apt to feel that life . . . is worthwhile, even if it is usually drab, pedestrian, painful, or ungratifying, since beauty, truth, and meaningfulness have been demonstrated to exist. . . . I think these aftereffects can all be generalized and a feeling of them communicated if the peak-experience could be likened to a visit to a personally defined Heaven from which the person then returns to earth."[13]

Maslow ended his riveting address by noting that any person in any of the peak experiences can temporarily take on many of the characteristics of self-actualizing people. "For the time they become self-actualizers," he wrote, "not only are these [their] happiest and most thrilling moments, but they are also moments of greatest maturity, individuation, fulfillment— in a word, [their] healthiest moments."[14, 15] What really distinguishes self-actualizing people, Maslow argued, is that peak experiences come much more frequently and intensely. "This makes self-actualization a matter of degree and of frequency rather than an all-or-none affair, and thereby makes it more amenable to available research procedures."[16, 17]

Maslow's talk was well received, but unfortunately it wasn't published until 1959, so its broadened reception was delayed. Still, Maslow lectured widely on peak experiences and worked on a book called *Religions, Values, and Peak Experiences,* which was published in 1964.[18] In that book, Maslow wrote: "The very beginning, the intrinsic core, the essence, the universal nucleus of every known high religion . . . has been the private, lonely, personal illumination, revelation or ecstasy of some acutely sensitive prophet or seer. . . . But it has recently begun to appear that these 'revelations' or mystical illuminations can be subsumed under the head of the 'peak-experiences' or 'ecstasies' or 'transcendent' experiences which are now being eagerly investigated by many psychologists."[19]

Today, the scientific investigation of transcendent experiences is, in my view, one of the most exciting frontiers in the science of well-being.

THE SCIENCE OF TRANSCENDENT EXPERIENCES

Our orientation toward the Transcendent arises from needs hard-wired into
our genetic makeup.

—Ralph Piedmont, "Does Spirituality Represent
the Sixth Factor of Personality?" (1999)

Many people (perhaps most people) see religion or spirituality as central to
their lives. . . . Any complete theory of human nature has to make sense of
this.

—Paul Bloom, "Religion Is Natural" (2007)

Freshman year in college, David Yaden was feeling lost and confused. He
didn't feel as though he knew who he was or where he was going with his
life. He was struggling to form his views of the world. A lot was in flux.
He was even a bit depressed and withdrew from the college party scene
and social life. One evening, as he lay on his dorm room bed, feeling "so
be it, come what may"—an acceptance of moving forward despite all the
confusion and uncertainty—something spontaneously happened that
would change Yaden's life forever:

> It really truly felt like it came out of nowhere, this feeling of heat in my
> chest. It felt physical, like heartburn. This heat spread throughout my
> entire body, and at some point, a voice in my mind spoke and said this is
> love. At that point it felt like I went out of my body, or into my mind,
> somewhere I could see 360-degree boundaryless horizons, and this
> intricate fabric I felt completely part of, as if there were no difference
> between me and that fabric. And that feeling, that heat, which now felt
> like love, reached the boiling point. I couldn't take it anymore. It felt
> like the cup was being filled and spilling over. After what felt like
> eternity, but was probably only a minute or two, I open my eyes and
> I'm laughing and crying at the same time. I could cry right now just
> thinking about it. Which is such a confusing, paradoxical feeling. A
> feeling of weeping and laughing. It was a release, a relief, a joy
> fountaining through me. It felt poignant and beautiful and powerful.
> My first thoughts are: Everything is different. I feel different. I don't

know who I am now that I had this. Everything around me is new and fresh. The world went from feeling distant and like a wall between me and everyone else, to completely part of it and included in it all. It all seemed new and interesting, including my future. All of a sudden the worries melted away and I felt many avenues forward would be so interesting. Opening my eyes, I was seeing myself, the world, and my future differently. But most of all, I was wondering: What the hell just happened to me?[20]

That question was so deep that it struck to his core. For Yaden, this experience was life changing: "This was a period of time that was the lowest low, and in that moment, it was the highest high I ever had." He started to eat his vegetables. He started exercising. All of a sudden he wanted to take good care of himself. He also started reading more. A lot more. Yaden was in the library every single day after the experience. At first, the only framework he had to place the experience was religion. He grew up in a religious family and went to church every Sunday. While he was always questioning as a child and didn't consider himself a believer at the time of his experience, he has a deep appreciation for the benefits of religious community. For a while after this experience, however, he was a believer.

Yaden began reading comparative religion literature. It felt as if what he had seen somehow showed him that all religions are different avenues to the same truth, and he felt that a deep study of religious comparisons would reveal the ultimate truth to him. His reading soon led him to philosophy, which, he says, gave him a greater sense of humility about the conclusions he could draw from his experience; he became, and remains, an agnostic.

"Seeing is believing went to seeing is perceiving, and you can question your perceptions," Yaden told me. That brought him to William James and *The Varieties of Religious Experience*. Yaden was struck by how sensitive, nonjudgmental, and open-minded James was in presenting the stories of people from so many different walks of life (some stories much further out than others). James was interested in the "fruits, not the roots" of the mystical experience—the effects of the experiences rather than where they came from. He realized that you could study the experiences scientifically while largely setting aside the question of beliefs. More important for Yaden, "That book convinced me I wasn't crazy." It has become part of his calling in life to pay this forward by helping people to understand their own experiences:

> When people talk about these experiences, they are viewed as suspect. Most people think through pathological causes first. That is definitely true of psychologists. I had some of that feeling in me. I am a very critical, self-questioning person. Maybe I was going crazy. Nothing about it led me to think that was the case, but we get that kind of messaging in our culture. *The Varieties of Religious Experience* showed me that no, many people throughout history and through many different cultures have had such experiences and they are very often very positive. It gave me such a relief. It gave me a feeling of coming home.[21]

Reading William James eventually led Yaden to reading more modern experimental psychology and then to the neuroscience work of Andrew Newberg at Thomas Jefferson University. The creator of a new field—neurotheology—Newberg and his colleagues published the book *Why God Won't Go Away* in 2001, in which they presented their findings on the neuroscience of spiritual experiences. From Tibetan monks to Franciscan nuns, Newberg scanned the brains of expert meditators who had encountered the same sort of intense feelings of unity that Yaden experienced. Newberg found that regardless of their religion or spiritual belief, the very same brain area was implicated—the superior parietal lobe, a region of the brain associated with spatial body awareness.[22]

Yaden was so inspired by his readings that he completed a senior honors thesis on the topic of rites of passage and self-transcendent experiences among adolescents. For personal research, he went on a Zen meditation retreat and completed Marine Corps boot camp, two modern rites of passage. Yaden then went on to do a master's thesis on the good death and self-transcendence, drawing from his work as a hospice volunteer as part of the Master of Applied Positive Psychology (MAPP) program at the University of Pennsylvania, where he studied with both Newberg and the founder of modern positive psychology, Martin Seligman. Yaden is now completing his doctoral degree in psychology with Seligman at the University of Pennsylvania and aims to devote his life to understanding the causes and effects of these experiences through scientific research.

It is this precise intersection of self-transcendence and well-being that inspired Yaden's 2017 review article, "The Varieties of Self-Transcendent Experience," co-authored with Jonathan Haidt, Ralph Hood, David Vago, and Andrew Newberg—a dream team of experts—in *Review of General Psychology*.[23] The article integrates the growing psychological literature on self-transcendent experiences (which, to be consistent with Maslow's language, I will refer to as simply transcendent experiences).

Alternate Names for the Transcendent Experience[24]

Mystic Experience

Peak Experience

Religious, Spiritual, and Mystical Experiences (RSMEs)

Clear Light

Cosmic Consciousness

Deautomatization

Fana

Mystical Union

Flow Experience

Optimal Experience

Elevating Experience

God Experience

Intensity Experience

Inward Light

Living Flame of Love

Love-Fire

Numinous Experience

Objective Consciousness

The Peace of God, which Passeth All Understanding

Samadhi

Satori

Shamanic Ecstasy

The Silence Beyond Sound

Subliminal Consciousness

The researchers define transcendent experiences as "transient mental states marked by decreased self-salience and increased feelings of connectedness." Further studies since Newberg's earlier work have confirmed that people reporting mystical and out-of-body experiences show decreases in activation of the superior and inferior parietal lobe, as well as the nearby temporo-parietal junction—a cluster of brain regions that represent self-other boundaries and egocentric spatial awareness.[25] As Yaden and his colleagues note, "This line of reasoning emphasizes how most fears and anxieties come from the prospect of damage to one's physical or social self. Therefore, when the self temporarily disappears, so, too, may some of these fears and anxieties."

At its most extreme, transcendence is a feeling of complete unity with everything ("Absolute Unitary Being"),[26] including other humans (the social environment), as well as all of existence, nature, and the cosmos (the spatial environment).* James observed that one extreme outcome from mystical experiences can be the feeling of being at home in the universe.[27]

Not all transcendent experiences are mystical.

But not all transcendent experiences are mystical. There are a variety of transcendent experiences that differ in their intensity and degree of unity with the world. There is a "unitary continuum,"[28] ranging from the experience

_____

* One prominent measure of mystical experiences is the Mystical Experience Questionnaire, which consists of four facets: mystical, positive mood, transcendence of time and space, and ineffability. Researchers classify a "complete mystical experience" as scores greater than or equal to 60 percent of the maximum possible score on each of the four subscales. See: Barrett, F. S., Johnson, M. W., & Griffiths, R. R. (2015). Validation of the revised Mystical Experience Questionnaire in experimental sessions with psilocybin. *Journal of Psychopharmacology, 29*(11), 1182–1190.

The Unitary Continuum

Increasing Degrees of Perceived Unity

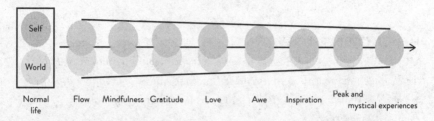

This conceptual graph was adapted from Yaden et al. (2017), "The Varieties of Self-Transcendent Experience." It suggests a range of transcendent experiences with varying levels of connection with the world and is included for suggestive, demonstrative purposes. Further research is required to further flesh out this model.

of becoming deeply absorbed in an engrossing book, sports performance, or creative activity (what psychologist Mihaly Csikszentmihalyi refers to as the flow experience),[29] to experiencing an extended mindful meditation retreat,[30] to feeling gratitude for a selfless act of kindness,[31] to merging with a loved one,[32] to experiencing awe at a beautiful sunset or the stars above,[33] to being so inspired by something—whether an inspiring role model, virtuoso performance, intellectual idea, or act of moral beauty—that you have a "transcendent awakening,"[34] all the way up to the great mystical illumination.[35]

While transcendent experiences differ in various ways, they all have in common weakening of the boundaries to connectedness with others, the world, and one's own self. William James personally observed this core aspect of the transcendent experience: "Looking back on my own experiences, they all converge towards a kind of insight to which I cannot help ascribing some metaphysical significance. . . . It is as if the opposites of the world, whose contradictoriness and conflict make all our difficulties and troubles, were melted into unity." Modern research suggests that the transcendent state of consciousness is related to positive mental health—including positive changes in family life, reduced fear of death, better health, and a greater sense of purpose—as well as a motivation for increased altruism and prosocial behaviors.[36] The sort of self-loss that occurs during transcendent experiences appears to be very conducive to health and growth. Which raises the question: What form of self-loss is specifically associated with these experiences?

HEALTHY SELF-LOSS

We may spend most of our waking hours advancing our own interests, but we all have the capacity to transcend self-interest and become simply a part of a whole. It's not just a capacity; it's the portal to many of life's most cherished experiences.

—Jonathan Haidt, *The Righteous Mind* (2012)

When we're in the grips of insecurity—when we don't feel safe, accepted, or respected—there is often a sense that we don't know who we are or what our real identity is. The world often feels less real, and we feel more disconnected from others. This form of self-loss, which is deeply impacted by our environment, often results in excessive self-focus, including a fear of loss of control of one's self and a lack of a healthy integration with the rest of one's personality structure.

However, in transcendent moments of self-loss, there is often a heightened sense of pure Being, and the experience often feels "realer than real."[37] William James referred to this as the "noetic" quality of the mystic experience.[38] What's more, the language associated with feelings of realness suggest a great connection with a larger whole, inclusiveness, and physical proximity—such as "all," "everything," "we," and "close"—and the use of fewer first-person pronouns such as "I" and "my."[39] Healthy self-loss does not involve fear. Rather, it is characterized by curiosity and openness to the present moment and one's inner experience.

Healthy self-loss is akin to what Mark Leary refers to as the "hypoegoic" state of consciousness.[40] According to Leary, people who are in a "hypoegoic state focus primarily on the present situation; introspect minimally on their thoughts, motives, and feelings; think about and evaluate themselves primarily in concrete, as opposed to abstract, ways; and pay relatively little attention to other people's perceptions and evaluations of them."[41] The hypoegoic state is similar to the quiet ego (see Chapter 5).

Having a substantial quieting of the ego is strongly related to having a strong, not weak, sense of self and with increased, not weakened, authenticity. Indeed, *those with the quietest ego defenses often have the strongest sense of self.* As the Buddhist Harvard psychotherapist Jack Engler put it, "You have to be somebody before you can be nobody."[42]

In his 1962 article "Peak Experiences as Acute Identity Experiences," Maslow tried to make sense of this seeming paradox, noting that "the greatest attainment of identity, autonomy, or selfhood is itself simultaneously a transcending of itself, a going beyond and above selfhood. The person can then become egoless."[43] While Maslow admits that he doesn't fully understand the paradox, he attempts to further describe the particular aspect of self that becomes transcended in these moments: "[There is] the total loss of self-consciousness or self-observation which is normally with us but which we feel to lower in any absorption or interest or concentration or distraction, or being taken 'out of ourselves,' whether on the high level of peak experiences, or on the lower level of becoming so interested in a movie or a novel or a football game as to become forgetful of oneself and one's minor pains, one's appearance, one's worries, etc. This is practically always felt as a pleasant state."[44, 45]

Once again, we see that self-actualizing people resolve ordinary dichotomies. We tend to think of a heightened sense of connectedness as contrary to a heightened sense of individuality. However, as Maslow pointed out, the dichotomy is resolved among self-actualizing individuals: "The fact is that self-actualizing people are simultaneously the most individualistic and the most altruistic and social and loving of all human beings. The fact that we have in our culture put these qualities at opposite ends of a single continuum is apparently a mistake that must now be corrected. These qualities go together and the dichotomy is resolved in self-actualizing people."[46]

One of the most unifying transcendent experiences is a sense of awe. David Yaden told me that when he is giving lectures, he asks people to raise their hand if they have ever "felt at one with all things," and only about one-third of the people in the audience raise their hands. He then asks people to raise their hands if they have "had a profound religious experience or awakening that changed the direction of their life." Slightly more hands are typically raised. Finally, Yaden asks if anyone has ever "felt awe," and nearly everyone's hands shoot up. For this reason, Yaden refers to awe as "the everyperson's spiritual experience."

AWE: THE EVERYPERSON'S SPIRITUAL EXPERIENCE

The most fortunate are those who have a wonderful capacity to appreciate again and again, freshly and naively, the basic goods of life, with awe, pleasure, wonder and even ecstasy.

—Abraham Maslow, *Toward a Psychology of Being* (1962)

While the concepts of awe and wonder have a long history in philosophy and religion, James and Maslow helped bring them to psychology. Today, much of the contemporary investigation of awe stems from a 2003 paper, "Approaching Awe, a Moral, Spiritual, and Aesthetic Emotion," written by Dacher Keltner and Jonathan Haidt.[47] The authors argued that there are two main cognitive appraisals that are central to awe experiences: the perception of vastness and the struggle to mentally process the experience. Vastness need not be perceptual, such as seeing the Grand Canyon, but can also be conceptual, such as contemplating eternity. Awe is an unusual and complex emotion because it mixes emotions that don't tend to go with each other, such as ecstasy and fear.[48]

Studies conducted since that 2003 paper have linked awe with increased life satisfaction,[49] a feeling that there is more time available,[50] increased generosity and helping,[51] and decreased aggressive attitudes.[52] Awe can also affect the way we perceive our bodies, leading us to underestimate their size,[53] temporarily increase religious and spiritual feelings and actions,[54] and temporarily increase both supernatural belief and the tendency to perceive human agency in random events.[55]

When my path crossed with Yaden's in 2014 at the University of Pennsylvania, we bonded over mutual research interests and almost immediately collaborated on multiple projects, including the light triad research I presented in Chapter 5. Yaden observed that the experimental literature on awe lacked a robust state measure of awe. So to be as comprehensive as possible, we created a scale based on the various aspects of awe that have been described in the literature.[56] Along with our other collaborators on the project—Elizabeth Hyde, Andrea Gaggioli, Jua Wei Zhang, and Dacher Keltner—we asked participants, "Please take a few minutes to think about a particular time, fairly recently, when you felt intense awe," and we had participants write a few paragraphs about their experience.[57] Here are some of the anonymous responses:

The moment I set my eyes on the view of the lake during the winter holidays I was immediately in awe. My jaw literally dropped and I was just blown away. The view was jaw-droppingly beautiful. My eyes lit up and my face was all grinning from intense amounts of joy, relief, and awe at the spectacle in front of my eyes.

My last time experiencing awe was watching my daughter play "Silent Night" on her sax. My daughter plays in the jazz ensemble in school and was given the solo for this year's convocation. . . . Watching her play recently, she amazed me.

The time that I felt intense awe was when my wife and I went into the Rocky Mountains for our honeymoon. I had never been outside the state of Missouri and couldn't contemplate something being as large as the mountains are.

The majority of the participants rated their awe experience as "strongly positive." We asked participants to specifically indicate what elicited their experience of awe. "Natural scenery" was described as the most frequent trigger, although other triggers were also represented: great skill, encounter with God, great virtue, building or monument, powerful leader, grand theory or idea, music, art, epiphany. The second most represented trigger was the "other" category. Consistent with what Maslow observed, a number of the write-in responses referred to childbirth as a trigger for intense awe experiences.

We then had participants fill out a survey that included our new items about the specific experience of awe. The six facets of the Awe Experience Scale include Vastness (e.g., "I experienced something greater than myself"), Need for Accommodation (e.g., "I found it hard to comprehend the experience in full"), Time (e.g., "I sensed things momentarily slow down"), Self-Diminishment (e.g., "I felt that my sense of self was diminished"), Connectedness (e.g., "I felt closely connected to humanity"), and Physical Sensations (e.g., "I had chills").

We found that all six of these facets of the awe experience were substantially related to one another, suggesting that they do tend to co-occur during the awe experience. (You can take the Awe Experience Scale at *selfactualizationtests.com*.) The total scale was related to a number of important variables. First, the greater the experience of awe, the higher the rated intensity of the experience. The experience of awe was related to heightened feelings of wonder, curiosity, inspiration, contentedness, appreciation, love, trust, happiness, and joyfulness.

The only uncomfortable emotions that were uniquely related to the awe experience were "stressed, nervous, overwhelmed." This is consistent with awe being a unique mix of exaltation and fear/reverence.[58] The largest personality trait associated with the awe experience was openness to experience. This makes sense, considering that openness to experience is also related to flow, absorption, appreciation of beauty, and other transcendent experiences (see Chapter 4).

Finally, we found that the awe experience was not associated with religiosity, but it was significantly related to spirituality, religious service attendance, and practices such as prayer and meditation. Therefore, while religion certainly encompasses more than just transcendent experiences—religion also serves a fundamentally social, community-binding function[59]—our findings do suggest that certain spiritual practices, rituals, and interventions might be able to increase awe and other transcendent experiences in all of us—regardless of our religious beliefs.[60]

MIND-ALTERING INTERVENTIONS

It may be that these drugs [especially LSD and psilocybin] . . . could be used to produce a peak-experience, with core-religious revelation, in non-peakers, thus bridging the chasm between these two separated halves of mankind.

—Abraham Maslow, *Religions, Values, and Peak-Experiences* (1964)

On April 15, 2012, on an airplane somewhere between Tuscon and Las Vegas, Katherine MacLean "died." MacLean was always an anxious person. Certain things would make the anxiety go away temporarily, such as meditating, getting deeply absorbed in work, or dabbling in "psychedelic extracurricular activities." But that day, everything changed.

MacLean was two years into her postdoc in psychopharmacology with Roland Griffiths at the Johns Hopkins University School of Medicine, where she worked as a psychedelic scientist, conducting legal trials of psilocybin (the primary chemical found in "magic mushrooms"). One day at a conference while she was on a walking path with a teacher, the teacher said something thought-provoking to her.

After their conversation, MacLean visited a waterfall and sat down and meditated on her breath, when a question popped into her mind: Where am I? As soon as she asked herself the question, everything "dissolved into this vortex of energy. It was terrifying, because I felt as though I was going to get sucked into this vortex of energy that didn't care about humans or life on earth or whether I was going to come back." But when she came back into her body, everything was "shiny, brilliant, and I felt a lot of gratitude for having a body and being alive. And I saw the earth as just this paradise of biological life." As it turns out, this was just the preliminary to her "death."

A couple of days later, after giving her first big public talk about psilocybin, MacLean was heading home. As her feet started down the jetway to the plane, "That's when I knew I was about to die. I knew it." As she approached her seat, panic began to rise. "I was sweating. I was going to come up with some excuse to just leave, get off the airplane," she recounts. But she stayed. Maybe it was the meditation experience a few days before, but she surrendered to the moment, a moment she had no control over, and began meditating on her breath as if each breath were her last. That's when it happened.

"The moment of death was actually kind of anticlimactic," she notes. "Instead, nothing happened. It was just like the light switch labeled 'Katherine MacLean' went off. I remember opening up my eyes and looking out the window and thinking, 'Oh, that was it.'" She felt an immediate sense of relief and total freedom. But then the panic set in. "I knew there was no going back. When I stepped off the plane, everything seemed strange and unreal. It felt like the volume had been turned up on everything, and it was difficult to orient." For months afterward, she felt as though she were stuck between the living and the dead. "The ground under my feet felt fluid, and sometimes when I looked in the mirror, a sickly corpse looked back at me." MacLean struggled to adjust to a new reality of having "died" but still being alive.

Eventually, MacLean gave up trying to understand what had happened to her and just started enjoying the experience. She fully accepted what had happened: "It was like a big chunk of that fear that I had been living with was gone. But a lot of other parts of me were still around. I forgot how to be afraid. And that was when the world opened up. In those moments, everything and everyone around me seemed so perfect I could hardly stand it. Everything seemed possible and I felt lucky to be alive in a world of shiny wonder."

MacLean admits she'll never know the precise causes of her experience, but she attributes part of the experience to facilitating over one hundred high-dose psychedelic sessions with people from all different walks of life. "It's as though my brain had been permanently rewired to expect transcendent experiences and death," she notes.[61] While at Johns Hopkins, MacLean led a pathbreaking study demonstrating significant changes in openness to experience after a mystical-experience-inducing psilocybin session.[62] As we've seen throughout this book, openness to experience is a strong predictor of creativity, love, and other transcendent experiences. MacLean and her colleagues found that openness remained high a year after having the mystical experience.

Over the years, as studies have accumulated—the number of studies counterbalancing the small sample size of each—the overall effects of psychedelics on personality, well-being, and an expanded worldview have been strikingly consistent.[63] One study found that experiences induced by psychedelic substances were rated as more intensely mystical, resulted in a reduced fear of death, increased one's sense of purpose, and increased spirituality as compared with non-psychedelically triggered religious, spiritual, or mystical experiences.[64] Other research has found that after a two-month follow-up, participants in a controlled psychedelic session in the laboratory showed positive changes in mood, altruism, and a sense of well-being or life satisfaction.[65] The majority of participants even rated the experience among the top five most personally meaningful experiences of their entire lives.

Psychedelics have helped addicted smokers quit smoking; terminal cancer patients face death with less depression and anxiety and even increased well-being and life satisfaction;[66] treatment-resistant depression (TD) patients decrease their levels of anxiety and increase their mood and openness to experience; and veterans substantially lower their PTSD and intrusive flashbacks. (MDMA-assisted psychotherapy also shows promise in treating PTSD as well as improving social anxiety among autistic adults.)[67] In the case of depression, psilocybin therapy may show even more progress in improving mood and openness to experience than traditional antidepressant treatment.[68]

If anyone has deep insight into the mechanism underlying these effects, it's Mary Cosimano. Cosimano served as a social worker, head session guide, and research coordinator for the Johns Hopkins Psilocybin Research Project for over nineteen years and personally guided more than 380 study sessions and participated in over one thousand preparation and integration meetings. MacLean told me that Cosimano is "very humble and quiet" and that "the entire enterprise at Hopkins would not exist without her. She's a true saint, in my opinion."[69]

In a 2014 article, "Love: The Nature of Our True Self," Cosimano reflected on her experience as head session guide: "Based on my clinical perspective, I would like to share what I personally believe to be one of the most important outcomes of this work: that psilocybin can offer a means to reconnect to our true nature—our authentic self—and thereby help find meaning in our lives. . . . I believe that what humans really want is to receive and to give love. I believe that love is what connects us to each other and that such a connection is brought about by being intimate with each other, by sharing ourselves with others. I believe that the nature of our true self is love. . . . Yet very often we're afraid to open ourselves to this connection so we put up barriers and wear masks. If we are able to remove the barriers, to let down our defenses, we can begin to know and accept ourselves, thus allowing ourselves to receive and to give love."[70]

Cosimano believes that the study sessions are so life-changing because of the combination of the preparatory sessions and the effects of psilocybin itself. In the preparatory meetings, researchers make sure that the participants feel safe and secure. They create an environment of trust and encourage participants to feel comfortable being vulnerable in telling their story. Intimate conversation and self-disclosure are encouraged. Cosimano believes such groundwork allows participants to enter the psilocybin session in a state of deep relaxation, ready for an especially expansive experience.

Some participants report that the session was the first time they felt they had been fully seen. One participant wrote: "Once I was past the darkness, I began to feel an increasing feeling of peace and connectedness. . . . An intense feeling of love and joy emanated from all over my body and I can't imagine feeling any happier. I knew that the worries of everyday life were meaningless and that all that mattered were my connections with the wonderful people who are my family and friends."

In their study on cancer patients, Cosimano observed, patients entered the study feeling "'disconnected'—not only from their place in the world but also more importantly from themselves, their lives having changed dramatically since their diagnosis." Many were too weak to continue to work, and many lost their jobs. At the start of the study, they felt weak, tired, and lacking vitality. What once gave them purpose and meaning now seemed meaningless.

After the experiment, however, the cancer patients showed a high positive response rate to the following two questions: (a) Have you all of a sudden changed your sense of who you are and where you are headed? (b) Do you often feel empty inside? Cosimano believes that the session helped patients reconnect to their "true self, to believing that they are worthy of love and connection." While the "true self" probably doesn't exist (see Appendix I), these studies do support the notion that there is a growth-oriented core to each of us that is full of openness, love, and meaning, but which is held back by our ordinary perceptions, fears, and anxieties.

Of course, psychedelics aren't the only path to such a colossal shift in perspective. Transcendent experiences can also be induced through various meditation and prayer practices.[71] Recent research suggests that a mystical-experience-inducing psilocybin session in combination with meditation and other spiritual practices produces the largest and most enduring positive changes in psychological functioning, including decreased anxiety and fearfulness and increased feelings of peace/harmony, joy/intense happiness, interpersonal closeness, gratitude, life meaning/ purpose, forgiveness, death acceptance, and increases in prosocial attitudes and behaviors.[72]

A number of researchers, including Barbara Fredrickson, Dacher Keltner, Patty Van Cappellen, and Vassilis Saroglou, have begun incorporating "awe induction" techniques in their work; they show participants awe-inspiring images and videos of architecture and natural scenery, then have participants write or read about an awe experience or have them engage in loving-kindness meditation.[73]

There are also promising technologies that can be enlisted to intensify transcendent experiences. As the historian Yuval Harari notes, they have the potential to change the course of humanity's future: "In the future, however, powerful drugs, genetic engineering, electronic helmets and direct brain-computer interfaces may open passages to these places. Just as Columbus and Magellan sailed beyond the horizon to explore new islands and unknown continents, so we may one day embark for the antipodes of the mind."[74]

One such technology is virtual reality (VR), a particularly promising tool for generating feelings of awe. Some of the most awe-inspiring experiences—such as reaching the peak of a high mountain or viewing earth from the vantage point of space[75]—are difficult to re-create in laboratory settings but are getting increasingly more realistic in VR technology. As Harari puts it, "It should be theoretically feasible to simulate an entire virtual world that I could not possibly distinguish from the 'real' world."[76,77]

VR can also help hospitalized or physically disabled individuals who would ordinarily not have the opportunity to walk the streets of Paris, climb Mount Everest, or orbit Earth. (Well, most of us are not capable of climbing Everest or orbiting Earth.)[78] Alice Chirico and her colleagues have been inducing awe in the laboratory by showing participants forests of tall trees in a 360-degree VR environment. They are able to increase the intensity of the awe experience as well as increase a sense of presence and enhance creative thinking.[79]

Noninvasive brain stimulation is another promising technology for inducing transcendent experiences. While some forms of invasive brain stimulation technology exist—such as deep brain stimulation and electro-convulsive therapy—noninvasive forms of brain stimulation are beginning to show promise in effecting well-being and transcendent experience. One noninvasive technology is transcranial magnetic stimulation (TMS), which involves passing magnetic pulses through the skull and into the cortex, affecting specific clusters of neurons.[80] Another noninvasive technology is transcranial direct current stimulation (tDCS), which increases or decreases cortical excitability and spontaneous neuronal firing in targeted regions of the brain, depending on the electrical charge of the current (which is low voltage).[81] Recent research shows that both TMS and tDCS can affect cognition and behavior in a number of ways, including increased insight, imagination, morality, learning, and attention, as well as reductions in depressive rumination.[82] tDSC even shows promise in reducing the desire to carry out physical and sexual assault and can increase the perception that such violence is morally wrong.[83]

Healthy Integration of Mind-Altering Interventions

As technologies develop, it will be increasingly important to consider the ethical implications of their use.[84] One important consideration is the extent to which such technologies run the risk of limiting human autonomy and meaning. Part of what gives us meaning in life is the struggle to overcome adversity. Most of us would choose a life of autonomy and the occasional struggle than a life in which we could receive an instant dose of happiness or feelings of transcendence whenever we wanted.[85]

I am struck by the similarities between Yaden's and MacLean's experiences. For both of them, the highest high seemed to follow the lowest low. Maslow recognized that peak experiences are seen in high proportion among those "who have overcome adversity and who have been strengthened by it rather than weakened."[86] Newberg told me that this is actually a common finding in his studies: many people have their greatest peak experience during a meditation session that directly follows an intense episode of some sort.[87] It appears the most profound experiences in life are those in which we overcome a seemingly life-threatening or impossible struggle, and then fully accept or meditate on the experience and acquire deep insight: *Wow, I don't need to live with the fear.*

Therefore, just as important as the question "How can we increase transcendent experiences?" may be the question "How can we integrate transcendent experiences into the ongoing stream of everyday life?" In 2014, Katherine MacLean left academia to focus on creating avenues for "healthy psychedelic integration" and increased community for those who have experienced intense transcendent experiences as a result of the use of psychedelics. A key question guiding MacLean's current work is the following: "How can we use these peak experiences to help people create community that is healthy and to be better human beings?"[88]

In an unpublished paper written on November 29, 1966, called "Drugs—Critique," Maslow noted that if you have achieved a victory, whether earning your income through hard work or through mastering a difficult craft, then the victory is "health-fostering," but if you have not earned the victory, then it is "sickness-fostering."[89] Maslow believed there are no shortcuts to authentic, long-lasting self-actualization, and that a quick hit of transcendence without the hard work of inner integration can be dangerous. "I think it's clearly better to work for your blessings, instead of to buy them," Maslow wrote in a separate correspondence. "I think an unearned Paradise becomes worthless."[90] "Should we build an escalator to the top of Mt. Everest or should we put more automobile roads through the wilderness or should we make life easier in general?"[91]

While acknowledging the incredible importance of peak experiences and their potential to be truly transformative and show people that a heaven on earth is at least possible, Maslow became increasingly convinced that a full understanding of the whole person requires a healthy *integration* of peak experiences with one's ongoing stream of consciousness, used in the service of making yourself and the world a better place to live.

In the spring of 1968, Maslow sat down for an extensive interview with his friend Warren Bennis for a documentary called *Being Abraham Maslow*. The interview took place in Buffalo, just as Maslow was about to head off to Columbus, Ohio, to celebrate the birth of his granddaughter Jeannie. (Maslow would report in his journals a number of peak experiences from spending time with her.) During the filming of the documentary, Maslow told Bennis that he was on the verge of a new image of humanity, of society, and of religion—"a basis for universalism." As he noted, "The good society has to be one world. Nationalism is dead, although it doesn't know it yet." He continued: "The good man has to be a member of the species. He has to know it too." To Maslow, the most central two questions were *How good a society does human nature permit?* and *How good of human nature does society permit?*

With the cameras turned off, Maslow turned to Bennis and remarked: "I have to make an important decision." Ever since his recent heart attack, he had suffered intermittent chest pains, heart palpitations, insomnia, "sick exhaustion," general fatigue, feebleness, trembling, and depression.[92] He knew how much energy it now took for him to write. "Have I written all the good psychology I can expect to write?" he asked. Maslow explained that his friend Bill Laughlin, the chairman and CEO of Saga Foods, had offered him an incredible opportunity to return to California and occasionally consult for the company, which would give him an abundance of free time to write. Continuing, Maslow told Bennis, "I hesitated for days and then, with Bertha's approval, I refused all the other offers from the major universities to go out West and to spend my full-time writing. I am about to cut myself adrift from all external circumstances—no Harvards, no Brandeises, I want to make a last song, sweet and exultant."[93]

CHAPTER 8

Theory Z: Toward the Farther Reaches of Human Nature

Human life will never be understood unless its highest aspirations are taken into account.

—Abraham Maslow, *Motivation and Personality*
(Preface to the 1970 Revised Edition)

This third psychology is giving rise to a fourth, "transhumanistic psychology" dealing with transcendent experiences and with transcendent values.

—Abraham Maslow, "The Farther Reaches of Human Nature" lecture,
San Francisco Unitarian Church (1967)

Perhaps no word has been used in so many different ways as the word "transcendence." Indeed, when I told people I was writing a book on transcendence, I was inevitably asked, "But what do you mean by transcendence?" In his 1969 paper "Various Meanings of Transcendence," Maslow put forward thirty-five conceptualizations of the word "transcendence"—from the sense of loss of self-consciousness; to the transcendence of one's ego; to acceptance of the natural world; to transcendence of dichotomies; to transcending one's own dependency on others; to rising above the dichotomized "us vs. them" nationalism, patriotism, or ethnocentrism; to transcending space and time; to the transcendence of ordinary, everyday humanness in favor of a higher nature; to transcending humanity and experiencing "cosmic consciousness."

It's tempting to look at this large potpourri of definitions and ask: So which is the *real* transcendence? *Will the real transcendence please stand up?* I hope by now you realize that this question itself is not the right question. In my view, the healthiest form of transcendence does not lie in any one aspect of your being but involves the healthy integration of your *entire* being.

Considering the writings of Maslow and modern psychological research relating to self-actualization and the heights of human nature, I propose the following definition of healthy transcendence:

> Healthy transcendence is an emergent phenomenon resulting from the harmonious integration of one's whole self in the service of cultivating the good society.

This view of transcendence, which I believe is the healthiest form of transcendence, is not about leaving any parts of ourselves or anyone else behind or singularly rising above the rest of humanity. Healthy transcendence is not about being outside of the whole, or feeling superior to the whole, but being a harmonious part of the whole of human existence. It's also not a level any human ever *actually* achieves, but it is a north star for all of humanity. In a nutshell: healthy transcendence involves harnessing all that you are in the service of realizing the best version of yourself so you can help raise the bar for the whole of humanity.

There are those among us who are consistently motivated by these higher values and higher experiences. For these "transcenders," self-actualization is merely a bridge to transcendent states of being. These transcenders show us what is possible in all of us and what we could become as a species.

TRANSCENDERS

As early as 1967, Maslow was beginning to wonder whether there are actually different types of self-actualizing people. In a private journal entry on May 28, 1967, he talked about "all sorts of insights," including "one big one" about self-actualization. "Meant to write & publish a self-actualization critique, but somehow never did," Maslow wrote in his journal. "Now I think I know why. I think I had used a hidden, uncon-scious hence mistaken criterion of selection for examples of self-actualization *beyond* health."[1]

In a journal entry a few weeks later, Maslow wrote further about this insight after a discussion with his friend Henry Murray, the founder of personology:

> I told him [i.e., Henry Murray] of my new discovery. . . . The B-person
> may be *more* symptom-loaded and have more value pathology than the
> symptom-free "healthies." Maybe one is symptom free *only* by virtue of
> not knowing or caring about the B-realm, never having experienced
> the B-realm in the highest peaks (now *that* must be changed also . . .).
> Having value-pathology symptoms is "higher" (& B-healthier?) than
> being symptom-free. . . . Value pathologies can be a *very* high
> achievement. And one can respect profoundly those in whom one can
> see—*through* the symptoms of frustrated idealism—the beautiful B-
> realm that they are reaching for and may therefore get to. . . . The ones
> who are struggling & reaching upward really have a better prognosis
> than the ones who rest perfectly content at the [self-actualization]
> level. . . . (I've really been *touting* value pathology & singing its praises!)[2]

The weight of this insight shouldn't be understated. What Maslow realized is that there belongs an additional *motivation* in his hierarchy of needs, not just a temporary peak experience.[3] This is an important dis-tinction. While peak experiences have immense transformative potential, *anyone*, regardless of their highest motivation in life, can undergo a peak experience (just as anyone, regardless of their highest motivation, can temporarily experience hunger, loneliness, or a blow to self-esteem). However, while many of the people he included under the umbrella of "self-actualizing people" were regularly motivated by health and growth, their highest motivation seemed to be a continual striving for transcen-dent experiences and transcendent values. Importantly, these people were not primarily motivated by happiness, and in fact many of them were continually frustrated as they struggled to realize their higher vision for humanity (visions that were often gleaned from peak experiences).

In an interview with humanistic psychologist Willard Frick the following year, Maslow further pointed out that "we can talk about self-actualizing people at different levels much more than I ever thought 10 years ago."[4] He noted that he became acquainted with people who "had everything . . . yet could be quite unhappy and not know their way and stagger, and stumble around and do all sorts of dopey things, and stupid things." He differentiated that sort of person from the person who had all their needs met, were neuroses-free and using their capacities well, and yet were "merely healthy."

Then he pointed out another sort of person who is self-actualizing but who is a "transcender." To Maslow, these were people whose value system implied the "Bodhisattva path" to enlightenment—"that is, the helping service to humanity or the helping of other people . . . and of simply becoming better human beings for others, as well as for themselves, and finally of transcending the ego."

Maslow took his exciting new insights and put them into a 1969 paper called "Theory Z," which was published in the second volume of the *Journal of Transpersonal Psychology*. Echoing the distinction between "transcenders" and "merely healthy people," Maslow argued that the merely healthy fulfill the expectations of Douglas MacGregor's Theory Y: they are free of deficiency needs and are driven by the desire for actualization of their personal potential and development of their identity, individuality, and uniqueness. "Such people live in the world, coming to fulfillment in it," Maslow noted. "They master it, lead it, use it for good purposes, as (healthy) politicians or practical people do."[5]

While arguing that transcenders also fulfill the expectations of Theory Y, Maslow argued that they also *transcend* Theory Y, having more frequent "illuminations or insights or cognitions which changed their view of the world and of themselves, perhaps occasionally, perhaps as a usual thing."[6] Maslow proposed that transcenders are "metamotivated" by higher ideals and values that go beyond the satisfaction of basic needs and the fulfillment of one's unique self. These metamotivations include a devotion to a calling outside oneself, as well as a commitment to the ultimate values, or the B-values, the values of Being. Maslow's list of B-values includes truth,

goodness, beauty, justice, meaningfulness, playfulness, aliveness, uniqueness, excellence, simplicity, elegance, and wholeness.

Maslow observed that when he asked transcenders why they do what
they do and what makes their life worth living, they often cited those
values. There was no *further* reason why they devoted so much time to
their work; the values were not in service of anything else, nor were they
instrumental in achieving any other goal. When Maslow asked, "But why
do you care about justice so much?" respondents would say something
along the lines of "I just do." Maslow believed that satisfaction of the "metaneeds" are necessary "to avoid illness and to achieve fullest humanness
or growth. . . . They are worth living for and dying for. Contemplating
them, or fusing with them gives the greatest joy that a human being is
capable of."

Maslow also put forward the intriguing suggestion that deprivation of
the B-values may result in "metapathologies," and that such frustrated
idealism may result in "metagrumbles." Maslow believed that the metagrumbles of transcenders may be an indicator of their mental *health*.
Indeed, grumbling about a lack of safety, status, money, power, respect, acceptance, and affection does seem to be of a different sort than
grumbling about a profound lack of beauty, humor, goodness, justice,
uniqueness, wholeness, and meaningfulness in the world.

In his paper, Maslow outlined a number of differences in degree
between transcenders and the "merely healthy," emphasizing that both
nontranscending and transcending self-actualizers share in common all
the characteristics he originally described for self-actualizing people but
also transcend those characteristics in the following ways:

Maslow's Characteristics of Transcenders[7]

- For the transcenders, peak experiences and plateau experiences
  become the most important things in their lives, the high spots, the
  validators of life, the most precious aspect of life.

- The transcenders speak easily, naturally, and unconsciously the language of Being (B-language), the language of poets, of mystics, of seers, of profoundly religious people, of those who live under the aspect of eternity.
- They perceive the sacred within the secular, i.e., the sacredness in all things at the same time that they also see them at the practical, everyday level. They can sacrilize everything at will, i.e., perceive it under the aspect of eternity. This ability is in addition to—not mutually exclusive from—good reality testing.
- They are much more consciously and deliberately motivated by B-values, such as perfection, truth, beauty, goodness, unity, dichotomy-transcendence, B-amusement, etc.
- They seem somehow to recognize one another and to come to an almost instant intimacy and mutual understanding even upon first meeting.
- They are more responsive to beauty, or rather they tend to beautify all things—including things that may seem ugly to most people.
- They are more holistic about the world than are the "healthy" or practical self-actualizers (who are also holistic in this same sense). Humankind is one, and the cosmos is one, and such concepts as the "national interest" or "the religion of my father" or "different grades of people or of IQ" either cease to exist or are easily transcended.
- Overlapping this statement of holistic perceiving is a strengthening of the self-actualizer's natural tendency to synergy—intrapsychic, interpersonal, intracultural, and international. Synergy transcends the dichotomy between selfishness and unselfishness and includes them both under a single superordinate concept. It is transcendence of competitiveness, of zero-sum, of win-lose gamesmanship.
- They transcend the ego more often and more easily.
- Not only are such people lovable, as are all of the most self-actualizing people, they are also more awe-inspiring, more "unearthly, more easily revered." They have more often produced the thought "This is a great man."

- Transcenders are far more apt to be innovators, discoverers of the new, of what actually could be, what exists in potential—and therefore of what might be brought to pass.
- Transcenders are less "happy" than the healthy ones. They can be more ecstatic, more rapturous, and experience greater heights of "happiness," but they are as prone—or maybe more prone—to a kind of cosmic sadness or B-sadness over the stupidity of people, their self-defeat, their blindness, their cruelty to one another, their shortsightedness. Perhaps this comes from the contrast between what actually is and the ideal world that the transcenders can see so easily and so vividly, and which is in principle so easily attainable. Perhaps this is a price these people have to pay for their direct seeing of the beauty of the world, of the saintly possibilities in human nature, of the nonnecessity of so much of human evil, of the seemingly obvious necessities for a good world; for human goodness rather than for higher IQs or greater expertness at some atomistic job, etc.
- Transcenders can more easily live in both the D- and B-realms simultaneously because they can sacralize everybody so much more easily. The sacredness of every person and even of every living thing, even of nonliving things that are beautiful, etc., is so easily and directly perceived in its reality by every transcender that they can hardly forget it for a moment.
- Transcenders find that increasing knowledge is associated with an increased sense of mystery, awe, humility, ultimate ignorance, reverence, and a sense of oblation. Most people pursue knowledge to lessen mystery and to reduce anxiety. But for peak experiencers and transcenders in particular, as well as for self-actualizers in general, mystery is attractive and challenging rather than frightening.
- Transcenders are more likely to be good selectors of creators (who sometimes look nutty or kooky). On the flip side, transcenders are also more able to screen out the nuts and kooks who are not creative.
- Transcenders tend to be more "reconciled with evil" in the sense of understanding its occasional inevitability and necessity in the larger

holistic sense. Since this implies a better understanding of it, it should generate both a greater compassion with it and a less ambivalent and a more unyielding fight against it. To understand more deeply means, at this level, to be more decisive, to have less conflict, ambivalence, regret, and thus to act more swiftly, surely, and effectively. One can compassionately strike down an evil person if this is necessary.

- Transcenders are more apt to regard themselves as carriers of talent, instruments of the transpersonal. This means a certain particular kind of objectivity or detachment toward themselves that to nontranscenders might sound like arrogance, grandiosity, or even paranoia.
- Transcenders are more apt to be profoundly "religious" or "spiritual" in either the theistic or nontheistic sense, excluding their historical, conventional, superstitious, or institutional meanings.
- Transcenders find it easier to transcend the ego, the self, and the identity and to go beyond self-actualization. Nontranscending self-actualizers are described primarily as having strong identities, people who know who they are, where they are going, what they want, what they are good for, in a word, as strong Selves, using themselves well and authentically and in accordance with their own true nature. And this of course does not sufficiently describe the transcenders. They are certainly this, but they are also more than this.
- Transcenders, because of their easier perception of the B-realm, have more end experiences, more of the fascinations that we see in children who get hypnotized by the colors in a puddle, by raindrops dripping down a windowpane, by the smoothness of skin, or by the movements of a caterpillar.
- Transcenders are somewhat more Taoistic, and the merely healthy somewhat more pragmatic. B-cognition makes everything look more miraculous, more perfect, just as it should be. It therefore breeds less impulse to do anything to the object that is fine just as it is, less needing improvement, or intruding upon it. There should

then be more impulse simply to stare at it and examine it than to do anything about it or with it.

- "Postambivalence" tends to be more characteristic of all self-actualizers and may turn out to be a little more so in some transcenders. Originating in Freudian theory, this term means total wholehearted and unconflicted love, acceptance, expressiveness, rather than the more usual mixture of love and hate that passes for "love" or friendship or sexuality or authority or power, etc.

- With increasing maturity of character, higher levels of pay ("metapay") and reward ("metareward") other than money and accolades increase in importance. Of course, a large proportion of self-actualizing people have probably fused work and play anyway; i.e., they love their work. Of them, one could say, they get paid for what they would do as a hobby anyway, for doing work that is intrinsically satisfying. However, transcenders additionally actively seek out jobs that make peak experiences and B-cognition more likely.[8]

Viewed holistically, the characteristics of "transcenders" represent a complete *Weltanschauung*, or worldview, similar to what Maslow referred to as "healthy childishness," or a "second naivete," in which there is a "true integration of the person at all levels."[9] This worldview includes the satisfaction of the security and growth needs but also transcends them. A transcender is able to fluidly navigate both the D-realm and the B-realm of existence.

The Theory Z worldview is full of awe, beauty, wonder, savoring, exploration, discovery, openness, holistic perception, unconditional acceptance, gratitude, B-love, B-humility (honest assessment of one's capacities rather than hiding one's self),[10] B-playfulness,[11] ego transcendence, synergy, unity, intrinsic motivation for work, and a motivation for the ultimate values in life. A key emergence of the Theory Z worldview is "dichotomy-transcendence": ordinary dichotomies—such as male vs. female, heart vs. head, lust vs. love, good vs. evil, national vs. global, selfish vs. unselfish, kindness vs. ruthlessness, happy vs. sad, or mystical vs.

realistic—are no longer seen as dichotomies but are all seen as simply parts of a larger integrated whole.

The Theory Z worldview is congruent with other prominent theories of ego development in the psychological literature, such as the "integrated" level in Jane Loevinger's stages of development, the "ego integrity" and "generativity" stages of Erik Erikson's stages of psychosocial development, the interindividual stage of Robert Kegan's constructive developmental theory, and the postconventional stages of Susanne Cook-Greuter's theory of ego development. Outside of the classical psychological literature, there are also connections to the highest states of consciousness in Ken Wilber's integral theory and the "second tier" of Clare Graves's spiral dynamics.[12]

The Theory Z worldview is strikingly similar to the modern psychological research on wisdom.[13, 14] Wisdom is often conceptualized in psychological literature as involving an integration among cognitive, affective, and behavioral dimensions. This includes the ability to accept multiple perspectives, to respond nondefensively when challenged, to express a wide array of emotions in order to derive meaning, to critically evaluate human truths, and to become aware of the uncertain and paradoxical nature of human problems.[15]

As clinical psychologist Deirdre Kramer puts it, "Wise people have learned to view the positive and negative and synthesize them to create a more human, more integrated sense of self, in all its frailty and vulnerability. . . . They seem able to first embrace and then transcend self-concerns to integrate their capacity for introspection with a deep and abiding concern for human relationships and generative concern for others."[16] Wisdom tends to increase with age and is most common among those with high levels of openness to experience, the capacity for self-examination and introspection, a motivation for personal growth, and the willingness to remain skeptical of one's self-views, continually questioning assumptions and beliefs, and exploring and evaluating new information that is relevant to one's identities.[17]

From the perspective of Theory Z, you are able to look at all of the human needs—lovingly and nonjudgmentally—from the highest vantage point possible, viewing them not as separate from one another but as integrated and harmonious. This vantage point isn't tethered to your own self or identity, although if need be, it can still clearly see all of it. Rather, it's like the vantage point of a seabird, free to soar above or dive within the landscape of human experience, viewing it from any angle. In this way, healthy transcendence helps you to navigate life's winds and waves.

> # This vantage point isn't tethered to your own self or identity, although if need be, it can still clearly see all of it.

By this point, it should be clear that self-actualization and self-transcendence can very much be *harmonious* with each other.[18] I believe that a true integration of Eastern, Western, and indigenous philosophical notions of self-actualization is not only possible but *necessary* for reaching the highest ceilings of human nature. Becoming a whole person involves a hierarchical integration of security, growth, and transcendence. We need not pit these realms of being against one another; at the highest level of integration they fuse into a single whole.

"I hope I have made my point clear," Maslow remarked at a public lecture in 1961. "Only by resolving and transcending the dichotomy between primary and secondary processes, conscious and unconscious, rational and intuitive, scientific and aesthetic, work and play, abstract and concrete, rubricizing and direct experiencing, can we perceive all of the world and of ourselves. Only there-by can we create whole-science, whole-language, whole-mathematics, whole-art, whole-education, and whole-people."[19]

WHAT HUMANS *COULD* BE

Perhaps human nature has been sold short. . . .

—Abraham Maslow, "The Farther Reaches of Human Nature,"
lecture, San Francisco Unitarian Church (1967)

The time has come to integrate our understanding of all aspects of human nature and, in so doing, create a truly comprehensive psychology.

—Abraham Maslow, "Building a New Politics Based on
Humanistic Psychology" (unpublished essay) (1969)

The Theory Z worldview has deep implications for the good person and the good society and offers an inspiring vision of what humans *could* be. I believe this vision is essential in the polarized, dehumanized world we are living in today. In this section, I will offer my own thoughts on what humans could be, building upon Maslow's lifelong mission to infuse the core principles of humanistic psychology into every aspect of human endeavor and experience.

First, Theory Z expands the scope of topics that are open to scientific investigation.* In his "Farther Reaches of Human Nature" lecture, Maslow noted: "When you open the door to value and to value experiences and peak or transcendent experiences, a whole new level of possibilities is open to investigation."[20] Indeed, a number of modern-day researchers from a variety of disciplines within psychology are examining the cultural, evolutionary, and biological foundations of our higher nature, including our human capacity for altruism, morality, love, connection, hope, forgiveness, laughter, gratitude, meditation, inspiration, spirituality, peak experiences, and even the great mystical illumination.[21] While there always needs to be more research, I'd like to think that if Maslow were alive today, he'd be quite pleased to see the progress that has been made in understanding the intrinsic potentiality of our higher nature.

Second, Theory Z offers a new image of relationships—from friendship to family to romantic love to sex. Maslow saw each of these relations as part of a hierarchy, with love at the highest level as something "considerably more than mutual customer satisfaction."[22] As we've seen throughout this book, B-love looks very different from D-love, whether in the teacher–child relationship, student–teacher relationship, therapist–patient relationship, in industry, or in management and leadership.

Take education. A true humanistic education involves educating the whole child and treating children and their own unique personal goals, dreams, and aspirations as valuable, regardless of how tightly aligned

---

* In his 1966 book *The Psychology of Science*, Maslow criticized the "desacralizing" of science: "The banishment of all the experiences of transcendence from the realm of the respectably known and the respectably knowable, and the denial of a systematic place in science for awe, wonder, mystery, ecstasy, beauty, and peak experiences." See: Maslow, *The psychology of science: A reconnaissance*, p. 121.

they are to the teacher's curriculum.[23] Imagine if schools weren't only a place to learn standardized academic material but were also places full of wonder, awe, and self-actualization— as well as hope for humanity. What's more, imagine if school weren't so separate from life. What if children went home at the end of the day inspired to continue being learners of the world throughout the rest of their day? Instilling a love of learning would be instilling an important B-value into students. As Maslow pointed out: "Humanistic education means educationalizing the whole of life, rather than having education take place in one kind of building and not outside it."[24]

> Imagine if schools weren't only a place to learn standardized academic material but were also places full of wonder, awe, and self-actualization—as well as hope for humanity.

These same principles also apply to the therapeutic experience. Imagine if we treated clinical patients as whole people first and foremost, and their clinical *DSM*-related symptoms as secondary. Many transcenders who find themselves on the clinician's couch show healthy symptoms of frustrated idealism that could be encouraged, rather than as something that needs to be medicated and cut off from the rest of their being. What many patients need is healthy integration of their "dark side," not a cordoning off of their strongest potentialities.

The Theory Z worldview also allows us to experience greater depths of joy. Calling the sort of joy associated with B-values "metahedonism," Maslow put forward the idea that there may exist a hierarchy of pleasures, ranging from "relief from pain, through the contentment of a hot tub, the happiness of being with good friends, the joy of great music, the bliss of having a child, the ecstasy of the highest love-experiences, on up to the fusion with the B-values."[25]

Imagine if we were all taught about the depths of joy that are possible. Research shows that clinically depressed and anxious individuals who were given a moral elevation intervention for ten days—observing acts of virtue, generosity, and courage—showed an increased striving to help others, an increased closeness to others, and lower interpersonal conflict and distress symptoms.[26] Sometimes the antidote to feelings of discontent and stress is a push toward the B-realm of existence and the metahedonism that can be experienced as a result.

This also applies to the sexual experience. What would a metahedonistic sexual experience look like? As Maslow noted, sex "can be seen at its higher levels, especially in a love relationship, as a trigger for peak-experiences, for mystical, unitive experiences—in short, as one of the gates to Heaven. This opens up a realm for science to explore because if you actually examined the sexual lives of most people, if you take a sample of the total population, you'd find that 99% of the population doesn't really know what the possibilities of sexuality are. They don't know how high the feelings can be."[27] As discussed earlier (see Chapter 5), B-love affords a more satisfying, transcendent experience of sex (B-sex).

There are also implications for the many divisions we see today. The Theory Z worldview allows for the possibility of healthy interactions among those who have different religious or political beliefs. As Maslow noted, it's possible to talk of the "religionizing" or the "sacralizing" of all of life, and for all individuals, not just among those we feel most connected to based on a common identity or common religious or political beliefs.

Take religion. Regardless of our religious beliefs, we can all unite over common spiritual experiences that unite us as a species. "Characteristically there are holy places, or places when you walk in the door, then you are supposed to feel that religious feeling and have that religious feeling until you walk out the door," Maslow noted. "Then you drop it and you don't have a religious feeling until the next time or the next building."[28] However, "I can report that [peak] experiences can take place any place at any time to practically anyone," Maslow declared.

While the word "sacred" often has religious connotations, Maslow pointed out one can have the felt sense of the sacred—experiencing reverence, mystery, wonder, and awe—just about anywhere and for anyone. Imagine if instead of only feeling a deep sense of connectedness and oneness with all of humanity in a church on Sundays, and immediately going on Twitter after church and calling out people who we disagree with, we maintained that feeling of the sacred in every encounter during the course of our lives. Imagine if we *all* did that with each other.

There are also deep implications for our current political landscape. Maslow was working on a new approach to politics that he called "psychopolitics," grounded in the humanistic psychology axiom that *human similarities are deeper than human differences*. Imagine a one-world type of politics in which we treat others as part of humanity first and their political affiliation as secondary.

A humanistic politics would also be based on a realistic understanding of human nature, including both our security needs as well as our growth and transcendence needs. To be sure, it's essential for politicians to value safety, security, and belongingness while maintaining coherence in the environment. It's hard to grow to our full heights without adequate stability. However, Maslow argued that we must not neglect our possibilities toward self-actualization and transcendence. "No real growth is possible without a firm basis of law and order," Maslow noted. "Yet, it is also possible for a society to become stuck or immobilized at the law-and-order level and to emphasize this condition so much that an individual's possibilities for growth are limited."[29]

This is why conservatives and liberals can complement each other; societies need those in power who care deeply about preserving traditional culture and the stability of society as well as those who are more concerned with egalitarianism and the suffering of those who are most vulnerable and in need of support.[30] Indeed, both liberals and conservatives are agreeable, just in different ways: conservatism is correlated with politeness, traditional moral values, and commitment to parochial aspects of life such as one's friends, family, and nation, whereas liberalism is correlated with universal compassion and egalitarianism.[31] Both aspects of agreeableness can make an important contribution to a one-world politics.

Instead, the greatest threat to a healthy democracy is really our antagonistic orientation toward one another and the rise of antagonism among those who wield great political power. Political chaos and inequality breed antagonism, distrust, and cynicism because they activate our deepest insecurities. In a highly insecure society, people's higher motivations are put aside as the needs for orderliness, stability, and belonging become much more pressing. However, it's these situations of unrest in which we must be careful that we aren't neglecting our strivings toward B-love and the B-values, or else we can run the risk of fanning the flames of populism and authoritarianism.

This is relevant to the current state of the world. Dutch political scientist Cas Mudde points out that populist discourse has become mainstream in the politics of Western democracies.[32] The core feature of populism is an anti-establishment message and a focus on the central importance of "the pure people."[33] The divide is not between liberal or conservative values but between the people and the powerful.

Opportunistic politicians with a quest for glory can craft their messaging in just such a way to tap into the power of the D-realm of existence, speaking the language of hate and fear.[34] Large-scale studies around the world have shown that the anti-establishment message of populists resonates the most with highly antagonistic people.[35] Physiologically, those who tend to have an antagonistic orientation toward others find anti-establishment messaging *particularly* emotionally arousing. This downward spiral of antagonism toward others is extremely threatening to a healthy democracy. As Maslow noted in an unpublished essay in 1969 titled "Building a New Politics Based on Humanistic Psychology":

> It is, therefore, vital to emphasize that a democratic society is rooted in a set of feelings toward other people—feelings like compassion and respect—and that certainly can be integrated with a very realistic understanding of the human capacity for evil. If we did not trust other people, if we did not like them, if we did not pity them, if we did not have brotherly or sisterly feelings for them, then a democratic society would of course be out of the question. Obviously, human history provides many examples to prove this point.[36]

Finally, the realization of healthy transcendence offers a new vision of civilization. Historically, the interests of society and the interests of the individual have been seen as mutually exclusive, sometimes even antagonistic (whatever is good for the person is bad for civilization). However, as we've seen as we have been climbing to higher heights of integration, this need not be the case. The purpose and values of the person can be *synergistic* with what's good for the society. The healthiest societies are built on a realistic understanding of human needs and offer the greatest growth-fostering potential for the individuals who are part of the society. How much are we allowing for opportunities for all people to fulfill their needs, including their security, growth, and transcendence needs?

There are concrete changes to our societal structures that can increase this synergy. As noted earlier, Maslow suggested that the healthiest societies are those in which "virtue pays"—in other words, societies (such as seen among the Blackfoot Indians) that reward people who behave virtuously, rather than only rewarding those with the most money or the most prestigious accomplishments. This could start with early education, by rewarding goodness and the love of learning over one's standardized test results relative to everyone else. This would not only benefit the collective but would also raise the ceiling on what the individuals in the society are striving toward.

It's time for us to take responsibility for the society we live in and to help create the conditions that will help all people not only self-actualize but also transcend. We can simultaneously work on making the good society better and making *ourselves* better. Improving the good society starts from *within*, as we shift our own perspective on human nature. In so doing, we can even transcend our physical existence, impacting future generations long after we're gone.

THE ULTIMATE UNKNOWN

The irony of [the human condition] is that the deepest need is to be free of the anxiety of death and annihilation; but it is life itself which awakens it, and so we must shrink from being fully alive.

—Ernest Becker, *The Denial of Death* (1973)

We can experience union with something larger than ourselves and in that union find our greatest peace.

—William James, *The Varieties of Religious Experience* (1902)

A few years ago, just as I was starting to write this book, I had an existential crisis. I underwent a very benign medical procedure, for which I was told that the probability of death was very low. I remember wanting to respond, "You mean not zero? You mean there's a chance I could die?" The procedure went according to plan, but I was left with a sudden awareness of my mortality. For some strange reason, I went nearly forty years of my life without the deliberate conscious awareness that this life, at least in this body, won't last forever. And quite frankly, the thought *terrified* me.

To get a grip, I read the classic book *The Denial of Death* by anthropologist Ernest Becker. Drawing heavily on the work of the Austrian psychoanalyst Otto Rank, Becker declares that there is a "rumble of panic underlying everything." According to Becker, this is the result of an "existential paradox":

> This is the terror: to have emerged from nothing, to have a name,
> consciousness of self, deep inner feelings, an excruciating inner
> yearning for life, and self-expression—and with all this yet to die.[37]

I definitely apprehended the "rumble of panic" that Becker described, but his proposed solutions—which included taking a "leap of faith" into the "invisible mystery" of creation that has a design beyond human comprehension—offered no guidance as to how to actually live my life even if I took such a leap of faith.

Coincidentally, an opportunity fell in my lap. A friend who worked for an experimental theater company called Swim Pony was putting together an interactive game called The End. I was asked to participate, and I could assess whether playing the game led to any improvements in well-being. I signed on.

Soon after I did, a package arrived containing a journal, a deck of cards with evocative images on each card, and an invitation to attend a party in twenty-eight days, the location to be announced. I also received a text message that read, "Hi, I'm The End. Text me when you're ready to play." Uh-oh, what had I gotten myself into here?

The entity that identified itself as The End explained the rules of the game to me. Each day, for twenty-eight consecutive days, I was to draw a new card, each directing I go on a quest. Then I was to reflect with The End on the lessons I learned from the experience, anything I noticed about myself as a result of the experience, and any patterns that connected the experience to cards I had already played. With that "rumble of panic," I fully engaged.

For twenty-eight days I embarked on quests of increasing intensity and poignancy, from engaging in a guided meditation on the expansiveness of the universe, to writing my own obituary, to walking through a cemetery and noticing how I felt, to imagining the ideal day of my life and who I'd want to spend it with, to actually experiencing what it would feel like to hear that I would have only a little time left to live, to researching what I wanted to do with my body after death and which medical procedures would be OK if I were incapacitated. For twenty-eight extremely emotional days, I confronted head on—with no defenses—what it *really* was about death that made me so afraid.

At multiple points, I was explicitly asked to provide a personal mission statement as to why I was playing this game. At the beginning, my statement was "Because I'm scared of the ultimate unknown, but also extremely curious about it." Halfway, I was asked if I wanted to adjust my statement based on my experiences so far, and I said, "I'd like to somehow change my default state from anxiety to curiosity. I'm a very curious person, but my default can get in the way."

Once The End was complete, I gathered with the rest of the players at a cemetery (of course) to reflect on the experience. We all agreed that the "game" was nothing short of life-changing. We understood what was most important in our lives, and while we were more aware of death than ever, we were also more aware of life than ever. When I looked at the data of all the players (including myself), it confirmed the conversations I had at the cemetery. There was a statistically significant increase in ratings from pre-game to post-game on the following aspects of well-being:

* Receiving help and support from others when it is needed
* Feeling a sense of direction in life
* Feeling less anxious
* Generally feeling happy

At first the data was perplexing. According to Becker and an entire line of research based on his theory, called Terror Management Theory (TMT), awareness of death should cause an increase in insecurity and defensiveness.[38] Yet that's not what any of us participants of The End actually experienced. Rather, we felt a renewed sense of wonder and joy for our lives and a greater focus on what we most care about. How to explain this discrepancy?

Now, upon completing this book, I can see more clearly that, like many other seeming paradoxes throughout the book, this paradox is only an *apparent* paradox. (That's Theory Z thinking for you.) When it comes to the fear of death, I think there is much more going on than simply a fear of "absolute annihilation."[39] Contrary to Terror Management Theory, I don't believe that humans evolved defenses *specifically* in order to cope with the existential reality of death. After all, research shows that people are often more afraid of the unknown, separation from loved ones, and eternal damnation than they are afraid of no longer existing.[40] In fact, when given a choice between living forever alone or dying prematurely surrounded by loved ones, most people choose *death*.[41]

Instead, I believe the "rumble of panic" that Ernest Becker describes arises not because of our fear of annihilation per se but because the *idea* of annihilation is so extremely threatening to the needs that most of us are so often preoccupied with satisfying.[42] It's likely that death awareness is a *by-product* of our uniquely developed capacities for imagination and self-awareness, and the idea of death just so happens to activate so many of our defenses. In particular, the awareness of our mortality activates our deep-seated fear of uncertainty (death is the ultimate uncertainty, after all), threatens the stability of our belonging and connection with others (death separates us from others), and threatens self-esteem, especially our narcissistic self-esteem (there's nothing more disruptive to our incessant quest to become godly than death).

No wonder people display so many defenses when confronted with the awareness of their mortality and why, when we feel most unsafe and uncertain, we tend to shift our focus to more immediate, egoistic concerns. But things don't have to be this way, at least insofar as we are able to climb our way out of the insecurity trap. As Irvin Yalom notes, "Though the physicality of death destroys us, the *idea* of death may save us."[43] In the state of full-mindfulness of one's existence, he says, "one marvels not about the *way* things are but *that* they are."[44]

In studying a number of individuals who actually confronted death, including his own psychotherapy work with terminally ill cancer patients, Yalom noticed that the experience is often highly transformative, leading to a rearrangement of life's priorities, a sense of liberation, an enhanced sense of living in the present, a vivid appreciation and acceptance of the elemental facts of life (changing seasons, falling leaves), deeper communication with loved ones, and fewer interpersonal fears.[45] This is from a person who survived a suicide attempt:

> I was refilled with a new hope and purpose in being alive. It's beyond most people's comprehension. I appreciate the miracles of life—like watching a bird fly—everything is more meaningful when you come close to losing it. I experienced a feeling of unity with all things and a oneness with all people. After my psychic rebirth I also feel for everyone's pain. Everything was clear and bright.[46]

There are indications that such transformations are possible for anyone who has the opportunity to repeatedly confront the ultimate unknown. Eric Weiner, author of *The Geography of Bliss,* visited Bhutan, a Buddhist kingdom well-known for its Gross National Happiness—a collective index used to measure the happiness and well-being of large swaths of its citizens. In Bhutan, death and gruesome images of death are openly confronted every day, and no one, not even children, is protected from the constant awareness of mortality.[47] There are many ways to die in Bhutan, and elaborate, lengthy rituals are performed when someone does die. As Weiner was told by one of the inhabitants of Thimphu, the capital of Bhutan, "You need to think about death for five minutes every day. . . . It will cure you. . . . It is this thing, this fear of death, this fear of dying before we have accomplished what we want or seen our children grow. This is what is troubling you."[48]

Recent research shows that even in the psychological laboratory, when given the opportunity to reflect more deeply and personally about their mortality over a sustained period of time, people tend to show a shift toward growth-oriented values—self-acceptance, intimacy, and community feeling—and away from extrinsic, status-oriented values such as money, image, and popularity.[49] Three characteristics that seem to be especially predictive of growth after an extended period of death awareness are mindfulness, openness to experiences, and having a quiet ego,[50] characteristics that are part and parcel of the B-realm of existence. Exploring your mortality with openness, curiosity, deep reflection, mindfulness, humility, and self-compassion helps you to move beyond the defenses that insecurity begets.[51]

Of course, easier said than done! The D-realm of existence is a potent force. These ways of being in the world have to be continually practiced, as we are prone to slip back into defense and insecurity in the face of threats to our security as even Yalom himself found after an automobile accident: "My fundamental death anxiety thus had only a brief efflorescence before being secularized to such lesser concerns as self-esteem, fear of interpersonal rejection, or humiliation."[52]

> At the end of the day, the best way to have a good death is to live a good *life*.

At the end of the day, the best way to have a good death is to live a good *life*. Developmental psychologist Gary Reker and existential positive psychologist Paul Wong argue that there are depths of meaning—ranging from purely hedonic pleasure and comfort to personal growth, creativity, and self-actualization, to service to others and dedication to a larger societal or political cause, to living values that transcend individuals and encompass cosmic meaning and ultimate purpose. They contend personal meaning in life increases in proportion to commitment to higher levels of meaning.[53]

More recent research by meaning researcher Tatjana Schnell has found striking support for this theory.[54] They found that the sources of meaning in one's life that are most strongly related to a sense of meaningfulness involve things that integrate self-actualization with transcendence, such as generativity, appreciation, inner harmony, growth, values, spirituality, creativity, care, and love. Lower down on the list are things like fun, individualism, achievement, tradition, order, and comfort.

As I dived into Maslow's private journals written during the last few years of his life, I saw a remarkable shift in his own depths of meaning, facilitated by the awareness of his own mortality, as well as the development of his own full humanness.

THE PLATEAU EXPERIENCE

The great lesson from the true mystics—from the Zen monks, and now also from the Humanistic and Transpersonal psychologists—is that the sacred is in the ordinary, that it is to be found in one's daily life, in one's neighbors, friends, and family, in one's back yard.

—Abraham Maslow, *Religions, Values, and Peak-Experiences* (1970)

Does death-awareness produce the transcendent, transpersonal, transhuman?

—Abraham Maslow, as quoted in Richard Lowry,
The Journals of A. H. Maslow (March 28, 1970)

At a conference just a few months before he died, Maslow announced, "My heart attack brought about a real confrontation with death. Ever since then, I've been living with what I've been calling to myself 'the post-mortem life.' I've already gone through the process of dying, so everything from then on is gravy."[55]

His private diaries tell a different story, however. They reveal a man increasingly facing his inner conflicts, struggles, and insecurities as honestly as possible right up to his death. One inner conflict that dogged his life was an insatiable need to be connected and liked by others, and for others to validate his sense of importance. Yet he also had a grandiose side in which he saw himself as a Messiah who "felt the great weight of responsibility & authority on my shoulders . . . & felt the responsibility of being the authority *so* heavily that it threw me into tension & exhaustion."[56] According to Becker, we all face the same conflict to some degree—between wanting to be God-like but also yearning to be part of a larger whole.[57]

Another prominent inner conflict that wove through Maslow's life involved his ultra-rational scientific side and his intuitive, spiritual side. On the one hand, Maslow believed it was his "duty to fight back against the forces of chaos, destruction, hatred, & counter-values," and he often criticized unrealistic liberals (whom he viewed as weak-minded), utopian thinkers, and superstitious people.[58,59] On the other hand, a genuinely tender side appreciated "wholehearted, boundless, ecstatic experience"[60] and deeply resented the cynicism and negativity of most scientists toward exploring the higher reaches of human nature.

The last few years of his life, Maslow constantly switched back and forth defending the two self-concepts and often reported feeling alienated from his friends and colleagues as a result. As clinical psychologist A. Lynn Heitzman, who conducted an extensive analysis of Maslow's later journal entries, noted, "His emerging spiritual sensibilities, which were in direct conflict with his self-image as a crusader against religious hypocrisy, superstition, and chaos, must have caused him considerable anxiety."[61,62]

Despite these inner conflicts, during the last months of his life, Maslow was nevertheless "temporarily able to transcend those conflicts, if only momentarily, to glimpse a world larger and more magnificent than himself."[63] He was able to relax his incessant striving for perfection and grandiosity, integrate his warring inner conflicts, and accept life on its own terms. He even became reconciled with the existence of human imperfection and the existence of evil, a topic he had long obsessed over. In a journal entry he wrote on April 28, 1970, he shows that he reached a higher integration and level of acceptance that allowed him to transcend "good" vs. "evil":

> One must be good humored about human frailties & *expect* them in advance & therefore not be disillusioned by their appearance, i.e., not perfectionistic or *a priori*, but "realistic" about human nature. . . . I guess the best way to describe this is "realism about human nature," on the same order as "realism about trees or cats or horses." So maybe I'd better offer the alternative of saying, "I am realistic & accepting of human frailties" rather than talking of good or evil insisting that I can

define it into being "basically good." *Ultimately* I'll have to stop using the words "good" & "evil," *either* for trees, tigers, or humans.[64]

This deep integration and acceptance allowed Maslow to tap deeply into the transcendent realm of experience more frequently and poignantly than ever before. As Heitzman put it, "Rather than diminishing his experience of living, he discovered that by accepting the harsh realities and ambivalent nature of the human condition, which he had previously fled, life became more poignant, vibrant, and miraculous. . . . Rather than reaching for the stars, he found that the miracle of life could be found in a tiny flower."[65]

Maslow's journal entries from the last few months of his life flow with the overwhelming poignancy of surrendering to the reality of the world. Here is an entry from March 26, 1970:

I've been writing in my back yard in the sun, facing the bougainvillea vines, & with birds on it & twittering all over the place . . . & it all adds up to the edge of tears. But it's from the piling-up of sheer beauty & the good luck of it all. They're really esthetic tears too. . . . But I think we have to add to that the fact that sheer beauty is too great to be borne. It's just "too much." More than we can assimilate or comprehend. It goes beyond our powers & is more than we can assimilate or control. Maybe the tears are the happy giving up of control? Of will? A sign of happy helplessness?[66]

A few days later, on March 28, 1970, a long journal entry reflected on the effects of making peace with one's mortality on one's tenderness toward others:

The ones who have made their peace with their mortality give up competition. (I still wonder that maybe what I've called SA [self-actualization] has reconciliation with mortality as a sine qua non.) . . . To the extent that death is a depriver, it produces the enlarged awareness of many things otherwise not perceived, as well as helping to produce sympathy, compassion, pity, identification with others, empathy, intuition & understanding of others.

At a transpersonal conference in Council Grove, Kansas, a few weeks later, Maslow provided a term for what he was experiencing: "the plateau experience."[67] Maslow co-opted this term from his East Indian colleague U. A. Asrani (who actually credited the term to the English writer Arthur Osborne). While peak experiences are ecstatic and momentary, Maslow argued that plateau experiences are more enduring and cognitive and involve seeing the extraordinary in the ordinary.[68] Maslow referred to the form of consciousness present in the plateau experience as "unitive consciousness," which he defined "as the simultaneous perception of the sacred and the ordinary . . . I now perceive under the aspect of eternity and become mystic, poetic, and symbolic about ordinary things. . . . There is a paradox because it is miraculous and yet doesn't produce an autonomic burst."[69] Elaborating on this in the preface to the 1970 edition of *Religions, Values, and Peak Experiences*, he noted that the plateau state of consciousness "becomes a witnessing, an appreciating . . . which can, however, have a quality of casualness and of lounging about."[70]

At the Council Grove conference in April 1970, Maslow mentioned that a key trigger of the plateau experience is the confrontation with mortality:

The death experience makes life much more precious and poignant and more vivid, and you're required to appreciate it and you hang on to it. . . . With surf, you sense a contrast between your own temporary nature and the surf's eternity—the fact that it will be there always, was there always, and that you are witnessing something that's a million years old and will be there a million years from now. I pass, and my own reaction to that is one of sadness on the one hand, and of great appreciation on the other hand. It seems to me that the surf is more beautiful to me now than it used to be, and more touching. That would be perhaps an example of the simultaneous perception of the temporal and the eternal which, in that sense of witnessing, is apocryphal. In thinking of the surf, I realize I am mortal, and the surf is not. This makes a strong contrast.*

Maslow believed that plateau experiences were more voluntary than peak experiences and could be deliberately sought ("I can go to an art museum or a meadow rather than into a subway"), and even taught: "I think you can teach plateau experiences; you could hold classes in miraculousness."[71] In a journal entry dated March 28, 1970, Maslow also mentioned his intention to develop exercises to help bring on the plateau state: "Think this through including the B-exercises, unitive exercises, sacralizing exercises, etc. They would automatically help toward B-love."

In that journal entry, Maslow said something else that really struck me. He suggested that he was able to resolve his long-standing inner conflicts, but "that 'working through' took years." I get the sense that the development of his motivational theory and ultimately his Theory Z was partly for the benefit of the world—and partly aspirational for himself. As he was working through his issues, he was *simultaneously* discovering higher possibilities within himself, which he was then eager to share as possibilities that lie within all of human nature.[72]

Thankfully for all of humanity, Maslow was willing to embrace the full complexities of his own existence. As A. Lynn Heitzman put it: "I believe Maslow's very humanness was a living tribute to the tenets of humanistic psychology. . . . I believe that his personal struggles gave depth and meaning to his plateau experience. Most importantly, as he apparently began to come to terms with his human imperfections and relish his remaining time on earth, he remained as human as anyone else—possibly more so."[73] By embracing his own full humanness and opening himself up to a deeper connection with the everyday world, Maslow eventually found his greatest peace, deepest sense of completion, and confidence that future generations would carry on his life's work and vision.

---

* In his own private reflections five days after the conference, Maslow wrote: "In talking about plateaus, I had to stay away from the surf & from Jeannie [his granddaughter]. Got too quavery, too touched." So much for the plateau experience being "essentially cognitive"!

In a journal entry on February 12, 1970, Maslow wrote, "I had thought that I'm at the peak of my powers & usefulness now, so *whenever* I die will be like chopping down a tree, leaving a whole crop of apples yet to be harvested. That *would* be sad. And yet acceptable. Because if life has been so rich, then hanging on to it would be greedy & ungrateful."

A few days later, Maslow echoed this sentiment in a tape he sent to *Psychology Today*:

> I had really spent myself. This was the best I could do, and here was not only a good time to die but I was even willing to die. . . . It was what David M. Levy called the "completion of the act." It was like a good ending, a good close. . . . If you're reconciled with death or even if you are pretty well assured that you will have a good death, a dignified one, then every single moment of every single day is transformed because the pervasive undercurrent—the fear of death—is removed. . . . I am living an end-life where everything ought to be an end in itself, where I shouldn't waste any time preparing for the future, or occupying myself with means to later ends. . . .
>
> Sometimes I get the feeling of my writing being a communication to my great-great-grandchildren who, of course, are not yet born. It's a kind of an expression of love for them, leaving them not money but in effect affectionate notes, bits of counsel, lessons I have learned that might help them. . . .

Maslow's message ends there.[74]

Live More in the B-Realm[1]

I was able to track down some of the B-exercises that Maslow was working on during the last few years of his life. I include some of them here in the hopes that they can further help you in your own journey of integration, wholeness, and transcendent experience. Feel free to return to these again and again, as they are timeless.

- Sample things.
- Keep your eye on the ends, not only on the means.
- Fight familiarization. Seek fresh experiences.
- Solve the Deficiency-problem (i.e., don't always regard the Deficiency-realm as prepotent over the Being-realm).
- Get out of the Deficiency-world by deliberately going into the B-realm. Seek out art galleries, libraries, museums, beautiful or grand trees, and the mountains or seashore.
- Avoid dichotomizing the D-realm and the B-realm. They are (or should be) hierarchically integrated. An either/or choice is not necessary. The firmest foundation for the Being-realm is to have satisfied Deficiency-needs (such as for safety, connection, or self-esteem).
- Cultivate periods of quiet, meditation, "getting out of the world," and getting out of our usual locality, immediate concerns, apprehensions, and forebodings. Periodically get away from time-and-space concerns, away from clocks, calendars, responsibilities, demands from the world, duties, and other people.
- Go into the dreamy state.

- Perceive the eternal, intrinsic laws of the cosmos. To accept or even love these laws is Taoistic and the essence of a good citizen of the universe.
- Embrace your past.
- Embrace your guilt rather than running from it.
- Be compassionate with yourself. Be understanding, accepting, forgiving, and perhaps even loving about your foibles as expressions of human nature. Enjoy and smile at yourself.
- Ask yourself: How would this situation look to a child? To the innocent? To a very old person who is beyond personal ambition and competition?
- Try to recover the sense of the miraculous about life. For example, a baby is a miracle. Think, for that baby now, "anything could happen" and "the sky is the limit." Cultivate that sense of infinite possibility. The sense of admiration, awe, respect, and wonder.
- To better appreciate your own present life situation, compare yourself not with those seemingly luckier than you but rather with others less fortunate than you.
- You musn't be ashamed to be good in a cynical world.
- Never underestimate the power of a single individual to affect the world. Remember, one candle in a cave lights everything.
- In order to regain authentic dignity and pride, try not concealing, not relying on external signs of validation (uniforms, medals, a cap and gown, labels, social roles). Show yourself as ultimately naked and self-revealing. Show your secret scars, shames, and guilts.
- Remember, it took one child in the fairy tale to say, "The Emperor has no clothes!" and then everyone saw it.
- Do not let anyone force roles on you. That is, do not act the way other people think that a doctor, minister, or teacher should act if it is not natural for you.
- Do not conceal your ignorance. Admit it.
- Engage in deliberate, experimental philanthropy. If sometimes you are no good for yourself (depressed, anxious), at least you can be good for someone else.

- If you find yourself becoming egoistic, arrogant, conceited, or puffed up, think of mortality. Or think of other arrogant and conceited people and see how they look. Do you want to look like that? Do you want to take yourself that seriously? To be that unhumorous?
- Contemplate people who are admirable, beautiful, lovable, or respectworthy.
- Try narrowed-down absorption or close-up fascination with the small world—for instance, the anthills, insects on the ground. Closely inspect flowers or blades of grass, grains of sand, or the earth. Watch intently without interfering.
- Use the artist's or photographer's trick of seeing the object in itself. For instance, frame it and thereby cut it away from its surroundings, away from your preconceptions, expectations, and theories of how it should look. Enlarge the object. Or squint at it so you see only general outlines. Or gaze at it from unexpected angles, such as upside down. Look at the object reflected in a mirror. Put it in unexpected backgrounds, in out-of-the-ordinary juxtapositions, or through unusual color filters. Gaze at it for a very long time. Gaze while free associating or daydreaming.
- Be with babies or children for a long period of time. They are closer to the Being-realm. Sometimes, you can experience the Being-realm in the presence of animals, like kittens, puppies, monkeys, or apes.
- Contemplate your life from a historian's viewpoint—one hundred or even one thousand years in the future.
- Contemplate your life from the viewpoint of a nonhuman species—for example, as it might appear to ants.
- Imagine that you have only one year left to live.
- Contemplate your daily life as though being seen from a great distance, such as from a remote village in Africa.
- Look at a familiar person or situation as if viewing for the very first time.
- Look at the same person or situation as if viewing for the very last time; imagine, for instance, that the person is going to die before you see him or her again. Think as vividly as you can how you would

feel, what you would truly lose, and about what you would be sorry. Would you have any regret or remorse? How would you conduct an effective good-bye to avoid later feeling a sense of gnawing incompleteness? And how would you best preserve your fullest memory of this person?

- Imagine yourself to be dying—or to be on the edge of execution. Then imagine how vivid and precious everything and everyone looks. Imagine vividly saying good-bye to each of the persons you love best. What would you say to each one? What would you do? How would you feel?

"Wonderful Possibilities and Inscrutable Depths," Reprised

I t was the final moments of a long few days in the Archives of the History of American Psychology at the University of Akron. I was tired—physically and mentally—from looking so deeply into the existence of this one human. So many correspondences, transcripts, journal entries, and unpublished essays. My head was spinning. Yet I was determined to find it. I *had* to find it—a document that had reached mythical proportions in my head but which I knew existed in the hundreds and hundreds of folders.[1]

As the clock was running down on my time in the library, I raced through the remaining folders on my desk. And there it was: Maslow's last writings. At the top of the notepad was a handwritten note that read: "This was the last piece of writing A.H.M. did before he died June 8, 1970. B.G.M. [Bertha G. Maslow]."

I couldn't bear to look at it. This really was it. The closing statement of an individual's existence—and not just anyone's existence. These were the final writings of a human being who had personally inspired me to formally investigate so many ideas, to see greater possibilities for myself and others, and to always be on the lookout for the farther reaches of human nature—while at the same time remaining fully aware of the realities of human struggles. Not only that, but I had grown quite fond of this person as a whole person, not in spite of, but precisely because of, the contradictions and paradoxes in which he courageously struggled throughout his life.

But I looked anyway. As I flipped through the pages, my eyes welling up with tears, I saw that Maslow was working on a set of axioms or propositions that would lay the foundation for a humanistic revolution. Devouring his last words and the contents of the neighboring folders, I discovered that these axioms were part of a book he was working on that would offer a new image of humanity and society. Up to the very end, Maslow was working on a book that would take the foundational axioms of humanistic psychology and lay out the implications for as many swaths of human endeavor as possible—science, religion, management, politics, economics, education, art, journalism. I also saw that he was planning to write a book entirely dedicated to humanistic education.

He even planned on having a chapter of his book proposing the need for a fifth force in psychology—*transhumanism*—that would transcend human interests and focus on species-transcending values.[2] "Being able to stand aside from the interests of the species," Maslow wrote, "so that one can look through the eyes of the tiger who threatens us, and who, after all, has species values also, this is an extremely difficult thing to do. But to become Transhuman, though difficult, is at times and for moments possible and does happen."

Sure, Maslow was grandiose, but such vision was, and remains, an important corrective to a psychology that truly sold humans short. At his eulogy at the Stanford Memorial Church in Palo Alto, California, on June 10, 1970, Warren Bennis noted that "two big things which Abe gave to all of us: the art and science of becoming more fully human, and the democratization of the soul. For these we will be forever indebted."[3]

As I read a draft of a chapter in Maslow's unpublished book entitled *The Possibilities for Human Nature,* I reached a summary statement of what he intended for the book. I was astounded—it was strikingly similar to the concluding paragraph of the essay the young twenty-year-old Abe Maslow wrote for his undergraduate philosophy class:

> If I had to condense this whole book into a single sentence, I think I could come close to the essence of it by saying that it spells out the consequences of the discovery that man has a higher nature and that this is part of his essence. Or more simply, human beings can be wonderful out of their own human and biological nature. We need not take refuge in super-natural gods to explain our saints and sages and heroes and statesmen, as if to explain our disbelief that mere unaided human beings could be that good or wise.[4]

In so many ways, we change throughout our lives. But there are many ways in which the seeds are there all along, in need of actualization. After flipping through the pages of Maslow's handwritten notes in his notepad, I reached a blank page. Then another blank page. And then another, and another. I imagined him putting down this very notepad I am holding in my hand on that last day of his life as he got up to do his physical exercises, only to forever leave the notepad behind. And it hit me: *this is what life is about.*

> # Each of us is capable of transcendence in this brief, suffering, and yet sometimes miraculous lifetime.

While we should not strive for perfection, each of us is capable of transcendence in this brief, suffering, and yet sometimes miraculous lifetime. We each have the potential to be a guide to future generations, to help them fill out the rest of the pages in their own style.

That's precisely what Maslow has done for me, and I will forever be grateful for the privilege of witnessing his own life's journey, and the inspiration and solid ground it provided for my own journey, the fruits of which lie in your hands. In return, I hope the information and humanity in this book inspires you to get out there and live your own full existence. There's a wide world out there, with many blank pages for you to fill in your own style, and in such a way that you not only existed but existed well.

Acknowledgments

This book is the result of a synthesis of many ideas, research findings, and personal collaborations. I have transcendent feelings of love and gratitude for a great number of people who have inspired me, influenced my thinking, and directly contributed to the research discussed in this book. While the number of people who deserve mention far outstrip the space limitations of this section, a few people must be highlighted at once.

Most immediately, thanks to my editor, Marian Lizzi, and my agent, Jim Levine, for making this book happen. Without them, this project would have remained a pipe dream.

Warm feelings of appreciation are directed toward Maslow's remaining friends, family, and former students who helped give me a deeper understanding of his complex psychology and generous nature: Paul Costa, James Fadiman, Tom Greening, Jeanne Kaplan, Miriam Kauderer, L. Ari Koplow, Stanley Krippner, Richard Lowry, Ann Maslow, Ricardo Morant, Michael Murphy, and Miles Vich. While I am saddened by the idea that I will never actually have a chance to have a conversation with Abraham Maslow, I had many peak experiences hearing what it was like to know him personally, and I must say, it was very gratifying to hear from some of the people who knew him that they thought he would have been pleased with how I represented his life's work.

Thanks to Edward Hoffman for meeting with me, for discussing my project, and for writing such a comprehensive and balanced biography of Maslow (*The Right to Be Human: A Biography of Abraham Maslow*), as well as putting together an essential collection of some of Maslow's unpublished papers (*Future Visions: The Unpublished Papers of Abraham Maslow*).

These were essential resources for my book, and I am deeply appreciative that they existed.

Big thanks to Lizette Royer Barton, reference archivist at the Archives of the History of American Psychology at the University of Akron's Cummings Center for the History of Psychology. Lizette was beyond helpful as I tried to track down so many of Maslow's unpublished correspondences, journal entries, essays, and unfinished manuscripts. Also, thanks to Don Blohowiak for helping me to track down the notepad Maslow was writing on during his last days of existence.

Thanks to a number of generous people who offered valuable feedback on earlier drafts of the manuscript: Sara Algoe, Colin DeYoung, R. Chris Fraley, Jane Dutton, Mark Leary, Hara Estroff Marano, Daniel Nettle, Reb Rebele, Kirk Schneider, Kennon Sheldon, Brandon Weiss, and David Yaden. I must give a special shout-out to Hara Estroff Marano for her continual and long-standing support of my writing, and for her editing help on this project in particular.

I have immeasurable appreciation for the many collaborators I've had the delight of working with over the past twenty years. Those who deserve particular mention due to their association with the research presented in this book include Roger Beaty, W. Keith Campbell, Colin DeYoung, Angela Duckworth, Rebecca Gotlieb, Elizabeth Hyde, Todd Kashdan, Taylor Kreiss, Mary Helen Immordino-Yang, Emanuel Jauk, James C. Kaufman, Joshua Miller, Reb Rebele, Martin Seligman, Luke Smillie, Jessie Sun, Eli Tsukayama, Brandon Weiss, and David Yaden. Special thanks to Martin Seligman for giving me the opportunity at the Imagination Institute to advance our understanding of the science of imagination and creativity, to interact and work with so many awesome people who came through the Positive Psychology Center, and for giving me the opportunity to learn about the field of positive psychology from the inside.

Thanks to those who had discussions with me surrounding various topics in this book. First and foremost, thanks to Kirk Schneider, a legend in the field of humanistic psychology, for both his support of this project and for offering helpful suggestions on various aspects of the manuscript at various stages in the process. I stand in awe at the mentors and collaborators he has had the delight of working with, including Rollo May and James Bugental. I really appreciate what Kirk has done for modern-day humanistic psychology, and I look forward to continuing to work with him to help bridge humanistic psychology with the rest of the field of psychology. Thanks to Adam Grant for riffing with me about the meaning of authenticity. I appreciated hearing his views on the topic, and I appreciate his encouragement of this book. Thanks to Andy Clark for explaining to me how the brain is a prediction engine and working through with me some of my ideas on how to link his work to the need for security. Thanks to Michael Gervais, host of the wonderful podcast *Finding Mastery,* for discussing the need for purpose and for offering his own unique and enlightening perspective on the topic as a sports psychologist. Thanks to Andrew Bland and Eugene DeRobertis for discussing how best to visually represent Maslow's hierarchy of needs and for teaching me about Maslow's contributions to developmental psychology. As always, thanks to Steven Kotler for the chats about flow and everything else under the sun.

A major thanks also goes to Andy Ogden, who is the illustrator and designer of the sailboat illustrations in this book and the originator of the sailboat metaphor. As soon as Ogden presented the idea to me, I knew right away it was just perfect. Also, thanks to Sacha Brown and Charlotte Livingston for helping with some illustrations in earliest drafts of the manuscript.

A number of friends ought to be thanked for their continual moral support, something that should not be underestimated in its importance for a highly sensitive writer such as myself: Naomi Arbit, Joshua Aronson, Susan Baum, Susan Cain, Skye Cleary, Jennifer Cory, Colin DeYoung, Jordyn Feingold, James C. Kaufman, Todd Kashdan, Daniel Lerner, Erica Liebman, Hara Estroff Marano, Cory Muscara, Elliot Samuel Paul, Zorana Ivcevic Pringle, Deborah Reber, Emma Seppälä, Emily Esfahani Smith, Daniel Tomasulo, Laura Taylor, Alice Wilder, and David Yaden. The list could go on and on. I am very fortunate to have such need-gratifying friends.

It always goes without saying, but immense love and appreciation to my mom and dad—Barbara and Michael Kaufman—for their B-love and unconditional positive regard. I love them with the full depth of my being. Words just cannot describe how much I value and appreciate their existence.

Finally, thank you, Abe. I realize it was a one-sided friendship, but I enjoyed having imaginary conversations with you and learning about your life and thinking. Thanks for continually showing me the "wonderful possibilities and inscrutable depths" of humanity. I hope I made you proud.

Seven Principles for Becoming a Whole Person

As the German humanistic developmental psychologist Charlotte Bühler noted at the First International Conference on Humanistic Psychology in 1970, "One of the most generally agreed upon aspects of humanistic psychology is that we strive to find access to the study and understanding of the person as a whole."[1]

Wholeness is an aspiration, not a destination; it's a process, not a state that is ever achieved. If anyone tells you they are completely whole, you might want to check to see whether they have any electrical wires growing out of their back; they're probably not human. The process of becoming a whole person is *an ongoing journey of discovery, openness, and courage, in which you reach higher and higher levels of integration and harmony within yourself and with the outside world, allowing greater flexibility and freedom to become who you truly want to become.* Since you are always in a state of change, you are always in a state of becoming.

> **Wholeness is an aspiration, not a destination.**

In this appendix, I will outline seven core principles for becoming a whole person that can serve as a healthy foundation for your own personal journey to self-actualize in your own style, and to ultimately experience the most satisfying and profound moments of transcendence.

PRINCIPLE #1: ACCEPT YOUR WHOLE SELF, NOT JUST YOUR BEST SELF[2]

In his book *On Becoming a Person,* Carl Rogers noted that while the problems people present during psychotherapy "run the gamut of life's experiences"—troubles with school, or spouse, or employer, or with one's own uncontrollable or bizarre behavior, or with one's frightening feelings—"there is perhaps only one problem."[3] Rogers observes that below the level of the complaint, each person is really asking, "Who am I, really? How can I get in touch with this real self, underlying all my surface behavior? How can I become myself?"

In my view, this is the wrong question. All the aspects of your mind are part of you. It's rather difficult to think of any intentional behavior that does not reflect some genuine part of your psychological makeup, whether it's your dispositions, attitudes, values, or goals.[4] We each contain multitudes. For personal growth, I believe a better question you should ask yourself is: "Which potentialities within me do I most wish to spend my limited time cultivating, developing, and actualizing in this world?" In order to have the greatest freedom in answering that question, you must plumb the depths of your own consciousness and accept your whole self.

Most people, however, only identify with the drives that make them feel the best about themselves. All around the globe, regardless of culture, people tend to show an *authenticity positivity bias*: people include their most positive and moral qualities—such as kind, giving, and honest—in their description of their "true self."[5] In fact, people judge their positive behaviors as more authentic than their negative behaviors even when both behaviors are consistent with their personal characteristics and desires.[6] What we think of as our true self really just seems to be our *most valued self.*[7]

Contrary to common sense, we don't feel most authentic when we are simply acting in accord with our actual nature, warts and all. Regardless of our individual personality, we all tend to feel most authentic and connected to ourselves when we are feeling content, calm, joyful, loving, self-accepting, sociable, free, competent, making progress toward a goal, mindful of the present moment, and open to new experiences.[8] In other words, we tend to feel most authentic when our basic needs are being met and we feel as though we have freely chosen to behave in a particular way and are assuming ownership of our subjective experiences.[9]

Also, there is a distinctly social aspect to authenticity, which is to be expected considering how social we are as a species and how important reputation and acquiring a unique role within a group was across the course of human evolution.[10] People tend to feel most authentic when they are spending time with close others, are in harmony with others and their environments, and acting in socially desirable ways.[11] On the contrary, we tend to feel most inauthentic when we are feeling socially isolated, having conflicts and misunderstandings in our relationships, or are in an evaluative situation where we are falling short of our standards or the standards of others.[12]

Due to this strong link between feeling authentic and engaging in socially desirable behaviors, what people think of as their true self may actually just be *what people want to be seen as*.[13] According to social psychologist Roy Baumeister, when the way others think of you matches how you want to be seen, you will feel authentic and satisfied. As he notes, it's not enough for people to simply convince themselves that they have positive traits; people also tend to need others to hold them in the same high regard.[14] If you think back on your own personal experiences of when you've felt most authentic, you can probably recall moments of glow when your most valued characteristics and talents were also being valued by others.

On the flip side, Baumeister argues that when people fail to achieve their desired reputation, they will dismiss their actions as inauthentic, as not reflecting their true self ("That's not who I am"). As Baumeister notes, "As familiar examples, such repudiation seems central to many of the public appeals by celebrities and politicians caught abusing illegal drugs, having illicit sex, embezzling or bribing, and other reputation-damaging actions."[15]

This would explain why people's evaluations of their authenticity are so strongly linked to their morality and most valued goals and why merely reflecting on moral past experiences increases feelings of authenticity.[16] After all, behaving in ways that are consistent with your "higher" goals (such as announcing your new humanitarian nonprofit) is typically perceived as more authentic by yourself and others than authentically watching Netflix while enjoying rocky road ice cream. Even though, sorry to say it, both behaviors are really you.

All of this casts great doubt indeed on the existence of a one true self.[17] Nevertheless, at least feeling *in touch* with a true self is a strong predictor of many indicators of well-being.[18] Also, the notion of the true self can serve as a useful guide to evaluate whether you are living up to your ideal.[19] As the philosopher Valerie Tiberius has noted, the "value-full life" is a major source of well-being.[20]

Also, while the true self may be a convenient fiction, I truly believe that there are, within each of us, aspects of our self that are most conducive to health and growth as a whole person. I believe we each have best selves— aspects of who we are that are healthy, creative, and growth-motivated—that make us feel most connected to ourselves and to others.* The more we can drop our social facades and the defenses that we erect to protect ourselves, the more we open ourselves up to greater opportunities for growth, development, and creativity.

> I believe we each have best selves—aspects of who we are that are healthy, creative, and growth-motivated— that make us feel most connected to ourselves and to others.

An important first step to getting in touch with your best self is becoming aware as much as possible of your whole self and accepting the totality of your being. This includes accepting all of the aspects of yourself that you dislike and are too quick to disown. Indeed, the existential psycho-

---

* What I am defining as "best selves" is similar to Karen Horney's notion of the "real "or "actual" self, which she argued is the "alive, unique, personal center of ourselves." I don't believe there is just one center, though, as a number of aspects of ourselves can give us this sense of aliveness. Nevertheless, I agree with Horney's focus on the detrimental effects of self-alienation. According to Horney, self-alienation is akin to striking the "devil's pact." In return for promises of glory, we lose touch with our own feelings, wishes, beliefs, energies, and the feeling of being an active determining force in our own life. As a result of this loss of feeling oneself as an organic whole, Horney argues we lose our "soul" and must go to "the hell within oneself." See: Horney, *Neurosis and human growth*.

therapist Irvin Yalom asked his successful patients to rank sixty factors in therapy according to their degree of effectiveness. He found that the single most frequently chosen item by far was "discovering and accepting previously unknown or unacceptable parts of myself."[21]

Of course, acceptance doesn't necessarily mean liking. It's perfectly reasonable to be repulsed by your intense desire to eat a stack of glazed donuts topped with cheese, for instance.[22] However, as Carl Rogers noted, "The curious paradox is that when I accept myself just as I am, then I can change."[23] Part of acceptance is taking responsibility for your whole self, not just the aspects of your mind or your actions that you like or make you feel the best about yourself.*[24]

Discovering and ultimately deciding which potentialities you most wish to spend your limited time actualizing in your lifetime is no easy task. You know that you have some large and unknown number of potentialities that are part of who you could become, but there are real external realities (environmental conditions) and internal realities (extreme traits that dominate your personality structure) that affect the probability of cultivating some potentialities. Even worse, some potential selves, if actualized, would surely conflict with one another. Rogers acknowledged these difficulties but argued that with the right environmental conditions, over time you can gradually learn to identify and trust those aspects of yourself that are most growth-oriented and bring you a sense of vitality, creativity, and wholeness.

PRINCIPLE #2: LEARN TO TRUST YOUR SELF-ACTUALIZING TENDENCY

At a very young age, we feel hungry, or tired, or fearful, but are often given messages by well-meaning (and, sadly, often not-so-well-meaning) parents and other caretakers that "if you feel that way, I won't love you." This can happen in a number of subtle and unsubtle ways anytime an expression of a need is disregarded as not as important as the needs of the caretaker. And so we start acting how we *should* feel, not how we *actually*

---

* In Yalom's study on the most effective therapeutic factors, he found that a close second to acceptance was "Learning that I must take ultimate responsibility for the way I live my life no matter how much guidance and support I get from others." See: Yalom, *Existential psychotherapy*.

feel. As a result, so many of us grow up being constantly swayed by the opinions and thoughts of others, driven by our own insecurities and fears of facing our actual self, that we introject the beliefs, needs, and values of others into the essence of our being. Not only do we lose touch with our real felt needs, but we also alienate ourselves from our *best* selves.

To the psychotherapist Carl Rogers, one of the founders of humanistic psychology, the loneliest state of all is not the loneliness of social relationships, but an almost complete separation from one's own experience. Based on his observations with a large number of patients with healthy development of their whole self, he developed the notion of the "fully functioning person."[25] Like many of the other founding humanistic psychologists, Rogers was inspired by the existential philosopher Søren Kierkegaard, who noted that "to will to be that self which one truly is, is indeed the opposite of despair."[26] According to Rogers, the fully functioning person:

- Is open to all of the elements of their experience,
- Develops a trust in their own experiences as an instrument of sensitive living,
- Is accepting of the locus of evaluation as residing within themselves, and
- Is learning to live their life as a participant in a fluid, ongoing process, in which they are continually discovering new aspects of themselves in the flow of their experience.[27]

Rogers believed that we each have an innate self-actualizing tendency that can be explained by the existence of an organismic valuing process (OVP). According to Rogers, the OVP is a vital part of humanity and evolved in order to help the organism move in the direction of growth, constantly responding to feedback from the environment, and correcting choices that consistently move against the current of growth.[28] Rogers believed that when people are inwardly free to choose their deepest values, they tend to value experiences and goals that further survival, growth, and development, as well as the survival and development of others.

Modern research supports the existence and importance of an OVP in humans. Positive organizational psychologists Reena Govindji and

P. Alex Linley created a scale to measure OVP and found that it was positively correlated with greater happiness, knowledge and use of one's greatest strengths, and a sense of vitality in daily life.[29] Here are some statements that can give you a rough estimate of how in touch you are with your deepest feelings, needs, and values:

ORGANISMIC VALUING SCALE
- I know the things that are right for me.
- I get what I need from life.
- The decisions I make are the right ones for me.
- I feel that I am in touch with myself.
- I feel integrated with myself.
- I do the things that are right for me.
- The decisions I make are based on what is right for me.
- I am able to listen to myself.

In another line of research on OVP, Kennon Sheldon conducted a series of clever experiments demonstrating that when given autonomy, people do tend to favor the growth choice over time.[30] Sheldon gave people free choice over time to choose from a wide menu of goals and found that the goals naturally grouped into two main clusters: security vs. growth.

SECURITY VS. GROWTH GOALS
Security Goals
- Have well-respected opinions.
- Have many nice things.
- Be admired by many others.
- Be well-known to many.
- Be financially successful.
- Be well-liked and popular.
- Find a good, high-paying job.

Growth Goals
- Help those who need it.
- Show affection to loved ones.

- Feel much loved by intimates.
- Make others' lives better.
- Be accepted for who I am.
- Help improve the world.
- Contribute something lasting.

Sheldon found that under conditions of complete freedom to choose, people tend to move toward growth, changing their minds over time in directions most likely to be growth-enhancing. Of course, the goal isn't to become 100 percent growth-oriented and 0 percent security-driven; we need both security goals and growth goals. The point here is that under optimal conditions for choosing, the relative balance over time tends to tip toward growth. In fact, Sheldon found that those with the highest initial adoption of security goals shifted the most toward growth goals over time. As Sheldon notes, those holding "unrewarding values are most in need of [growth-relevant] motivational change and are thus most likely to evidence such change."[31] Therefore, the research suggests that when free of anxiety, fear, and guilt, most people do tend to not only move in the direction of the realization of their unique potential but also tend to move in the direction of goodness.

This should give us hope and point to what is possible under optimal conditions. But it should also give us a healthy dose of realism, considering that in the real world, most people are not entirely free to choose their most valued direction. The cultural climate matters a lot. For instance, many individuals with marginalized identities—whether based on ethnicity, race, religion, gender, socioeconomic status, sexual orientation, disability, or even special education status ("learning disabled," "gifted," "twice-exceptional")—often do not receive the environmental support and encouragement they need to feel comfortable fully expressing themselves.[32] For such individuals, they may have greater difficulty feeling authentic in environments where they truly do not feel as though they fit in, or in which their minority status is so salient to them and everyone around them.[33]

The culture of an institution can also have an effect on everyone within it. Sheldon found that new law students shifted toward security goals and away from growth goals during their first year of law school, presumably because "traditional legal education induces profound insecurity, which serves to alienate students from their feelings, values, and ideals."[34] As we'll see later, there are many other harsh and unpredictable environmental conditions that can lead people to be more present-focused, less cooperative, and less connected to one's whole self. Not only can environmental conditions impede the realization of our self-actualizing tendency, but even within ourselves, we have so many different (often unconscious) aspects of our mind constantly clamoring for our attention. Which is why awareness is so important, including awareness of our inner conflicts and extreme traits.

PRINCIPLE #3: BECOME AWARE OF YOUR INNER CONFLICTS

To have conflicts is human. Conflicts with others, conflicts with ourselves. While there is a universal set of basic needs, we each have dramatically different ways of satisfying those needs. We also differ as to which needs we consider most important and when in our lives they are most prominent. Such differences can lead to considerable conflict among people. But equally important, and related, is the conflict within ourselves. Our inner conflicts typically penetrate the boundaries of self and cause us to take out our frustration and aggressive impulses on others. Our inner conflicts are a significant component of our struggle toward self-realization.

If sometimes it feels as though there are multiple personalities within you that are constantly warring with one another, well, *that's because there are multiple personalities within you that are constantly warring with one another*! Each of us contains a bundle of dispositions, emotional tendencies, values, attitudes, beliefs, and motives that are often contradictory and incompatible.[35] While the early psychoanalysts and humanistic psychologists talked a lot about our "inner conflicts," modern psychological research—encompassing evolutionary psychology, social psychology, cognitive science, and cybernetics—shows empirically that our minds really are divided.[36]

Human beings, like every other living organism on the planet, are *cybernetic systems*—simply put, we are goal-directed systems.[37] As such, humans have multiple, often conflicting goals, some of which are conscious, many of which are not. Each of our goals has its own imagined future of what the world would look like with the goal completed, and it has some representation of the steps to be taken that will hopefully allow us to reach the goal. While our vision of the future is not always clear, it nevertheless drives behavior and how we experience the world. We are constantly comparing our present experiences with where we want to be, directing our attention to the most relevant features of the world that will help us reduce the discrepancy between our current state and our goal state.

Since we have many goals, we have many drives. As Maslow put it, "Man is a wanting animal. . . . It is characteristic of the human being that he is practically always desiring something."[38] Many of our goals are preprogrammed into our DNA because they increased the survival and reproduction of our distant ancestors.[39] However, it's important to recognize that the more we engage in a particular "sub-self"—or evolved component of the mind—the stronger that sub-self becomes and the quicker it is to activate in the future. Vice versa, the less we engage in that corner of the mind, the weaker the signal.

Also, many of our goals are not preprogrammed. Human beings show a flexibility in goal pursuit that is unprecedented in the animal kingdom. The astounding variety of goals humans can invent—from running a successful humanitarian nonprofit, to Skee-Ball champion of the world, to biggest Instagram influencer, to having the world's biggest bum[40]—often leads to profound inner conflicts. Just knowing that all of us face these conflicts should make us more forgiving of our own foibles as well as the foibles of others.

Given the brains we have, and our unique capacity for awareness of the often bewildering outputs arising from the complex computations of our brains, we actually do a pretty great job of managing our inner conflicts. To be sure, at times reality can feel unbearable, and despite the general satisfaction most people feel with their lives, mental illness is actually a lot more common than people realize. In fact, most people develop a diagnosable mental illness at some point in their lives.[41] Nevertheless, most people report being fairly happy in life, show positive developmental change across their life-spans, and display extraordinary capacities for resilience, dignity, and grace.[42] As resilience researcher Froma Walsh puts it, humans have the capacity to "struggle well."[43]

If you want a really good example of the civil war that exists all across the spectrum of humanity, and which often leads to momentary states of insanity, look no further than the domain of romantic love! There are many sorts of relationships that contribute to becoming a whole person—between friends, siblings, parents, children, and all of humanity. But the most actively pursued, exhilarating, fulfilling, despairing, maddening, and confusing form of love is romantic love.*

The typical romantic relationship can be thought of as blending some combination of attachment, caregiving, lust, and romantic passion.[44] While these elements are often deeply intertwined in romantic relationships, each element has, quite literally, a mind of its own. Each is the hallmark of a specific system that evolved to facilitate a specific problem associated with survival and reproduction.

Each of the elements of romantic love—attachment, caregiving, lust, and romantic passion—works with the others in differing degrees of intensity to produce the myriad ways people express romantic love around the world. The fact that each element of romantic love has different goals helps explain many human dramas seen around the globe. As anthropologist

---

* Romantic love is so powerful and universal that anthropologist Helen Fisher argues that it is a distinctively fundamental need separate from other forms of love. Indeed, the expressions of romantic love, including the joys as well as the sorrows, can be found cross-culturally and do not vary substantially based on age, gender, sexual orientation, or ethnic group. Of course, this doesn't mean cultural factors are unimportant. As psychologist Lisa Diamond put it, "Human experiences of sexual arousal and romantic love are always mediated by social, cultural, and interpersonal contexts. Love is neither biological nor cultural; the powerful mechanisms in our brain that we bring to bear when in love are exquisitely tuned to respond to particular information from the environment." See: Diamond, L. M. (2003). What does sexual orientation orient? A biobehavioral model distinguishing romantic love and sexual desire. *Psychological Review, 110*(1), 173–192; Fisher, H. E. (1998). Lust, attraction, and attachment in mammalian reproduction. *Human Nature, 9*(1), 23–52; Fisher, H. E. (2004). *Why we love: The nature and chemistry of romantic love.* New York: Henry Holt; Tolman, D. L., & Diamond, L. M. (2001). Desegregating sexuality research: Cultural and biological perspectives on gender and desire. *Annual Review of Sex Research, 12*, 33–74; Jenkins, C. (2017). *What love is: And what it could be.* New York: Basic Books.

Helen Fisher puts it, "The relative neurological independence of these . . . mating drives helps to explain contemporary cross-cultural patterns of philandering, sexual jealousy, stalking, spousal abuse, love homicide, love suicide, and the clinical depression associated with unstable and disbanded partnerships."[45]

Different environmental triggers can activate different goals within us, so that, as Fisher notes, "one can feel deep attachment for one individual while feeling romantic passion for someone else while feeling the sex drive for a range of others."[46] Any combination of the elements of romantic love is theoretically possible. We can become attached to people whom we do not like—or even those we despise—developing a dependency on them. We can care deeply about people we do not even know but are nevertheless motivated to alleviate their suffering, such as starving children in a third world country. We can become intensely lustful toward people we otherwise find repulsive and fall in love with people whom we do not sexually desire even one iota, even if the attraction violates our stated sexual orientation.[47] Walt Whitman was right, humans contain multitudes.

Of course, there need not be such a war among the elements of romantic love, and the greatest satisfaction in relationships tends to occur when the elements are harmoniously aligned and integrated. A more whole, transcendent version of love is possible (see Chapter 5). Nevertheless, a failure to integrate these various systems in a healthy way in relationships and within ourselves can create enormous confusion and frustration.

PRINCIPLE #4: LOOK OUT FOR LOPSIDED DEVELOPMENT

Swiss psychiatrist Carl Jung argued that a major goal of therapy is to help move a person toward the "path of individuation," in which one accepts the inherent contradictions within themselves so that they are able to fulfill their unique potential. Jung proposed a general principle—the principle of enantiodromia—"running counter to"—which states that the presence of any extreme element in one's personality also produces the opposite extreme in order to restore balance, even though the contradiction may remain hidden in the shadows of the subconscious.[48] While Jung believed that the neurotic person is stranded in one-sided development, he believed therapy had the great potential to help people accept all sides of themselves and approximate wholeness.

Karen Horney extended Jung's ideas and identified a number of lopsided patterns of human social behavior, which she referred to as "neurotic trends." Horney argued that these trends are attitudes toward other people and life that provide a feeling of safety and security during times of confusion and distress but which ultimately stunt growth. She grouped a large number of these trends under three main categories: (a) The extreme need for compliance and to be liked by others ("Moving Toward People"), (b) The extreme need to be antagonistic toward others and to constantly be rebellious ("Moving Against People"), and (c) The extreme need to become detached from people and always prove one's capacity for self-sufficiency ("Moving Away from People").[49]

To be sure, it is perfectly normal and healthy to desire the affection and adulation of others, to value your solitude, and to want to express frustration and anger when your needs are thwarted. The problem is when these needs become so outsize that they become compulsive and have the ability to seize upon the whole person. Remember, one of the goals of becoming a whole person is having maximum freedom to move in the direction of growth toward your highest potentialities. The healthy personality is able to flexibly switch between various strivings and regulate behavior in a productive manner that actually moves the person toward growth as a whole person.

In the grip of a lopsided striving, we are often unaware of the extent to which it is determining and taking over our life. In such moments, we are so hung up on our "tyrannical shoulds" that we aren't actually moving in the direction we truly value. Horney gives the example of the neurotic counterpart of the basic human striving for affection: "A wish for affection from others is meaningful only if there is affection for them, a feeling of having something in common with them. . . . But the neurotic need for affection is devoid of the value of reciprocity. For the neurotic person his own feelings of affection count as little as they would if he were surrounded by strange and dangerous animals. To be accurate, he does not even really want the others' affection, but is merely concerned, keenly and strenuously, that they make no aggressive move against him. The singular value lying in mutual understanding, tolerance, concern, sympathy, has no place in the relationship."[50] The compulsive nature of our neurotic trends have two main characteristics:

- Neurotic trends are often pursued indiscriminately (e.g., we must have everyone like us, even if we don't even like a person in return).
- Thwarting of the neurotic trend in any situation often leads to panic and anxiety (e.g., a person with a compulsive need for unlimited freedom panics at the slightest hint of a tie, whether it's a marriage engagement or the need to sign a contract for a gym membership).[51]

As Horney points out, neurotic trends serve an immensely important function in maintaining a sense of safety and security, which is why such individuals feel great terror if their neurotic trend is threatened in any way. They are soothing illusions. George Vaillant, who has studied the "wisdom of our ego," likens the mind's defense mechanisms to the body's immune mechanisms: "They protect us by providing a variety of illusions to filter pain and to allow self-soothing." According to Vaillant, our "defenses creatively rearrange the sources of conflict so that they become manageable. . . . The ego struggles to cope and to reduce the forces that work on it into some kind of harmony."[52] Horney argues that there are two ways in which our neurotic trends create "artificial harmony":

- We repress certain aspects of our personality and bring their opposite to the fore (e.g., we overemphasize our ability to be a kind, caring person who would never, ever, under any circumstance act aggressively toward others; we overemphasize our ability to control our environment and dominate others and make it clear that we will, under no circumstances, back down, apologize, or look "weak" by showing kindness), or
- We put such a distance between ourselves and others that we don't even allow the conflicts to arise in the first place (e.g., we value solitude so much that we will never engage in anything that may even have the slightest hint of jeopardizing our precious space and bring attention to our neurotic trend).

Both strategies induce a false sense of unity that may allow a person to function in the moment. Ultimately, however, Horney believed in the great potential for growth and development. In fact, she referred to her theory as a "constructive" theory and believed the highest goal of therapy is the striving for wholeheartedness: "to be without pretense, to be emotionally sincere, to be able to put the whole of oneself into one's feeling, one's work, one's beliefs."[53,54] As accumulating research shows, this is not blind optimism, as long-lasting personality change is possible.

PRINCIPLE #5: CREATE THE BEST VERSION OF YOURSELF

All of us retain the capacity to change, even to change in fundamental ways, as long as we live.

—Karen Horney, *Self-Analysis* (1942)

Horney agreed with Jung that acceptance was a critical first step to self-realization, but she differed from him in one important aspect: she believed mere acceptance wasn't enough. Horney argued that people also have to be willing to undergo extensive self-analysis and put in the considerable effort and hardship required for growth.[55] Only then, she argued, can they begin the process of growing, gradually, by becoming more consciously aware of the triggers of their neurotic trends, testing their irrational beliefs, and changing their maladaptive attitudes about the world through experience and insight. Maslow echoed this approach to therapy when he wrote, "The process of therapy helps the adult to discover that the childish (repressed) necessity for the approval of others no longer need exist in the childish form and degree, and that the terror of losing these others with the accompanying fear of being weak, helpless and abandoned is no longer realistic and justified as it was for the child. For the adult, others can be and should be less important than for the child."[56]

This approach is similar to modern-day cognitive-behavioral therapy, and indeed, the founder of CBT, Aaron Beck, told me that he was deeply influenced by humanistic thinkers such as Karen Horney, Abraham Maslow, and Gordon Allport.[57] In his more recent research on recovery-oriented cognitive therapy, Beck has found that when he and his team treat their schizophrenic patients as human beings with real human concerns, they have witnessed tremendous growth among their patients.[58] The patients need not only medication but also love, care, and treatment as a whole human being.

To be sure, modern-day science confirms that we aren't born blank slates; each of us is born with the potential to become a human being, even though that potential is for the development of a unique variation on the theme.[59] While this means no human has the potential to develop into an elephant or a tiger (and vice versa, in fact), and most of us don't have the potential to become as good a basketball player as Michael Jordan, it does mean that, given favorable conditions, you have the potential to become the best you in the whole entire world. Put another way, no one else in the entire world has as much potential to become you than you. Through a lifetime of exquisitely intricate interactions among thousands of genes interacting with one another and with the environment, you make decisions that determine your existence.[60,61] During the process of becoming, you still very much create yourself.

Recent research shows that while enduring personality change isn't easy, people really can change their personality in very substantial ways throughout life with intentional effort and therapy, as well as by making changes to one's environment that have long-lasting influences on one's personality, such as changing one's job, social roles, or relationship partners, or by adopting new identities.[62]

Modern personality psychologists prefer to think of personality traits as "density distributions." While environmental triggers do have a substantial effect on which self comes to the fore in which moment, it nevertheless still makes sense to talk about personality differences between people, because when whole distributions of behavior are observed, there are consistent individual differences. For instance, everyone craves at least some solitude throughout the day, but some prefer *a lot more* solitude throughout the day.

> We shouldn't think of personality as something cast in stone or always consistent.

Nevertheless, we shouldn't think of personality as something cast in stone or always consistent.[63] Throughout the course of the day, everyone fluctuates in their personality and even their intellectual functioning quite a lot.[64] Personality psychologist William Fleeson has found that people fluctuate in their personality traits throughout the day just as much as people differ from one another. Acting out of character is actually quite common.[65] This likely applies to all of our traits, including our morality. Even those we consider "saints" display many different levels of moral behavior throughout the day; they just display a much higher frequency of moral behaviors throughout the day compared to other people.[66] As psychologists Dawn Berger and Robert McGrath put it, it's better to think of virtue "as something we must continuously pursue rather than a state we ever achieve."[67] Indeed, Maslow repeatedly emphasized that self-actualized people are still human and are still very much prone to displaying imperfections (albeit less habitually so). This emerging understanding of personality is consistent with the humanistic psychology emphasis on experience. Viewing personality as our daily pattern of experiences, or states, we can talk about the *experience* of being extroverted, the *experience* of being moral, the *experience* of being cruel, the *experience* of being neurotic, etc., thus integrating the psychology of personality and the psychology of being.

This new understanding of personality, which has only emerged in the past thirty years or so, has deep implications for personality change because it suggests that we are only "extroverted," "caring," "conscientious," "neurotic"—even "intelligent"—to the extent to which our repeated patterns of thoughts, feelings, and behaviors say we are.[68] While genes can certainly have a strong influence on our patterns of behavior—we have what personality psychologist Brian Little refers to as our "biogenic" nature[69]—there is nothing sacred or unalterable about being a certain way; with enough adjustments to these patterns over time, we literally change our being.

Of course, this doesn't mean personality change is easy. Trying to change yourself too quickly can be very draining, and you have to want to change. While it is true that all people tend to feel authentic when naturally experiencing certain states—such as being competent or connecting with others—recent research suggests that forcing people to continually act contrary to their natural dispositions over a prolonged period of time can lead to increased anxiety and tiredness and decreased feelings of authenticity.[70]

Some people may simply not wish to change their default way of being just to reach some societal ideal. For instance, many people who score high in introversion may be perfectly accepting of their levels of introversion and not see any reason why they should have to care more about socializing with strangers rather than cultivate their already existing relationships.[71] Indeed, one study found that introverts who were comfortable with their introversion showed higher levels of authenticity than introverts who reported a greater desire to be more extroverted. The introverts who were more self-accepting were able to achieve a level of well-being that came close to the level experienced by extroverts.[72]

The key here is that for long-lasting personality change, you must want to change and be willing to follow through on your personality change goals and actively and successfully implement behaviors to change yourself.[73] The good news, though, is that by making enough changes to our states over time, we are capable of making long-lasting changes not only to our traits but also to our most valued goals in life.[74]

PRINCIPLE #6: STRIVE FOR GROWTH, NOT HAPPINESS

The founding humanistic psychologists were not focused on happiness or achievement, topics that receive so much attention in modern-day psychology and in self-help books. Instead, they were primarily interested in personal routes to health and growth. This process often involves experiencing uncomfortable emotions fully and accepting and integrating them with the rest of human experience.[75] This is why I personally prefer terms that describe the emotional experience—such as "exuberant," "comfortable," "uncomfortable," and "painful"—instead of outright labeling the emotions as "positive" or "negative."

Researchers are increasingly taking a more nuanced understanding of our traits, emotions, and behaviors, one that takes into account the importance of context.[76] Many emotions that make people uncomfortable or are painful to bear can be incredibly conducive to growth, just as the more comfortable or even ebullient emotions can sometimes sabotage our growth. The point is to embrace the full richness and complexities of our emotional landscape and bring them to a healthy integration. As Carl Rogers observed in his psychotherapy practice, "It seems to me that clients who have moved significantly in therapy live more intimately with their feelings of pain, but also more vividly with their feelings of ecstasy; that anger is more clearly felt, but so also is love; that fear is an experience they know more deeply, but so is courage. And the reason they can thus live fully in a wider range is that they have this underlying confidence in themselves as trustworthy instruments for encountering life."[77]

Of course, most of us want to feel good. On average, people tend to prefer more feel-good feelings in their daily lives relative to uncomfortable or painful emotions. The good news is that when people consistently move in the direction of growth, feelings of happiness and life satisfaction tend to come along for the ride as an epiphenomenon of growth.[78] In other words, the best route to happiness and life satisfaction is through transcending your egoistic insecurities, becoming the best version of yourself, and making a positive contribution to the world around you.

Consider the Dark Horse project, a long-term Harvard University study that looked at people who achieve impressive success that nobody saw coming.[79] Their list of "dark horses" include in-home chefs, master sommeliers, puppeteers, life coaches, embalmers, dog trainers, and air-balloon pilots. How did these trailblazers reach personal fulfillment and success? The researchers found that the key to their success was that they stayed focused on growing the things they cared most about, and they paid little attention to how they were doing in comparison to others or to traditional definitions of success.[80] They were able to find fulfillment and achievement by cultivating their unique interests, abilities, and circumstances.

PRINCIPLE #7: HARNESS THE POWER OF YOUR DARK SIDE

I criticize the classical Freudians for tending (in the extreme instance) to pathologize everything and for not seeing clearly enough the healthward possibilities in the human being, for seeing everything through brown-colored glasses. But the growth school (in the extreme instance) is equally vulnerable, for they tend to see through rose-colored glasses and generally slide over the problems of pathology, of weakness, of failure to grow. One is like a theology of evil and sin exclusively; the other is like a theology without any evil at all, and is therefore equally incorrect and unrealistic.

—Abraham Maslow, *Toward a Psychology of Being* (1962)

Carl Rogers noted that a common fear among his patients was that therapy would "release the beast" within themselves as they remove their defenses and fully experience previously unknown aspects of themselves. However, Rogers found that just the opposite actually occurs: "There is no beast in man. There is only man in man, and this we have been able to release."[81]

As people become more open to all their impulses, Rogers noted that people tend to strike more of a balance among their competing needs, and they are able to show aggression when it is realistically appropriate, but not display a "runaway" need for aggression. It is only when people deny awareness of various aspects of their experience, Rogers argued, that we have reason to fear them. However, when one is most fully human, one's varied feelings operate in a constructive harmony: "It is not always conventional. It will not always be conforming. It will be individualized. But it will also be socialized."[82]

Rollo May had a similar although in his view an even more realistic approach to human evil.[83] May highlighted the "daimonic" that exists in all of us (not to be confused with the demonic). May believed that humans are neither fundamentally good nor fundamentally evil but "are bundles of both evil and good potentialities."[84] May defined the daimonic as whatever potentiality within us "has the power to take over the whole person."[85] Integrating the daimonic into the personality can result in creativity and can be constructive. However, if the daimonic is not integrated, "it can take over the total personality . . . destructive activity is then the result."[86] May believed that the healthy integration of hostility, aggression, and anger was essential for growth, not by avoiding the potential for evil but by directly confronting it.[87]

While May believed we have the potential for both good and evil, he agreed with the other humanistic psychologists of the day that the environment can play an important role in helping to guide these potentialities in healthy directions. Indeed, Maslow repeatedly pointed out that we can help create good conditions for choosing.[88]

George Vaillant, who has revitalized the importance of our mind's defenses for healthy adaption to life, has also emphasized our great potential for change.[89] Not by suppressing our inner conflicts, or by pretending that everything is perfectly fine when it's not, but by transforming our defenses "from thunderstorms to rainbows," and in doing so, contributing to some of our highest heights of creative expression and wisdom. "The maladaptive defenses of adolescence can evolve into the virtues of maturity," Vaillant writes. "If we use defenses well, we are deemed mentally healthy, conscientious, funny, creative, and altruistic. If we use them badly, the psychiatrist diagnoses us ill, our neighbors label us unpleasant, and society brands us immoral."[90]

The founding humanistic psychologists were neither wide-eyed optimists nor cynical naysayers.* Maslow referred to himself as an "optimistic realist," arguing for a balance of perspectives on human nature.[91] While acknowledging our inner conflicts and defenses, humanistic psychologists also dared to show us the human possibilities for growth and goodness.

---

* Well, the one exception may have been Carl Rogers. He did seem particularly optimistic about human nature!

Growth Challenges
(co-authored with Jordyn Feingold)

One can choose to go back toward safety or forward toward growth. Growth must be chosen again and again; fear must be overcome again and again.

—Abraham Maslow[1]

Congratulations! If you are reading this text, you have likely begun your own personal journey toward growth, integration, and transcendence. The growth challenges presented on the following pages are designed to usher you, providing prompts, activities, and thought experiments to foster your development toward becoming a whole person.

Each exercise accompanies the science found throughout the chapters of this book and builds on the previous challenges, so we suggest that you go through them in sequence.[2] Some challenges might require more of your time and attention than others, based on how each exercise resonates with you and your unique life circumstances. We advise that you proceed with these exercises mindfully, consciously reserving judgment for yourself and any of your perceived shortcomings; this journey is about leaning into your whole self, capitalizing on what is working, and using those strengths to help you ascend your own hierarchy. Feel free to take your time with each exercise, but in some instances you might mindfully decide that it's better to move on to another exercise and return to a prior one when you are more ready. Remember, *life is not a video game*, and human development is often a two-steps-forward, one-step-back contiguous dynamic.[3] Finally, we recommend that you keep a journal dedicated to reflecting on each challenge so that you can chart your journey.

We hope you remain on this brave path, choosing growth again and again. Good luck sailing!

GROWTH CHALLENGE #1: SPOT YOUR LOPSIDED DEVELOPMENT

One crucial step on the path to becoming a whole person is awareness of your lopsided development. This growth challenge is a start toward identifying and facing your own outsize reactions to the world, so that you can begin moving in a direction to live more by your values, rather than falling for many of the illusions that we tend to live by mindlessly every day. Certainly, there are times when it is important to be compliant, aggressive, and detached from the world around you. However, if you find yourself disproportionately falling into one of these categories more than the others, this may indicate that you are stuck in the boat of insecurity without setting sail and moving forward.

The Challenge

Start by reading through the various items under each heading (Compliance, Aggressive, and Detached; see next page).[4] Tally up the number of statements you agree with under each heading to determine your "neurotic trend," as the humanistic psychoanalyst Karen Horney put it.[5] This is where we will first bring our attention.

Most Prominent Neurotic Trend: _____

(You might find that you affiliate with many statements under each heading, so you can simply choose the one you want to work on first.)

Now elaborate on the concrete beliefs or behaviors you exhibit that reflect each of the statements you agree with, i.e., how do these thoughts manifest themselves in your life?

Consider: How do these beliefs and behaviors help you? How might they get in the way of you living most by your values and feeling whole? How can you question the beliefs that are impeding you so that you may live with greater inner freedom?

COMPLIANT	AGGRESSIVE	DETACHED
1. I need to be liked by everyone.	1. It's a hostile world.	1. I am totally self-sufficient.
2. I am completely self-sacrificing.	2. Life is a struggle.	2. I don't really need people.
3. I'd almost always rather be with someone else than be alone.	3. I like to be in command.	3. I could live quite well without anyone.
4. I care too much what other people think of me.	4. Only the strongest survive.	4. I avoid long-term obligations.
5. I feel crushed if I am rejected.	5. I enjoy feeling powerful.	5. I resent people trying to influence me.
6. I feel weak and helpless when I'm alone.	6. I enjoy outsmarting other people.	6. I try to avoid advice from others.
7. I try to avoid fighting or arguing.	7. Other people are too sentimental.	7. I could live fine without friends or family.
8. I tend to feel it's my fault if something goes wrong.	8. I am uninhibited and brave.	8. I like it better when people do not share their thoughts or feelings with me.
9. I tend to be the one who apologizes first.	9. To survive in this world, you have to look out for yourself first.	9. I feel I'd be better off without people than with people.
10. I constantly need the company of others.	10. It's a fact of life most successful people step on others to get ahead.	10. I try to avoid conflicts.

Commit to being more aware of these beliefs as they come up in your life—how can you continue to challenge these beliefs and free yourself so that you can become the person you most wish to become?

GROWTH CHALLENGE #2: EXPLORE YOUR DARK SIDE

The latest research suggests the importance of not only cultivating positive emotions and events in our lives, but also accepting and exploring our most difficult or uncomfortable emotions, acknowledging them nonjudgmentally, and hopefully finding a healthy outlet for them.[6] For instance, emotions like pride, guilt, anger, or embarrassment can serve as cues that we may find useful in repenting, resolving a conflict, or evaluating the reasons for these negative emotions so that we may respond to them. Similarly, features of our lives that may sometimes feel to us like scars, such as struggling with physical or mental illness, harboring a particular insecurity, and so on, can actually become sources of great strength, giving us a unique ability to help or understand other people.

This activity involves reacting mindfully to our own uncomfortable emotions or life experiences and thinking about ways to harness these emotions for optimal growth and creativity.

The Challenge
In your journal, reflect upon your "dark side," using some or all of the following questions to guide you:

• What might come to mind when thinking about your own dark side?
• What are a few situations in your life that make you feel particularly negative (i.e., time spent in a particular place, with certain people, things you often dread but have to do, etc.)?
• What is something in your life that you struggle with or see as a potential scar?
• Consider in what ways have you coped with the negative emotions, emotional scars, or negative parts of your identity?
• In what new ways might you be able to take these negative emotions or scars and do something productive with them, such as making small personal improvements or connecting with others, rather than judging yourself? How might your dark side make you a better friend, student, or person? How does your dark side serve you in helping you become a whole person?

GROWTH CHALLENGE #3: FACE YOUR FEARS
This growth challenge involves identifying and facing your psychological fear(s) so that you may better combat the persistent anxieties in daily life

that interfere with your health and overall capacity to thrive. You will start by reading through the following Psychological Fears Scale and continue with the exercise prompt.[7]

PSYCHOLOGICAL FEARS SCALE

Fear of Failure

1. I am afraid of failing in somewhat difficult situations when a lot depends on me.
2. I feel uneasy doing something if I am not sure of succeeding.
3. If I do not understand a problem immediately, I start feeling anxious.

Fear of Rejection

4. When I get to know new people, I often fear being rejected by them.
5. Being given the cold shoulder when approaching strangers makes me feel insecure.
6. Being rejected is a big deal for me.

Fear of Losing Control

7. I become scared when I lose control over things.
8. I start worrying instantly when I notice that I don't have an impact on some things.
9. The idea of not having any control in a situation frightens me.

Fear of Losing Emotional Contact

10. I am absolutely devastated if a good friend breaks off contact with me.
11. I become agitated when I lose emotional contact with my loved ones.
12. If a close friend blows me off, I become anxious about our relationship.

Fear of Losing Reputation

13. I would be very worried if my good reputation was in danger.

14. I'm very keen on an undamaged reputation.

The Challenge

Think about some of your own fears. For some, these might come immediately to mind, or you may read through the Psychological Fears Scale to see which statements resonate with you most.

Determine which fear(s) you would most like to work on, based on your current life experiences and taking into account the Psychological Fears Scale.

In a written reflection, explore the following:

• What am I afraid of? Why is this so scary to me? What is the worst possible outcome of this happening to me?

• What could be a potentially favorable outcome of this fear unfolding? In what ways might I grow as a person? What might I learn? What parts of myself can I rely on (i.e., specific qualities, strengths) that could help me overcome my greatest fear?

Throughout your daily life, try to notice when your fears are getting in your way. Commit yourself to facing this fear and being even-handed with what positive things might ensue as you feel yourself panicking or avoiding these aversive stimuli.

GROWTH CHALLENGE #4: GROW TOGETHER, CULTIVATE A SECURE RELATIONSHIP

At one time or another, we have all felt insecure in a relationship, whether due to external stressors or because of our own more deep-seated tendencies toward avoidance or anxiety. However, when couples express their fears and needs with one another, previously silenced concerns can be tackled directly, and partners may be relieved of the pressure to mind-read or assume how their partner might be feeling. This exercise is designed for dyads (couples, friends, siblings, etc.) to engage in to deepen your most valued relationships, demystify hidden feelings or anxieties, and secure a foundation of trust and acceptance.

The Challenge

Sit with a partner (a significant other, close friend, etc.) in a comfortable setting without distractions (put away cell phones and bring your full presence to the moment).

Together, start by coming up with at least two or three elements of your relationship that you cherish the most and which bring you the most satisfaction (i.e., the fun you have together, your common vision of the future, what you learn from each other, etc.). Feel free to really delve into those elements that make your relationship successful, citing specific memories or stories, perhaps sharing feelings you have not expressed before.

Once you feel that you have a sufficient list of the strongest parts of the relationship, allow each partner to share one concern or insecurity that they may harbor. As you share, try to use only "I" statements rather than "you" statements, sharing your experience without placing blame on the partner. The listener should wait to respond in any way until the speaker is entirely done sharing. The listener should then repeat back their partner's statement to ensure mutual understanding.

Together, devise a plan to address this concern, drawing upon your mutual strengths from the first part of the exercise to formulate a solution.

Note: You will likely not be able to solve these problems or concerns in one sitting. The goal of this challenge is to create an environment where it is safe to share your insecurities, in which both partners commit to being more mindful of their partner's needs. Drawing upon your strengths together and as individuals can be a great approach to dealing with insecurity and anxiety.

Switch places so that each partner has had a chance to share and that you have a plan for beginning to address each partner's concerns.

GROWTH CHALLENGE #5: FOSTER A HIGH-QUALITY CONNECTION

Even brief moments of connection with other people can enliven our days and bring us closer to experiencing wholeness. Imagine how different your day might feel if, instead of feeling tension and awkwardness with your classmate or neighbor, your interactions were defined by trust, humor, and mutual positive regard. This exercise is about transforming a subpar or even neutral relationship in your life into a source of energy and sustaining connection.

Tips for Building High-Quality Connections (HQCs) in Four Domains[8]

RESPECTFUL ENGAGEMENT	TASK ENABLING	TRUSTING	PLAYING
• Be present • Listen, really listen • Be punctual • Be affirming, yet authentic • Communicate	• Coach • Facilitate • Accommodate • Nurture	• Share with others • Self-disclose • Ask for feedback and proceed accordingly	• Make meetings playful • Let your guard down • Create fun rituals

The Challenge

Choose a relationship in your personal or professional life in which your interactions with another person are less than ideal. In writing, describe and reflect on the current state of this relationship. What about this connection might be subpar?

Strategize about potential steps that you can take to improve your quality of connection with this person. What specific actions can you take to enhance the relationship quality and build genuine positive regard?

When you feel ready, actually start by reflecting on what you observe. Have you noticed any changes in the quality of this connection? How does this impact your energy level? How can you continue to ensure this connection, and other connections, remain high quality?

GROWTH CHALLENGE #6: ACTIVE CONSTRUCTIVE RESPONDING

A central part of Carl Rogers's person-centered therapy was what he referred to as "active listening."[9] Rogers viewed active listening as essential for effective communication and resolving conflicts. His approach involves having the listener paraphrase what they have heard to make sure that both people have a mutual understanding of what was said, as it is core to the "Grow Together, Cultivate a Secure Relationship" growth challenge. Today, scientists have elaborated on this through the Active Constructive Responding technique.[10] This growth challenge will help you practice this technique within the context of responding to positive news.

Ways of Responding to Positive News

Example: Your friend shares with you that they have received a job promotion.

ACTIVE-DESTRUCTIVE	ACTIVE-CONSTRUCTIVE
Demeaning the event	Enthusiastic support, asking questions, helping others capitalize on the positive
"Isn't that new job just going to make you more stressed and unhappy than you already are?"	"That's wonderful! Tell me everything from start to finish!"
PASSIVE-DESTRUCTIVE	PASSIVE-CONSTRUCTIVE
Ignoring the event, shifting focus to the self	Providing quiet, understated support
"You're not going to believe what happened to me today!"	"I'm happy to hear that, but I'm super busy right now. Can you tell me about this later?"

The Challenge

Choose a person in your life with whom you are close (a friend, classmate, significant other, etc.). Start paying attention to how you respond to them when they relay good news, such as "My interview went so well today!" or "I'm cleared by work to take a long vacation this summer!" Do this long enough to discern a stable pattern.

Do you respond enthusiastically, asking questions and reveling in the other person's success? Do you do this more frequently than any other sort of response? If so, you are demonstrating active–constructive responding. You most likely already have an excellent relationship with this person. If that is the case, choose another target for this exercise.

Continue observing your responses to others until you find someone to whom you do not typically respond this way. Reflect: What keeps you from responding actively/constructively with this person? (It might be because you care deeply about this person, and a critical response indicates a desire to protect them. You may not want a friend to get too excited about something that could fall through.) However, a steady stream of tempered enthusiasm or seemingly "constructive" criticism can take a toll on the relationship if your partner does not feel supported or if this is all that he or she hears from you.

Accordingly, resolve to respond to this person's good news in an active and constructive manner. Find at least three opportunities to use Active Constructive Responding with this person.

Reflect in a journal about the interactions you had, both in terms of what you did and how the other person reacted. Was it challenging to change your response style? How did your partner respond? Did you notice anything change in the dynamic between the two of you? What, if anything, did you learn from this exercise?

GROWTH CHALLENGE #7: PRACTICE HEALTHY ASSERTIVENESS

Practicing assertiveness involves employing a communication style that enables open and honest exchange with others and demonstrates that you

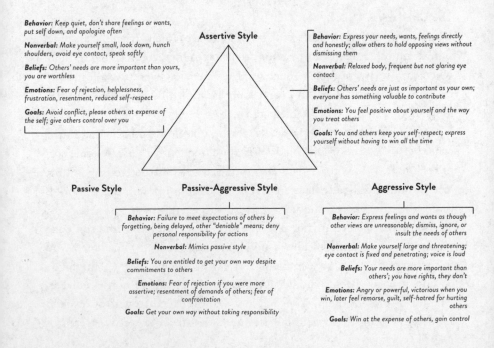

Assertive Style

Passive Style

Behavior: Keep quiet, don't share feelings or wants, put self down, and apologize often

Nonverbal: Make yourself small, look down, hunch shoulders, avoid eye contact, speak softly

Beliefs: Others' needs are more important than yours, you are worthless

Emotions: Fear of rejection, helplessness, frustration, resentment, reduced self-respect

Goals: Avoid conflict, please others at expense of the self; give others control over you

Behavior: Express your needs, wants, feelings directly and honestly; allow others to hold opposing views without dismissing them

Nonverbal: Relaxed body, frequent but not glaring eye contact

Beliefs: Others' needs are just as important as your own; everyone has something valuable to contribute

Emotions: You feel positive about yourself and the way you treat others

Goals: You and others keep your self-respect; express yourself without having to win all the time

Passive-Aggressive Style

Behavior: Failure to meet expectations of others by forgetting, being delayed, other "deniable" means; deny personal responsibility for actions

Nonverbal: Mimics passive style

Beliefs: You are entitled to get your own way despite commitments to others

Emotions: Fear of rejection if you were more assertive; resentment of demands of others; fear of confrontation

Goals: Get your own way without taking responsibility

Aggressive Style

Behavior: Express feelings and wants as though other views are unreasonable; dismiss, ignore, or insult the needs of others

Nonverbal: Make yourself large and threatening; eye contact is fixed and penetrating; voice is loud

Beliefs: Your needs are more important than others'; you have rights, they don't

Emotions: Angry or powerful, victorious when you win, later feel remorse, guilt, self-hatred for hurting others

Goals: Win at the expense of others, gain control

are in control of your own behavior and actions. An assertive style is one of four communication styles, which include passive, aggressive, passive-aggressive, and alternating.

The Challenge[11]
Review the pyramid graphic, including the behaviors, nonverbal communication, beliefs, emotions, and goals of each of the communication styles. Determine which communication style is your dominant response. If you are already an assertive communicator in most domains of your life, consider choosing another exercise to complete this week. If you are nearly always assertive except in certain situations, focus this exercise on those situations in which you could be more assertive.

Briefly list one to three situations in your life in which you would like to become more assertive (and less passive, passive-aggressive, or aggressive).

Complete the following sentences:

- I act most passive when: _____
- I often become aggressive when: _____
- My biggest fear of being assertive is: _____
- The one to three people in my life with whom I find it hardest to be assertive are: _____
- I am already quite assertive when: _____

Reflect upon your answers to these questions and practice acting in a more assertive manner in one domain in your life. Write a brief reflection after you endeavor to practice some assertiveness skills, as highlighted on the diagram on page 288. Here are some additional tips for being more assertive as you complete this exercise:[12]

- Assertiveness is about controlling our own behavior, not the behavior of others. You always have a choice. You can't stop people from asking of you, but you can say no.
- People are not psychic. If you want something, ask for it! If others say no, do not take it personally.

- Symbolic value (i.e., what actions represent, as opposed to the action itself) is often what makes confrontation hard. Try to get others to change a behavior, not their personality.

GROWTH CHALLENGE #8: UNPLUG

This exercise is about detaching from the virtual world of cell phones, television, tablets, email, smartwatches, and anything with a screen, and plugging in to the present moment—being with yourself, your friends, your family. Not only do phones and other electronic devices get in the way of quality time during meals, other quality time with family and friends, and time alone decompressing from a difficult day or savoring a great one, but these devices may also hamper our sleep quality. The blue light in our cell phones and televisions interferes with melatonin and may disrupt our circadian rhythms.[13] Therefore, unplugging from electronic devices at least two hours before bed and sleeping in a dark room may greatly enhance sleep quality.

The Challenge

Set an evening to unplug. Invite friends or family to participate in the Unplug Challenge with you. You, alone or with your friends/family members, will shut off all electronic devices, including the television, cell phones, tablets, computers, etc. Use clean socks as "sleeping bags" for participants' cell phones.

Set yourself up to complete an activity while you are "unplugged." This can include cooking dinner, reading, writing, going for a walk or hike, or creating a piece of art. If you are completing the Unplug Challenge with others, you can cook together, discuss a book, co-create art, play board games, hike, play charades, or create a family tree if completing the challenge with family.

After an evening of unplugged fun, remain unplugged until bedtime. Resist the temptation to turn on your phone or browse the web before bed. Get to bed at a reasonable hour so that you can get as close to eight hours of sleep as possible.

Complete a written reflection, detailing your experience of unplugging either by yourself or with others. What did you do while unplugged?

How did you feel? How do you feel now? What did you learn from this exercise?

GROWTH CHALLENGE #9: DITCH PERFECT!

Securing our self-esteem involves worrying less about what other people think, taking more risks, and spending less of our energy projecting a persona of perfection. Many of us spend too much of our own precious time and energy striving for perfection, worrying about how we are doing at any given task, rather than what we are doing in the moment. This quest for perfectionism can leave us feeling exhausted, isolated, and constantly dissatisfied with others and ourselves. This exercise is about questioning the pressures that we place on ourselves and receive from others to be perfect and settling for "good enough" so that we can move in the direction of greater self-actualization.

The Challenge

Think about an area in your life in which you find yourself striving for perfection. Explore the following questions in a written reflection:

- Why might I feel pressure to be perfect?
- What does striving for perfection require of me? How does it impact my energy?
- How does it impact my feelings of self-worth?
- How might seeking perfection actually interfere with my performance?
- What am I putting at risk by not achieving perfection?
- What is the worst thing that will happen if I am not perfect?
- How likely is this outcome?

After reflecting on these questions, identify some ways that you can "ditch perfect" in your life. Devise an explicit plan to increase your tolerance for "good enough" in yourself and others. Note that this does not mean settling for mediocrity—rather, it means shifting our focus of attention from outcome to process, the how to the what, and enabling ourselves to learn and grow, even through failure.

GROWTH CHALLENGE #10: CHALLENGE COGNITIVE DISTORTIONS

Throughout our evolution, humans have developed ways of navigating the world to make it easier to make decisions when we are inundated with information. Confirmation bias is one such shortcut, defined as the tendency to notice, remember, and value information that supports our beliefs and disregard and devalue evidence that conflicts with our beliefs. The problem is, our beliefs themselves are often fraught with cognitive distortions or irrational patterns in our thinking (elaborated on below).[14]

We often then rely on faulty beliefs to make judgments about the world, others, and ourselves. This faulty reasoning can leave us feeling exhausted, isolated, and constantly disappointed by others and dissatisfied with ourselves. This exercise is about identifying and understanding some of the thinking errors that you are subject to, and actively challenging and testing the truth of them so that you may break *negative thought patterns* and change core beliefs that aren't serving your growth.[15] In doing so, you can eventually learn to take your negative automatic thoughts less seriously and free yourself from some of our own angst, frustration, shame, and neuroticism.

Common cognitive distortions include but are certainly not limited to (these examples may or may not have been taken from Scott's personal life):[16]

- Black-and-white thinking: Viewing everything in extreme terms. *("If I get rejected by this woman, I'm a total loser in life.")*
- Catastrophizing: Believing that the worst will happen in a given situation. *("If I approach this woman I really like, I am 100 percent going to get rejected harshly and everyone will see and I will feel totally humiliated and the video of this happening will appear on Instagram somewhere and my mom will see and . . .")*
- False sense of hopelessness: Believing we have less power to reach an outcome than we really do. *("There's no point in approaching her anyway, I'll probably just come across as shady.")*
- Minimizing: Undervaluing positive events. *("She seems interested in me, but I don't think I really deserve it. It was probably my new jacket she really liked and not anything I said or did in that interaction.")*

- Personalizing: Attributing the outcome of a situation as solely the result of one's own actions or behaviors. *("She said she has a girlfriend; she must be saying that because she really is not interested in me and was probably repulsed by me.")*
- Shoulding: Thinking the way we want things to turn out is how they ought to have turned out. *("She really should have liked me, it seemed so meant to be.")*
- Entitlement: Expecting a particular outcome based on our status of behavior. *("I deserve for her to like me because I'm such a nice person.")*
- Jumping to conclusions: Feeling certain of the meaning of a situation despite little evidence to support that conclusion. *("She hasn't texted me back in two days; I know that she is actively trying to avoid me.")*
- Overgeneralizing: Drawing conclusions or settling on a global belief based on a single situation. *("Since I was rejected by her, I might as well never approach any other woman I'm interested in ever again because I am obviously unlovable.")*
- Mind reading: Assuming others know what you are thinking or that you know what another is thinking, despite not communicating directly. *("She should know that I am interested in her romantically; it doesn't need to be said.")*
- Emotional reasoning: Reasoning that what we feel is true, without evidence. *("I feel jealous when I see my new partner talking to other guys. She must be cheating on me, or why else would I feel this way?")*
- Outsourcing happiness: Making outside factors the ultimate arbiter of our happiness. *("I can't be happy in life unless I am attractive to as many women as possible.")*

The Challenge

Pick out some of these cognitive distortions that you find yourself falling subject to regularly. Ask yourself: When do you typically fall into these patterns? How do these patterns impact your sense of self-worth and sense of competence? How do they affect the way you view others?

How might you prevent yourself from falling into some of these patterns in the future?

Think about a specific example of when you fell into one of these cognitive distortions. Write down an outline of the specific example, note what trap you fell into, and ask yourself the critical questions for each distortion:

- Black-and-white thinking: What might the gray area be here? *("If I get rejected by this woman, might there be some alternative explanation other than 'I'm a total loser'?")*
- Catastrophizing: How likely is it that this worst-case scenario will happen? What evidence do you have to believe that this will happen? Do you have a sense of agency here to improve the outcome? *("If I do happen to get rejected, what can I do to ensure I maintain my dignity and self-respect?")*
- False sense of hopelessness: What could come of taking a risk here, even if the odds of success are low? *("She may downright reject me, but what if she doesn't? What do I have to lose?")*
- Minimizing: What could you have done to contribute to the situation? *("Other than my cool new jacket, what else did she like about Me?")*
- Personalizing: What could others have done to contribute to the situation? *("She very well might have liked me, but she has a boyfriend. Sometimes it's just not the right timing.")*
- Shoulding: Is this thought rational? *("What about the situation led me to think we 'should' be together?")*
- Entitlement: Is this thought rational? *("Does my being a nice guy automatically mean that she should be attracted to me romantically? Why do I deserve this particular woman in this particular instance, without her even getting a chance to get to know me? Or are there other factors at play?")*
- Jumping to conclusions: Could there be other explanations for this situation? *("She hasn't texted me back in two days; other than avoiding me, could she be busy? Without reception? Working?")*
- Overgeneralizing: Is this a fair global assessment? *("Am I universally unlovable, or is there another explanation for why this did not work out?")*
- Mind reading: Were you clear in communicating your feelings? Are you missing critical information? *("Did I adequately express my feelings to her? How could I have been clearer in getting my message across?")*

- Emotional reasoning: Do your feelings accurately reflect the facts of the situation? *("Do I have factual evidence to support my feelings of jealousy? Is it possible that I am wrong here?")*
- Outsourcing happiness: How can you rely on your inner self for happiness in this moment? *("What do I love about myself, and how can I use my own strengths to get me through this moment?")*

How might you notice when you are falling into a distortion in real time, and how can you avoid some of these patterns in the future? Be a scientist—test the evidence for your negative core beliefs. Keep track of the evidence for and against your belief during the course of your day. Look at your journal and analyze the data. How strong is the case for your belief, *really*?[17]

How can you build new core beliefs that are more conducive to growth? *Tip*: See if you can identify a more realistic belief. As clinical psychologist Seth Gillihan notes, "Don't worry if you have a hard time feeling like your alternative belief is true. Negative core beliefs can be persistent, and modifying them takes time and repetition."[18]

GROWTH CHALLENGE #11: BE SOCIALLY CURIOUS!

This growth challenge is about cultivating social curiosity in order to see the people in our lives for who they really are, rather than who we want them to be.

The Challenge

Choose someone in your life with whom you will practice your social curiosity. This can be someone you know very well, or it can be with a newer relationship. The next time you engage with this person, try to learn or notice something about them that you never knew before. You can start out subtly, by just paying more attention to their expressions, their smile, their voice, etc.

When you feel comfortable, start to ask questions that demonstrate your interest in this person. Some question suggestions might include:

- What would your perfect day be like?
- If you could have a meal with anyone in the world, who would it be with and why?
- What would others say is your greatest strength, and why?
- What are you fearful of, and why?
- What is a dream you have for the near future? For the distant future?

Be sure to use your judgment about when showing this curiosity is appropriate, and be ready to reciprocate and allow your partner to ask questions as well. See what you notice about the quality of your connection, and try to practice this curiosity with others in your life.

Write a written reflection about the experience of pursuing social curiosity, what came of this exercise, and anything that you might have learned.

GROWTH CHALLENGE #12: TEST THE WATERS, EXPAND YOUR COMFORT ZONE, AND GROW FROM ADVERSITY

Humans are creatures of habit, and expanding our comfort zones or changing up our usual routines can be challenging and uncomfortable. In addition, each of us has experienced some sort of adversity or loss in life, and confronting these difficult situations can bring back the negative emotions or overwhelming sensations. However, embracing change, stepping out of our comfort zones, and confronting past loss (in a safe way) can lead to growth, discovery, and a greater sense of mastery.

The Challenge

Set yourself up to do something that at first makes you feel slightly uncomfortable—something that you would normally *not* do. If you tend to be more introverted, consider hosting a dinner party, inviting a new friend over for coffee, stirring up a conversation with a stranger or potential relationship partner, or going to a new event in your community, such as an art show or workout class. If you tend to be more social, consider going out for a meal or to a concert, movie, or sporting event alone. Whatever activity you choose, the goal should be to try something new: to expand the boundaries of what you're comfortable with. If you tend to have a difficult time confronting past adversity or loss, practice sitting with a past hardship in a written contemplative reflection. Think about your loss or challenge, and think about what doors closed for you in the aftermath of that loss, what it felt like in the moment, and how it feels now.

While completing this activity, lean into the discomfort. Try to understand the physical sensations you may experience and what you can do to make yourself more comfortable in the situation.

After completing this exercise, explore what doors it opened for you in a written reflection. What good came out of this uncomfortable situation? What good came out of the adversity you reflected on? How did you decide what type of activity to complete? What were the barriers (if any) to your feeling comfortable immediately? How did your comfort level with the activity change throughout the process of engaging? What, if anything, did you learn about yourself through this personal exploration?

Feel free to do this activity again and again, choosing a new reflection/adventure to complete each time!

GROWTH CHALLENGE #13: EXERCISE LOVING-KINDNESS

Practicing loving-kindness toward yourself and toward others is a powerful way to build your capacity for compassion and exercise your vagal tone, which is strongly associated with physical, mental, and social flexibility, as well as adaptation to stress.[19] This exercise involves cultivating your capacity to practice love and kindness toward others and yourself.

The Challenge

Sit down in a quiet place where you can meditate without interruption, even for just five to ten minutes. Relax your body and bring your awareness to any places in your body where you may be holding tension. Without judgment, let those areas soften.

Allow your mind to think about a person in your life who loves you and whom you love very much. This can be someone living or someone who has passed. Imagine the warmth radiating from this person and the emotions you feel when you are with them. Imagining this person as vividly as possible standing beside you, send them all of your love and kindness with the following phrases:

- May you be safe.
- May you live your life in peace, free from pain.
- May you always feel supported and loved.

Next, turn your attention to someone in your life who is neutral to you, perhaps an acquaintance or even a stranger. Imagine this person standing beside you, and when you are ready, send them all of your love and kindness with the following phrases:

- May you be safe.
- May you live your life in peace, free from pain.
- May you always feel supported and loved.

Finally, turn your attention to yourself. Imagine yourself in a room, surrounded by all of those people who love you and wish you well. Allow yourself to feel the warmth radiating from your loved ones, and bask in this moment. When you are ready, repeat the following phrases:

- May I be safe.
- May I live my life in peace, free from pain.
- May I always feel supported and loved.

When you feel ready, bring your awareness back into the present moment. Reflect on what it felt like to send love toward someone you love, a stranger, and yourself. How can you bring this loving-kindness into your daily life?

Try to complete this practice for five days in a row—see what you notice. In a written reflection, describe the experience of practicing loving-kindness to others and yourself. For whom is it most difficult to channel positive sentiment? What, if anything, did you learn or gain from this exercise?

GROWTH CHALLENGE #14: TREAT YOURSELF
LIKE YOU WOULD TREAT A BEST FRIEND[20]

Often, our own inner dialogues can be cold and even downright cruel. Practicing self-kindness can be a great challenge compared to practicing kindness directed toward others, including friends and loved ones.

The Challenge

Think about a time when a close friend or family member came to you for advice after struggling with or feeling really down about something. How did you (or would you) respond to your friend in this situation, being the best possible friend that you could? Write down what you typically do, what you say, and note the tone in which you typically talk to your friends.

Now think about a time in your life (this could be now or in the past) when you really struggled with something or felt down about yourself. Think about how you typically respond to yourself in these situations: What do you do, what do you say, and what tone do you take with yourself?

Now write a letter to yourself in which you treat yourself and your difficult situation as though you are your own best friend. Write a letter in the second person about this experience. Allow yourself to remember the situation or think about your stress/suffering. Then acknowledge your feelings or thoughts, as well as what you were (or are) hoping for and needing. For example: "Dear Kelly, I know that you are feeling [sad/afraid/angry/disappointed in yourself, etc.]. You were really [looking forward to . . . /trying your best to . . . / etc.]."

Write about both the stress/suffering and the core need underneath it: a desire for health, safety, love, appreciation, connection, achievement, and so on. Offer a message of common humanity (e.g., that all humans make mistakes, sometimes fail, get angry, experience disappointment, know loss, and so forth). Mentor yourself with some compassionate advice or encouragement.

After writing the letter, consider reading it out loud to yourself or putting it away and bringing it out when you need self-compassion.

GROWTH CHALLENGE #15: HARMONIZE YOUR IDENTITIES

As each of us has many dimensions to our identity, integrating these facets can sometimes feel like a tremendous task. We each play many different roles in our lives, and bringing these roles into harmony can lead to experiencing a greater sense of wholeness.

The Challenge

Sit down in a quiet place and write down all the different roles that you play in your life. This list may include words like "son," "daughter," "student," "girlfriend/boyfriend," "neighbor," "brother," "sister," "friend," "uncle," "leader," "community member," "writer," "teacher," and more. You may also consider different parts of your personality that manifest in each role. For example, being a student brings out your diligence; as a brother, you are very protective; as a significant other, you are goofy, etc.

Consider how these roles can come into conflict with one another in your daily life—be as specific as possible:

- "Sometimes it can be challenging to be a goofy friend when I also have to be diligent and serious while I run my business."
- "As a leader of my religious organization, I have to be constantly available for my congregants. As a father, I want to be completely available for my children. It sometimes feels as though I don't have the bandwidth to do it all."

Next, consider how these same roles can complement each other.

- "Being goofy with my friends and family recharges me so that I can be fully present and more serious in my workplace. It is also sometimes an advantage to be slightly goofy with my clients. After all, we are all human."
- "I can use my knowledge and growth from being a father to help my congregants in my role as a spiritual leader."

For the next week or so, begin to focus on these reinforcing aspects of the roles in your life. Reflect on potential conflicts as opportunities to find new ways to harmonize the various parts of your identity and what it feels like to transform a challenge into an opportunity.

GROWTH CHALLENGE #16: USE YOUR SIGNATURE STRENGTHS IN NEW WAYS

In this growth challenge, you will take the VIA Survey of Character Strengths[21] to become aware of your strengths, then explore your strengths, and finally to apply your strengths in new ways. As you may discover when answering the survey and reviewing your results, strengths are not fixed traits across settings and time; rather, strengths are malleable, subject to growth, and largely context-specific.[22] Thus, strengths that you may rank high in in life, such as perspective or humor, may seem to go out the

	Strength	Opposite	Absence	Excess
Wisdom and Knowledge	Creativity	Triteness	Conformity	Eccentricity
	Curiosity	Boredom	Disinterest	Nosiness
	Judgment	Gullibility	Uneffectiveness	Cynicism
	Love of learning	Orthodoxy	Complacency	"Know-it-all"-ism
	Perspective	Foolishness	Shallowness	Ivory tower
Courage	Bravery	Cowardice	Fright	Foolhardiness
	Persistence	Helplessness	Laziness	Obsessiveness
	Authenticity	Deceit	Phoniness	Righteousness
	Vitality	Lifelessness	Restraint	Hyperactivity
Love	Intimacy	Loneliness	Isolation/autism	Emotional promiscuity
	Kindness	Cruelty	Indifference	Intrusiveness
	Social intelligence	Self-deception	Obtuseness	Psychobabbling
Justice	Citizenship	Narcissism	Selfishness	Chauvinism
	Fairness	Prejudice	Partisanship	Detachment
	Leadership	Sabotage	Compliance	Despotism
Temperance	Forgiveness	Vengefulness	Mercilessness	Permissiveness
	Humility	Arrogance	Footless self-esteem	Self-deprecation
	Prudence	Recklessness	Sensation-seeking	Prudishness
	Self-regulation	Impulsivity	Self-indulgence	Inhibition
Transcendence	Awe	Criticism	Oblivion	Snobbery
	Gratitude	Entitlement	Rudeness	Ingratiation
	Hope	Despair	Present orientation	Pollyannaism
	Humor	Dourness	Humorlessness	Buffoonery
	Spirituality	Alienation	Anomie	Fanaticism

window when it comes to your financial planning. Similarly, you may not be very prudent or self-regulated when it comes to putting yourself at risk, but when it comes to your loved ones, you are highly cautious and reserved. It is important to note that strengths may sometimes be overused or applied in a situation where they may not be appropriate or warranted. When it comes to strengths, there tends to be a "golden mean," or right amount, of exercising a strength that leads to optimal results (see the figure on page 301).

This exercise is intended to help you channel your top strengths in your work to increase your engagement, meaning, and mastery in everyday life. Note that when you complete the VIA survey, your strengths will be ranked from top to bottom; lower strengths are not necessarily your weaknesses. While this intervention is specifically designed for you to use your top strengths, also consider focusing on some of your bottom strengths. Further information about this is provided in the challenge prompt.

The Challenge

Complete the VIA Survey of Character Strengths. Do this by visiting *viacharacter.org* and then clicking "Take the Free Survey." After creating an account and registering, take the survey. It should take you about twenty minutes to complete. Once you are done, review your results. You can see your rank-ordered twenty-four strengths with explanations of what each strength means. You do not need to purchase a detailed report, but you are welcome to if you would like.

Complete a written reflection about the following. Do any of your top strengths surprise you? What about your lower strengths? What would your life look like if you were unable to use your number-one top strength? Do you think you would find it more helpful to focus on using your top strengths or improving your lesser strengths?

Find three new ways to use your top strengths this week. Can you use these top strengths to help you be a better person? To help you be a better friend/family member? To overcome some obstacle? To create a positive experience? Please reflect on the three new ways you used your top strengths this week, and how it made you feel when you did so. Use the following template to record how you are using your strengths in new ways. (You can use the same strength three times, or three different strengths.)

Note: You don't have to stop finding new ways to use your top strengths this week. You can keep it up for the next month, year, and for the rest of your life!

Using Strengths in New Ways

STRENGTH 1:
How did you use this strength in a new way this week? How did this make you feel?

STRENGTH 2:
How did you use this strength in a new way this week? How did this make you feel?

STRENGTH 3:
How did you use this strength in a new way this week? How did this make you feel?

GROWTH CHALLENGE #17: WHAT'S YOUR *IKIGAI*?

To find one's *ikigai*, or "reason for being," requires an exploration of the things in our lives most central to who we are—that which excites us, brings us meaning, and helps us feel whole. Hopefully, through this book, you have and will continue to come to greater awareness of your own

Ikigai

A Japanese concept meaning "a reason for being"

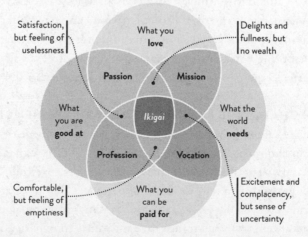

ikigai and learn new ways to deliberately engage in the things that sustain you most. This exercise is designed to move you forward on this journey.

The Challenge
In writing, reflect on the following questions:

• What in my life am I best at? What sorts of things feel effortless for me (i.e., they energize me and light me up)?
• What in my life do I choose to pursue, even though it is challenging?
• What in life do I most value?
• What in my life provides me with a sense that I am part of something larger than myself?
• What in my life focuses my attention most completely and allows me to enter the flow state of consciousness?
• If I could quit school tomorrow and do absolutely anything in the world, what would I do?

Reflect on any themes that emerge, attending to aspects that come up in more than one of these questions. Spend time over the next several days reflecting on your *ikigai* and how you are spending time in your life engaging in the things that bring you a sense of meaning and vitality.

What is one thing you can do to live more in line with your *ikigai*? How can you attend to your *ikigai* on a daily or at least weekly basis?

Note: Venturing to discover a singular *ikigai* can seem daunting—do not fret! Living by your *ikigai* is simply about doing more of the things in your life that bring you a sense of meaning and purpose. As you continue on this journey, consider how engaging in such activities affects you.

GROWTH CHALLENGE #18: CREATE A PEAK EXPERIENCE
This exercise is about increasing peak experiences in your life, in any domain of your choosing, for example, at school, at work, or with family and friends. Maslow described peak experiences as "rare, exciting, oceanic, deeply moving, exhilarating, elevating experiences that generate an advanced form of perceiving reality, and are even mystic and magical . . ."[23] While it may seem daunting to just dive into such an experience, which

Maslow considered one of the most transformative of our lives, we will start by understanding related concepts that can help facilitate peak experiences: flow and awe.

Flow is about intense absorption in an activity in which you are fully concentrating, completely immersed, and even unaware of yourself.[24] To induce flow, the idea is to find the optimal balance between skill and challenge: you do not want to do something that is so difficult that you are anxious while doing it, and you don't want to do something so simple that you are bored. Cultivating one's ability to experience flow in as many circumstances as possible may lead to a happier, more fulfilling life. Ideally, you would be able to find flow in your favorite hobbies or activities, such as cooking, painting, or running, and also in your professional pursuits—where most people spend the majority of their waking hours.

Finding flow involves challenging the body and mind to its limits; striving to accomplish something new, difficult, or worthwhile; and discovering rewards in the process of each moment. Eight tools for enhancing flow are presented in the following table:[25]

CONTROL ATTENTION	Flow is about mastering control over your attention so that you may be completely immersed in the task at hand. While very strict control over your attention may take a great deal of effort in the moment, it is an important ingredient toward long-term mastery.
OPEN YOURSELF TO NEW EXPERIENCES	Be open to new and different experiences, such as: going camping, playing a new sport, traveling to a foreign place, or trying new types of cuisine. Keep challenging yourself, and do not become complacent!
BE A LIFELONG LEARNER	Leaning and embracing new challenges throughout the course of life is a key component of finding flow when you've already mastered many skills.
LEARN WHAT FLOWS	Often, individuals fail to recognize when they experience flow. Pay close attention and establish precise time periods and activities during which you are in flow, and seek to amplify these activities.

TRANSFORM ROUTINE TASKS	You can find "micro-flow" states even in mundane activities, such as running errands, cleaning up a workspace, waiting for a train, or listening to a lecture. Transform routine tasks by solving puzzles in your head, doodling, rewriting song lyrics to tell a funny story, or writing a poem or riddle.
FLOW IN CONVERSATION	Develop goals within your conversation to learn more about the person you're speaking with: What is on her mind? What emotions is she experiencing? Have I learned something about her that I didn't know before? Focus your full attention on the speaker and on your reactions to her works. Prompt with follow-up questions: "And then what happened?" "Why did you think that?"
ENGAGE IN SMART LEISURE	Consider making your leisure time "smarter" by engaging in activities in which you are using your mind and exercising your skills—ideally different skills from the ones you use all day at work or at home.
ENGAGE IN SMART WORK	Tailor the tasks you need to do to align with your skills, passions, and values.

The concept of awe has been described as a complex mixing of the emotions of ecstasy and fear. It can be deeply personal to experience awe, and researchers have explained two primary cognitive appraisals that are central to awe experiences: 1) the perception of vastness, and 2) a struggle to mentally process the experience.[26] Experiencing awe is associated with many positive outcomes, including enhanced life satisfaction, a feeling that there is more time available to experience the world, increased helping behaviors and generosity, and decreased aggressive attitudes.

This exercise is intended to increase your experience and understanding of awe and reflect upon your own awe experience.

The Challenge

First, reflect on a previous peak experience you've had (if you've had one). Alternatively, think about a time that you felt immense awe or experienced a deep sense of flow in your life. In short, think about the closest experience you might have ever had to a peak experience.

The experience can be from any part of your life, but should be recent enough that you remember the details. Consider what has facilitated this peak experience or awe or flow state awe (i.e., what features of the experience induced your "peak" state). Features might include:

- Vastness (being in the presence of something grand)
- Self-diminishment (feeling small in a large universe)
- Feeling challenged to mentally process the experience
- Connectedness (having the sense of being connected to everything around you)
- A distorted sense of time and space (time may speed up or move much more slowly than usual)
- The feeling of being one whole harmonious self, free of inner conflict
- Being without fear, doubt, or negative self-talk
- Experiencing distinct physical sensations (such as the chills, having your jaw drop, etc.)

Consider both what has facilitated the experience and what, if anything, may have impeded it. Then consider how you might solve the potential obstacles to experiencing these peak states.

Then intentionally set yourself up for a peak experience, to the best of your ability! Go out and complete this activity (safely) and continue to write about this experience reflectively. What did you do, and how did it feel? This may be a solitary activity or something you engage in with others. For some potential prompts, see "Live More in the B-Realm" on page 245.

GROWTH CHALLENGE #19: PRACTICE SAVORING

Maslow's notion of the plateau experience shares a number of attributes with modern-day notions of "savoring."[27] Modern science has identified four main types of savoring: basking, luxuriating, thanksgiving, and marveling. Of the four types of savoring, which type(s) are you most inclined to do naturally?

Think through the three temporal forms of savoring (savoring something about the past,[28] savoring the present, or anticipatory savoring of the future); what type(s) are you most inclined to do naturally?

Set yourself up for a savoring experience using a temporal form and savoring type of your choice. Use at least one strategy to enhance savoring from the following table. For example, if you are a reminiscer and are naturally inclined toward gratitude, take out an old photo album and look through photos of your childhood. Engage a sibling or parent to do it with you for your savoring strategy of "share good things with others."

Four Types of Savoring

	INTERNAL SELF	EXTERNAL WORLD
COGNITIVE REFLECTION (THINKING)	Basking (pride) Being receptive to praise and congratulations For example, enjoying the afterglow of winning a soccer game, acing an exam, etc.	Thanksgiving (gratitude) Experiencing and expressing gratitude For example, spending the afternoon with your mother, expressing gratitude that you have such a beautiful, close relationship.
EXPERIENTIAL ABSORPTION (DOING)	Luxuriating (pleasure) Engaging the senses fully For example, enjoying a relaxing bubble bath, slowly eating a piece of delicious chocolate, or sipping a glass of fine wine.	Marveling (awe) Losing yourself in the wonder of experience For example, waking up early to watch the sunrise or going outside during a thunderstorm to marvel at the sky's action.

CAPSTONE GROWTH CHALLENGE: ACCEPT YOUR WHOLE SELF

It's time once and for all to accept the totality of your being, including the parts of yourself that you most struggle with. Part of acceptance is taking responsibility for your whole self, not just the aspects of your mind or your actions that you like or that make you feel the best about yourself.

The Challenge

Settle into a comfortable position and relax into your body. Focus on allowing your muscles to relax, bringing your attention to your breath. Inhale deeply as you bring yourself fully into the present moment, imaging yourself sipping in air as if to breathe in the world around you as it is happening right now, and exhale to release everything that has come before this moment.

As you breathe, allow your mind to focus on one or two things you like about yourself. Repeat these qualities in your head, basking in the parts of yourself that you consider your greatest assets.

When you feel ready, allow your mind to wander to some of the qualities about yourself that you may struggle with. Maybe these are qualities you consider to be less desirable or perhaps wish you did not possess. It may feel uncomfortable, but allow yourself to soak in these qualities as you breathe in and out.

Once you have summoned these qualities, repeat the following phrases in your mind:

- I take responsibility for my whole self, including my flaws.
- My weaknesses are the raw material for personal growth.
- I accept my whole self in this moment.

As you repeat this mantra, accept whatever sensations or urges arise, without trying to control or change them.

Complete a written reflection about how it felt to complete this exercise; you may also write your own mantra that is different from the one provided, which can help you to better accept the totality of your being.

Notes

PREFACE

1. Brooks, D. (2017). When life asks for everything. *The New York Times*. Retrieved from https://www.nytimes.com/2017/09/19/opinion/when-life-asks-for-everything.html; Brooks, D. (2019). *The second mountain: The quest for a moral life*. NY: Random House.

2. Maslow, A. H. (1966/1996). Critique of self-actualization theory. In E. Hoffman (Ed.), *Future visions: The unpublished papers of Abraham Maslow* (pp. 26–32). Thousand Oaks, CA: Sage Publications.

3. Maslow, A. H. (1961). Peak experiences as acute identity experiences. *The American Journal of Psychoanalysis, 21,* 254–262, p. 260.

4. Maslow, A. H. (1998; originally published in 1962). *Toward a psychology of being* (3rd ed.) New York: Wiley, p. 231.

5. Maslow, A. H. (1969). The farther reaches of human nature. *Journal of Transpersonal Psychology, 1*(1), 1–9, p. 1. The entire lecture at the Unitarian church can be found on YouTube at https://www.youtube.com/watch?v=pagvjnTEEvg.

6. Maslow, The farther reaches of human nature, pp. 3–4.

7. Lowry, R. (1979). *The journals of A. H. Maslow—two volumes (The A. H. Maslow series)*. Monterey, CA: Brooks/Cole, p. 1261.

8. Krippner, S. (1972). The plateau experience: A. H. Maslow and others. *Journal of Transpersonal Psychology, 4*(2), 107–120, p. 119.

9. International Study Project, Inc. (1972). *Abraham H. Maslow: A memorial volume*. Monterey, CA: Brooks/Cole, p. 53.

10. Lowry, *The journals of A. H. Maslow*, p. 869.

11. Michael Murphy, personal correspondence, May 10, 2018.

12. https://www.abrahammaslow.com/audio.html. *The Abraham Maslow audio collection: Volume 2, The farther reaches of human nature, part 8*, 1967.

13. Schneider, K. J. (2018). The chief peril is not a DSM diagnosis but the polarized mind. *Journal of Humanistic Psychology,* doi: 10.1177/0022167818789274; Peters, S. (2018). "The polarized mind" as alternative framework for human suffering. *Mad in America*. Retrieved from https://www.madinamerica.com/2018/07/polarized-mind-alternative-framework-human-suffering.

14. Kaufman, S. B. (2013). *Ungifted: Intelligence redefined*. New York: Basic Books. Kaufman, S. B. (2018) (Ed.). *Twice exceptional: Supporting and educating bright and creative students with learning difficulties*. New York: Oxford University Press.

15. Kaufman, S. B., Weiss, B., Miller, J. D., & Campbell, W. K. (2018). Clinical correlates of vulnerable and grandiose narcissism: A personality perspective. *Journal of Personality Disorders, 32,* 384.

16. Maslow, *Toward a psychology of being*, p. 66.

17. Maslow, A. H. (1969). *The psychology of science: A reconnaissance*. Washington, DC: Gateway Editions, p. 15.

18. Maslow, *Toward a psychology of being*, p. 85.

19. Fromm, E. (1989). *The art of being*. New York: Bloomsbury Academic.

INTRODUCTION: A NEW HIERARCHY OF NEEDS

1. Maslow, Critique of self-actualization theory, p. 28.

2. In the first edition of his book *Motivation and Personality*, Maslow included an entire chapter titled "Toward a Positive Psychology," in which he set out a vision for such a field. Later, in an appendix to the revised edition, he wrote: "Of course the most pertinent and obvious choice of subject for a positive psychology is the study of psychological health (and other kinds of health, aesthetic health, value health, physical health, and the like). But a positive psychology also calls for more study of the good man, of the secure and of the confident, of the democratic character, of the happy man, of the serene, the calm, the peaceful, the compassionate, the generous, the kind, of the creator, of the saint, of the hero, of the strong man, of the genius, and other good specimens of humanity."

3. Maslow, *Toward a psychology of being*, p. 85.

4. Schneider, K. J., Pierson, J. F., & Bugental, J. F. T. (Eds.). (2015). *The handbook of humanistic psychology: Theory, research, and practice* (2nd ed.). Thousand Oaks, CA: Sage Publications, p. xix.

5. van Deurzen, E., et al. (Eds.). (2019). *The Wiley world handbook of existential therapy*. Hoboken, NJ: Wiley-Blackwell; Schneider, K. J., & Krug, O. T. (2017). *Existential-humanistic therapy* (2nd ed.). London: APA Books.

6. Bland, A. M., & DeRobertis, E. M. (2020). Humanistic perspective. In V. Zeigler-Hill & T. K. Shackelford (Eds.), *Encyclopedia of personality and individual differences*. Cham, Switzerland: Springer. Advance online publication. doi: 10.1007/978-3-319-28099-8_1484-2.

7. Jourard, S. M., & Landsman, T. (1980). *Healthy personality: An approach from the viewpoint of humanistic psychology*. New York: Macmillan; Kaufman, S. B. (2018). Do you have a healthy personality? *Scientific American Blogs*. Retrieved from https://blogs.scientific american.com/beautiful-minds/do-you-have-a-healthy-personality.

8. Compton, W. C., & Hoffman, E. L. (2019). *Positive psychology: The science of happiness and flourishing*. New York: Sage Publications; Basic Books; Lopez, S. J., Pedrotti, J. T., & Snyder, C. R. (2018). *Positive psychology: The scientific and practical explorations of human strengths*. New York: Sage Publications; Seligman, M. E. P. (2011). *Flourish: A visionary*

new understanding of happiness and well-being. New York: Free Press; Seligman, M. E. P., & Csikszentmihalyi, M. (2000). Positive psychology: An introduction. *American Psychologist, 55,* 5–14. The quote "makes life worth living" is from Seligman & Csikszentmihalyi (2000), p. 5.

9. It should be noted that some humanistic psychologists and positive psychologists have called for a greater focus on the inherent paradoxes of human existence within positive psychology research, seeing that as a major limitation of the field. I agree with this criticism. See: DeRobertis, E. M., & Bland, A. M. (2018). Tapping the humanistic potential of self-determination theory: Awakening to paradox. *The Humanistic Psychologist, 46*(2), 105–128; Wong, P. T. P. (2010). What is existential positive psychology? *International Journal of Existential Psychology & Psychotherapy, 3,* 1–10; Wong, P. T. P. (2011). Positive psychology 2.0: Towards a balanced interactive model of the good life, *Canadian Psychology, 52*(2), 69–81.

10. Sheldon, K. M., & Kasser, T. (2001). Goals, congruence, and positive well-being: New empirical support for humanistic theories. *Journal of Humanistic Psychology, 41*(1), 30–50.

11. Diener, E., Suh, E. N., Lucas, R. E., & Smith, H. L. (1999). Subjective well-being: Three decades of progress. *Psychological Bulletin, 125*(2), 276–302; Kaufman, S. B. (2017). Which personality traits are most predictive of well-being? *Scientific American Blogs.* Retrieved from https://blogs.scientificamerican.com/beautiful-minds/which-personality-traits-are-most-predictive-of-well-being; Kern, M. L., Waters, L. E., Adler, A., & White, M. A. (2013). A multidimensional approach to measuring well-being in students: Application of the PERMA framework. *The Journal of Positive Psychology, 10*(3), 262–271; Ryan & Deci, Self-determination theory and the facilitation of intrinsic motivation, social development, and well-being; Ryff, C. D., & Keyes, C. L. M. (1995). The structure of psychological well-being revisited. *Journal of Personality and Social Psychology, 69*(4), 719–727; Seligman, M. E. P. (2011). *Flourish: A visionary new understanding of happiness and well-being.* New York: Simon & Schuster; Sun, J., Kaufman, S. B., & Smillie, L. D. (2016). Unique associations between Big Five personality aspects and multiple dimensions of well-being. *Journal of Personality, 86,* 158–172; Yaden, D. B., Haidt, J., Hood, R. W., Vago, D. R., & Newberg, A. B. (2017). The varieties of self-transcendent experience. *Review of General Psychology, 21*(2), 143–160.

12. Bland, A. M., & DeRobertis, E. M. (2017). Maslow's unacknowledged contributions to developmental psychology. *Journal of Humanistic Psychology,* doi: 10.1177/0022167 817739732.

13. Maslow, *Toward a psychology of being,* 212–213.

14. Maslow, A. H. (1987). *Motivation and personality* (3rd ed.). New York: HarperCollins, pp. 27–28.

15. Maslow, *Motivation and personality,* p. 37.

16. Maslow, *Motivation and personality,* p. 388.

17. Maslow, *Motivation and personality,* p. 390.

18. Maslow, *Toward a Psychology of Being,* p. 190.

19. Rowan, J. (1999). Ascent and descent in Maslow's theory. *Journal of Humanistic Psychology, 39*(3), 125–133.

20. Bland, A. M., & DeRobertis, E. M. (2017). Maslow's unacknowledged contributions to developmental psychology. *Journal of Humanistic Psychology*, doi: 10.1177/0022167817 739732.

21. Bland & DeRobertis, Maslow's unacknowledged contributions to developmental psychology; Bridgman, T., Cummings, S., & Ballard, J. (2019). Who built Maslow's pyramid? A history of the creation of management studies' most famous symbol and its implications for management education. *Academy of Management Learning & Education*, *18*(1), https://doi.org/10.5465/amle.2017.0351; Eaton, S. E. (2012). Maslow's hierarchy of needs: Is the pyramid a hoax? *Learning, Teaching and Leadership*. Retrieved from https://drsaraheaton.wordpress.com/2012/08/04/maslows-hierarchy-of-needs; Kaufman, S. B. (2019). Who created Maslow's iconic pyramid? *Scientific American Blogs*. Retrieved from https://blogs.scientificamerican.com/beautiful-minds/who-created -maslows-iconic-pyramid; Rowan, J. (1998). Maslow amended. *Journal of Humanistic Psychology*, *38*(1), 81–92.

22. Miriam Kauderer, one of Maslow's students at Brooklyn College, told me that in his class he did present to the students something resembling a pyramid to describe his hierarchy of needs. Nevertheless, it's likely he was reproducing something, rather than being the originator of the pyramid. L. Ari Kopolow, another one of his former students, told me that in personal correspondence Maslow said he didn't like the pyramid representation of his theory.

23. Bridgman et al., p. 90.

24. Mills, A. J., Simmons, T., & Helms Mills, J. C. (2005). *Reading organization theory: A critical approach to the study of behaviour and structure in organizations* (3rd ed.). Toronto: Garamond Press, p. 133.

25. Bridgman, Cummings, & Ballard, Who built Maslow's pyramid?, p. 94.

26. Sheldon, K. M., Elliot, A. J., Kim, Y., & Kasser, T. (2001). What is satisfying about satisfying events? Testing 10 candidate psychological needs. *Journal of Personality and Social Psychology*, *80*(2), 325–339; Oishi, S., Diener, E., Suh, E. M., & Lucas, R. E. (1999). Value as a moderator in subjective well-being. *Journal of Personality*, *67*(1), 157–184; Tay, L., & Diener, E. (2011). Needs and subjective well-being around the world. *Journal of Personality and Social Psychology*, *101*(2), 354–365.

27. MacLellan, L. (2019). "Maslow's pyramid" is based on an elitist misreading of the psychologist's work. *Quartz at Work*. Retrieved from https://qz.com/work/1588491 /maslow-didnt-make-the-pyramid-that-changed-management-history.

28. Lowry, R. J., foreword to Maslow, *Toward a psychology of being*, p. x.

29. On the surface, Maslow's notion of growth motivation seems similar to Carol Dweck's distinction between a "growth mindset" and a "fixed mindset." To be sure, Dweck has done a lot of important work showing that the extent to which one thinks ability can grow and improve is related to levels of achievement, success, and high performance across a wide range of human endeavors—from education to sports to coaching to business to relationships. However, Maslow's notion of growth motivation is much broader. Whereas Dweck's theory is about beliefs about ability, and the work is often applied in high-performance settings, Maslow's theory of motivation was not focused on external

metrics of performance and achievement, instead focused on growth of one's full powers as an integrated whole person, regardless of the environment pressures and sometimes *in spite of* environmental conditions. I've argued elsewhere for a personal growth mindset, which I believe is more in line with Maslow's notion of a growth motivation. A personal growth mindset consists of a motivation to engage in a wide variety of activities that will expand your horizons, challenge how you think about yourself and the world, and lead to continuous learning, growth, and understanding of your whole self. There are a lot of people who may have a growth mindset for an activity—i.e., believe that they are capable of change and growth—yet are still highly motivated by neurotic defenses and unhealthy forms of motivation. Not all areas one can grow in are necessarily worth growing in. For instance, a student could apply a growth mindset to putting their full energies into getting the best score on a standardized test of achievement, while thwarting their own best potentialities in a specific domain, such as art, music, history, or math. There are certainly cases in which a personal growth mindset would lead to greater growth of the whole person than simply a belief that intelligence and ability can change. See: Dweck, C. S. (2007). *Mindset: The new psychology of success.* New York: Ballantine Books; Kaufman, S. B. (2015). Is it time for a personal growth mindset? *Scientific American Blogs.* Retrieved from https://blogs.scientificamerican.com/beautiful-minds /is-it-time-for-a-personal-growth-mindset.

30. Wright, R. (2018). *Why Buddhism is true: The science and philosophy of meditation and enlightenment.* New York: Simon & Schuster, p. 3.

31. In particular, modern personality psychologists have observed that people differ from one another in a certain number of predictable ways that form a personality hierarchy. At the top of the hierarchy are just two "metatraits": stability and plasticity. Personality neuroscientist Colin DeYoung defines them as follows:

- Stability: protection of goals, interpretations, and strategies from disruption of impulses.
- Plasticity: exploration and creation of new goals, interpretations, and strategies.

Every organism (including human beings) must have the capacity for both stability and plasticity in order to survive and adapt on its own. Stability allows for staying on task in reasonably predictable situations, but stability is not enough; the organism must also be able to cope with a constantly changing and complex environment. Since perfect prediction is never possible, any fully functioning system must have the capacity for stability as well as plasticity. This is referred to as the "stability-plasticity dilemma" in the field of artificial intelligence; researchers are attempting to build artificial systems that, like humans, can learn and adapt on their own, without the need for constant input from a programmer. Building on these insights, DeYoung proposed a link between cybernetics and personality variation among humans. DeYoung argues that every major source of human personality variation can ultimately be tied to a motivation for either stability or plasticity. Critically, stability and plasticity *depend on* each other in an integrated fashion and work together to enable the cybernetic system to pursue its goals in a constantly complex and changing environment. In a recently published paper in the *Journal of Humanistic Psychol-*

ogy, I tested and confirmed the idea that Maslow's descriptions of self-actualizing people are akin to a finely tuned, optimally functioning cybernetic system. See: DeYoung, C. G., & Weisberg, Y. J. (2018). Cybernetic approaches to personality and social behavior. In K. Deaux & M. Snyder (Eds.), *The Oxford handbook of personality and social psychology* (2nd ed.) (pp. 387–413). New York, NY: Oxford University Press; Kaufman, S. B. (2018). Self-actualizing people in the 21st century: Integration with contemporary theory and research on personality and well-being. *Journal of Humanistic Psychology,* https:/doi.org /10.1177/0022167818809187.

32. Kenrick, D. T., Griskevicius, V., Neuberg, S. L., & Schaller, M. (2010). Renovating the pyramid of needs: Contemporary extensions built upon ancient foundations. *Perspectives on Psychological Science, 5*(3), 292–314.

33. Kashdan, T. B., & Silvia, P. J. (2011). Curiosity and interest: The benefits of thriving on novelty and challenge. In S. J. Lopez & C. R. Snyder (Eds.), *The Oxford handbook of positive psychology* (2nd ed.) (pp. 367–74). New York: Oxford University Press.

34. Kenrick, Griskevicius, Neuberg, & Schaller, Renovating the pyramid of needs, 292–314.

35. Portions of this chapter were adapted from the foreword to: Geher, G., & Wedberg, N. (2019). *Positive Evolutionary Psychology: Darwin's Guide to Living a Richer Life.* New York: Oxford University Press.

36. Colin DeYoung, personal correspondence, December 23, 2017.

37. Buss, D. (2015). *Evolutionary psychology: The new science of the mind* (5th ed.). New York: Psychology Press.

38. Fromm, E. (1955). *The sane society.* New York: Henry Holt, p. 25.

39. Yalom, I. D. (1989). *Love's executioner: & other tales of psychotherapy.* New York: Basic Books.

40. Yalom, I. D. (1980). *Existential psychotherapy.* New York: Basic Books.

41. Rogers, C. R. (1961). *On becoming a person: A therapist's view of psychotherapy.* New York: Houghton Mifflin, p. 186.

42. Rogers, *On becoming a person,* p. 196.

43. Tillich, P. (1952). *The courage to be.* New Haven, CT: Yale University Press.

PART 1. SECURITY

1. Walters, J., & Gardner, H. (1992). The crystallizing experience: Discovering an intellectual gift. In R. S. Albert (Ed.), *Genius & Eminence* (2nd ed.). (pp. 135–56). Tarrytown, NY: Pergamon Press.

2. Unpublished notes from 1962, as quoted in Lowry, R. J. (1973). *A. H. Maslow: An intellectual portrait (The A.J. Maslow series).* Monterey, CA: Brooks/Cole.

3. Sumner, W. G. (1906/2017). *Folkways: A study of the sociological importance of usages, manners, customs, mores, and morals.* CreateSpace Independent Publishing Platform, p. 7.

4. Hoffman, E. (1988). *The right to be human: A biography of Abraham Maslow.* Los Angeles: Tarcher.

5. Maslow, A. H., & Honigmann, J. (ca. 1943). *Northern Blackfoot culture and personality* (Unpublished manuscript; Maslow Papers, M443). Archives of the History of American

Psychology, Cummings Center for the History of Psychology, University of Akron, Akron, OH.

6. Martin Heavy Head [mheavyhead]. (2017, October 21). Abraham Maslow had spent six weeks with Blackfoot People, an experience which he said "shook him to his knees." He was inspired by us. [Tweet]. Retrieved from https://twitter.com/mheavyhead/status /921946655577927680.

7. Hoffman, *The right to be human*, p. 121.

8. Maslow, A. H. (1993/1971). *The farther reaches of human nature*. New York: Penguin Books, p. 218.

9. Blackstock, C. (2011). The emergence of the breath of life theory. *Journal of Social Work Values and Ethics, 8*(1); Kaufman, S. B. (2019). Honoring the wisdom of indigenous people with Richard Katz. *The Psychology Podcast*. Retrieved from https://scottbarrykaufman .com/podcast/honoring-the-wisdom-of-indigenous-peoples-with-richard-katz.

10. Some people have gone further, however, and suggested that Maslow's entire theory of motivation and the pyramid representation of his theory may have been inspired by the First Nations' perspective and the design of the tipi. While I certainly do think Maslow was deeply inspired by his visit, and the general philosophy of life of the indigenous peoples played a part in his thinking, I think it's also important to recognize the many other influences on Maslow's theory, including William Sumner's description of the impelling force of human needs, Kurt Goldstein's research on self-actualization, and the work of Alfred Adler, Harry Harlow, and Karen Horney, among a great many others I'll be covering in this book. What's more, in his 1943 formulation, Maslow put self-actualization at the top of his hierarchy of needs, whereas the First Nations' perspective places self-actualization at the base of the tipi. Most relevant, however, Maslow didn't even represent his hierarchy of needs as a pyramid! Taking this issue seriously, however, I had a chat with the psychologist Richard Katz, who was a personal friend of Maslow's. Katz has spent his career studying indigenous people and does not believe that Maslow's idea for a hierarchy of needs originated solely from his visit among the Blackfoot Indians. Nevertheless, we both agreed that Maslow's visit did have an important impact on his thinking about human nature more generally and that it's very important to honor the wisdom of indigenous peoples. In fact, I believe that Maslow's later writings in life on spirituality and transcendence, and my own revised hierarchy of needs, is more in line with the First Nations' perspective, which includes self-actualization as the foundation for "community actualization" and "cultural perpetuity." In essence, I think we can have an integrated model that respects and acknowledges everyone's contribution. See: Blackstock, The emergence of the breath of life theory; Kaufman, Honoring the wisdom of indigenous people with Richard Katz; Michel, K. L. (2014). Maslow's hierarchy connected to Blackfoot beliefs. *A Digital Native American*. Retrieved from https://lincolnmi chel.wordpress.com/2014/04/19/maslows-hierarchy-connected-to-blackfoot-beliefs.

11. Lowry, *A. H. Maslow: An intellectual portrait*.

12. Taylor, S. (2019). Original influences. *Psychology Today*. Retrieved from https://www .psychologytoday.com/us/blog/out-the-darkness/201903/original-influences.

13. Maslow, A. H. (1938). *Report to the National Research Council*.

14. Lowry, *A. H. Maslow: An intellectual portrait*, p. 20.

15. Lowry, *A. H. Maslow: An intellectual portrait*.

16. Unpublished note, quoted in Lowry, *A. H. Maslow: An intellectual portrait*, p. 17.

CHAPTER 1. SAFETY

1. Pinker, S. (2018). *Enlightenment now: The case for reason, science, humanism, and progress.* New York: Viking.

2. Whippman, R. (2017). Where were we while the pyramid was collapsing? At a yoga class. *Society, 54*(6), 527–529.

3. Whippman, Where were we while the pyramid was collapsing? At a yoga class, p. 528.

4. Bland & DeRobertis, Maslow's unacknowledged contributions to developmental psychology; Hoffman, *The right to be human*.

5. George, L., & Park, C. (2016). Meaning in life as comprehension, purpose, and mattering: Toward integration and new research questions. *Review of General Psychology, 20*(3), 205–220; Martela, F., & Steger, M. F. (2016). The three meanings of meaning in life: Distinguishing coherence, purpose, and significance. *The Journal of Positive Psychology, 11*(5), 531–545.

6. Morgan, J., & Farsides, T. (2009). Measuring meaning in life. *Journal of Happiness Studies, 10*(2), 197–214; Morgan, J., & Farsides, T. (2009). Psychometric evaluation of the meaningful life measure. *Journal of Happiness Studies, 10*(3), 351–366.

7. Martela & Steger, The three meanings of meaning in life, p. 539.

8. George, L. S., & Park, C. L. (2013). Are meaning and purpose distinct? An examination of correlates and predictors. *The Journal of Positive Psychology, 8*(5), 365–375.

9. Hirsh, J. B., Mar, R. A., & Peterson, J. B. (2012). Psychological entropy: A framework for understanding uncertainty-related anxiety. *Psychological Review, 119*(2), 304–320.

10. Clark, A. (2013). Whatever next?: Predictive brains, situated agents, and the future of cognitive science. *Behavioral and Brain Sciences, 36*(3), 181–204.

11. Friston, K. (2009). The free-energy principle: A rough guide to the brain? *Trends in Cognitive Sciences, 13*(7), 293–301; Friston, K. (2010). The free-energy principle: A unified brain theory? *Nature Reviews Neuroscience, 11*, 127–138; Hirsh, Mar, & Peterson, Psychological entropy; Kelso, J. (1995). *Dynamic patterns: The self-organization of brain and behavior.* Cambridge, MA: MIT Press.

12. Kauffman, S. A. (1993). *The origins of order: Self-organization and selection in evolution.* New York: Oxford University Press.

13. McEwen, B. S. (2007). Physiology and neurobiology of stress and adaptation: Central role of the brain. *Physiological Review, 87*(3), 873–904.

14. Bateson, M., & Nettle, D. (2016). The telomere lengthening conundrum—it could be biology. *Aging Cell, 16*(2), 312–319; Fox, N. A., & Shonkoff, J. P. (2011). How persistent fear and anxiety can affect young children's learning, behavior and health. *Early childhood matters*; Nettle, D., et al. (2017). Early-life adversity accelerates cellular ageing and affects adult inflammation: Experimental evidence from the European starling. *Scientific Reports, 7*, 40794; Storoni, M. (2019). *Stress-proof: The ultimate guide to living a stress-free life.* London: Yellow Kite.

15. Watts, A. W. (1951). *The wisdom of insecurity: A message for an age of anxiety.* New York: Vintage Books, p. 77.

16. Paulos, J. A. (2003). *A mathematician plays the stock market.* New York: Routledge.

17. Hirsh, J. B., & Inzlicht, M. (2008). The devil you know: Neuroticism predicts neural response to uncertainty. *Psychological Science, 19*(10), 962–967.

18. Cuijpers, P., et al. (2010). Economic costs of neuroticism: A population-based study. *Archives of General Psychiatry, 67*(10), 1086–1093; Lahey, B. B. (2009). Public health significance of neuroticism. *American Psychologist, 64*(4), 241–256; Tackett, J. L., et al. (2013). Common genetic influences on negative emotionality and a general psychopathology factor in childhood and adolescence. *Journal of Abnormal Psychology, 122*(4), 1142–1153.

19. Schönbrodt, F. D., & Gerstenberg, F. X. R. (2012). An IRT analysis of motive questionnaires: The unified motive scales. *Journal of Research in Personality, 46*(6), 725–742.

20. Fox & Shonkoff, How persistent fear and anxiety can affect young children's learning, behavior and health.

21. Maslow, *Motivation and personality,* p. 66.

22. Nettle, D. (2017). Does hunger contribute to socioeconomic gradients in behavior? *Frontiers in Psychology, 8,* https://doi.org/10.3389/fpsyg.2017.00358.

23. Fessler, D. M. (2002). Pseudoparadoxical impulsivity in restrictive anorexia nervosa: A consequence of the logic of scarcity. *International Journal of Eating Disorders, 31*(4), 376–388; Swanson, D. W., & Dinello, F. A. (1970). Severe obesity as a habituation syndrome: Evidence during a starvation study. *Archives of General Psychiatry, 22*(2), 120–127.

24. Swanson & Dinello, Severe obesity as a habituation syndrome, p. 124.

25. Orquin, J. L., & Kurzban, R. (2016). A meta-analysis of blood glucose effects on human decision making. *Psychological Bulletin, 142*(5), 546–567.

26. Nettle, Does hunger contribute to socioeconomic gradients in behavior?; Orquin & Kurzban, A meta-analysis of blood glucose effects on human decision making.

27. Nettle, Does hunger contribute to socioeconomic gradients in behavior?

28. Fessler, Pseudoparadoxical impulsivity in restrictive anorexia nervosa.

29. Bowlby, J. (1982; originally published in 1969). *Attachment and loss: Vol. 1. Attachment* (2nd ed.). New York: Basic Books; Bowlby, J. (1973). *Attachment and loss: Vol. 2. Separation: Anxiety and anger.* New York: Basic Books; Bowlby, J. (1980). *Attachment and loss: Vol. 3. Loss: Sadness and depression.* New York: Basic Books.

30. Fraley, R. C. (2019). Attachment in adulthood: Recent developments, emerging debates, and future directions. *Annual Review of Psychology, 70,* 401–422; Fraley, R. C., & Shaver, P. R. (2008). Attachment theory and its place in contemporary personality research. In O. P. John, R. W. Robins, & L. A. Pervin (Eds.), *Handbook of personality: Theory and research* (3rd ed.) (pp. 518–541). New York: Guilford Press.

31. Ainsworth, M. D. S., Blehar, M. C., Waters, E., & Wall, S. N. (1978). *Patterns of attachment.* Hillsdale, NJ: Erlbaum.

32. Kaufman, S. B. (2017). The latest science of attachment with R. Chris Fraley. *The Psychology Podcast.* Retrieved from https://scottbarrykaufman.com/podcast/latest-science-attachment-r-chris-fraley.

33. Bartholomew, K., & Horowitz, L. M. (1991). Attachment styles among young adults: A

test of the four-category model. *Journal of Personality and Social Psychology, 61*(2), 226–244; Hazan, C., & Shaver, P. R. (1987). Romantic love conceptualized as an attachment process. *Journal of Personality and Social Psychology, 52*(3), 511–524.

34. Fraley, R. C., Hudson, N. W., Heffernan, M. E., & Segal, N. (2015). Are adult attachment styles categorical or dimensional? A taxometric analysis of general and relationship-specific attachment orientations. *Journal of Personality and Social Psychology, 109*(2), 354–368; Fraley, R. C., & Spieker, S. J. (2003). Are infant attachment patterns continuously or categorically distributed? A taxometric analysis of strange situation behavior. *Developmental Psychology, 39*(3), 387–404.

35. Edenfield, J. L., Adams, K. S., & Briihl, D. S. (2012). Relationship maintenance strategy use by romantic attachment style. *North American Journal of Psychology, 14,* 149–162; Noftle, E. E., & Shaver, P. R. (2006). Attachment dimensions and the big five personality traits: Associations and comparative ability to predict relationship quality. *Journal of Research in Personality, 40*(2), 179–208; Mikulincer, M., & Shaver, P. R. (2005). Mental representations of attachment security: Theoretical foundation for a positive social psychology. In M. W. Baldwin (Ed.), *Interpersonal cognition* (pp. 233–66). New York: Guilford Press; Shaver, P. R., Mikulincer, M., Gross, J. T., Stern, J. A., & Cassidy, J. (2016). A lifespan perspective on attachment and care for others: Empathy, altruism, and prosocial behavior. In J. Cassidy & P. R. Shaver (Eds.), *Handbook of attachment: Theory, research, and clinical applications* (3rd ed.) (pp. 878–916). New York: Guilford Press; Mikulincer, M., & Shaver, P. R. (2016). *Attachment in adulthood: Structure, dynamics, and change* (2nd ed.). New York: Guilford Press; Mikulincer, M., Shaver, P. R., Gillath, O., & Nitzberg, R. A. (2005). Attachment, caregiving, and altruism: Boosting attachment security increases compassion and helping. *Journal of Personality and Social Psychology, 89*(5), 817–839.

36. Mikulincer & Shaver, *Attachment in adulthood.*

37. Gouin, J-P., et al. (2009). Attachment avoidance predicts inflammatory responses to marital conflict. *Brain, Behavior, and Immunity, 23*(7), 898–904; Pietromonaco, P. R., & Beck, L. A. (2019). Adult attachment and physical health. *Current Opinion in Psychology,* 25, 115–120; Plotsky, P. M., et al. (2005). Long-term consequences of neonatal rearing on central corticotropin-releasing factor systems in adult male rat offspring, *Neuropsychopharmacology, 30*(12), 2192–2204; Robles, T. F., Brooks, K. P., Kane, H. S., & Schetter, C. D. (2013). Attachment, skin deep? Relationships between adult attachment and skin barrier recovery. *International Journal of Psychophysiology, 88*(3), 241–252.

38. Collins, N. L. (1996). Working models of attachment: Implications for explanation, emotion, and behavior. *Journal of Personality and Social Psychology, 71*(4), 810–832.

39. Vicary, A. M., & Fraley, R. C. (2007). Choose your own adventure: Attachment dynamics in a simulated relationship. *Personality and Social Psychology Bulletin, 33*(9), 1279–1291.

40. Wiebe, S. A., & Johnson, S. M. (2017). Creating relationships that foster resilience in Emotionally Focused Therapy. *Current Opinion in Psychology, 13,* 65–69.

41. Simpson, J. A., & Rholes, W. S. (2017). Adult attachment, stress, and romantic relationships. *Current Opinion in Psychology, 13,* 19–24.

42. Simpson & Rholes, Adult attachment, stress, and romantic relationships.

43. Simpson & Rholes, Adult attachment, stress, and romantic relationships.

44. Groh, A. M., et al. (2014). The significance of attachment security for children's social competence with peers: A meta-analytic study. *Attachment & Human Development, 16*(2), 103–136; Pinquart, M., Feussner, C., & Ahnert, L. (2013). Meta-analytic evidence for stability in attachments from infancy to early adulthood. *Attachment & Human Development, 15*(2), 189–218.

45. Carnelley, K. B., Otway, L. J., & Rowe, A. C. (2015). The effects of attachment priming on depressed and anxious mood. *Clinical Psychological Science, 4*(3), 433–450.

46. Bakermans-Kranenburg, M. J., van IJzendoon, M. H., & Juffer, F. (2003). Less is more: Meta-analyses of sensitivity and attachment interventions in early childhood. *Psychological Bulletin, 129*(2), 195–215; Bakermans-Kranenburg, M. J., Van IJzendoorn, M. H., & Juffer, F. (2005). Disorganized infant attachment and preventive interventions: A review and meta-analysis. *Infant Mental Health Journal, 26*(3), 191–216; Bernard, K., et al. (2012). Enhancing attachment organization among maltreated children: Results of a randomized clinical trial. *Child Development, 83*(2), 623–636; van den Boom, D. C. (1994). The influence of temperament and mothering on attachment and exploration: An experimental manipulation of sensitive responsiveness among lower-class mothers with irritable infants. *Child Development, 65*(5), 1457–1477.

47. Belsky, J., & Pluess, M. (2013). Beyond risk, resilience, and dysregulation: Phenotypic plasticity and human development. *Development and Psychopathology, 25*(4, part 2), 1243–1261.

48. Influenced by Adler's perspective—after informally studying with him in the 1930s—Maslow wrote a brief unpublished essay in 1957 called "Limits, Controls, and the Safety Need in Children." In the essay, Maslow points out that young children *need* external controls and can even feel "contempt, scorn, and disgust for their weak parents." He argues that young children *seek* firm limits to avoid what Kurt Goldstein—the German-born American psychiatrist who coined the term "self-actualization"—referred to as the "catastrophic anxiety" of being on one's own. See: Maslow, Limits, controls, and the safety need in children. In Hoffman, *Future visions*, pp. 45–46.

49. Maslow, Limits, controls, and the safety need in children. In Hoffman, *Future visions*, p. 46.

50. Fraley, R. C., & Roisman, G. I. (2015). Do early caregiving experiences leave an enduring or transient mark on developmental adaptation? *Current Opinion in Psychology, 1*, 101–106; Simpson, J. A., Collins, W. A., Farrell, A. K., & Raby, K. L. (2015). Attachment and relationships across time: An organizational-developmental perspective. In V. Zayas & C. Hazan (Eds.), *Bases of Adult Attachment* (pp. 61–78). New York: Springer.

51. Kaufman, The latest science of attachment with R. Chris Fraley.

52. Plomin, R. (2018). *Blueprint: How DNA makes us who we are.* Cambridge, MA: MIT Press.

53. Bowlby, J. (1944). Forty-four juvenile thieves: Their characters and home life. *The International Journal of Psychoanalysis, 25*, 19–53.

54. Finkelhor, D., Ormrod, R., Turner, H., & Hamby, S. L. (2005). The victimization of children and youth: A comprehensive, national survey. *Child Maltreatment, 10*(1), 5–25; Fox & Shonkoff, How persistent fear and anxiety can affect young children's learning, behavior and health.

55. Belsky, J., Steinberg, L., Houts, R. M., Halpern-Felsher, B. L., & NICH Early Child Care Research Network. (2010). The development of reproductive strategy in females: Early maternal harshness → earlier menarche → increased sexual risk taking. *Developmental Psychology, 46*(1), 120–128; Hartman, S., Li, Z., Nettle, D., & Belsky, J. (2017). External-environmental and internal-health early predictors of adolescent development. *Development and Psychopathology, 29*(5), 1839–1849; Nettle, N., Frankenhuis, W. E., & Rickard, I. J. (2013). The evolution of predictive adaptive responses in human life history. *Proceedings of the Royal Society B*, 280, 1766.

56. Takesian, A. E., & Hensch, T. K. (2013). Balancing plasticity/stability across brain development. *Progress in Brain Research, 207*, 3–34.

57. Teicher, M. H., & Samson, J. A. (2016). Annual research review: Enduring neurobiological effects of childhood abuse and neglect. *Journal of Child Psychology and Psychiatry, 57*(3), 241–266; Teicher, M. H., Samson, J. A., Anderson, C. M., & Ohashi, K. (2016). The effects of childhood maltreatment on brain structure, function and connectivity. *Nature Reviews Neuroscience, 17*(10), 652–656.

58. Teicher, Samson, Anderson, & Ohashi, The effects of childhood maltreatment on brain structure, function and connectivity.

59. Teicher, Samson, Anderson, & Ohashi, The effects of childhood maltreatment on brain structure, function and connectivity.

60. Jonason, P. K., Icho, A., & Ireland, K. (2016). Resources, harshness, and unpredictability: The socioeconomic conditions associated with the dark triad traits. *Evolutionary Psychology*, p. 8.

61. Tiecher, M. H., & Samson, J. A. (2013). Childhood maltreatment and psychopathology: A case for ecophenotypic variants as clinically and neurobiologically distinct subtypes. *American Journal of Psychiatry, 170*(10), 1114–1133; Teicher, Samson, Anderson, & Ohashi, The effects of childhood maltreatment on brain structure, function and connectivity.

62. Fox & Shonkoff, How persistent fear and anxiety can affect young children's learning, behavior and health.

63. Fox & Shonkoff, How persistent fear and anxiety can affect young children's learning, behavior and health.

64. Carew, M. B., & Rudy, J. W. (1991). Multiple functions of context during conditioning: A developmental analysis. *Developmental Psychobiology, 24*(3), 191–209; Kim, J. H., & Richardson, R. (2008). The effect of temporary amygdala inactivation on extinction and reextinction of fear in the developing rat: Unlearning as a potential mechanism for extinction early in development. *Journal of Neuroscience, 28*(6), 1282–1290; Maier, S. F., & Seligman, M. E. (2016). Learned helplessness at fifty: Insights from neuroscience. *Psychological Review, 123*(4), 349–367; Teicher, Samson, Anderson, & Ohashi, The effects of childhood maltreatment on brain structure, function and connectivity; Thompson, J. V., Sullivan, R. M., & Wilson, D. A. (2008). Developmental emergence of fear learning corresponds with changes in amygdala synaptic plasticity. *Brain Research, 1200*, 58–65.

65. Maier, S. F., & Seligman, M. E. (1976). Learned helplessness: Theory and evidence. *Journal of Experimental Psychology: General, 105*(1), 3–46.

66. Maier & Seligman, Learned helplessness at fifty.

67. Bolland, J. M. (2003). Hopelessness and risk behaviour among adolescents living in high-poverty inner-city neighborhoods. *Journal of Adolescence, 26*(2), 145–58; Brezina, T., Tekin, E., & Topalli, V. (2009). "Might not be a tomorrow": A multimethods approach to anticipated early death and youth crime. *Criminology, 47*(4), 1091–1129; Haushofer, J., & Fehr, E. (2014). On the psychology of poverty. *Science, 344*(6186), 862–867.

68. Infurna, F. J., Gerstorf, D., Ram, N., Schupp, J., & Wagner, G. G. (2011). Long-term antecedents and outcomes of perceived control. *Psychology and Aging, 26*(3), 559–575.

69. Pepper, G. V., & Nettle, D. (2014). Out of control mortality matters: The effect of perceived uncontrollable mortality risk on a health-related decision. *PeerJ, 2,* e459.

70. Nettle, D., Pepper, G. V., Jobling, R., & Schroeder, K. B. (2014). Being there: A brief visit to a neighbourhood induces the social attitudes of that neighbourhood. *PeerJ, 2,* e236.

71. Nettle, Pepper, Jobling, & Schroeder, Being there: A brief visit to a neighbourhood induces the social attitudes of that neighbourhood.

72. The social attitudes and levels of trust in a community have real implications for understanding the cultural evolution of crime and punishment. Study findings suggest there are multiple, simultaneous, mutually reinforcing mechanisms that can explain how socially aversive behaviors—for example, generally cheating—can become widespread. In a culture in which low levels of cooperation and minimal punishment are the norm, noncooperative strategies may indeed be more adaptive, especially under extreme poverty and harsh environmental conditions. See: Cialdini, R. B., Reno, R. R., & Kallgren, C. A. (1990). A focus theory of normative conduct: Recycling the concept of norms to reduce littering in public places. *Journal of Personality and Social Psychology, 58*(6), 1015–1126; Traxler, C., & Winter, J. (2012). Survey evidence on conditional norm enforcement. *European Journal of Political Economy, 28*(3), 390–398; Wilson, D. S., & Csikszentmihalyi, M. (2007). Health and the ecology of altruism. In S. G. Post (Ed.), *Altruism and health: Perspectives from empirical research.* New York: Oxford University Press, pp. 314–331.

73. Costello, E. J., Compton, S. N., Keeler, G., & Angold, A. (2003). Relationships between poverty and psychopathology: A natural experiment. *JAMA, 290*(15), 2023–2029.

74. Costello, Relationships between poverty and psychopathology, p. 2028.

75. Maslow, *Motivation and personality.*

76. Ellis, B. J., Bianchi, J., Griskevicius, V., & Frankenhuis, W. E. (2017). Beyond risk and protective factors: An adaptation-based approach to resilience. *Perspectives on Psychological Science, 12*(4), 561–587, https://doi.org/10.1177/1745691617693054.

77. Sternberg, R. J. (1997). *Successful intelligence: How practical and creative intelligence determine success in life.* New York: Plume; Sternberg, R. J. (2014). The development of adaptive competence: Why cultural psychology is necessary and not just nice. *Developmental Review, 34*(3), 208–224.

78. Sternberg, The development of adaptive competence, p. 209.

79. Ellis, Bianchi, Griskevicius, & Frankenhuis, Beyond risk and protective factors, p. 561.

80. Ellis, Bianchi, Griskevicius, & Frankenhuis, Beyond risk and protective factors.

81. Kraus, M. W., Piff, P. K., Mendoza-Denton, R., Rheinschmidt, M. L., & Keltner, D. (2012). Social class, solipsism, and contextualism: How the rich are different from the poor. *Psychological Review, 119*(3), 546–572.

82. Mayer, J. D., Salovey, P., & Caruso, D. R. (2002). *Manual for the MSCEIT (Mayer-Salovey-Caruso Emotional Intelligence Test)*. Toronto: Multi-Health Systems.

83. Kaufman, S. B. (2014). The creative gifts of ADHD. *Scientific American Blogs*. Retrieved from https://blogs.scientificamerican.com/beautiful-minds/the-creative-gifts-of-adhd.

84. Hatt, B. (2007). Street smarts vs. book smarts: The figured world of smartness in the lives of marginalized, urban youth. *The Urban Review, 39*(2), 145–166.

85. Nakkula, M. (2013). A crooked path to success. *Phi Delta Kappan, 94*(6), 60–63, https://doi.org/10.1177/003172171309400615.

86. Fielding, M. (2001). Students as radical agents of change. *Journal of Educational Change, 2*(2), 123–141; Toshalis, E., & Nakkula, M. J. (2012). *Motivation, engagement, and student voice: The students at the center series*. Boston: Jobs for the Future.

87. van Gelder, J-L., Hershfield, H. E., & Nordgren, L. F. (2013). Vividness of the future self predicts delinquency. *Psychological Science, 24*(6), 974–980.

88. Cohen, G. L., Garcia, J., Apfel, N., & Master, A. (2006). Reducing the racial achievement gap: A social-psychological intervention. *Science, 313*(5791), 1307–1310; Cohen, G. L., Garcia, J., Purdie-Vaughns, V., Apfel, N., & Brzustoski, P. (2009). Recursive processes in self-affirmation: Intervening to close the minority achievement gap. *Science, 324*(5925), 400–403.

89. Oyserman, D., Bybee, D., & Terry, K. (2006). Possible selves and academic outcomes: How and when possible selves impel action. *Journal of Personality and Social Psychology, 91*(1), 188–204; Oyserman, D., Terry, K., & Bybee, D. (2002). A possible selves intervention to enhance school involvement. *Journal of Adolescence, 25*, 313–326.

90. Grant, A. (2018). What straight-A students get wrong. *The New York Times*. Retrieved from https://www.nytimes.com/2018/12/08/opinion/college-gpa-career-success.html.

91. Seale, C. (2018). Today's disruptors can be tomorrow's innovators. *thinkLaw*. Retrieved from https://www.thinklaw.us/todays-disruptors-tomorrows-innovators; Kaufman, S. B., (2019). Closing the critical thinking gap. *The Psychology Podcast*. Retrieved from https://scottbarrykaufman.com/podcast/closing-the-critical-thinking-gap-with-colin-seale.

CHAPTER 2. CONNECTION

1. Hoffman, *The right to be human*, p. 50.

2. Hoffman, *The right to be human*, p. 49.

3. Hoffman, *The right to be human*, p. 51.

4. Covin, R. (2011). *The need to be liked*. Self-published; Leary, M. R., & Guadagno, J. (2011). The sociometer, self-esteem, and the regulation of interpersonal behavior. In K. D. Vohs & R. F. Baumeister (Eds.), *Handbook of self-regulation: Research, theory, and applications* (pp. 339–354). New York: Guilford Press.

5. Baumeister, R. F., & Leary, M. R. (1995). The need to belong: Desire for interpersonal attachments as a fundamental human motivation. *Psychological Bulletin, 117*(3), 497–529.

6. Leary, M. R., Koch, E. J., & Hechenbleikner, N. R. (2001). Emotional responses to interpersonal rejection. In M. R. Leary (Ed.), *Interpersonal rejection* (pp. 145–166). New York: Oxford University Press.

7. Cacioppo, J. T., & Patrick, W. (2009). *Loneliness: Human nature and the need for social connection*. New York: W. W. Norton.

8. Cacioppo, J. T., et al. (2002). Do lonely days invade the nights? Potential social modulation of sleep efficiency. *Psychological Science, 13*(4), 384–387; Kurina, L. M., et al. (2011). Loneliness is associated with sleep fragmentation in a communal society. *Sleep, 34*(11), 1519–1526; Luo, Y., Hawkley, L. C., Waite, L. J., & Cacioppo, J. T. (2012). Loneliness, health, and mortality in old age: A national longitudinal study. *Social Science & Medicine, 74*(6), 907–914; Quora contributor. (2017). Loneliness might be a bigger health risk than smoking or obesity. *Forbes*. Retrieved from https://www.forbes.com/sites/quora/2017/01/18/loneliness-might-be-a-bigger-health-risk-than-smoking-or-obesity/amp.

9. Scelfo, J. (2015). Suicide on campus and the pressure of perfection. *The New York Times*. Retrieved from https://www.nytimes.com/2015/08/02/education/edlife/stress-social-media-and-suicide-on-campus.html; Firger, J. (2016). Suicide rate has increased 24 percent since 1999 in the U.S., says CDC. *Newsweek*. Retrieved from http://www.newsweek.com/us-suicide-rates-cdc-increase-24-percent-cdc-1999-2014-451606; Routledge, C. (2018). Suicides have increased. Is there an existential crisis? *The New York Times*. Retrieved from https://www.nytimes.com/2018/06/23/opinion/sunday/suicide-rate-existential-crisis.html.

10. Sherif, M., Harvey, O. J., White, B. J., Hood, W. R., & Sherif, C. W. (1961). *The Robbers Cave Experiment: Intergroup conflict and cooperation*. Norman, OK: Institute of Group Relations, the University of Oklahoma.

11. McCauley, C. R., & Segal, M. E. (1987). Social psychology of terrorist groups. In C. Hendrick (Ed.), *Group processes and intergroup relations: Review of personality and social psychology, 9*, 231–256. Thousand Oaks, CA: Sage Publications.

12. Rabbie, J. M., & Horwitz, M. (1969). Arousal of ingroup-outgroup bias by a chance win or loss. *Journal of Personality and Social Psychology, 13*(3), 269–277.

13. Yang, X., & Dunham, Y. (2019). Minimal but meaningful: Probing the limits of randomly assigned social identities. *Journal of Experimental Child Psychology, 185*, 19–34; Kaufman, S. B. (2019). In-group favoritism is difficult to change, even when the social groups are meaningless. *Scientific American Blogs*. Retrieved from https://blogs.scientificamerican.com/beautiful-minds/in-group-favoritism-is-difficult-to-change-even-when-the-social-groups-are-meaningless.

14. Leary, M. R., Kelly, K. M., Cottrell, C. A., & Schreindorfer, L. S. (2013). Construct validity of the need to belong scale: Mapping the nomological network. *Journal of Personality Assessment, 95*(6), 610–624.

15. Leary, Kelly, Cottrell, & Schreindorfer, Construct validity of the need to belong scale.

16. Mellor, D., Stokes, M., Firth, L., Hayashi, Y., & Cummins, R. (2008). Need for belonging, relationship satisfaction, loneliness, and life satisfaction. *Personality and Individual Differences, 45*(3), 213–218.

17. Schöonbrodt , F. D., & Gerstenberg, F. X. R. (2012). An IRT analysis of motive questionnaires: The Unified Motive Scales. *Journal of Research in Personality, 46*, 725–742.

18. Dutton, J., & Heaphy, E. D. (2003). The power of high-quality connections. In K. S. Cameron, J. E. Dutton, & R. E. Quinn (Eds.), *Positive organizational scholarship* (pp. 263–279). San Francisco: Berrett-Koehler Publishers, p. 264.

19. Dutton & Heaphy, The power of high-quality connections. In Cameron, Dutton, & Quinn, *Positive organizational scholarship*, p. 265.

20. Rogers, C. R. (1951). *Client-centered therapy: Its current practice, implications, and theory.* Boston: Houghton-Mifflin.

21. Sandelands, L. E. (2003). *Thinking about social life.* Lanham, MD: University Press of America, p. 250.

22. Dutton & Heaphy, The power of high-quality connections. In Cameron, Dutton, & Quinn, *Positive organizational scholarship*, p. 267.

23. Dutton & Heaphy, The power of high-quality connections. In Cameron, Dutton, & Quinn, *Positive organizational scholarship*, p. 266.

24. Cummings, L. L., & Bromiley, P. (1996). The Organizational Trust Inventory (OTI): Development and validation. In R. M. Kramer & T. R. Tyler (Eds.), *Trust in organization: Frontiers of theory and research* (pp. 302–30). Thousand Oaks, CA: Sage Publications; Diener, E., Oishi, S., & Lucas, R. E. (2003). Personality, culture, and subjective well-being: Emotional and cognitive evaluations of life. *Annual Review of Psychology, 54,* 403–425.

25. Algoe, S. B. (2019). Positive interpersonal processes. *Current Directions in Psychological Science, 28*(2), 183–188, doi: 10.1177/0963721419827272; Pawelski, S. P., & Pawleski, J. O. (2018). *Happy together: Using the science of positive psychology to build love that lasts.* New York: TarcherPerigee.

26. Diener, E., & Seligman, M. E. P. (2002). Very happy people. *Psychological Science, 13*(1), 81–84.

27. Compton, W. C., & Hoffman, E. (2019). *Positive psychology: The science of happiness and flourishing* (3rd ed.). Thousand Oaks, CA: Sage Publications.

28. Fredrickson, B.L. (2013). *Love 2.0: Finding happiness and health in moments of connection.* New York: Plume.

29. Hasson, U., Ghazanfar, A. A., Galantucci, B., Garrod, S., Keysers, C. (2012). Brain-to-brain coupling: A mechanism for creating and sharing a social world. *Trends in Cognitive Science, 16*(2), 114–121; Stephens, G. J., Silbert, L. J., & Hasson, U. (2010). Speaker-listener neural coupling underlies successful communication. *PNAS, 107*(32), 14425–14430; Zaki, J. (2019). *The war for kindness: Building empathy in a fractured world.* New York: Crown.

30. Fredrickson, *Love 2.0*, p. 8.

31. Depue, R. A., & Morrone-Strupinsky, J. V. (2005). A neurobehavioral model of affiliative bonding: Implications for conceptualizing a human trait of affiliation. *Behavioral and Brain Sciences, 28*(3), 313–350.

32. Panksepp, J., Siviy, S. M., & Normansell, L. A. (1985). Brain opioids and social emotions. In M. Reite & T. Field (Eds.), *The psychobiology of attachment and separation* (pp. 3–49). New York: Academic Press.

33. Panksepp, Brain opioids and social emotions, pp. 3-49.

34. Bartz, J. A., Zaki, J., Bolger, N., & Ochsner, K. N. (2011). Social effects of oxytocin in humans: Context and person matter. *Trends in Cognitive Sciences, 15*(7), 301–09; Donaldson, Z. R., & Young, L. J. (2008). Oxytocin, vasopressin, and the neurogenetics of sociality. *Science, 322*(5903), 900–904.

35. Guastella, A. J., & MacLeod, C. (2012). A critical review of the influence of oxytocin nasal spray on social cognition in humans: Evidence and future directions. *Hormones and Behavior, 61*(3), 410–418; Kosfeld, M., Heinrichs, M., Zak, P. J., Fischbacher, U., & Fehr, E. (2005). Oxytocin increases trust in humans. *Nature, 435,* 673–676.

36. It's still an open research question the extent to which interventions such as intranasal oxytocin administration produce significant effects on behavior. In fact, one recent randomized, double-blind, placebo-controlled, between-subjects study found no main effects of oxytocin and vasopressin on a host of social outcomes. See: Tabak, B.A., et al. (2019). Null results of oxytocin and vasopressin administration across a range of social cognitive and behavioral paradigms: Evidence from a randomized controlled trial. *Psychoneuroendocrinology, 107,* 124–132.

37. Debiec, J. (2005). Peptides of love and fear: Vasopressin and oxytocin modulate the integration of information in the amygdala. *BioEssays, 27*(9), 869–873; Kirsch, P., et al. (2005). Oxytocin modulates neural circuitry for social cognition and fear in humans. *Journal of Neuroscience, 25*(49), 11489–93.

38. Bartz, Zaki, Bolger, & Ochsner, Social effects of oxytocin in humans; Kemp, A. H., & Guastella, A. J. (2011). The role of oxytocin in human affect: A novel hypothesis. *Current Directions in Psychological Science, 20*(4), 222–231.

39. De Dreu, C. K., & Kret, M. E. (2016). Oxytocin conditions intergroup relations through upregulated in-group empathy, cooperation, conformity, and defense. *Biological Psychiatry, 79*(3), 165–173.

40. Declerck, C. H., Boone, C., & Kiyonari, T. (2010). Oxytocin and cooperation under conditions of uncertainty: The modulating role of incentives and social information. *Hormones and Behavior, 57*(3), 368–374; De Dreue, C. K., et al. (2010). The neuropeptide oxytocin regulates parochial altruism in intergroup conflict among humans. *Science, 328*(5984), 1408–1411; Mikolajczak, M., Pinon, N., Lane, A., de Timary, P., & Luminet, O. (2010). Oxytocin not only increases trust when money is at stake, but also when confidential information is in the balance. *Biological Psychology, 85*(1), 182–184; Stallen, M., De Dreu, C. K., Shalvi, S., Smidts, A., & Sanfey, A. G. (2012). The herding hormone: Oxytocin stimulates in-group conformity. *Psychological Science, 23*(11), 1288–1292.

41. Stallen, De Dreue, Shalvi, Smidts, & Sanfey, The herding hormone.

42. De Dreu & Kret, Oxytocin conditions intergroup relations through upregulated in-group empathy, cooperation, conformity, and defense; Stallen, De Dreu, Shalvi, Smidts, & Sanfey, The herding hormone.

43. Kok, B. E., & Fredrickson, B. L. (2011). Upward spirals of the heart: Autonomic flexibility, as indexed by vagal tone, reciprocally and prospectively predicts positive emotions and social connectedness. *Biological Psychology, 85*(3), 432–436.

44. Knowledge Networks and Insight Policy Research. (2010). *Loneliness among older adults: A national survey of adults 45+.* Retrieved from https://assets.aarp.org/rgcenter/general

/loneliness_2010.pdf; Wood, J. (2018). Loneliness epidemic growing into biggest threat to public health. *PsychCentral.* Retrieved from https://psychcentral.com/news/2017/08 /06/loneliness-epidemic-growing-into-biggest-threat-to-public-health/124226.html.

45. Cacioppo & Patrick, *Loneliness,* p. 5.

46. Wood, Loneliness epidemic growing into biggest threat to public health.

47. Hawkley, L. C., & Cacioppo, J. T. (2010). Loneliness matters: A theoretical and empirical review of consequences and mechanisms. *Annals of Behavioral Medicine, 40*(2), 218–227.

48. Valtorta, N. K., Kanaan, M., Gilbody, S., Ronzi, S., & Hanratty, B. (2016). Loneliness and social isolation as risk factors for coronary heart disease and stroke: Systematic review and meta-analysis of longitudinal observational studies. *Heart, 102*(13), 1009–1016; Storrs, C. (2016). People who are alone and lonely are at greater risk of heart disease. *CNN.* Retrieved from http://www.cnn.com/2016/04/20/health/can-loneliness -lead-to-heart-disease/index.html.

49. Luo, Hawkley, Waite, & Cacioppo, Loneliness, health, and mortality in old age.

50. Holt-Lunstad, J., Smith, T. B., Baker, M., Harris, T., & Stephenson, D. (2015). Loneliness and social isolation as risk factors for mortality: A meta-analytic review. *Perspectives on Psychological Science, 10*(2), 227–237; Worland, J. (2015). Why loneliness may be the next big public-health issue. *Time.* Retrieved from http://time.com/3747784/loneliness -mortality.

51. Holt-Lunstad, J., Smith, T. B., & Layton, J. B. (2010). Social relationships and mortality risk: A meta-analytic review. *PLOS Medicine, 7*(7): e1000316, https://doi.org/10.1371 /journal.pmed.1000316.

52. Braudy, L. (1997). *The frenzy of renown: Fame and its history.* New York: Vintage Books.

53. Roberts, John Cacioppo, who studied effects of loneliness, is dead at 66.

54. Levine, N. (2016). Stephen Fry reveals he attempted suicide after interviewing a homophobic Uganda politician. *NME.* Retrieved from http://www.nme.com/news/tv /stephen-fry-reveals-he-attempted-suicide-after-int-884674.

55. Fry, S. (2013). Only the lonely. *Stephen Fry.* Retrieved from http://www.stephenfry .com/2013/06/only-the-lonely.

56. Emma Seppälä, personal communication, July 1, 2016.

57. Emma Seppälä, personal communication, July 1, 2016.

58. Biswas-Diener, R., & Diener, E. (2006). The subjective well-being of the homeless, and lessons for happiness. *Social Indicators Research, 76*(2), 185–205.

59. Brown, K. W., & Kasser, T. (2005). Are psychological and ecological well-being compatible? The role of values, mindfulness, and lifestyle. *Social Indicators Research, 74*(2), 349–368; Jacob, J. C., & Brinkerhoff, M. B. (1999). Mindfulness and subjective well-being in the sustainability movement: A further elaboration of multiple discrepancies theory. *Social Indicators Research, 46*(3), 341–368.

60. Kasser, T., Ryan, R. M., Couchman, C. E., & Sheldon, K. M. (2004). Materialistic values: Their causes and consequences. In T. Kasser & A. D. Kanner (Eds.), *Psychology and consumer culture: The struggle for a good life in a materialistic world* (pp. 11–28). Washington, DC: American Psychological Association.

61. Hanniball, K. B., Aknin, L. B., & Wiwad, D. (2018). Spending money well. In D. S. Dunn (Ed.), *Positive psychology: Established and emerging issues* (pp. 61–79). New York: Routledge.

62. Kahneman, D., Krueger, A. B., Schkade, D., Schwarz, N., & Stone, A. A. (2006). Would you be happier if you were richer? A focusing illusion. *Science, 312*(5782), 1908–1910.

63. Piff, P. K., Kraus, M. W., Côté, S., Cheng, B. H., & Keltner, D. (2010). Having less, giving more: The influence of social class on prosocial behavior. *Journal of Personality and Social Psychology, 99*(5), 771–784.

64. Hanniball, Aknin, & Wiwad, Spending money well. In Dunn, *Positive psychology*; Piff, Kraus, Côté, Cheng, & Keltner, Having less, giving more.

65. Niemiec, C. P., Ryan, R. M., & Deci, E. L. (2009). The path taken: Consequences of attaining intrinsic and extrinsic aspirations in post-college life. *Journal of Research in Personality, 73*(3), 291–306.

66. Quoidbach, J., Dunn, E. W., Petrides, K. V., & Mikolajczak, M. (2010). Money giveth, money taketh away: The dual effect of wealth on happiness. *Psychological Science, 21*(6), 759–763.

67. Hanniball, Aknin, & Wiwad, Spending money well. In Dunn, *Positive psychology*.

68. Whillans, A. V., Dunn, E. W., Smeets, P., Bekkers, R., & Norton, M. I. (2017). Buying time promotes happiness. *PNAS, 114*(32), 8523–8527.

69. Van Boven, L., & Gilovich, T. (2003). To do or to have? That is the question. *Journal of Personality and Social Psychology, 85*(6), 1193–1202.

70. Mogilner, C. (2010). The pursuit of happiness: Time, money, and social connection. *Psychological Science, 21*(9), 1348–1354.

71. Powdthavee, N. (2010). *The happiness equation: The surprising economics of our most valuable asset.* London: Icon Books.

72. Boyce, C. J., & Wood, A. M. (2011). Personality and marginal unity of income: Personality interacts with increases in household income to determine life satisfaction. *Journal of Economic Behavior & Organization, 78*(1–2), 183–191.

73. Park, A. (2019). I'm a disabled teenager, and social media is my lifeline. *The New York Times.* Retrieved from https://www.nytimes.com/2019/06/05/learning/im-a-disabled-teenager-and-social-media-is-my-lifeline.html.

74. Utz, S., Jonas, K. J., & Tonkens, E. (2012). Effects of passion for massively multiplayer online role-playing games on interpersonal relationships. *Journal of Media Psychology: Theories, Methods, and Applications, 24*(2), 77–86.

75. Szalavitz, M. (2013). More satisfaction, less divorce for people who meet spouses online. *Time.* Retrieved from http://healthland.time.com/2013/06/03/more-satisfaction-less-divorce-for-people-who-meet-spouses-online.

76. Kross, E., et al. (2013). Facebook use predicts declines in subjective well-being in young adults. *PLOS One, 8*(8): e69841, https://doi.org/10.1371/journal.pone.0069841.

77. Emma Seppälä, personal correspondence, July 1, 2016.

78. Buettner, D. (2017). *The blue zones solution: Eating and living like the world's healthiest people.* Washington, DC: National Geographic; Buettner, D. (2012). The island where people forget to die. *The New York Times.* Retrieved from http://www.nytimes.com/2012/10/28/magazine/the-island-where-people-forget-to-die.html.

79. Buettner, The island where people forget to die.

80. Emma Seppälä, personal communication, July 1, 2016.

81. Lavigne, G. L., Vallerand, R. J., & Crevier-Braud, L. (2011). The fundamental need to belong: On the distinction between growth and deficit-reduction orientations. *Personality and Social Psychology Bulletin, 37*(9), 1185–1201.

CHAPTER 3. SELF-ESTEEM

1. Hoffman, *The right to be human.*

2. As quoted in Hoffman, *The right to be human,* p. 61.

3. Maslow, A. H. (1942). Self-esteem (dominance-feeling) and sexuality in women. *The Journal of Social Psychology, 16,* 259–294, p. 282.

4. Friedan, B. (1963). *The feminine mystique.* New York: W. W. Norton.

5. Hoffman, *The right to be human.*

6. Hoffman, *The right to be human.*

7. Hoffman, *The right to be human.*

8. Hoffman, *The right to be human.*

9. Maslow, A. H. (1937). Dominance-feeling, behavior, and status. *Psychological Review, 44*(5), 404–429.

10. Maslow, Dominance-feeling, behavior, and status.

11. Maslow, *Motivation and personality,* p. 13.

12. Baumeister, R. F., Campbell, J. D., Krueger, J. I., Vohs, K. D. (2003). Does high self-esteem cause better performance, interpersonal success, happiness, or healthier lifestyles? *Psychological Science in the Public Interest, 4*(1), 1–44; Diener, E., & Diener, M. (1995). Cross-cultural correlates of life satisfaction and self-esteem. *Journal of Personality and Social Psychology, 68*(4), 653–663; Orth, U., Robins, R. W., Trzesniewski, K. H., Maes, J., & Schmitt, M. (2009). Low self-esteem is a risk factor for depressive symptoms from young adulthood to old age. *Journal of Abnormal Psychology, 118*(3), 472–478.

13. Brooks, D. (2017). When life asks for everything. *The New York Times.* Retrieved from https://www.nytimes.com/2017/09/19/opinion/when-life-asks-for-everything.html.

14. Crocker, J., & Park, L. E. (2004). The costly pursuit of self-esteem. *Psychological Bulletin, 130*(3), 392–414.

15. Ryan, R. M., & Brown, K. W. (2003). Why we don't need self-esteem: On fundamental needs, contingent love, and mindfulness. *Psychological Inquiry, 14*(1), 71–76.

16. Greenberg, J., Pyszczynski, T., & Solomon, S. (1986). The causes and consequences of a need for self-esteem: A terror management theory. In R.F . Baumeister (Ed.), *Public Self and Private Self.* Berlin: Springer-Verlag.

17. Tafarodi, R. W., & Swann, W. B., Jr. (1995). Self-liking and self-competence as dimensions of global self-esteem: Initial validation of a measure. *Journal of Personality Assessment, 65*(2), 322–342; Tafarodi, R. W., & Swann, W. B., Jr. (2001). Two-dimensional self-esteem: Theory and measurement. *Personality and Individual Differences, 31*(5), 653–673.

18. Items adapted from Tafarodi & Swann, Two-dimensional self-esteem.

19. Maslow made this point in a private journal entry on February 13, 1961: "The abyss between is & ought = depression, discouragement, hopelessness. So, one must somehow

love one's ideal self & at the same time one's current self (so far actualized) so that one can be & become simultaneously—i.e., enjoy one's current being & yet press on toward higher levels of being. MUST FEEL WORTHY."

20. Maslow, *Motivation and personality*.

21. Leary & Guadagno, The sociometer, self-esteem, and the regulation of interpersonal behavior. In Vohs & Baumeister, *Handbook of self-regulation*.

22. Leary, M. R., Jongman-Sereno, K. P., & Diebels, K. J. (2016). The pursuit of status: A self-presentational perspective on the quest for social value. In J. T. Cheng, J. L. Tracy, & C. Anderson (Eds.), *The Psychology of Social Status* (pp. 159–78). New York: Springer.

23. Leary & Guadagno, The sociometer, self-esteem, and the regulation of interpersonal behavior. In Vohs & Baumeister, *Handbook of self-regulation*.

24. Tafarodi & Swann, Two-dimensional self-esteem, p. 656.

25. Damon, W., & Hart, D. (1988). *Self-understanding in childhood and adolescence*. New York: Cambridge University Press; Rosenberg, M. (1986). Self-concept from middle childhood through adolescence. In J. Suls & A. G. Greenwald (Eds.), *Psychological perspectives on the self* (Vol. 3, pp. 107–135). Hillsdale, NJ: Lawrence Erlbaum Associates.

26. Tafarodi & Swann, Two-dimensional self-esteem; Bandura, A. (1977). Self-efficacy: Toward a unifying theory of behavioral change. *Psychological Review, 84*(2), 191–215.

27. Tafarodi & Swann, Two-dimensional self-esteem, p. 655.

28. While Albert Bandura argued that self-efficacy is separate from self-esteem, personality research has shown an almost identical correlation between general self-efficacy and global self-esteem. See: Bandura, A. (1990). Conclusion: Reflections on nonability determinants of competence. In R. J. Sternberg & J. Kolligian Jr. (Eds.), *Competence considered* (pp. 315–62). New Haven, CT: Yale University Press; Bernard, L. C., Hutchison, S., Lavin, A., & Pennington, P. (1996). Ego-strength, hardiness, self-esteem, self-efficacy, optimism, and maladjustment: Health-related personality constructs and the "Big Five" model of personality. *Assessment, 3*(2), 115–131; Stanley, K. D., Murphy, M. R. (1997). A comparison of general self-efficacy with self-esteem. *Genetic, Social, and General Psychology Monographs, 123*(1), 79–99.

29. Tafarodi, R. W. (1998). Paradoxical self-esteem and selectivity in the processing of social information. *Journal of Personality and Social Psychology, 74*(5), 1181–1196.

30. Orth, U., Robins, R. W., Meier, L. L., & Conger, R. D. (2016). Refining the vulnerability model of low self-esteem and depression: Disentangling the effects of genuine self-esteem and narcissism. *Journal of Personality and Social Psychology, 110*(1), 133–149; Kaufamn, S. B. (2018). Why do people mistake narcissism for high self-esteem? *Scientific American Blogs*. Retrieved from https://blogs.scientificamerican.com/beautiful-minds /why-do-people-mistake-narcissism-for-high-self-esteem; Kaufman, S. B. (2017). Narcissism and self-esteem are very different. *Scientific American Blogs*. Retrieved from https:// blogs.scientificamerican.com/beautiful-minds/narcissism-and-self-esteem-are-very -different.

31. Harter, S. (2015). *The construction of the self: Developmental and sociocultural foundations* (2nd ed.). New York: Guilford Press.

32. Harter, *The construction of the self.*

33. Brummelman, E., et al. (2015). Origins of narcissism in children. *PNAS, 112*(12), 3659–3662; Brummelman, E., Thomaes, S., Nelemans, S. A., de Castro, B. O., & Bushman, B. J. (2015). My child is God's gift to humanity: Development and validation of the Parental Overvaluation Scale (POS). *Journal of Personality and Social Psychology, 108*(4), 665–679.

34. Gabbard, G. O. (1989). Two subtypes of narcissistic personality disorder. *Bulletin of the Menninger Clinic, 53*(6), 527–532; Kaufman, S. B., Weiss, B., Miller, J. D., & Campbell, W. K. (2018). Clinical correlates of vulnerable and grandiose narcissism: A personality perspective. *Journal of Personality Disorders, 32,* 384; Kohut, H. (1966). Forms and transformations of narcissism. *Journal of the American Psychoanalytic Association, 14*(2), 243–272; Kernberg, O. (1986). Narcissistic personality disorder. In A. A. Cooper, A. J. Frances, & M. H. Sachs (Eds.), *The personality disorders and neuroses* (Vol. 1, pp. 219–231). New York: Basic Books; Wink, P. (1991). Two faces of narcissism. *Journal of Personality and Social Psychology, 61*(4), 590–597.

35. Kernberg, Narcissistic personality disorder. In Cooper, Frances, & Sachs, *The personality disorders and neuroses.*

36. Kohut, Forms and transformations of narcissism.

37. On December 5, 1965, in New York City, Heinz Kohut made a presentation to the American Psychoanalytic Association in which he noted: "Although in theoretical discussions it will usually not be disputed that narcissism . . . is per se neither pathological nor obnoxious, there exists an understandable tendency to look at it with a negatively toned evaluation." Attempting to take a clear-eyed look at this cathexis of the self and the potential for harnessing the already existing narcissism that exists in all of us, Kohut continued:

In many instances, the reshaping of the narcissistic structures and their integration into the personality—the strengthening of ideals, and the achievement, even to a modest degree, of such wholesome transformation of narcissism as humor, creativity, empathy, and wisdom—must be rated as a more genuine and valid result of therapy than that patient's precarious compliance with demands for a change of his narcissism into object love.

In the prevailing "object relations" theory of the day, object love meant the drive to form close relationships with others, akin to Adler's notion of social interest. See: Kohut, Forms and transformations of narcissism.

38. Kohut, Forms and transformations of narcissism.

39. Case vignette adapted from Russ, E., Shedler, J., Bradley, R., & Westen, D. (2008). Refining the construct of narcissistic personality disorder: Diagnostic criteria and subtypes. *The American Journal of Psychiatry, 165*(11), 1473–1481.

40. Arkin, R. M., Oleson, K. C., & Carroll, P. J. (2009). *Handbook of the uncertain self.* New York: Psychology Press.

41. Baumeister, R. F., Tice, D. M., & Hutton, D. G. (1989). Self-presentational motivations and personality differences in self-esteem. *Journal of Personality, 57*(3), 547–579, https://doi.org/10.1111/j.1467-6494.1989.tb02384.x.

42. Items adapted from the following scales: Glover, N., Miller, J. D., Lynam, D. R., Crego, C., & Widiger, T. A. (2012). The Five-Factor Narcissism Inventory: A five-factor measure of narcissistic personality traits. *Journal of Personality Assessment, 94*, 500–512; Pincus, A. L., Ansell, E. B., Pimenel, C. A., Cain, N. M., Wright, A. G. C., and Levy, K. N. (2009). Initial construction and validation of the Pathological Narcissism Inventory. *Psychological Assessment, 21,* 365-379.

43. Leary & Guadagno, The sociometer, self-esteem, and the regulation of interpersonal behavior. In Vohs & Baumeister, *Handbook of self-regulation.*

44. Finzi-Dottan, R., & Karu, T. (2006). From emotional abuse in childhood to psychopathology in adulthood: A path mediated by immature defense mechanisms and self-esteem. *The Journal of Nervous and Mental Disease, 194*(8), 616–621; Riggs, S. A. (2010). Childhood emotional abuse and the attachment system across the life cycle: What theory and research tell us. *Journal of Aggression, Maltreatment & Trauma, 19,* 5–51.

45. Crowell, S. E., Beauchaine, T. P., & Linehan, M. M. (2009). A biosocial developmental model of borderline personality: Elaborating and extending Linehan's theory. *Psychological Bulletin, 135,* 495–510; Kaufman, S. B. (2019). There is no nature-nurture war. *Scientific American Blogs.* Retrieved from https://blogs.scientificamerican.com/beautiful-minds/there-is-no-nature-nurture-war.

46. Crowell, S. E., Beauchaine, T. P., & Linehan, M. M. (2009). A biosocial developmental model of borderline personality: Elaborating and extending Linehan's theory. *Psychological Bulletin, 135,* 495-510; Kaufman, S. B. (2019). There is no nature-nurture war. *Scientific American Blogs.* Retrieved from https://blogs.scientificamerican.com/beautiful-minds/there-is-no-nature-nurture-war.

47. Finzi-Dottan & Karu, From emotional abuse in childhood to psychopathology in adulthood.

48. Kaufman, Weiss, Miller, & Campbell, Clinical correlates of vulnerable and grandiose narcissism; Kaufman, S. B. (2018). Are narcissists more likely to experience impostor syndrome? *Scientific American Blogs.* Retrieved from https://blogs.scientificamerican.com/beautiful-minds/are-narcissists-more-likely-to-experience-impostor-syndrome.

49. Unsurprisingly, while not exactly the same, vulnerable narcissism is strongly correlated with scales measuring the characteristics of borderline personality disorder (BPD). People who are diagnosed with BPD also describe a feeling of a "fragile sense of self." As one BPD patient put it, "I am only a response to other people—I have no identity of my own. Other people supply me with my existence." The psychoanalyst Otto Kernberg, who observed many patients with BPD as well as patients he diagnosed with vulnerable narcissism, noticed that his patients seemed to have a self the consistency of Jell-O, capable of being molded into any form but slipping through the hands if one tries to pick it up. See: Miller, J. D., et al. (2010). Grandiose and vulnerable narcissism: A nomological network analysis. *Journal of Personality, 79*(5), 1013–1042; Flury, J. M., & Ickes, W. (2005). Having a weak versus strong sense of self: The sense of self scale (SOSS). *Self and*

Identity, 6(4), 281–303; Kernberg, O. F. (1975). Transference and countertransference in the treatment of borderline patients. *Journal of the National Association of Private Psychiatric Hospitals, 7*(2), 14–24; Laing, R. D. (1965). *The divided self: An existential study in sanity and madness.* Oxford, UK: Penguin Books.

50. Cowman, S. E., & Ferrari, J. R. (2002). "Am I for real?" Predicting impostor tendencies from self-handicapping and affective components. *Social Behavior and Personality: An International Journal, 30*(2), 119–125; Leary, M. R., Patton, K. M., Orlando, A. E., & Funk, W. W. (2001). The impostor phenomenon: Self-perceptions, reflected appraisals, and interpersonal strategies. *Journal of Personality, 68*(4), 725–756; McElwee, R. O., & Yurak, T. J. (2007). Feeling versus acting like an impostor: Real feelings of fraudulence or self-presentation? *Individual Differences Research, 5*(3), 201–220.

51. Smith, M. M., et al. (2016). Perfectionism and narcissism: A meta-analytic review. *Journal of Research in Personality, 64,* 90–101.

52. Beck, A. T., Davis, D. D., & Freeman, A. (2015) (Eds.). *Cognitive therapy of personality disorders* (3rd ed.). New York: Guilford Press; Gillihan, S. J. (2018). *Cognitive behavioral therapy made simple: 10 strategies for managing anxiety, depression, anger, panic, and worry.* Emeryville, CA: Althea Press; Gillihan, S. J. (2016). *Retrain your brain: Cognitive behavioral therapy in 7 weeks: A workbook for managing depression and anxiety.* Emeryville, CA: Althea Press; Hayes, S. C. (2019). *A liberated mind: How to pivot toward what matters.* New York: Avery; Hayes, S. C. (2005). *Get out of your mind and into your life: The new acceptance & commitment therapy.* Oakland, CA: New Harbinger Publications; Hayes, S. C., Strosahl, K. D., & Wilson, K. G. (2016). *Acceptance and commitment therapy: The process and practice of mindful change* (2nd ed.). New York: Guilford Press; Linehan, M. M. (2014). *DBT skills training manual.* New York: Guilford Press; Linehan, M. M. (2014). *DBT skills training handouts and worksheets* (2nd ed.). New York: Guilford Press; McKay, M., Wood, J. C., & Brantley, J. (2007). *The dialectical behavioral therapy skills workbook: Practical DBT exercises for learning mindfulness, interpersonal effectiveness, emotion regulation & distress tolerance.* Oakland, CA: New Harbinger Publications.

53. Gillihan, S. J. (2016). *Retrain your brain: Cognitive behavioral therapy in 7 weeks: A workbook for managing depression and anxiety.* Emeryville, CA: Althea Press.

54. Kaufman, S. B. (2017). Get out of your mind and live a vital life with Steven Hayes. *The Psychology Podcast.* Retrieved from http://scottbarrykaufman.com/podcast/get-mind-live-vital-life-steven-hayes.

55. Kaufman, Weiss, Miller, & Campbell, Clinical correlates of vulnerable and grandiose narcissism.

56. Maslow, The Jonah Complex: Understanding our fear of growth. In Hoffman, *Future visions* (pp. 47–51), p. 48.

57. Maslow, The Jonah Complex: Understanding our fear of growth. In Hoffman, *Future visions,* p. 50.

58. Brown, B. (2017). *Braving the wilderness: The quest for true belonging and the courage to stand alone.* New York: Random House, p. 158.

59. Case vignette adapted from Russ, Shedler, Bradley, & Westen, Refining the construct of narcissistic personality disorder.

60. Items adapted from: Glover, N., Miller, J. D., Lynam, D. R., Crego, C., & Widiger, T. A. (2012). The Five-Factor Narcissism Inventory: A five-factor measure of narcissistic personality traits. *Journal of Personality Assessment, 94,* 500–512.

61. Gebauer, J. E., Sedikides, C., Verplanken, B., & Maio, G. R. (2012). Communal narcissism. *Journal of Personality and Social Psychology, 103*(5), 854–878.

62. Kaufman, Weiss, Miller, & Campbell, Clinical correlates of vulnerable and grandiose narcissism.

63. Beck, A. T., Davis, D. D., & Freeman, A. (2004). *Cognitive therapy of personality disorders* (3rd ed.). New York: Guilford Press; Ronningstam, E. (2010). Narcissistic personality disorder: A current review. *Current Psychiatry Reports, 12,* 68–75; Ronningstam, E. (2011). Narcissistic personality disorder: A clinical perspective. *Journal of Personality and Social Psychology, 17,* 89–99; Smith et al., Perfectionism and narcissism.

64. Smith et al., Perfectionism and narcissism.

65. Beck, Davis, & Freeman, *Cognitive therapy of personality disorders*; Flett, G. L., Sherry, S. B., Hewitt, P. L., & Nepon, T. (2014). Understanding the narcissistic perfectionists among us. In A. Besser (Ed.), *Handbook of the psychology of narcissism: Diverse perspectives* (pp. 43–66). New York: Nova Science Publishers; Smith et al., Perfectionism and narcissism.

66. Smith et al., Perfectionism and narcissism.

67. Herman, T. (2019). *The alter ego effect: The power of secret identities to transform your life.* New York: HarperBusiness.

68. Baumeister, R. F., & Vohs, K. D. (2001). Narcissism as addiction to esteem. *Psychological Inquiry, 12*(4), 206–210.

69. Jauk, E., & Kaufman, S. B. (2018). The higher the score, the darker the core: The nonlinear association between grandiose and vulnerable narcissism. *Frontiers in Psychology, 9,* https://doi.org/10.3389/fpsyg.2018.01305; Jauk, E., Weigle, E., Lehmann, K., Benedek, M., & Neubauer, A. C. (2017). The relationship between grandiose and vulnerable (hypersensitive) narcissism. *Frontiers in Psychology, 8.*

70. Gore, W. L., & Widiger, T. A. (2016). Fluctuation between grandiose and vulnerable narcissism. *Personality Disorders: Theory, Research, and Treatment, 7*(4), 363–371; Pincus, A. L., Cain, N. M., & Wright, A. G. (2014). Narcissistic grandiosity and narcissistic vulnerability in psychotherapy. *Personality Disorders: Theory, Research, and Treatment, 5*(4), 439–443; Hyatt, C. S., et al. (2016). Ratings of affective and interpersonal tendencies differ for grandiose and vulnerable narcissism: A replication and extension of Gore and Widiger (2016). *Journal of Personality, 86*(3), 422–434; Pincus, A. L., & Lukowitsky, M. R. (2010). Pathological narcissism and narcissistic personality disorder. *Annual Review of Clinical Psychology, 6,* 421–446; Wright, A. G., & Edershile, E. A. (2018). Issues resolved and unresolved in pathological narcissism. *Current Opinion in Psychology, 21,* 74–79.

71. Although narcissists aren't nearly as seductive the more you get to know them. See: Kaufman, S. B. (2015). Why do narcissists lose popularity over time? *Scientific American Blogs.* Retrieved from https://blogs.scientificamerican.com/beautiful-minds/why-do-narcissists-lose-popularity-over-time.

72. Baumeister & Vohs, Narcissism as addiction to esteem, p. 209.

73. Keltner, D. (2016). *The power paradox: How we gain and lose influence*. New York: Penguin Books.

74. de Zavala, A. G., Cichocka, A., Eidelson, R., & Jayawickreme, N. (2009). Collective narcissism and its social consequences. *Journal of Personality and Social Psychology, 97*(6), 1074–1096.

75. Cichocka, A. (2016). Understanding defensive and secure in-group positivity: The role of collective narcissism. *European Review of Social Psychology, 27*(1), 283–317.

76. de Zavala, A. G. (2019). Collective narcissism and in-group satisfaction are associated with different emotional profiles and psychological well-being. *Frontiers in Psychology, 10*, 203.

77. de Zavala, Collective narcissism and in-group satisfaction are associated with different emotional profiles and psychological well-being.

78. Tracy, J. (2016). *Take pride: Why the deadliest sin holds the secret to human success*. New York: Houghton Mifflin Harcourt.

79. Cheng, J. T., Tracy, J. L., Foulsham, T., Kingstone, A., & Henrich, J. (2013). Two ways to the top: Evidence that dominance and prestige are distinct yet viable avenues to social rank and influence. *Journal of Personality and Social Psychology, 104*, 103–125.

80. See Appendix to Kaufman, Self-actualizing people in the 21st century.

81. Keltner, *The power paradox*.

PART II. GROWTH

1. Hoffman, *The right to be human*.

2. Hoffman, *The right to be human*, p. 87.

3. Maslow, *The farther reaches of human nature*, p. 40.

4. Maslow, *The farther reaches of human nature*, p. 41.

5. Maslow, A. H., & Mittelmann, B. (1941). *Principles of abnormal psychology*. New York: Harper & Brothers.

6. Maslow and Mittelmann, *Principles of abnormal psychology*, p. 11.

7. Maslow and Mittelmann, *Principles of abnormal psychology*, p. 11.

8. Maslow and Mittelmann, *Principles of abnormal psychology*, p. 44.

9. Hoffman, E. (1992). Overcoming evil: An interview with Abraham Maslow, founder of humanistic psychology. *Psychology Today*. Retrieved from https://www.psychologyto day.com/articles/199201/abraham-maslow.

10. Here are some of his primary influences in addition to Kurt Goldstein (although this is far from an exhaustive list): From his encounter in college with William Sumner's work on cultural folkways he learned about the important influence of culture on the satisfaction of our needs and how culture influences which pathways we take to satisfy them; from Ruth Benedict he learned about how cultural institutions can have an effect on the holistic nature of the society; from his visit with the Blackfoot Indians he saw that "we are all the same underneath," and he also learned about the importance of community, gratitude for what one has, and giving back to future generations; from the psychoanalytic writings of Karen Horney he learned about the need to overcome neuroses for self-realization; from working with Harry Harlow he learned about the need for affection among monkeys; from Alfred Adler he learned about the needs for power and social

interest; from the Gestalt psychologists he learned that the whole is greater than the sum of its parts; and from Max Wertheimer's lectures he learned about the value of "unmotivated behavior" in psychology, such as playfulness, aesthetic enjoyment, and other ecstatic human experiences that weren't motivated by deficiency. See: Blackstock, The emergence of the breath of life theory; Kaufman, Honoring the wisdom of indigenous people with Richard Katz; Hoffman, *The right to be human*.

11. Foreword to Goldstein, K. (2000; originally published in 1934). *The organism*. New York: Zone Book, p. 7.

12. Maslow, *Motivation and personality*, p. 46.

13. Hoffman, *The right to be human*.

14. In this draft (which he never published), he wrote: "[But] the truth which we can see more and more clearly is that man has infinite potentiality, which, properly used, could make his life very much like fantasies of heaven. In potentiality, he is the most awe-inspiring phenomenon in the universe, the most creative, the most ingenuous. Throughout the ages, philosophers have sought to understand the true, the good, and the beautiful, and to speak for its forces. Now we know that the best place to look for them is in man himself." See: Hoffman, *The right to be human*, p. 165.

15. Lowry, *A. H. Maslow: An intellectual portrait*.

16. Lowry, *A. H. Maslow: An intellectual portrait*, p. 81.

17. Hoffman, Overcoming evil.

18. Lowry, *A. H. Maslow: An intellectual portrait*, p. 91.

19. See: Lowry, *A. H. Maslow: An intellectual portrait*.

20. Maslow would pick out students who appeared self-actualized in his class and then would look up their scores on his test of emotional security. Then he would interview them and give them the Rorschach inkblot test, which was considered a gold standard measure of psychopathology at the time. However, he quickly ran into lots of problems. First, virtually no college student could be considered self-actualized based on the tests he was using. Maslow also noticed that he was biased in his selection of students, unconsciously choosing a disproportionate number of attractive female students. Always the explorer, he "went ahead anyway."

CHAPTER 4. EXPLORATION

1. Kashdan, T. B., & Silvia, P. J. (2011). Curiosity and interest: The benefits of thriving on novelty and challenge. In S. J. Lopez & R. Snyder (Eds.), *The Oxford Handbook of Positive Psychology* (pp. 367–374).

2. Maslow, *Toward a psychology of being*.

3. Maslow, *Toward a psychology of being*, p. 67.

4. Maslow, *Toward a psychology of being*.

5. Let Grow: Future-proofing our kids and our country. Retrieved from https://letgrow.org.

6. Kashdan, T. B., et al. (2018). The five-dimensional curiosity scale: Capturing the bandwidth of curiosity and identifying four unique subgroups of curious people. *Journal of Research in Personality, 73,* 130–49.

7. Maslow, *Toward a psychology of being*, p. 76.
8. DeYoung, C. G. (2013). The neuromodulator of exploration: A unifying theory of the role of dopamine in personality. *Frontiers in Human Neuroscience, 7*; Peterson, J. B. (1999). *Maps of meaning: The architecture of belief.* New York: Routledge; Schwartenbeck, P., Fitz-Gerald, T., Dolan, R. J., & Friston, K. (2013). Exploration, novelty, surprise, and free energy minimization. *Frontiers in Psychology, 4,* 710.
9. DeYoung, The neuromodulator of exploration.
10. DeYoung, The neuromodulator of exploration.
11. DeYoung, The neuromodulator of exploration.
12. Lavigne, Vallerand, & Crevier-Braud, The fundamental need to belong.
13. Hartung, F-M., & Renner, B. (2013). Social curiosity and gossip: Related but different drives of social functioning. *PLOS One, 8*(7): e69996; Kashdan et al., The five-dimensional curiosity scale; Litman, J. A., & Pezzo, M. V. (2007). Dimensionality of interpersonal curiosity. *Personality and Individual Differences, 43*(6), 1448–1459.
14. Kashdan et al., The five-dimensional curiosity scale.
15. Litman & Pezzo, Dimensionality of interpersonal curiosity.
16. Hartung, F-M, & Renner, B. (2011). Social curiosity and interpersonal perception: A judge × trait interaction. *Personality and Social Psychology Bulletin, 37*(6), 796–814.
17. Hartung & Renner, Social curiosity and interpersonal perception; Vogt, D. W., & Colvin, C. R. (2003). Interpersonal orientation and the accuracy of personality judgments. *Journal of Personality, 71*(2), 267–295.
18. Vogt & Colvin, Interpersonal orientation and the accuracy of personality judgments.
19. Hartung & Renner, Social curiosity and gossip.
20. Baumeister, R. F., Zhang, L., & Vohs, K. D. (2004). Gossip as cultural learning. *Review of General Psychology, 8*(2), 111–121.
21. Baumeister, R. F. (2005). *The cultural animal: Human nature, meaning, and social life.* New York: Oxford University Press; Baumeister, R. F., Maranges, H. M., & Vohs, K. D. (2018). Human self as information agent: Functioning in a social environment based on shared meanings. *Review of General Psychology, 22*(1), 36–47; Baumeister, Zhang, & Vohs, Gossip as cultural learning.
22. Hirsh, J. B., DeYoung, C. G., & Peterson, J. B. (2009). Metatraits and the Big Five differentially predict engagement and restraint of behavior. *Journal of Personality, 77*(4), 1–17.
23. Renner, B. (2006). Curiosity about people: The development of a social curiosity measure in adults. *Journal of Personality Assessment, 87*(3), 305–16.
24. 60 Minutes (2011, December 27). The ascent of Alex Honnold. Retrieved from https://www.cbsnews.com/news/the-ascent-of-alex-honnold-27-12-2011/.
25. Synnott, M. (2015). Legendary climber Alex Honnold shares his closest call. *National Geographic.* Retrieved from https://www.nationalgeographic.com/adventure/adventure-blog/2015/12/30/ropeless-climber-alex-honnolds-closest-call.
26. Synnott, Legendary climber Alex Honnold shares his closest call.
27. Chen, C., Burton, M., Greenberger, E., & Dmitrieva, J. (1999). Population migration and the variation of dopamine D4 receptor (DRD4) allele frequencies around the globe. *Evolution and Human Behavior, 20*(5), 309–324.

28. Synnott, Legendary climber Alex Honnold shares his closest call.

29. wwwAAASorg. (2018, April 5). *Alex Honnold's amygdala: Analyzing a thrill-seeker's brain* [Video file]. Retrieved from https://www.youtube.com/watch?v=ib7SS49Kk-o.

30. Zuckerman, M. (2009). Sensation seeking. In M. R. Leary & R. H. Hoyle (Eds.). *Handbook of individual differences in social behavior* (pp. 455–465). New York/London: Guilford Press.

31. Bjork, J. M., Knutson, B., & Hommer, D. W. (2008). Incentive-elicited striatal activation in adolescent children of alcoholics. *Addiction, 103*(8), 1308–1319.

32. Kashdan et al., The five-dimensional curiosity scale.

33. Maples-Keller, J. L., Berke, D. S., Few, L. R., & Miller, J. D. (2016). A review of sensation seeking and its empirical correlates: Dark, bright, and neutral hues. In V. Zeigler-Hill & D. K. Marcus (Eds.), *The dark side of personality: Science and practice in social, personality, and clinical psychology* (Chapter 7). Washington, DC: American Psychological Association.

34. Breivik, G. (1996). Personality, sensation seeking, and risk-taking among Everest climbers. *International Journal of Sport Psychology, 27*(3), 308–320; Zuckerman, M. (1994). *Behavioral expressions and biosocial bases of sensation seeking.* New York: Cambridge University Press; Goma-i-Freixanet, M. (1995). Prosocial and antisocial aspects of personality. *Personality and Individual Differences, 19*(2), 125–34; Maples-Keller, Berke, Few, & Miller, A review of sensation seeking and its empirical correlates. In Zeigler-Hill & Marcus, *The dark side of personality*; Okamoto, K., & Takaki, E. (1992). Structure of creativity measurements and their correlates with sensation seeking and need for uniqueness. *Japanese Journal of Experimental Social Psychology, 31*(3), 203–10; Rawlings, D., & Leow, S. H. (2008). Investigating the role of psychoticism and sensation seeking in predicting emotional reactions to music. *Psychology of Music, 36*(3), 269–287; Wymer, W., Self, D. R., & Findley, C. (2008). Sensation seekers and civic participation: Exploring the influence of sensation seeking and gender on intention to lead and volunteer. *International Journal of Nonprofit and Voluntary Sector Marketing, 13*(4), 287–300.

35. Jonas, K., & Koçhansaka, G. (2018). An imbalance of approach and effortful control predicts externalizing problems: Support for extending the dual-systems model into early childhood. *Journal of Abnormal Child Psychology, 46*(8), 1573–1583.

36. Ravert, R. D., et al. (2013). The association between sensation seeking and well-being among college-attending emerging adults. *Journal of College Student Development, 54*(1), 17–28.

37. McKay, S., Skues, J. L., & Williams, B. J. (2018). With risk may come reward: Sensation seeking supports resilience through effective coping. *Personality and Individual Differences, 121*, 100–105.

38. Carroll, L. (2013). Problem-focused coping. In M. D. Gellman & J. R. Turner (Eds.), *Encyclopedia of Behavioral Medicine* (pp. 1540–1541). New York: Springer Science+Business, pp. 1540–41.

39. Bonanno, G. A. (2004). Loss, trauma, and human resilience: Have we underestimated the human capacity to thrive after extremely adversive events? *American Psychologist, 59*(1), 20–28.

40. Kessler, R. C., Sonnega, A., Bromet, E., Hughes, M., & Nelson, C. B. (1995). Posttraumatic stress disorder in the National Co-morbidity Survey. *Archives of General Psychiatry, 52*(12), 1048–60.

41. Sears, S. R., Stanton, A. L., & Danoff-Burg, S. (2003). The Yellow Brick Road and the Emerald City: Benefit finding, positive reappraisal coping and posttraumatic growth in women with early-stage breast cancer. *Health Psychology, 22*(5), 487–497; Tedeschi, R. G., & Calhoun, L. G. (1996). The Posttraumatic Growth Inventory: Measuring the positive legacy of trauma. *Journal of Traumatic Stress, 9*(3), 455–472; Tedeschi, R. G., & Calhoun, L. G. (2009). Posttraumatic growth: Conceptual foundations and empirical evidence. *Psychological Inquiry, 15*(1), 1–18.

42. Calhoun, L. G., & Tedeschi, R. G. (2001). Posttraumatic growth: The positive lesson of loss. In R. A. Neimeyer (Ed.), *Meaning reconstruction & the experience of loss* (pp. 157–172). Washington, DC: American Psychological Association.

43. Mangelsdorf, J., Eid, M., & Luhmann, M. (2019). Does growth require suffering? A systematic review and meta-analysis on genuine posttraumatic and postecastic growth. *Psychological Bulletin, 145*(3), 302–338.

44. Dabrowski, K. (2016; originally published in 1964). *Positive disintegration*. Anna Maria, FL: Maurice Bassett.

45. Yalom, I. D., & Lieberman, M. A. (2016). Bereavement and heightened existential awareness. *Interpersonal and Biological Processes, 54*(4), 334–45.

46. Viorst, J. (1986). *Necessary losses: The loves, illusions, dependencies and impossible expectations that all of us have to give up in order to grow.* London: Simon & Schuster, p. 295.

47. Dabrowski, K. (2016; originally published in 1964). *Positive disintegration*. Anna Maria, FL: Maurice Bassett.

48. DeYoung, C. G. (2014). Openness/intellect: A dimension of personality reflecting cognitive exploration. In M. L. Cooper and R. J. Larsen (Eds.), *APA handbook of personality and social psychology: Personality processes and individual differences* (Vol. 4, pp. 369–99). Washington, DC: American Psychological Association; Fayn, K., Silvia, P. J., Dejonckheere, E., Verdonck, S., & Kuppens, P. (2019). Confused or curious? Openness/intellect predicts more positive interest-confusion relations. *Journal of Personality and Social Psychology*, doi: 10.1037/pspp0000257; Oleynick, V. C., et al. (2019). Openness/intellect: The core of the creative personality. In G. J. Feist, R. Reiter-Palmon, & J. C. Kaufman (Eds.), *The Cambridge handbook of creativity and personality research* (pp. 9–27). New York: Cambridge University Press.

49. Kaufman, S. B., & Gregoire, C. (2016). *Wired to create: Unraveling the mysteries of the creative mind.* New York: TarcherPerigee; Tedeschi, R. G., & Calhoun, L. G. (2004). Posttrauamtic growth: Conceptual foundations and empirical evidence. *Psychological Inquiry, 15*, 1–18.

50. Brooks, M., Graham-Kevan, N., Robinson, S., & Lowe, M. (2019). Trauma characteristics and posttraumatic growth: The mediating role of avoidance coping, intrusive thoughts, and social support. *Psychological Trauma, 11*(2), 232–38.

51. Kaufman & Gregoire, *Wired to create.*

52. Batten, S. V., Orsillo, S. M., & Walser, R. D. (2005). Acceptance and mindfulness-based

approaches to the treatment of posttraumatic stress disorder. In S. M. Orsillo & L. Ro-emer (Eds.). *Acceptance and mindfulness-based approaches to anxiety: Conceptualization and treatment* (pp. 241–271). New York: Springer; Hayes, S. C., Luoma, J. B., Bond, F. W., Masuda, A., & Lillis, J. (2006). Acceptance and commitment therapy: Model, processes, and outcomes. *Behaviour Research and Therapy, 44*(1), 1–25; Kashdan, T. B., Breen, W. E., & Julian, T. (2010). Everyday strivings in combat veterans with posttraumatic stress disorder: Problems arise when avoidance and emotion regulation dominate. *Behavior Therapy, 41*(3), 350–363; Kashdan, T. B. (2010). Psychological flexibility as a fundamental aspect of health. *Clinical Psychology Review, 30*(7), 865–878.

53. Hayes, S. C. (2019). *A liberated mind: How to pivot toward what matters.* New York: Avery.

54. Kashdan, T. B., & Kane, J. Q. (2011). Posttraumatic distress and the presence of post-traumatic growth and meaning in life: Experiential avoidance as a moderator. *Personality and Individual Differences, 50*(1), 84–89.

55. Hayes, Luoma, Bond, Masuda, & Lillis, Acceptance and commitment therapy; Kashdan, T. B., & Breen, W. E. (2008). Social anxiety and positive emotions: A prospective examination of a self-regulatory model with tendencies to suppress or express emotions as a moderating variable. *Behavior Therapy, 39*(1), 1–12; Kashdan, T. B., Morina, N., & Priebe, S. (2008). Post-traumatic stress disorder, social anxiety disorder, and depression in survivors of the Kosovo War: Experiential avoidance as a contributor to distress and quality of life. *Journal of Anxiety Disorders, 23*(2), 185–196; Kashdan, T. B., & Steger, M. (2006). Expanding the topography of social anxiety: An experience-sampling assessment of positive emotions and events, and emotion suppression. *Psychological Science, 17*(2), 120–128.

56. Forgeard, M. J. C. (2013). Perceiving benefits after adversity: The relationship between self-reported posttraumatic growth and creativity. *Psychology of Aesthetics, Creativity, and the Arts, 7*(3), 245–264.

57. Zausner, T. (2007). *When walls become doorways: Creativity and the transforming illness.* New York: Harmony Books.

58. Kaufman, S. B. (2013). Turning adversity into creative growth. *Scientific American Blogs.* Retrieved from https://blogs.scientificamerican.com/beautiful-minds/turning-adversity -into-creative-growth.

59. Combs, A. W. (Ed.). (1962). *Perceiving, behaving, becoming: A new focus for education.* Washington, DC: National Education Association.

60. Combs, *Perceiving, behaving, becoming.*

61. Oleynick et al., Openness/intellect: The core of the creative personality. In Feist, Reiter-Palmon, & Kaufman, *The Cambridge handbook of creativity and personality.*

62. DeYoung, Openness/intellect: A dimension of personality reflecting cognitive exploration. In Cooper & Larsen, *APA handbook of personality and social psychology: Personality processes and individual differences*; Oleynick et al., Openness/intellect: The core of the creative personality. In Feist, Reiter-Palmon, & Kaufman, *The Cambridge handbook of creativity and personality research.*

63. Conner, T. S., & Silvia, P. J. (2015). Creative days: A daily diary study of emotion, personality, and everyday creativity. *Psychology of Aesthetics, Creativity, and the Arts, 9*(4),

463–470; Wolfradt, U., & Pretz, J. E. (2001). Individual differences in creativity: Personality, story writing, and hobbies. *European Journal of Personality, 15*(4), 297–310.

64. Silvia, P. J., et al. (2014). Everyday creativity in daily life: An experience-sampling study of "little c" creativity. *Psychology of Aesthetics, Creativity, and the Arts, 8*(2), 183–188.

65. The statements were adapted from these sources:

    Nelson, B., & Rawlings, D. (2010). Relating schizotypy and personality to the phenomenology of creativity. *Schizophrenia Bulletin*, 36, 388–399; Norris, P., & Epstein, S. (2011). An experiential thinking style: Its facets and relations with objective and subjective criterion measures. *Journal of Personality, 79*, 5; Soto, C. J., & John, O. P. (2017). The next Big Five Inventory (BFI-2): Developing and assessing a hierarchical model with 15 facets to enhance bandwidth, fidelity, and predictive power. *Journal of Personality and Social Psychology, 113*, 117–143; Tellegen, A., & Waller, N. G. (2008). Exploring personality through test construction: Development of the Multidimensional Personality Questionnaire. In G. J. Boyle, G. Matthews, & D. H. Saklofske (Eds.), *The Sage Handbook of personality theory and assessment* (pp. 261–292). London: Sage Publications; https://www.ocf.berkeley.edu/~jfkihlstrom/ConsciousnessWeb/Meditation/TAS.htm.

66. Kaufman & Gregoire, *Wired to create.*

67. For a review, see: Kaufman & Gregoire, *Wired to create.*

68. Lubow, R., & Weiner, I. (Eds.). (2010). *Latent inhibition: Cognition, neuroscience and applications to schizophrenia.* New York: Cambridge University Press.

69. Carson, S. J., Peterson, J. B., & Higgins, D. M. (2003). Decreased latent inhibition is associated with increased creative achievement in high-functioning individuals. *Journal of Personality and Social Psychology, 85*(3), 499–506; Peterson, J. B., & Carson, S. (2000). Latent inhibition and openness to experience in a high-achieving student population. *Personality and Individual Differences, 28*(2), 323–332.

70. Nelson, B., & Rawlings, D. (2008). Relating schizotypy and personality to the phenomenology of creativity. *Schizophrenia Bulletin, 36*(2), 388–399.

71. Maslow, *Motivation and personality*, p. 163.

72. Poe, E. A. (2016; originally published in 1842). *The mystery of Marie Roget.* CreateSpace Independent Publishing Platform, p. 29.

73. Barbey, A. K., et al. (2012). An integrative architecture for general intelligence and executive function revealed by lesion mapping. *Brain, 135*(4), 1154–1164; DeYoung, C. G., Shamosh, N. A., Green, A. E., Braver, T. S., & Gray, J. R. (2009). Intellect as distinct from openness: Differences revealed by fMRI of working memory. *Journal of Personality and Social Psychology, 97*(5), 883–892.

74. These statements were adapted from: Norris, P., & Epstein, S. (2011). An experiential thinking style: Its facets and relations with objective and subjective criterion measures. *Journal of Personality, 79*, 5; Soto, C. J., & John, O. P. (2017). The next Big Five Inventory (BFI-2): Developing and assessing a hierarchical model with 15 facets to enhance bandwidth, fidelity, and predictive power. *Journal of Personality and Social Psychology, 113*, 117–143.

75. Kashdan et al., The five-dimensional curiosity scale.

76. Kashdan et al., The five-dimensional curiosity scale.

77. Maslow, *Motivation and personality.*

78. Kaufman, S. B. (2013). Opening up openness to experience: A four-factor model and relations to creative achievement in the arts and sciences. *Journal of Creative Behavior, 47*(4), 233–255.

79. Kaufman, S. B. (2017). Schools are missing what matters about learning. *The Atlantic.* Retrieved from https://www.theatlantic.com/education/archive/2017/07/the-underrated -gift-of-curiosity/534573.

80. Kaufman, S. B., et al. (2015). Openness to experience and intellect differentially predict creative achievement in the arts and sciences. *Journal of Personality, 84*(2), 248–258.

81. Kaufman et al., Openness to experience and intellect differentially predict creative achievement in the arts and sciences.

82. As quoted in Paul, E., & Kaufman, S. B. (Eds.). (2014). *The philosophy of creativity.* New York: Oxford University Press.

83. Kaufman, S. B., & Paul, E. S. (2014). Creativity and schizophrenia spectrum disorders across the arts and sciences. *Frontiers in Psychology, 5,* 1145.

84. Beaty, R. E., et al. (2018). Robust prediction of individual creative ability from brain functional connectivity. *PNAS, 115*(5), 1087–1092.

85. Beaty, R. E., et al. (2018). Brain networks of the imaginative mind: Dynamic functional connectivity of default and cognitive control networks relates to openness to experience. *Human Brain Mapping, 39*(2), 811–821.

86. Kaufman, S. B. (2013). *Ungifted: Intelligence redefined.* New York: Basic Books.

87. May, R. (1979). *Psychology and the human dilemma.* New York: W. W. Norton, pp. 196–197.

CHAPTER 5. LOVE

1. Vaillant, G. (2009). *Spiritual evolution: How we are wired for faith, hope, and love.* New York: Harmony Books, p. 101.

2. Martela, F., & Ryan, R. M. (2015). The benefits of benevolence: Basic psychological needs, beneficence, and the enhancement of well-being. *Journal of Personality, 84,* 750–764; Martela, F., & Ryan, R. M. (2016). Prosocial behavior increases well-being and vitality even without contact with the beneficiary: Causal and behavioral evidence. *Motivation and Emotion, 40,* 351–357; Martela, F., Ryan, R. M., & Steger, M. F. (2018). Meaningfulness as satisfaction of autonomy, competence, relatedness, and beneficence: Comparing the four satisfactions and positive affect as predictors of meaning in life. *Journal of Happiness Studies, 19,* 1261–1282.

3. Nuer, C. (Chair). (1997, August). *Personal mastery in action.* Learning as Leadership Seminar, Sausolito, CA.

4. Maslow, *Toward a psychology of being,* p. 47.

5. Maslow, *Toward a psychology of being,* p. 47.

6. Maslow, *Toward a psychology of being,* p. 47.

7. Maslow, *Toward a psychology of being,* p. 47.

8. Maslow, *Toward a psychology of being,* p. 48.

9. Salzberg, S. (2017). *Real love: The art of authentic connection.* New York: Flatiron Books. https://scottbarrykaufman.com/podcast/real-love-sharon-salzberg/.

10. Fromm, E. (1956). *The art of loving.* New York: Harper.

11. Fredrickson, B. L. (2013). *Love 2.0: Finding happiness and health in moments of connection.* New York: Plume.

12. Fromm, *The art of loving,* p. 38.

13. Yalom, *Existential psychotherapy,* p. 377.

14. This section is adapted from Kaufman, S. B. (2019). The light triad vs. dark triad of personality. *Scientific American Blogs.* Retrieved from https://blogs.scientificamerican .com/beautiful-minds/the-light-triad-vs-dark-triad-of-personality.

15. Paulhus, D. L., & Williams, K. M. (2002). The dark triad of personality: Narcissism, Machiavellianism, and psychopathy. *Journal of Research in Personality, 36*(6), 556–563.

16. Dinić, B., & Wertag, A. (2018). Effects of dark triad and HEXACO traits on reactive/ proactive aggression: Exploring the gender differences. *Personality and Individual Differences, 123,* 44–49; Jonason, P. K., Zeigler-Hill, V., & Okan, C. (2017). Good v. evil: Predicting sinning with dark personality traits and moral foundations. *Personality and Individual Differences, 104,* 180–185; Muris, P., Merckelbach, H., Otgaar, H., & Meijer, E. (2017). The malevolent side of human nature: A meta-analysis and critical review of the literature on the dark triad (narcissism, Machavellianism, and psychopathy). *Perspectives on Psychological Science, 12*(2), 183–204; Pailing, A., Boon, J., & Egan, V. (2014). Personality, the Dark Triad and violence. *Personality and Individual Differences, 67,* 81–86; Veselka, L., Giammarco, E. A., & Vernon, P. A. (2014). The Dark Triad and the seven deadly sins. *Personality and Individual Differences, 67,* 75–80.

17. Kaufman, S. B. (2018). The dark core of personality. *Scientific American Blogs.* Retrieved from https://blogs.scientificamerican.com/beautiful-minds/the-dark-core-of -personality; Jones, D. N., & Figueredo, A. J. (2013). The core of darkness: Uncovering the heart of the dark triad. *European Journal of Personality, 27*(6), 521–531; Miller, J. D., Vize, C., Crowe, M. L., & Lynam, D. R. (2019). A critical appraisal of the dark-triad literature and suggestions for moving forward. *Current Directions in Psychological Science, 28*(4), 353–360, https://doi.org/10.1177/0963721419838233; Moshagen, M., Hilbig, B. E., & Zettler, I. (2018). The dark core of personality. *Psychological Review, 125*(5), 656–688.

18. Jones & Figueredo, The core of darkness.

19. Vachon, D. D., Lynam, D. R., & Johnson, J. A. (2014). The (non)relation between empathy and aggression: Surprising results from a meta-analysis. *Psychological Bulletin, 140*(3), 751–773.

20. Figueredo, A. J., & Jacobs, W. J. (2010). Aggression, risk-taking, and alternative life history strategies: The behavioral ecology of social deviance. In M. Frías-Armenta, & V. Corral-Verdugo (Eds.), *Bio-psycho-social perspectives on interpersonal violence* (pp. 3–28). Hauppauge, NY: Nova Science Publishers; Jones & Figueredo, The core of darkness.

21. These items are adapted from the Five-Factor Narcissism Inventory: Miller, J. D., et al. (2013). The Five-Factor Narcissism Inventory (FFNI): A test of the convergent, discriminant, and incremental validity of FFNI scores in clinical and community samples. *Psychological Assessment, 25*(3), 748–758. I found that this "antagonism" factor of the FFNI correlated extremely highly with a few different measures of the dark triad.

22. Maslow, Motivation and personality, p. 198.

23. Kant, I. (1993; originally published in 1785). *Grounding for the metaphysics of morals* (3rd ed.). Translated by J. W. Ellington. London: Hackett, p. 36.

24. Kaufman, S. B., Yaden, D. B., Hyde, E., & Tsukayama, E. (2019). The light vs. dark triad of personality: Contrasting two very different profiles of human nature. *Frontiers in Psychology*, https://doi.org/10.3389/fpsyg.2019.00467.

25. Kaufman, Yaden, Hyde, & Tsukayama, The light vs. dark triad of personality.

26. Schwartz, S. H., et al. (2012). Refining the theory of basic individual values. *Journal of Personality and Social Psychology, 103*(4), 663–688.

27. Niemiec, R. M., & McGrath, R. E. (2019). *The power of character strengths: Appreciate and ignite your positive personality*. Cincinnati: VIA Institute on Character.

28. Bakan, D. (1966). *The duality of human existence: Isolation and communion in Western man*. Boston: Beacon Press.

29. Helgeson, V. S. (1994). Relation of agency and communion to well-being: Evidence and potential explanations. *Psychological Bulletin, 116*(3), 412–428; Helgeson, V. S., & Fritz, H. L. (1998). A theory of unmitigated communion. *Personality and Social Psychology Review, 2*(3), 173–183; Helgeson, V. S., & Fritz, H. L. (1999). Unmitigated agency and unmitigated communion: Distinctions from agency and communion. *Journal of Research in Personality, 33*(2), 131–158.

30. Fritz, H. L., & Helgeson, V. S. (1998). Distinctions of unmitigated communion from communion: Self-neglect and overinvolvement with others. *Journal of Personality and Social Psychology, 75*(1), 121–140; Helgeson, Relation of agency and communion to well-being; Helgeson & Fritz, A theory of unmitigated communion; Helgeson & Fritz, Unmitigated agency and unmitigated communion.

31. Bloom, P. (2016). *Against empathy: The case for rational compassion*. New York: Ecco.

32. Oakley, B., Knafo, A., Madhavan, G., & Wilson, D. S. (Eds.). (2011). *Pathological altruism*. New York: Oxford University Press.

33. Blair, R. J. (2005). Responding to the emotions of others: Dissociating forms of empathy through the study of typical and psychiatric populations. *Consciousness and Cognition, 14*(4), 698–718; Vachon, Lynam, & Johnson, The (non)relation between empathy and aggression; Raine, A., & Chen, F. R. (2018). Cognitive, affective, and somatic empathy scale (CASES) for children. *Journal of Clinical Child & Adolescent Psychology, 47*(1), 24–37.

34. Wai, M., & Tiliopoulos, N. (2012). The affective and cognitive empathic nature of the dark triad of personality. *Personality and Individual Differences, 52*(7), 794–799; Kaufman, S. B. (2012). Are narcissists better at reading minds? *Psychology Today*. Retrieved from https://www.psychologytoday.com/us/blog/beautiful-minds/201202/are-narcissists-better-reading-minds.

35. Scale adapted from Raine & Chen, Cognitive, affective, and somatic empathy scale (CASES) for children.

36. Kaufman, S. B., & Jauk, E. (in preparation). Healthy selfishness and pathological altruism: Measuring two paradoxical forms of selfishness; Oakley, Knafo, Madhavan, & Wilson, *Pathological altruism*.

37. Grant, A., & Rebele, R. (2017). Beat generosity burnout. *Harvard Business Review*. Retrieved from https://hbr.org/cover-story/2017/01/beat-generosity-burnout.

38. Vaillant, G. E. (1992). *Ego mechanisms of defense: A guide for clinicians and researchers*. Washington, DC: American Psychiatric Publishing; Vaillant, G. E. (1998). *Adaptation to life*. Cambridge, MA: Harvard University Press.

39. Vaillant, *Adaptation to life*, p. 108.

40. Andrews, G., Singh, M., & Bond, M. (1993). The Defense Style Questionnaire. *The Journal of Nervous and Mental Disease, 181*(4), 246–256.

41. Vaillant, *Adaptation to life*, p. 119.

42. Andrews, Singh, & Bond, The Defense Style Questionnaire.

43. Vaillant, *Adaptation to life*, p. 116.

44. Kaufman, S. B. (2018). Self-actualizing people in the 21st century: Integration with contemporary theory and research on personality and well-being. *Journal of Humanistic Psychology*, https://doi.org/10.1177/0022167818809187.

45. Andrews, Singh, & Bond, The Defense Style Questionnaire.

46. Andrews, Singh, & Bond, The Defense Style Questionnaire.

47. Andrews, Singh, & Bond, The Defense Style Questionnaire.

48. Fromm, E. (1939). Selfishness and self-love. *Psychiatry, 2*(4), 507–523.

49. Maslow, Is human nature basically selfish? In Hoffman, *Future visions*, p. 110.

50. Fromm, Selfishness and self-love.

51. Kaufman & Jauk, Healthy selfishness and pathological altruism.

52. Fromm, Selfishness and self-love.

53. Neff, K. D. (2003). Self-compassion: An alternate conceptualization of a healthy attitude toward oneself. *Self and Identity, 2*(2), 85–101, p. 87.

54. Neff, K. D., Kirkpatrick, K. L., & Rude, S. S. (2007). Self-compassion and adaptive psychological functioning. *Journal of Research in Personality, 41*(1), 139–154; Neff, K. D., et al. (2018). The forest and the trees: Examining the association of self-compassion and its positive and negative components with psychological functioning. *Self and Identity, 17*(6), 627–645.

55. Interestingly, recent research suggests that self-coldness (e.g., "When I fail at something important to me, I become consumed by feelings of inadequacy," "When I'm feeling down I tend to obsess and fixate on everything that's wrong," "I'm disapproving and judgmental about my own flaws and inadequacies") is even more predictive of health and well-being than self-compassion. See: Brenner, R. E., Heath, P. J., Vogel, D. L., & Credé, M. (2017). Two is more valid than one: Examining the factor structure of the Self-Compassion Scale (SCS). *Journal of Counseling Psychology, 64*(6), 696–707.

56. Items adapted from Raes, F., Pommier, E. A., Neff, K. D., & Van Gucht, D. (2011). Construction and factorial validation of a short form of the Self-Compassion Scale. *Clinical Psychology & Psychotherapy, 18*(3), 250–255.

57. This section was reprinted in a similar form in an article for my blog at Scientific American: Kaufman, S. B. (2018). The pressing need for everyone to quiet their egos. *Scientific American Blogs*. Retrieved from https://blogs.scientificamerican.com/beautiful-minds/the-pressing-need-for-everyone-to-quiet-their-egos.

58. Leary, M. R. (2007). *The curse of the self: Self-awareness, egotism, and the quality of human life.* New York: Oxford University Press.

59. Tesser, A., Crepaz, N., Collins, J. C., Cornell, D., & Beach, S. R. H. (2000). Confluence of self-esteem regulation mechanisms: On integrating the self-zoo. *Personality and Social Psychology Bulletin, 26*(12), 1476–1489.

60. Wayment, H. A., & Bauer, J. J. (Eds.). (2008). *Transcending self-interest: Psychological explorations of the quiet ego.* Washington, DC: American Psychological Association; Heppner, W. L., & Kernis, M. H. (2007). "Quiet ego" functioning: The complementary roles of mindfulness, authenticity, and secure high self-esteem. *Psychological Inquiry, 18*(4), 248–251; Wayment, H. A., Wiist, B., Sullivan, B. M., & Warren, M. A. (2010). Doing and being: Mindfulness, health, and quiet ego characteristics among Buddhist practitioners. *Journal of Happiness Studies, 12*(4), 575–589; Kesebir, P. (2014). A quiet ego quiets death anxiety: Humility as an existential anxiety buffer. *Journal of Personality and Social Psychology, 106*(4), 610–623.

61. Wayment & Bauer, *Transcending self-interest.*

62. Kaufman, The pressing need for everyone to quiet their egos.

63. Wayment & Bauer, *Transcending self-interest.*

64. Wayment, H. A., & Bauer, J. J. (2017). The quiet ego: Motives for self-other balance and growth in relation to well-being. *Journal of Happiness Studies, 19*(3), 881–896.

65. Grant, A. (2016, June 4). Unless you're Oprah, "Be yourself" is terrible advice. Retrieved from https://www.nytimes.com/2016/06/05/opinion/sunday/unless-youre-oprah-be-yourself-is-terrible-advice.html.

66. Ibarra, H., (2017, July 18). The authenticity paradox. Retrieved from https://hbr.org/2015/01/the-authenticity-paradox.

67. Kaufman, S. B. (2019, June 14). Authenticity under fire. Retrieved from https://blogs.scientificamerican.com/beautiful-minds/authenticity-under-fire/.

68. Horney, K. (1959). *Neurosis and human growth.* New York: W. W. Norton, p. 155.

69. The Polish psychiatrist Kazimierz Dabrowski also talked at length about the healthy development of authenticity, suggesting that the person can be guided by constructing an idealization of the personality one wishes to bring into fruition. Dabrowski called this the "personality ideal," and he believed a critical part of this process was an ongoing examination of one's values from a multilevel perspective—examining the hierarchy of values and goals that we can pursue in our day-to-day behavior. With this road map, Dabrowski believed one can live life in pursuit of one's unique and authentic self. See: Tillier, W. (2018). *Personality development through positive disintegration: The work of Kazimierz Dabrowski.* Anna Maria, FL: Maurice Bassett.

70. Kernis, M. H., & Goldman, B. M. (2005). From thought and experience to behavior and interpersonal relationships: A multicomponent conceptualization of authenticity. In A. Tesser, J. V. Wood, & D. A. Stapel (Eds.), *On building, defending, and regulating the self: A psychological perspective* (pp. 31–52). New York: Psychology Press; Wood, A. M., Linley, P. A., Maltby, J., Baliousis, M., & Joseph, S. (2008). The authentic personality: A theoretical and empirical conceptualization and the development of the Authenticity Scale. *Journal of Counseling Psychology, 55*(3), 385–399.

71. de Botton, A. (2016). Why you will marry the wrong person. *The New York Times*. Retrieved from https://www.nytimes.com/2016/05/29/opinion/sunday/why-you-will-marry-the-wrong-person.html.
72. Aron, A., & Aron, E. N. (1986). *Love and the expansion of self: Understanding attraction and satisfaction*. New York: Hemisphere Publishing Corp./Harper & Row.
73. Maslow, *Motivation and personality*, p. 188.
74. Maslow, *Motivation and personality*, p. 199.
75. Adler, P. (1991). *Backboards & blackboards: College athletics and role engulfment*. New York: Columbia University Press; Carbonneau, N., Vallerand, R. J., Lavigne, G. L., & Paquet, Y. (2015). "I'm not the same person since I met you": The role of romantic passion in how people change when they get involved in a romantic relationship. *Motivation and Emotion, 40*(1), 101–17.
76. Carbonneau, Vallerand, Lavigne, & Paquet, "I'm not the same person since I met you."
77. Maslow, *Motivation and personality*, p. 199.
78. Maslow, *Motivation and personality*, p. 199.
79. Maslow, *Motivation and personality*, p. 199.
80. Sahdra, B. K., & Shaver, P. R. (2013). Comparing attachment theory and Buddhist psychology. *International Journal for the Psychology of Religion, 23*(4), 282–293.
81. Sahdra, B. K., Shaver, P. R., & Brown, K. W. (2009). A scale to measure nonattachment: A Buddhist complement to Western research on attachment and adaptive functioning. *Journal of Personality Assessment, 92*(2), 116–127.
82. Maslow, Acceptance of the beloved in being-love. In Hoffman, *Future visions*, p. 37.
83. Maslow, *Motivation and personality*, p. 200.
84. Aron, A., Aron, E. N., Tudor, M., & Nelson, G. (1991). Close relationships as including other in the self. *Journal of Personality and Social Psychology, 60*(2), 241–253.
85. Perel, E. (2016). *Mating in captivity: Unlocking erotic intelligence*. New York: Harper, p. 5.
86. Aron, A., Norman, C. C., Aron, E. N., McKenna, C., & Heyman, R. E. (2000). Couples' shared participation in novel and arousing activities and experienced relationship quality. *Journal of Personality and Social Psychology, 78*(2), 273–284; Reissman, C., Aron, A., & Bergen, M. R. (1993). Shared activities and marital satisfaction: Causal direction and self-expansion versus boredom. *Journal of Social and Personal Relationships, 10*(2), 243–254.
87. Kaufman, S. B. (2017). Real love with Sharon Salzberg. *The Psychology Podcast*. Retrieved from https://scottbarrykaufman.com/podcast/real-love-sharon-salzberg.
88. Berridge, K. C. (1995). Food reward: Brain substrates of wanting and liking. *Neuroscience and Biobehavioral Reviews, 20*(1), 1–25.
89. Perel, *Mating in captivity*.
90. Selterman, D., Gesselman, A. N., & Moors, A. C. (2019). Sexuality through the lens of secure base dynamics: Individual differences in sexploration. *Personality and Individual Differences, 147*, 229–236.
91. Manson, M. (2013). Sex and our psychological needs. *Mark Manson*. Retrieved from https://markmanson.net/sex-and-our-psychological-needs.

92. Meston, C. M., & Buss, D. M. (2007). Why humans have sex. *Archives of Sexual Behavior, 36*(4), 477–507.

93. Péloquin, K., Brassard, A., Delisle, G., & Bédard, M-M. (2013). Integrating the attachment, caregiving, and sexual systems into the understanding of sexual satisfaction. *Canadian Journal of Behavioral Science, 45*(3), 185–195.

94. Selterman, Gesselman, & Moors, Sexuality through the lens of secure base dynamics.

95. Impett, E. A., Gordon, A. M., & Strachman, A. (2008). Attachment and daily goals: A study of dating couples. *Personal Relationships, 15*(3), 375–390; Schachner, D. A., & Shaver, P. R. (2004). Attachment dimensions and sexual motives. *Personal Relationships, 11*(2), 179–195.

96. Péloquin, Brassard, Delisle, & Bédard, Integrating the attachment, caregiving, and sexual systems into the understanding of sexual satisfaction, p. 191.

97. Kashdan, T. B., et al. (2011). Effects of social anxiety and depressive symptoms on the frequency and quality of sexual activity: A daily process approach. *Behaviour Research and Therapy, 49*(5), 352–360.

98. Kaufman, S. B. (2017). The science of passionate sex. *Scientific American Blogs*. Retrieved from https://blogs.scientificamerican.com/beautiful-minds/the-science-of-passionate-sex; Philippe, F. L., Vallerand, R. J., Bernard-Desrosiers, L., Guilbault, V., & Rajotte, G. (2017). Understanding the cognitive and motivational underpinnings of sexual passion from a dualistic model. *Journal of Personality and Social Psychology, 113*(5), 769–785.

99. May, R. (1969). *Love & will*. New York: W. W. Norton, p. 74.

100. Maslow, *Motivation and personality*, p. 188.

101. Debrot, A., Meuwly, N., Muise, A., Impett, E. A., & Schoebi, D. (2017). More than just sex: Affection mediates the association between sexual activity and well-being. *Personality and Social Psychology Bulletin, 43*(3), 287–299.

102. Kashdan, T. B., Goodman, F. R., Stiksma, M., Milius, C. R., & McKnight, P. E. (2018). Sexuality leads to boosts in mood and meaning in life with no evidence for the reverse direction: A daily diary investigation. *Emotion, 18*(4), 563–576.

103. Rollo May *Love & Will*, pp. 96, 278.

104. Helgeson & Fritz, Unmitigated agency and unmitigated communion.

CHAPTER 6. PURPOSE

1. Hoffman, *The right to be human*, p. 219.

2. Hoffman, *The right to be human*, p. 220.

3. Hoffman, *The right to be human*, p. 219.

4. Burrows, L. (2013). Memory of Abraham Maslow faded, not forgotten. *Brandeis Now*. Retrieved from http://www.brandeis.edu/now/2013/may/maslow.html.

5. Lowry, *The journals of A. H. Maslow*, p. 93.

6. Maslow, A. H. (1965). *Eupsychian management: A journal*. Homewood, IL: Richard D. Irwin, Inc., and the Dorsey Press, p. 6.

7. Maslow. *Eupsychian management*.

8. Maslow, *Eupsychian management*, p. x.

9. Ruth Benedict had put forward her ideas about synergistic cultures in a series of lectures

at Bryn Mawr College in 1941, but she never published her manuscript on the topic. Maslow was "horrified" to discover that the manuscript she had given him was the only one in existence. "I was afraid that she would not publish it," Maslow wrote. "She seemed not to care much whether it was published or not. I was also afraid that it might be lost." His fears turned out to be well founded. After her death, the anthropologist Margaret Mead looked through Benedict's files and papers, but her manuscript on synergy was nowhere to be found. So Maslow felt a personal responsibility to share as much of the manuscript as possible and to extend the idea of synergy in fruitful directions. It should be noted, however, that not all scholars believe he extended her work in directions that she would have approved of. In fact, Rene Anne Smith and Kenneth Feigenbaum argue that Maslow's "later work indicated that he did not understand the synergic collective anthropological approach of Benedict but rather misused the concept of synergy to promote a person-centered psychological reductionist position mostly devoid of its cultural context." At any rate, it's clear that Maslow had a great affection for Benedict and deeply resonated with the idea of the importance of a synergy between a person and their culture. See: Maslow, *The farther reaches of human nature* (1993/1971, Chapter 14); Smith, R. A., & Feigenbaum, K. D. (2013). Maslow's intellectual betrayal of Ruth Benedict? *Journal of Humanistic Psychology, 53*(3), 307–321.

10. Smith & Feigenbaum, Maslow's intellectual betrayal of Ruth Benedict?

11. Maslow, *Eupsychian management*, p. 7.

12. Maslow, *Eupsychian management*, p. 103; Maslow, *The farther reaches of human nature* (1993/1971), chapter 14.

13. Maslow, *Eupsychian management*, p. 7.

14. Maslow, *Eupsychian Management*, p. 7.

15. Maslow, A. H., with Stephens, D. C., & Heil, G. (1998). *Maslow on management*. New York, NY: John Wiley & Sons, p. 6.

16. Maslow, *Eupsychian management*, p. 6.

17. Maslow, *Eupsychian management*, p. 6.

18. https://twitter.com/GretaThunberg/status/1167916944520908800?s=20.

19. Edge. (2016). The mattering instinct: A conversation with Rebecca Newberger Goldstein. *Edge.* Retrieved from https://www.edge.org/conversation/rebecca_newberger_goldstein-the-mattering-instinct.

20. Bugental, J. F. T. (1965). *The search for authenticity: An existential-analytic approach to psychotherapy.* New York: Holt, Rinehart and Winston, pp. 267–272.

21. Bugental, *The search for authenticity: An existential-analytic approach to psychotherapy*, pp. 267–272.

22. Maslow, The psychology of happiness. In Hoffman, *Future visions* (pp. 21–25).

23. Frankl, V. E. (1969). *The will to meaning: Foundations and applications of logotherapy.* Cleveland: World Publishing Co.

24. Frankl, V. E. (1966). Self-transcendence as a human phenomenon. *Journal of Humanistic Psychology, 6*(2), 97–106.

25. Marseille, J. (1997). The spiritual dimension in logotherapy: Viktor Frankl's contribution to transpersonal psychology. *The Journal of Transpersonal Psychology, 29*, 1–12.

26. Frankl, V. E. (2006; originally published in 1946). *Man's search for meaning*. Boston: Beacon Press, p. 112.

27. Viktor Frankl deeply influenced the emerging humanistic psychology of the fifties and sixties and may have had a particular influence on Maslow's thinking about self-actualization. According to his biographer Edward Hoffman, Maslow presented his work on self-actualization to a group of leading existential-humanistic psychotherapists in New York City in the early sixties. In attendance were Frankl and Rollo May. Both gave him helpful suggestions, but it was Frankl's comments that Maslow found particularly useful. Frankl noted that self-actualization doesn't operate in a vacuum; one is always actualizing in relation to the people and circumstances around oneself. Maslow agreed that a calling to service from the world, not merely a drive from within, is a central aspect of self-actualization. I can only speculate, but since the meeting occurred just before Maslow's visit to Non-Linear Dynamics in the summer of 1962, that may be one reason why the notion of calling was so prominent in Maslow's summer notes.

28. Yaden, D. B., McCall, T. D., & Ellens, J. H. (Eds.). (2015). *Being called: Scientific, secular, and sacred perspectives*. Santa Barbara, CA: Praeger; Seligman, M. E. P. (2018). *The hope circuit: A psychologist's journey from helplessness to optimism*. New York: PublicAffairs.

29. Wrzesniewkski, A., McCauley, C., Rozin, P., & Schwartz, B. (1997). Jobs, careers, and callings: People's relations to their work. *Journal of Research in Personality, 31*(1), 21–33.

30. Damon, W., & Bronk, K. C. (2007). Taking ultimate responsibility. In H. Gardner (Ed.), *Responsibility at work: How leading professionals act (or don't act) responsibly* (pp. 21–42). San Francisco: Jossey-Bass.

31. Kaufman, S. B. (2018). The path to purpose with William Damon. *The Psychology Podcast*. Retrieved from https://www.scottbarrykaufman.com/podcast/path-purpose-william -damon.

32. Fromm, E. (1955). *The sane society*. New York: Henry Holt.

33. Maslow, *Toward a psychology of being*, p. 9.

34. Emmons, R. A. (1986). Personal strivings: An approach to personality and subjective well-being. *Journal of Personality and Social Psychology, 51*(5), 1058–1068.

35. Hektner, J. M., Schmidt, J. A., & Csikszentmihalyi, M. (2007). *Experience sampling method: Measuring the quality of everyday life*. Thousand Oaks, CA: Sage Publications.

36. Sheldon, K. M. (2014). Becoming oneself: The central role of self-concordant goal selection. *Personality and Social Psychology Review, 18*(4), 349–365.

37. Tillich, P. (1957). *Dynamics of faith*. New York: Harper & Row.

38. Carver, C. S., & Scheier, M. F. (2001). *On the self-regulation of behavior*. New York: Cambridge University Press.

39. Sheldon, Becoming oneself.

40. Baer, J., Kaufman, J. C., & Baumeister, R. F. (2008). *Are we free? Psychology and free will*. New York: Oxford University Press; Harris, S. (2012). *Free will*. New York: Free Press.

41. Gollwitzer, P. M. (2012). Mindset theory of action phases. In P. A. M. Van Lange, A. W. Kruglanski, & T. T. Higgins (Eds.), *The handbook of theories of social psychology* (Vol. 1, pp. 526–45). Thousand Oaks, CA: Sage Publications; Sheldon, Becoming oneself.

42. Hyland, M. E. (1988). Motivational control theory: An integrative framework. *Journal of*

Personality and Social Psychology, 55(4), 642–651; Markus, H., & Ruvolo, A. (1989). Possible selves: Personalized representation of goals. In L. A. Pervin (Ed.), *Goal concepts in personality and social psychology* (pp. 211–241). Hillsdale, NJ: Lawrence Erlbaum.

43. Torrance, E. P. (1983). The importance of falling in love with "something." *Creative Child & Adult Quarterly, 8*(2), 72–78.

44. Torrance, The importance of falling in love with "something."

45. Sheldon, K. M., & Kasser, T. (1995). Coherence and congruence: Two aspects of personality integration. *Journal of Personality and Social Psychology, 68*(3), 531–543.

46. Ryan, R. M., & Deci, E. L. (2000). Self-determination theory and the facilitation of intrinsic motivation, social development, and well-being. *American Psychologist, 55*(1), 68–78.

47. Rigby, C. S., & Ryan, R. R. (2018). Self-determination theory in human resource development: New directions and practical considerations. *Advances in Developing Human Resources, 20*(2), 133–147; Rogers, Client-centered therapy: Its current practice, implications, and theory.

48. Sheldon, Becoming oneself.

49. Sheldon, Becoming oneself.

50. Grant, A. M. (2008). Does intrinsic motivation fuel the prosocial fire? Motivational synergy in predicting persistence, performance, and productivity. *Journal of Applied Psychology, 93*(1), 48–58.

51. Epstein, S. (2014). *Cognitive-experiential theory: An integrative theory of personality.* New York: Oxford University Press.

52. What the research says about character strengths. VIA Institute on Character. Retrieved from https://www.viacharacter.org/research/findings.

53. Kaufman, S. B. (2013). What is talent—and can science spot what we will be best at? *The Guardian.* Retrieved from https://www.theguardian.com/science/2013/jul/07/can-science-spot-talent-kaufman; Kaufman, Ungifted; Niemiec & McGrath, The power of character strengths.

54. Kruglanski, A., Katarzyna, J., Webber, D., Chernikova, M., & Molinario, E. (2018). The making of violent extremists. *Review of General Psychology, 22*(1), 107–120.

55. Frimer, J. A., Walker, L. J., Lee, B. H., Riches, A., & Dunlop, W. L. (2012). Hierarchical integration of agency and communion: A study of influential moral figures. *Journal of Personality, 80*(4), 1117–1145; Walker, L. J., & Frimer, J. A. (2007). Moral personality of brave and caring exemplars. *Journal of Personality and Social Psychology, 93*(5), 845–860.

56. Colby, A., & Damon, W. (1994). *Some do care: Contemporary lives of moral commitment.* New York: Free Press.

57. Frimer, J. A., Biesanz, J. C., Walker, L. J., & MacKinlay, C. W. (2013). Liberals and conservatives rely on common moral foundations when making moral jugments about influential people. *Journal of Personality and Social Psychology, 104*(6), 1040–1059; Haidt, J. (2012). *The righteous mind: Why good people are divided by politics and religion.* London: Allen Lane.

58. Kuszewski, A. (2011). Walking the line between good and evil: The common thread of heroes and villains. *Scientific American Blogs.* Retrieved from https://blogs.scientificamerican.com/guest-blog/walking-the-line-between-good-and-evil-the-common-thread-of-heroes-and-villains.

59. Frimer, J. A., Walker, L. J., Dunlop, W. L., Lee, B. H., & Riches, A. (2011). The integration of agency and communion in moral personality: Evidence of enlightened self-interest. *Journal of Personality and Social Psychology, 101*(1), 149–163.

60. Quote on pp. 1139–1140 of Frimer, J. A., Walker, L. J., Lee, B. H., Riches, A., & Dunlop, W. L. (2012). Hierarchical integration of agency and communion: A study of influential moral figures. *Journal of Personality, 80*, 1117–1145.

61. Frimer, Walker, Lee, Riches, & Dunlop, Hierarchical integration of agency and communion.

62. Grant, Does intrinsic motivation fuel the prosocial fire?

63. Kaufman, S. B. (2018). How to be an optimal human with Kennon Sheldon. *The Psychology Podcast*. Retrieved from https://scottbarrykaufman.com/podcast/optimal-human-kennon-sheldon.

64. Nasby, W., & Read, N. W. (1997). The life voyage of a solo circumnavigator: Integrating theoretical and methodological perspectives. *Journal of Personality, 65*(4), 785–1068, p. 976.

65. Doran, G. T. (1981). There's a S.M.A.R.T. way to write management's goals and objectives. *Management Review, 70*, 35–36.

66. Thanks to Jordyn Feingold for developing these examples.

67. Duffy, R. D., Allan, B. A., Autin, K. L., & Douglass, R. P. (2014). Living a calling and work well-being: A longitudinal study. *Journal of Counseling Psychology, 61*(4), 605–615; Hall, D. T., & Chandler, D. E. (2005). Psychological success: When the career is a calling. *Journal of Organizational Behavior, 26*(2), 155–176; Vianello, M., Galliani, E. M., Rosa, A. D., & Anselmi, P. (2019). The developmental trajectories of calling: Predictors and outcomes. *Journal of Career Assessment*. https://doi.org/10.1177/1069072719831276.

68. Vianello, Galliani, Rosa, & Anselmi, The developmental trajectories of calling.

69. Kaufman, Ungifted.

70. O'Keefe, P. A., Dweck, C. S., & Walton, G. M. (2018). Implicit theories of interest: Finding your passion or developing it? *Psychological Science, 29*(10), 1653–1664.

71. Duckworth, A. (2018). *Grit: The power of passion and perseverance*. New York: Scribner; Miller, C. A. (2017). *Getting grit: The evidence-based approach to cultivating passion, perseverance, and purpose*. Boulder, CO: Sounds True.

72. Q&A. Angela Duckworth. Retrieved from https://angeladuckworth.com/qa.

73. Duckworth, A. L., Peterson, C., Matthews, M. D., & Kelly, D. R. (2007). Grit: Perseverance and passion for long-term goals. *Journal of Personality and Social Psychology, 92*(6), 1087–1101.

74. Kaufman, S. B. (2016). Review of Grit: The power of passion and perseverance. *Scientific American Blogs*. Retrieved from https://blogs.scientificamerican.com/beautiful-minds/review-of-grit-the-power-of-passion-and-perseverance.

75. Manuscript in preparation by Scott Barry Kaufman, Reb Rebele, and Luke Smillie.

76. Epstein, D. (2019). *Range: Why generalists triumph in a specialized world*. New York: Riverhead Books.

77. Equanimity. Insight Meditation Center. Retrieved from https://www.insightmeditationcenter.org/books-articles/articles/equanimity.

78. Antonovsky, A. (1993). The structure and properties of the sense of coherence scale. *Social Science & Medicine, 36*(6), 725–33; Kaufman, S. B. (2016). Grit and authenticity. *Scientific American Blogs.* Retrieved from https://blogs.scientificamerican.com/beauti ful-minds/grit-and-authenticity; Vainio, M. M., & Daukantaité, D. (2015). Grit and different aspects of well-being: Direct and indirect relationships via sense of coherence and authenticity. *Journal of Happiness Studies, 17*(5), 2119–2147.

79. Maslow, *Toward a psychology of being*, p. 131.

80. Vallerand, R. J., et al. (2003). Les passions de l'ame: On obsessive and harmonious passion. *Journal of Personality and Social Psychology, 85*(4), 756–767.

81. Vallerand, R. J., & Rapaport, M. (2017). The role of passion in adult self-growth and de-velopment. In M. L. Wehmeyer, K. A. Shogren, T. D. Little, & S. J. Lopez (Eds.), *Develop-ment of self-determination through the life-course* (pp. 125–143). New York: Springer.

82. Schellenberg, B. J. I., et al. (2018). Testing the dualistic model of passion using a novel quadripartite approach: A look at physical and psychological well-being. *Journal of Per-sonality, 87*(2), 163–180.

83. Vallerand, R. J. (2017). On the two faces of passion: The harmonious and the obsessive. In P. A. O'Keefe & J. M. Harackiewicz (Eds.), *The science of interest* (pp. 149–173). New York: Springer.

84. Carpentier, J., Mageau, G. A., & Vallerand, R. J. (2012). Ruminations and flow: Why do people with a more harmonious passion experience higher well-being? *Journal of Happiness Studies, 13*(3), 501–518.

85. Schellenberg et al. (2018). Testing the dualistic model of passion using a novel quadri-partite approach; Vallerand & Rapaport, The role of passion in adult self-growth and development. In Wehmeyer, Shogren, Little, & Lopez, *Development of self-determination through the life-course.*

86. Niemiec & McGrath, The power of character strengths.

87. Proyer, R. T., Ruch, W., and Buschor, C. (2013). Testing strengths-based interventions: A preliminary study on the effectiveness of a program targeting curiosity, gratitude, hope, humor, and zest for enhancing life satisfaction. *Journal of Happiness Studies, 14*(1), 275–292, doi: 10.1007/s10902-012-9331-9; Proyer, R. T., Gander, F., Wellenzohn, S., & Ruch, W. (2015). Strengths-based positive psychology interventions: A randomized placebo-controlled online trial on long-term effects for a signature strengths-vs. a lesser strengths-intervention. *Frontiers in Psychology, 6,* https://doi.org/10.3389/fpsyg .2015.00456; What the research says about character strengths. VIA Institute on Char-acter; Jessie. (2016). Is there anything special about using character strengths? *Mindful Psych.* Retrieved from http://mindfulpsych.blogspot.com/2016/03/is-there-anything -special-about-using_14.html.

88. Kaufman, S. B. (2015). Which character strengths are most predictive of well-being? *Scientific American Blogs.* Retrieved from https://blogs.scientificamerican.com/beauti-ful-minds/which-character-strengths-are-most-predictive-of-well-being.

89. Bryant, F. B., & Cvengros, J. A. (2004). Distinguishing hope and optimism: Two sides of a coin, or two separate coins? *Journal of Social and Clinical Psychology, 23*(2), 273–302.

90. Lopez, S. J. (2014). *Making hope happen: Create the future you want for yourself and others.*

New York: Atria Books; Snyder, C. R. (1995). Conceptualizing, measuring, and nurturing hope. *Journal of Counseling & Development 73*(3), 355–60, https://doi.org/10.1002/j.1556-6676.1995.tb01764.x; Kaufman, S. B. (2011). The will and ways of hope. *Psychology Today.* Retrieved from https://www.psychologytoday.com/us/blog/beautiful-minds/201112/the-will-and-ways-hope. See also https://blogs.scientificamerican.com/beautiful-minds/2-beautiful-minds-we-lost-in-2016/.

91. Snyder, Conceptualizing, measuring, and nurturing hope.

92. Kashdan, T. B., & Rottenberg, J. (2010). Psychological flexibility as a fundamental aspect of health. *Clinical Psychology Review, 30*, 865–878.

93. Kashdan & Rottenberg. Psychological flexibility as a fundamental aspect of health, 865–878; Visser, P. L., Loess, P. Jeglic, E. L., & Hirsch, J. K. (2013). Hope as a moderator of negative life events and depressive symptoms in a diverse sample. *Stress and Health, 29*(1), 82–88.

94. Goodman, F. R., Disabato, D. J., Kashdan, T. B., & Machell, K. A. (2016). Personality strengths as resilience: A one-year multiwave study. *Journal of Personality, 85*(3), 423–434.

95. Arnold, J. A., Arad, S., Rhoades, J. A., & Drasgow, F. (2000). The empowering leadership questionnaire: The construction and validation of a new scale for measuring leader behaviors. *Journal of Organizational Behavior, 21*(3), 249–269; Bono, J. E., & Judge, T. A. (2018). Self-concordance at work: Toward understanding the motivational effects of transformational leaders. *Academy of Management, 46*(5), 554–571; Hon, A. H. Y. (2011). Enhancing employee creativity in the Chinese context: The mediating role of employee self-concordance. *International Journal of Hospitality Management, 30*(2), 375–384.

96. Deci, E. L., & Ryan, R. M. (2000). The "what" and "why" of goal pursuits: Human needs and the self-determination of behavior. *Psychological Inquiry, 11*(4), 227–268.

97. Sheldon, K. M., et al. (2018). Freedom and responsibility go together: Personality, experimental, and cultural demonstrations. *Journal of Research in Personality, 73*, 63–74.

98. Hon, Enhancing employee creativity in the Chinese context.

99. Rigby & Ryan, Self-determination theory in human resource development.

100. Grant, Does intrinsic motivation fuel the prosocial fire?; Rigby & Ryan, Self-determination theory in human resource development.

101. Woodman, R. W., Sawyer, J. E., & Griffin, R. W. (1993). Toward a theory of organizational creativity. *Academy of Management Review, 18*(2), 293–321.

102. George, J. M. (2007). Creativity in organizations. *Academy of Management Annals, 1*, 439–477; Hon, Enhancing employee creativity in the Chinese context; Wong, S., & Pang, L. (2003). Motivators to creativity in the hotel industry: Perspectives of managers and supervisors. *Tourism Management, 24*(5), 551–559; Woodman, Sawyer, & Griffin, Toward a theory of organizational creativity; Zhou, J., & Shalley, C. E. (2003). Research on employee creativity: A critical review and directions for future research. *Research in Personnel and Human Resources Management, 22*, 165–217.

103. Berg, J. M., Dutton, J. E., & Wrzesniewski, A. (2007). What is job crafting and why does it matter? Michigan Ross School of Business, Center for Positive Organizational Scholarship; Berg, J. M., Dutton, J. E., & Wrzesniewski, A. (2013). Job crafting and

meaningful work. In B. J. Dik, Z. S. Byrne, & M. F. Steger (Eds.), *Purpose and meaning in the workplace* (pp. 81–104). Washington, DC: American Psychological Association; Wrzesniewski, A., & Dutton, J. E. (2001). Crafting a job: Revisioning employees as active crafters of their work. *Academy of Management Review, 26*(2), 179–201.

104. Berg, Dutton, & Wrzesniewski, What is job crafting and why does it matter?

105. Berg, J. M., Grant, A. M., & Johnson, V. (2010). When callings are calling: Crafting work and leisure in pursuit of unanswered occupational callings. *Organization Science, 21*(5), 973–994.

106. Maslow, Toward a psychology of being, p. 10.

107. Wrosch, C., Miller, G. E., Scheier, M. F., & de Pontet, S. B. (2007). Giving up on unattainable goals: Benefits for health? *Personality and Social Psychology Bulletin, 33*(2), 251–265.

108. Brandtstädter, J., & Renner, G. (1990). Tenacious goal pursuit and flexible goal adjustment: Explication and age-related analysis of assimilative and accommodative strategies of coping. *Psychology and Aging, 5*(1), 58–67; Carver, C. S., & Scheier, M. F. (1990). Origins and functions of positive and negative affect: A control-process view. *Psychological Review, 97*(1), 19–35; Carver & Scheier, On the self-regulation of behavior; Heckhausen, J., & Schulz, R. (1995). A life-span theory of control. *Psychological Review, 102*(2), 284–304; Klinger, E. (1975). Consequences of commitment to and disengagement from incentives. *Psychological Review, 82*(1), 1–25; Nesse, R. M. (2000). Is depression an adaptation? *Archives of General Psychiatry, 57*(1), 14–20.

109. Wrosch, C., Scheier, M. F., Miller, G. E., Schulz, R., & Carver, C. S. (2003). Adaptive self-regulation of unattainable goals: Goal disengagement, goal reengagement, and subjective well-being. *Personality and Social Psychology Bulletin, 29*(12), 1494–1508.

110. Grogan, J. (2012). *Encountering America: Humanistic psychology, sixties culture, and the shaping of the modern self.* New York: Harper Perennial.

111. Michael Murphy, personal correspondence, May 10, 2018.

112. Feng is a fascinating case study in his own right. He served as an accountant (managing finances on an abacus), "keeper of the baths," and "crazy Taoist" at the upstart springs. Born into a wealthy Buddhist family in China (his father was one of the founders of the Bank of China), Feng came to the United States and earned a master's degree in international finance at the Wharton School at the University of Pennsylvania. After graduating from Penn, Feng wandered across the country, spending time in a Quaker community and living in a Georgia commune at the time when *Brown v. Board of Education of Topeka* was decided. In the mid-fifties, Feng moved out west, hanging out with Jack Kerouac, teaching Taoism, and translating Chinese classics for the philosopher Alan Watts. Watts considered Feng "the real thing" and recommended him to aspiring Beat and hippie Taoists.

Feng became interested in the spirituality movement then growing in Northern California, which soon spread globally. As Watts put it, "Between, say, 1958 and 1970 a huge tide of spiritual energy in the form of poetry, music, philosophy, painting, religion, communications techniques in radio, television, and cinema, dancing, theater, and general life-style swept out of [San Francisco] and its environs to affect America and the whole world." In the early sixties, Feng became friends with Richard Price and Michael Murphy, founders of Big Sur Hot Springs, soon to be Esalen Institute. He was drawn to the growing "human potential movement," which was deeply inspired by humanistic psychology. Indeed, Maslow's book *Toward a Psychology of Being* had just been published, and the young Esalen community resonated deeply with Maslow's notions of self-actualization and peak experience, which jibed so well with their own developing ideas about human potential and spirituality. Maslow's book also gave their ideas academic legitimacy. As Jeffrey Kripal notes in his book *Esalen: American and the Religion of No Religion*, "It was as if Abraham Maslow and this book had appeared on the cultural horizon just for them."

113. Hoffman, *The right to be human*.
114. Hoffman, *The right to be human*.
115. Grogan, *Encountering America*, p. 158.
116. Hoffman, *The right to be human,* p. 276.
117. Murphy, personal correspondence, May 10, 2018. In a journal entry dated April 30, 1970, Maslow described his relationship with Murphy as one defined by "self-exposure," "feedback of intimacies," and directness. Reciprocally, in another entry, Murphy was described as "far-out but still really open, curious, not tied to a system"—a description that clearly overlapped with the spirit residing deep within Maslow (September 19, 1967, journal entry).

PART III. HEALTHY TRANSCENDENCE

1. Lowry, *A. H. Maslow: An intellectual portrait*, p. 10.
2. Lowry, *A. H. Maslow: An intellectual portrait*, p. 11.
3. Lowry, *A. H. Maslow: An intellectual portrait*, p. 12.
4. Lowry, *A. H. Maslow: An intellectual portrait*, pp. 14–15.
5. Lowry, *A. H. Maslow: An intellectual portrait*, p. 16.
6. Richard Lowry's insight on Maslow's writing style: "His, for better or worse, was the style of a man who felt he had a great deal of truth to impart to the world and who, perceiving that life is short, could scarcely take time out for the conventional amenities. Whatever might have been Maslow's virtues and shortcomings, he was in any case a man of great passion and honesty. Perhaps at times his passion took the form of arrogance; perhaps, too, his honesty sometimes looked like naiveté. But throughout it all he was a man who took himself, his work, and the world around him with utter ingenuous seriousness. His early paper on Emerson was only the first of a great many instances in which he abhorred, or loved, or studied, or sought after something with all the vehemence that was in him." See: Lowry, *A. H. Maslow: An intellectual portrait*, p. 16.

CHAPTER 7. PEAK EXPERIENCES

1. Hoffman, *The right to be human*.
2. Be You Fully. (2016, May 24). Abraham Maslow on Peak Experiences [Video file]. Retrieved from https://www.youtube.com/watch?v=zcOHMGe7lYg.

3. Be You Fully. Abraham Maslow on Peak Experiences.

4. James, W. (1902). *The varieties of religious experience*. Cambridge, MA: Harvard University Press.

5. Hoffman, *The right to be human*, p. 224.

6. Hoffman, *The right to be human*, p. 224.

7. Maslow, A. H. (1957). Cognition of being in the peak experience. *The Journal of Genetic Psychology, 94*, 43–66.

8. Maslow, Cognition of being in the peak experience, p. 43.

9. Maslow, Cognition of being in the peak experience, p. 52.

10. Maslow, Cognition of being in the peak experience, p. 64.

11. It really frustrated Maslow that this point was so often overlooked. In a journal entry dated December 2, 1967, Maslow wrote, "Big question today [transcendence conference] with the philosophers: how can you best prove the validity of the 'reality' perceived in peak-experiences? I stressed the need for validation and confirmation in latter time by science, logic, reason, etc., i.e., that some revelations turn out to be correct, some incorrect. But they didn't seem to get it. Not presented well? Also mixed up with the question: Why should I not trust a Nazi's 'relevation'? They seemed to be convinced that I was glorifying experience & calling it necessarily valid. Nothing I could say could get this out of their heads. Better work this up some more. Examples of researches which do confirm these illuminations & which do not."

12. Maslow, Cognition of being in the peak experience, p. 65.

13. Maslow, Cognition of being in the peak experience, p. 65.

14. Maslow, Cognition of being in the peak experience, p. 62.

15. Maslow was so inspired to reconceptualize his definition of self-actualization that he wrote: "We may define [self-actualization] as an episode, or a spurt in which the powers of the person come together in a particularly efficient and intensely enjoyable way, and in which he is more integrated and less split, more open for experience, more idiosyncratic, more perfectly expressive or spontaneous, or fully functioning, more creative, more humorous, more ego-transcending, more independent of his lower needs, etc. He becomes in these episodes more truly himself, more perfectly actualizing his potentialities, closer to the core of his Being."

16. Maslow, Cognition of being in the peak experience, p. 62.

17. In digging through Maslow's personal correspondences with colleagues around this time, I stumbled upon a letter from the famed personality psychologist Gordon Allport that referenced a lecture on peak experiences that Maslow gave on April 12, 1957, entitled "Two Kinds of Cognition and Their Integration." Considering the similarity of their approaches to studying personality—Allport was interested in studying the whole person and mature religiosity—it should come as little surprise that Allport reacted with great enthusiasm to Maslow's lecture on peak experiences. As Allport wrote Maslow: "How much stimulation your paper brought! You can see how many angles it has for me. Thanks for writing it." In turn, he suggested that Maslow bring his notion of peak experience "closer to the literature on mysticism." It's not clear how much Allport's suggestion influenced Maslow's subsequent thinking and writing on the link between peak

experiences and religion, but it's interesting to think that Allport played a pivotal but uncredited role.

18. Maslow, A. H. (1964). *Religions, values, and peak experiences.* Columbus, OH: Ohio State University Press.

19. Maslow, *Religions, values, and peak experiences,* p. 19.

20. David Yaden, personal correspondence.

21. David Yaden, personal correspondence.

22. Newberg, A., et al. (2001). The measurement of regional cerebral blood flow during the complex cognitive task of mediation: A preliminary SPECT study. *Psychiatry Research: Neuroimaging, 106*(2), 113–122; Newberg, A. B., & Iversen, J. (2003). The neural basis of the complex mental task of meditation: Neurotransmitter and neurochemical considerations. *Medical Hypotheses, 61*(2), 282–291.

23. Yaden, D. B., Haidt, J., Hood, R. W., Vago, D. R., & Newberg, A. B. (2017). The varieties of self-transcendent experience. *Review of General Psychology, 21*(2), 143–160.

24. List adapted from Levin, J., & Steele, L. (2005). The transcendent experience: Conceptual, theoretical, and epidemiologic perspectives. *Explore, 1*(2), 89–101.

25. Azari, N. P., et al. (2001). Neural correlates of religious experience. *The European Journal of Neuroscience, 13*(8), 1649–1652; Beauregard, M., & Paquette, V. (2006). Neural correlates of a mystical experience in Carmelite nuns. *Neuroscience Letters, 405*(3), 186–190; Farrer, C., & Frith, C. D. (2002). Experiencing oneself vs. another person as being the cause of an action: The neural correlates of the experience of agency. *NeuroImage, 15*(3), 596–603; Johnstone, B., Bodling, A., Cohen, D., Christ, S. E., & Wegrzyn, A. (2012). Right parietal lobe-related "selflessness" as the neuropsychological basis of spiritual transcendence. *International Journal for the Psychology of Religion, 22*(4), 267–284.

26. d'Aquili, E., & Newberg, A. B. (1999). *The mystical mind: Probing the biology of religious experience.* Minneapolis: Fortress Press.

27. Sagan, C. (2011). *Pale blue dot: A vision of the human future in space.* New York: Ballantine Books.

28. Newberg, A. B., & d'Aquili, E. G. (2000). The neuropsychology of religious and spiritual experience. *Journal of Consciousness Studies, 7*(11–12), 251–266.

29. Csikszentmihalyi, M., & LeFevre, J. (1989). Optimal experience in work and leisure. *Journal of Personality and Social Psychology, 56*(5), 815–822; Csikszentmihalyi, M. (1990). *Flow: The psychology of optimal experience.* New York: Harper & Row; Kotler, S. (2014). *The rise of Superman: Decoding the science of ultimate human performance.* New York: Houghton Mifflin Harcourt; Kowal, J., & Fortier, M. S. (1999). Motivational determinants of flow: Contributions from self-determination theory. *The Journal of Social Psychology, 139*(3), 355–368; Walker, C. J. (2008). Experiencing flow: Is doing it together better than doing it alone? *The Journal of Positive Psychology, 5,* 3–11.

30. Goleman, D., & Davidson, R. J. (2017). *Altered traits: Science reveals how meditation changes your mind, brain, and body.* New York: Avery.

31. Watkins, P. C. (2013). *Gratitude and the good life: Toward a psychology of appreciation.* New York: Springer; Emmons, R. A. (2013). *Gratitude works!: A 21-day program for creating*

emotional prosperity. San Francisco: Jossey-Bass; Emmons, R. A., & McCullough, M. E. (Eds.). (2004). *The psychology of gratitude*. New York: Oxford University Press.

32. Fredrickson, *Love 2.0*; Sternberg, R. J., & Sternberg, K. (Eds.). (2019). *The new psychology of love* (2nd ed.). New York: Cambridge University Press.

33. Schneider, K. (2004). *Rediscovery of awe: Splendor, mystery and the fluid center of life*. St. Paul: Paragon House; Yaden, D. B., et al. (2018). The development of the Awe Experience Scale (AWE-S): A multifactorial measure for a complex emotion. *The Journal of Positive Psychology, 14*(4), 474–488.

34. Belzak, W. C. M., Thrash, T. M., Sim, Y. Y., & Wadsworth, L. M. (2017). Beyond hedonic and eudaimonic well-being: Inspiration and the self-transcendence tradition. In M. D. Robinson & M. Eid (Eds.), *The happy mind: Cognitive contributions to well-being* (pp. 117–138). New York: Springer; Erickson, T., & Abelson, J. L. (2012). Even the downhearted may be uplifted: Moral elevation in the daily life of clinically depressed and anxious adults. *Journal of Social and Clinical Psychology, 31*(7), 707–728; Haidt, J. (2000). The positive emotion of elevation. *Prevention & Treatment, 3*(1); Shiota, M. N., Thrash, T. M., Danvers, A. F., & Dombrowski, J. T. (2014). Transcending the self: Awe, elevation, and inspiration. In M. M. Tugade, M. N. Shiota, & L. D. Kirby (Eds.), *Handbook of positive emotions* (pp. 362–377). New York: Guilford Press.

35. Kotler, S., & Wheal, J. (2018). *Stealing fire: How Silicon Valley, the Navy SEALs, and maverick scientists are revolutionizing the way we live and work*. New York: Dey Street; Newberg, A., & Waldman, M. R. (2017). *How enlightenment changes your brain: The new science of transformation*. New York: Avery.

36. Koenig, H., King, D. E., & Carson, V. B. (2012). *Handbook of religion and health* (2nd ed.). New York: Oxford University Press; Yaden, D. B. et al. (2017). The noetic quality: A multimethod exploratory study. *Psychology of Consciousness: Theory, Research, and Practice, 4*(1), 54–62; Yaden, Haidt, Hood, Vago, & Newberg, The varieties of self-transcendent experience.

37. Yaden et al., The noetic quality.

38. James, *The varieties of religious experience*.

39. Yaden, D. B., et al. (2016). The language of ineffability: Linguistic analysis of mystical experiences. *Psychology of Religion and Spirituality, 8*(3), 244–252; Yaden et al., The noetic quality.

40. Leary, M. R., Diebels, K. J., Jongman-Sereno, K. P., & Hawkins, A. (2016). Perspectives on hypo-egoic phenomena from social and personality psychology. In K. W. Brown & M. R. Leary (Eds.), *The Oxford handbook of hypo-egoic phenomena* (pp. 47–62). New York: Oxford University Press.

41. Leary, Diebels, Jongman-Sereno, & Hawkins, Perspectives on hypo-egoic phenomena from social and personality psychology. In Brown & Leary, *The Oxford handbook of hypo-egoic phenomena*.

42. Engler, J. (1984). Therapeutic aims in psychotherapy and meditation: Developmental stages in the representation of self. *Journal of Transpersonal Psychology, 16*(1), 25–61; Shaheen, J. (2004). Just as it is. *Tricycle*. Retrieved from https://tricycle.org/magazine/just-as-it-is.

43. Maslow, Peak experiences as acute identity experiences, p. 255.

44. Maslow, Peak experiences as acute identity experiences, p. 255.

45. I, too, became fascinated with this paradox and looked at my own dataset for guidance. As I was constructing my Characteristics of Self-Actualization Scale, I found support for the notion that self-actualizing people tend to experience a greater frequency of peak experiences in their daily lives. So far so good. But then I looked at the correlations between the self-actualization scale and a new scale Yaden created to measure a tendency to experience transcendence in one's daily life. Yaden's scale consisted of the following two aspects of transcendence: oneness with all things (e.g., "I often have experiences of feeling entirely connected to humanity") and self-loss (e.g., "I often have experiences in which, for a moment, I lose my sense of self"). Participants were asked to rate how much they experience each of these aspects in their everyday lives. I found that both oneness and self-loss were positively correlated with the frequency of peak experiences in daily life. However, while a tendency toward oneness experiences was positively correlated with every other characteristic of self-actualization—including increased levels of authenticity, purpose, and humanitarian concern—a general tendency toward self-loss, viewed by itself, was negatively related to most of the other aspects of self-actualization, including authenticity. See: Kaufman, S. B. (2018). Self-actualizing people in the 21st century: Integration with contemporary theory and research on personality and well-being. *Journal of Humanistic Psychology,* https:/doi.org/10.1177/0022167818809187.

46. Maslow, *Toward a psychology of being,* p. 85.

47. Keltner, D., & Haidt, J. (2003). Approaching awe, a moral spiritual, and aesthetic emotion. *Cognition and Emotion, 17*(2), 297–314.

48. Piff, P. K., Dietze, P., Feinberg, M., Stancato, D. M., & Keltner, D. (2015). Awe, the small self, and prosocial behavior. *Journal of Personality and Social Psychology, 108*(6), 883–899; Gordon, A. M., et al. (2016). The dark side of the sublime: Distinguishing a threat-based variant of awe. *Journal of Social Psychology, 113*(12), 310–328; Bonner, E. T., & Friedman, H. L. (2011). A conceptual clarification of the experience of awe: An interpretative phenomenological analysis. *The Humanistic Psychologist, 39*(3), 222–235; Chirico, A., Yaden, D. B., Riva, G., & Gaggioli, A. (2016). The potential of virtual reality for the investigation of awe. *Frontiers in Psychology, 7,* Article ID 1766; Shiota, M. N., Keltner, D., & Mossman, A. (2007). The nature of awe: Elicitors, appraisals, and effects on self-concept. *Cognition and Emotion, 21*(5), 944–963.

49. Rudd, M., Vohs, K. D., & Aaker, J. (2012). Awe expands people's perception of time, alters decision making, and enhances well-being. *Psychological Science, 23*(10), 1130–1136; Krause, N., & Hayward, R. D. (2015). Assessing whether practical wisdom and awe of God are associated with life satisfaction. *Psychology of Religion and Spirituality, 7*(1), 51–59.

50. Rudd, Vohs, & Aaker, Awe expands people's perception of time, alters decision making, and enhances well-being.

51. Piff, Dietze, Feinberg, Stancato, & Keltner, Awe, the small self, and prosocial behavior; Prade, C., & Saroglou, V. (2016). Awe's effects on generosity and helping. *The Journal of Positive Psychology, 11*(5), 522–530.

52. Yang, Y., Yang, Z., Bao, T., Liu, Y., & Passmore, H-A. (2016). Elicited awe decreases aggression. *Journal of Pacific Rim Psychology, 10,* e11.

53. van Elk, M., Karinen, A., Specker, E., Stamkou, E., & Baas, M. (2016). "Standing in awe": The effects of awe on body perception and the relation with absorption. *Collabra, 2*(1), 4.

54. Van Cappellen, P., & Saroglou, V. (2012). Awe activates religious and spiritual feelings and behavioral intentions. *Psychology of Religion and Spirituality, 4*(3), 223–236.

55. Valdesolo, P., & Graham, J. (2014). Awe, uncertainty, and agency detection. *Psychological Science, 25*(1), 170–178.

56. Yaden et al., The development of the Awe Experience Scale (AWE-S).

57. Yaden et al., The development of the Awe Experience Scale (AWE-S).

58. Harrison, I. B. (1975). On the maternal origins of awe. *The Psychoanalytic Study of the Child, 30,* 181–195.

59. Graham, J., & Haidt, J. (2010). Beyond beliefs: Religions bind individuals into moral communities. *Personality and Social Psychology Review, 14*(1), 140–150.

60. de Botton, A. (2013). *Religion for atheists: A non-believer's guide to the uses of religion.* New York: Vintage.

61. TEDx Talks. (2016, June 20). "Open Wide and Say Awe," Katherine Maclean, TEDx-OrcasIsland [Video file]. Retrieved from https://www.youtube.com/watch?v=Zl jALxpt3iU.

62. MacLean, K. A., Johnson, M. W., & Griffiths, R. R. (2011). Mystical experience occasioned by the hallucinogen psilocybin lead to increases in the personality domain of openness. *Journal of Psychopharmacology, 25*(11), 1453–1461.

63. Pollan, M. (2018). *How to change your mind: What the new science of psychedelics teaches us about consciousness, dying, addiction, depression, and transcendence.* New York: Penguin Press.

64. Yaden, D. B., et al. (2016). Of roots and fruits: A comparison of psychedelic and nonpsychedelic mystical experiences. *Journal of Humanistic Psychology, 57*(4), 338–353.

65. Griffiths, R. R., Richards, W. A., McCann, U., & Jesse, R. (2006). Psilocybin can occasion mystical-type experiences having substantial and sustained personal meaning and spiritual significance. *Psychopharmacology, 187*(3), 268–283; Griffiths, R., Richards, W., Johnson, M., McCann, U., & Jesse, R. (2008). Mystical-type experiences occasioned by psilocybin mediate the attribution of personal meaning and spiritual significance 14 months later. *Journal of Psychopharmacology, 22*(6), 621–632.

66. Griffiths, R. R., et al. (2016). Psilocybin produces substantial and sustained decreases in depression and anxiety in patients with life-threatening cancer: A randomized double-blind trial. *Journal of Psychopharmacology, 30*(12), 1181–1197; Grob, C. S., et al. (2011). Pilot study of psilocybin treatment for anxiety in patients with advanced-stage cancer. *Archives of General Psychiatry, 68*(1), 71–78.

67. Danforth, A. L., Struble, C. M., Yazar-Klosinski, B., & Grob, C. S. (2016). MDMA-assisted therapy: A new treatment model for social anxiety in autistic adults. *Progress in Neuro-Psychopharmacology and Biological Psychiatry, 64,* 237–249.

68. Errizoe, D., et al. (2018). Effects of psilocybin therapy on personality structure. *Acta Psychiatrica Scandinavica, 138*(1), 368–378.

69. Katherine MacLean, personal correspondence, June 14, 2018.

70. Cosimano, M. (2014). Love: The nature of our true self. MAPS Bulletin Annual Report, 39–41. https://pdfs.semanticscholar.org/82bd/2468ba88d088146f4065658b02 b7785b3603.pdf .

71. Hood, R. W. (1975). The construction and preliminary validation of a measure of reported mystical experience. *Journal for the Scientific Study of Religion, 14*(1), 29–41; Newberg, et al., The measurement of regional cerebral blood flow during the complex cognitive task of meditation; Zanesco, A. P., King, B. G., MacLean, K. A., & Saron, C. D. (2018). Cognitive aging and long-term maintenance of attentional improvements following meditation training. *Journal of Cognitive Enhancement, 2*(3), 259–275.

72. Griffiths, R. R., et al. (2018). Psilocybin-occasioned mystical-type experience in combination with meditation and other spiritual practices produces enduring positive changes in psychological functioning and in trait measure of prosocial attitudes and behaviors. *Journal of Psychopharmacology, 32*(1), 49–69.

73. Shiota, Keltner, & Mossman, The nature of awe.

74. Harari, Y. N. (2017). *Homo deus: A brief history of tomorrow.* New York: HarperCollins.

75. Yaden, D. B., et al. (2016). The overview effect: Awe and self-transcendent experience in space flight. *Psychology of Consciousness: Theory, Research, and Practice, 3*(1), 1–11.

76. Harari, Homo deus.

77. The philosopher David Chalmers makes a similar argument. See: Kaufman, S. B. (2017). Philosopher David Chalmers thinks we might be living in a simulated reality. *The Psychology Podcast.* Retrieved from https://scottbarrykaufman.com/podcast/philosopher -david-chalmers-thinks-we-might-be-living-in-a-simulated-reality.

78. Yaden, D. B., Eichstaedt, J. C., & Medaglia, J. D. (2018). The future of technology in positive psychology: Methodological advances in the science of well-being. *Frontiers in Psychology, 9,* https://doi.org/10.3389/fpsyg.2018.00962.

79. Chirico, Yaden, Riva, & Gaggioli, The potential of virtual reality for the investigation of awe; Chirico, A., et al. (2017). Effectiveness of immersive videos in inducing awe: An experimental study. *Scientific Reports, 7*(1); Chirico, A. & Yaden, D. B. (2018). Awe: A self-transcendent and sometimes transformative emotion. In H. C. Lench (Ed.), *The function of emotions: When and why emotions help us* (pp. 221–233): New York: Springer; Chirico, A., Glaveanu, V. P., Cipresso, P., Riva, G., & Gaggioli, A. (2018). Awe enhances creative thinking: An experimental study. *Creativity Research Journal, 30*(2), 123–31.

80. Hallett, M. (2000). Transcranial magnetic stimulation and the human brain. *Nature, 406*(6792), 147–150.

81. Fregni, F., & Pascual-Leone, A. (2007). Technology insight: Noninvasive brain stimulation in neurology—perspectives on the therapeutic potential of rTMS and tDSC. *Nature Clinical Practice Neurology, 3,* 383–393.

82. Hamilton, R., Messing, S., and Chatterjee, A. (2011). Rethinking the thinking cap: Ethics of neural enhancement using noninvasive brain stimulation. *Neurology, 76*(2), 187–193; O'Reardon, J. P., et al. (2007). Efficacy and safety of transcranial magnetic stimulation in the acute treatment of major depression: A multisite randomized controlled trial. *Biological Psychiatry, 62*(11), 1208–1216; Smith, K. S., Mahler, S. V., Peciña,

S., & Berridge, K. C. (2010). Hedonic hotspots: Generating sensory pleasure in the brain. In M. L. Kringelbach, & K. C. Berridge (Eds.), *Pleasures of the Brain* (pp. 27–49). New York: Oxford University Press; Medaglia, J. D., Zurn, P., Sinnott-Armstrong, W., & Bassett, D. S. (2017). Mind control as a guide for the mind. *Nature Human Behaviour, 1,* Article ID 0119, doi: 10.1038/s41562-017-0119; Medaglia, J. D., Yaden, D. B., Helion, C., & Haslam, M. (2019). Moral attitudes and willingness to enhance and repair cognition with brain stimulation. *Brain Stimulation, 12*(1), 44–53.

83. Berger, M. W. (2018). Brain stimulation decreases intent to commit assault. *Penn Today.* Retrieved from https://penntoday.upenn.edu/news/brain-stimulation-decreases-intent -commit-physical-sexual-assault.

84. Yaden, Eichstaedt, & Medaglia, The future of technology in positive psychology.

85. Nozick, R. (1974). *Anarchy, state, and utopia.* New York: Basic Books.

86. Maslow, *The farther reaches of human nature,* p. 271.

87. Kaufman, S. B. (2017). Your brain on enlightenment with Dr. Andrew Newberg. *The Psychology Podcast.* Retrieved from https://scottbarrykaufman.com/podcast/your-brain -on-enlightenment-with-dr-andrew-newberg.

88. Kaufman, S. B. (2018). Open wide and say awe with Katherine MacLean. *The Psychology Podcast.* Retrieved from https://scottbarrykaufman.com/podcast/open-wide-say-awe -katherine-maclean.

89. Maslow, A. H. (1966, November 22). Drugs—Critique. Maslow Papers, Box M 4448, Archives of the History of American Psychology, Cummings Center for the History of Psychology, University of Akron, Akron, OH.

90. Maslow, A. H. (1966, May 11). Letter to Mrs. Paula Gordon from Maslow, 5/11/1966, discussing peak experiences and the use of psychaedelic [*sic*] drugs in research. Maslow Papers, Box M 4471, Archives of the History of American Psychology, Cummings Center for the History of Psychology, University of Akron, Akron, OH.

91. According to Edward Hoffman, when Timothy Leary arrived at Harvard in 1960, Maslow and Leary "became quite friendly, and spent many hours discussing their mutual interests in creativity, superior mental functioning, and peak experiences." In 1962, Maslow even collaborated with Leary on a panel on drug-induced peak experiences, and his daughter Ellen worked for Leary as a research assistant. In theory, Maslow supported rigorous research on psychedelics. But he was unwilling to try any of the drugs himself and grew increasingly concerned about reliance on drugs as a fast track to self-actualization, warning that LSD abuse was likely to result in intellectual atrophy, aimlessness, and disconnection rather than self-actualization. "It's too easy," Maslow told Leary during their frequent lunches together. "To have a peak experience, you have to sweat." Upon which Leary teased Maslow, "All right, then, Abe, you want to sweat? Well, do you plan to walk back from Harvard Square to Brandeis, or are you going to drive? You mentioned going to California next month. Do you plan to walk there or take a plane? You want to sweat, don't you?" See: Hoffman, *The right to be human* (pp. 265–266). Maslow, A. H. (1963, October 24). Z. M. Schachter and Maslow, 1963, discussing various research implication of LSD and peak experiences. Maslow Papers, Folder LSD—Drugs, Box M 4471, Archives of the History of American Psychol-

ogy, Cummings Center for the History of Psychology, University of Akron, Akron, OH.; Maslow, A. H. (1963, October 24). Letter to Rabbi Zalman Schachter. Maslow Papers, Folder LSD—Drugs, Box M 449.7, Archives of the History of American Psychology, Cummings Center for the History of Psychology, University of Akron, Akron, OH.

92. Grogan, *Encountering America*.

93. Foreword by Warren Bennis to the new edition of Maslow, A. H. (1998). *Maslow on management*. New York: Wiley, pp. x–xi.

CHAPTER 8. THEORY Z: TOWARD THE FARTHER REACHES OF HUMAN NATURE

1. Lowry, *The journals of A. H. Maslow*, p. 794.

2. Lowry, *The journals of A. H. Maslow*, pp. 798–799.

3. Koltko-Rivera, M. E. (2006). Rediscovering the later version of Maslow's hierarchy of needs: Self-transcendence and opportunities for theory, research, and unification. *Review of General Psychology, 10*(4), 302–317.

4. Frick, W. B. (2000). Remembering Maslow: Reflections on a 1968 interview. *Journal of Humanistic Psychology, 40*(2), 128–147, p. 142.

5. Maslow, *The farther reaches of human nature*, p. 271.

6. Maslow, *The farther reaches of human nature*, p. 271.

7. Adapted from Maslow, *The farther reaches of human nature*, pp. 273–285.

8. Maslow further made this intriguing suggestion: "To avoid resentments, from the impotent envy of the weak, of the underprivileged, of the less capable, of those who need to be helped, is to pay them, not with more money, but with less, to pay them rather with 'higher pay' and with 'metapay.' It follows from the principles so far set further here and elsewhere that this would please both the self-actualizers and the less psychologically developed, and would abort the development of the mutually exclusive and antagonistic classes or castes that we have seen throughout human history. All we need to do to make practical this post-Marxian, post-historical possibility is to learn not to pay too much for money, i.e., to value the higher rather than the lower. Also it would be necessary here to desymbolize money; i.e., it must not symbolize success, respect worthiness, or loveworthiness. These changes should in principle be quite easily possible since they already accord with the preconscious value-life of self-actualizing people. Whether or not this *Weltanschauung* is or is not more characteristic of transcenders remains to be discovered. So perhaps this could be a help in designing a world in which the most capable, the most awakened, the most idealistic would be chosen and loved as leaders, as teachers, as obviously benevolent and unselfish authority." In support of this, research has found that people are indeed willing to accept lower salaries for more meaningful work. So it is possible to make "virtue" pay, or at the very least to make *meaning* pay. See Hu, J., and Hirsch, J. B. (2017). Accepting lower salaries for meaningful work. *Frontiers in Psychology, 29*, 1649.

9. Maslow, *Toward a psychology of being*.

10. In recent years, Aaron Weidman and his colleagues have found that people have two fundamentally different conceptualizations of humility. Some people, when asked to think about humility, conjure up images of humiliation and self-abasement (D-humility).

Those scoring high in this form of self-abasing humility are characterized by a low opinion of themselves, feelings of meekness and insignificance, a hiding from the evaluations of others, and a deep loathing of their flaws. Such people tend to display greater shame, embarrassment, submissive behavior, insecure self-esteem, and neuroticism. Another way people conceptualize humility—which humility researcher Pelin Kesebir believes is closer to the real meaning of humility—is an accurate assessment and acceptance of one's strengths and limitations, a lack of egotism and self-focus, and an appreciation of the world surrounding oneself. Those with an abundance of this form of appreciative humility (or B-humility) tend to have higher levels of authentic pride, prestige, agency, secure self-esteem, a tendency toward the celebration of others, openness to experience, and more enduring happiness. While it hasn't been tested yet, I suspect they also tend to experience more transcendent experiences in their daily lives. See: Weidman, A. C., Cheng, J. T., & Tracy, J. L. (2016). The psychological structure of humility. *Journal of Personality and Social Psychology, 114*(1), 153–178.

11. In *Toward a Psychology of Being*, Maslow described B-playfulness in the following way: "It is very hard to describe this B-playfulness since the English language falls far short here (as in general it is unable to describe the 'higher' subjective experiences). It has a cosmic or a godlike, good-humored quality, certainly transcending hostility of any kind. It could as easily be called happy joy, or gay exuberance or delight. It has a quality of spilling over as of richness or surplus (not D-motivated). It is existential in the sense that it is an amusement or delight with both the smallness (weakness) and the largeness (strength) of the human being, transcending the dominance-subordinance polarity. It has a certain quality of triumph in it, sometimes perhaps also of relief. It is simultaneously mature and childlike." (p. 123).

12. Loevinger, J. (1976). *Ego development: Conceptions and theories*. San Francisco: Jossey-Bass; Erikson, E. H. (1982). *The life cycle completed*. New York: W. W. Norton; McAdams, D. P., & de St. Aubin, E. (1992). A theory of generativity and its assessment through self-report, behavioral acts, and narrative themes in autobiography. *Journal of Personality and Social Psychology, 62*(6), 1003–1015; Kegan, R. (1982). *The evolving self*. Cambridge, MA: Harvard University Press; Eriksen, K. (2006). The constructive developmental theory of Robert Kegan. *The Family Journal: Counseling and Therapy for Couples and Families, 14*(3), 290–298; Melvin, E., & Cook-Greuter, S. (Eds.). (2000). *Creativity, spirituality, and transcendence: Paths to integrity and wisdom in the mature self*. Stamford, CT: Ablex Publication Corporation; Pfaffenberger, A. H., Marko, P. W., & Combs, A. (2011). *The postconventional personality*. Albany: State University of New York Press; Wilber, K. (2000). *Integral psychology: Consciousness, spirit, psychology, therapy*. Boston: Shambhala Publications; Cowan, C. C., & Todorovic, N. (Eds.). (2005). *The never ending quest: Dr. Clare W. Graves explores human nature*. Santa Barbara, CA: ECLET Publishing.

13. Kramer, D. A. (2000). Wisdom as a classical source of human strength: Conceptualization and empirical inquiry. *Journal of Social and Clinical Psychology, 19*(1), 83–101; Staudinger, U. M., Lopez, D. F., & Baltes, P. B. (1997). The psychometric location of wisdom-related performance: Intelligence, personality, and more? *Personality and Social Bulletin, 23*(11), 1200–1214.

14. See: Loevinger, J. (1976). *Ego development: Conceptions and theories*. San Francisco: Jossey-Bass; Erikson, E. H. (1982). *The life cycle completed*. New York: W. W. Norton; McAdams, D. P., & de St. Aubin, E. (1992). A theory of generativity and its assessment through self-report, behavioral acts, and narrative themes in autobiography. *Journal of Personality and Social Psychology, 62*(6), 1003–1015; Kegan, R. (1982). *The evolving self*. Cambridge, MA: Harvard University Press; Eriksen, K. (2006). The constructive developmental theory of Robert Kegan. *The Family Journal: Counseling and Therapy for Couples and Families, 14*(3), 290–298; Melvin, E., & Cook-Greuter, S. (Eds.). (2000). *Creativity, spirituality, and transcendence: Paths to integrity and wisdom in the mature self*. Stamford, CT: Ablex Publishing; Pfaffenberger, A. H., Marko, P. W., & Combs, A. (2011). *The postconventional personality*. Albany: State University of New York Press; Wilbur, K. (2000). *Integral psychology: Consciousness, spirit, psychology, therapy*. Boston: Shambhala Publications; Cowan, C. C., & Todorovic, N. (Eds.). (2005). *The never ending quest: Dr. Clare W. Graves explores human nature*. Santa Barbara, CA: ECLET Publishing.
15. Kramer, Wisdom as a classical source of human strength.
16. Kramer, Wisdom as a classical source of human strength.
17. Beaumont, S. L. (2009). Identity processing and personal wisdom: An information-oriented identity style predicts self-actualization and self-transcendence. *Identity: An International Journal of Theory and Research, 9*(2), 95–115; Berzonsky, M. D. (1992). Identity style and coping strategies. *Journal of Personality, 60*(4), 771–788; Berzonsky, M. D., & Sullivan, C. (1992). Social-cognitive aspects of identity style: Need for cognition, experiential openness, and introspection. *Journal of Adolescent Research, 7*(2), 140–155; Kramer, Wisdom as a classical source of human strength; Kunzmann, U., & Baltes, P. B. (2003). Wisdom-related knowledge: Affective, motivational, and interpersonal correlates. *Personality and Social Psychology Bulletin, 29*(9), 1104–1119; Staudinger, Lopez, & Baltes, The psychometric location of wisdom-related performance; Sternberg, R. J. (1998). A balance theory of wisdom. *Review of General Psychology, 2*(4), 347–365.
18. Beaumont, Identity processing and personal wisdom.
19. Maslow, A. H. (1957). Alfred Korzybski memorial lecture: Two kinds of cognition and their integration. General Semantic Bulletin, 20 & 21, 17–22, p. 22.
20. Maslow, The farther reaches of human nature. *The Journal of Transpersonal Psychology*, p. 5.
21. Christakis, N. A. (2019). *Blueprint: The evolutionary origins of a good society*. New York: Little, Brown Spark; Fredrickson, *Love 2.0*; Friedman, H. L., & Hartelius, G. (Eds.). (2015). *The Wiley-Blackwell handbook of transpersonal psychology*. Hoboken, NJ: Wiley-Blackwell; Goleman & Davidson, Altered traits; Harari, Homo deus; Keltner, D. (2009). *Born to be good: The science of a meaningful life*. New York: W. W. Norton; Vaillant, Spiritual evolution. Harmony; Kotler & Wheal, Stealing fire; Newberg & Waldman, How enlightenment changes your brain.
22. Maslow, The farther reaches of human nature. *The Journal of Transpersonal Psychology,* p. 6.
23. Kaufman, Ungifted.
24. Maslow, The farther reaches of human nature (1969), p. 8.
25. Maslow, *The farther reaches of human nature* (1993/1971), p. 317.
26. Ericson & Abelson, Even the downhearted may be uplifted.

27. Maslow, The farther reaches of human nature. *The Journal of Transpersonal Psychology*, p. 6.

28. Maslow, The farther reaches of human nature. *The Journal of Transpersonal Psychology*, p. 8.

29. Maslow, Building a new politics based on humanistic psychology. In Hoffman, *Future visions* (pp. 147–152), p. 148.

30. Hirsh, J. B., DeYoung, C. G., Xiaowen, X., & Peterson, J. B. (2010). Compassionate liberals and polite conservatives: Associations of agreeableness with political ideology and moral values. *Personality and Social Psychology Bulletin, 36*(5), 655–664; Waytz, A., Iyer, R., Young, L., and Haidt, J. (2019). Ideological differences in the expanse of the moral circle. *Nature Communications, 10*, doi: 10.1038/s41467-019-12227-0.

31. Hirsh, DeYoung, Xiaowen, & Peterson, Compassionate liberals and polite conservatives.

32. Mudde, C. (2004). The populist zeitgeist. *Government and Opposition*, 39, 541–563.

33. Judis, J. B., & Teixeira, R. (2004). *The emerging democratic majority*. New York: Scribner; Mudde, The populist zeitgeist; Taggart, P. (2000). *Populism*. Buckingham, UK: Open University Press.

34. Caprara, G. V., & Zimbardo, P. G. (2004). Personalizing politics: A congruency model of political preference. *American Psychologist, 59*(7), 581–594; Valkenburg, P. M., & Jochen, P. (2013). The differential susceptibility to media effects model. *Journal of Communication, 63*(2), 221–243; Kaufman, S. B. (2016). Donald Trump's real ambition. *Scientific American Blogs*. Retrieved from https://blogs.scientificamerican.com/beautiful-minds/donald-trump-s-real-ambition.

35. Dunn, K. (2013). Preference for radical right-wing populist parties among exclusive-nationalists and authoritarians. *Party Politics, 21*(3), 367–380; Kaufman, S. B. (2018). The personality trait that is ripping America (and the world) apart. *Scientific American Blogs*. Retrieved from https://blogs.scientificamerican.com/beautiful-minds/the-personality -trait-that-is-ripping-america-and-the-world-apart; Rooduijn, M. (2018). Populist appeal: Personality and anti-establishment communication. Retrieved from https://www .mzes.uni-mannheim.de/d7/en/events/populist-appeal-personality-and-anti -establishment-communication.

36. Maslow, Building a new politics based on humanistic psychology. In Hoffman, *Future visions* (pp. 147–152), p. 151.

37. Becker, E. (1997; originally published in 1973). *Denial of death*. New York: Free Press, p. 87.

38. Solomon, S., Greenberg, J., & Pyszczynski, T. (2004). The cultural animal: Twenty years of terror management theory and research. In J. Greenberg, S. L. Koole, & T. Pyszczynski (Eds.), *Handbook of experimental existential psychology* (pp. 13–34). New York: Guilford Press.

39. Solomon, S., Greenberg, J., & Pyszczynski, T. (1986). A terror management theory of social behavior: The psychological functions of self-esteem. *Advances in Experimental Social Psychology, 24*, 93–159.

40. Feifel, H., & Nagy, V. T. (1981). Another look at fear of death. *Journal of Consulting and Clinical Psychology, 49*(2), 278–286.

41. Also, some recent preregistered research has found that previous effects of mortality salience found in the published literature may be more difficult to reproduce than previously assumed. See: Sætrevik, B. & Sjåstad, H. (2019). A pre-registered attempt to

replicate the mortality salience effect in traditional and novel measures, https://psyarxiv
.com/dkg53.

42. Leary, M. R., & Schreindorfer, L. S. (1997). Unresolved issues with terror management
theory. *Psychological Inquiry, 8*(1), 26–29.

43. Yalom, *Existential psychotherapy*, p. 40.

44. Yalom, *Existential psychotherapy*, p. 31.

45. Yalom, *Existential psychotherapy*.

46. Yalom, *Existential psychotherapy*, p. 34.

47. Weiner, E. (2015). Bhutan's dark secret of happiness. *BBC Travel*. Retrieved from http://
www.bbc.com/travel/story/20150408-bhutans-dark-secret-to-happiness.

48. Weiner, Bhutan's dark secret of happiness.

49. Cozzolino, P. J., Blackie, L. E. R., & Meyers, L. S. (2014). Self-related consequences of
death fear and death denial. *Death Studies, 38*(6), 418–422; Lykins, E. L., Segerstrom,
S. C., Averill, A. J., Evans, D. R., & Kemeny, M. E. (2007). Goal shifts following reminders of mortality: Reconciling posttraumatic growth and terror management theory. *Personality and Social Psychology Bulletin, 33*(8), 1088–1099.

50. Kesebir, A quiet ego quiets death anxiety; Moon, H. G. (2019). Mindfulness of death as
a tool for mortality salience induction with reference to terror management theory.
Religions, 10, doi: 10.3390/rel10060353; Niemiec, C. P., Brown, K. W., Kashdan, T. B.,
Cozzolino, P. J., and Ryan, R. M. (2010). Being present in the face of existential threat:
The role of trait mindfulness in reducing defensive responses to mortality salience. *Jour-
nal of Personality and Social Psychology, 99,* 344–365. Prentice, M., Kasser, T., & Sheldon,
K. M. (2018). Openness to experience predicts intrinsic value shifts after deliberating
one's own death. *Death Studies, 42*(4), 205–215.

51. Yalom, *Existential psychotherapy,* p. 45.

52. Yalom, *Existential psychotherapy,* p. 45.

53. Reker, G. T., & Wong. P. T. P (1988). Aging as an individual process: Toward a theory
of personal meaning. In J. E. Birren & V. L. Bengston (Eds.), *Emergent theories of aging*
(pp. 214–246). New York: Springer. Also see: Steger, M. F. (2020). Meaning in life: A
unified model. In S. J. Lopez, L. M. Edwards, S. C. Marques (Eds.), *Oxford handbook of
positive psychology* (3rd Ed.). Oxford, UK: Oxford University Press.

54. Schnell, T. (2009). The sources of meaning in life questionnaire (SoMe): Relations to
demographics and well-being. *Journal of Positive Psychology, 4,* 483–499; Schnell, T. (2011).
Individual differences in meaning-making: Considering the variety of sources of meaning, their density and diversity. *Personality and Individual Differences, 51,* 667–673.

55. Krippner, *The plateau experience*, p. 119.

56. Lowry, *The journals of A. H. Maslow,* p. 1306.

57. Becker, *Denial of death*; Solomon, S., Greenberg, J., & Pyszczynski, T. (2015). *The worm
at the core: On the role of death in life.* New York: Random House.

58. Lowry, *The journals of A. H. Maslow,* p. 998.

59. Maslow particularly resented his mother's superstitious thinking when he was a child.
Here is a very elucidating journal entry from Maslow, written April 16, 1969: "Big insight
over breakfast conversation. B. was talking about her cleanliness as a reaction against

childhood filth & evil. And suddenly it dawned on me that it had been the same thing for my mother (father too). What I had reacted against & totally hated & rejected was not only her physical appearance, but also her values & world view, her stinginess, her total selfishness, her lack of love for anyone else in the world, even her own husband & children, her narcissism. . . . I've always wondered where my Utopianism, ethical stress, humanism, stress on kindness, love, friendship, & all the rest came from. I knew certainly of the direct consequences of having no mother-love. But the whole thrust of my life-philosophy & all my research & theorizing also has its roots in a hatred for & revulsion against everything she stood for—which I hated so early that I was never tempted to seek her love or to want it or expect it. All so simple, so obvious—& to discover it at the age of 61! And after all the psychoanalysis & self-analysis! And after all the talk about Bertha being the opposite in many respects of the world view of her foster-parents! Insight never ceases."

60. Heitzman, A. L. (2003). The plateau experience in context: An intensive in-depth psychobiographical case study of Abraham Maslow's "post-mortem life" (Doctoral dissertation). Saybrook Graduate School and Research Center.

61. Heitzman, The plateau experience in context, p. 251.

62. Richard Lowry had a similar take on Maslow's dueling self-concepts: "There was always a part of him that was the antisentimentalist, skeptic, 'realist,' and 'scientist.' . . . There was another part of him that was ever the mystic, the poet, the rhapsodist, the seer of 'wonderful vistas' who could be shamelessly moved to tears by beauty, joy, and tragedy. The great risk that a man runs when he is host to two such contrary tendencies of personality is that he will embrace one tendency in the extreme and then set about to persecute all signs of the reformed sinner." See: Lowry, *A. H. Maslow: An intellectual portrait*, p. 15.

63. Heitzman, The plateau experience in context, p. 292.

64. Lowry, *The journals of A. H. Maslow*, p. 1284–1285.

65. Heitzman, The plateau experience in context, p. 301.

66. Lowry, *The journals of A. H. Maslow*, p. 1256.

67. In a letter to U. A. Asrani, dated May 5, 1967, Maslow wrote: "I think your suggested term Plateau Experience is excellent and I shall use it henceforce to describe what I have been calling 'serene B-cognition.' Apparently, this tends to come with aging or at least that is my experience. The acute and climactic peak experiences seem to lessen in number while the 'awakened' cognition or unitive perceiving seems to increase and even to come under voluntary control. The happiness then tends to be mild and constant rather than poignant and acute." For more on Maslow's genesis of the plateau experience, see: Gruel, N. (2015). The plateau experience: An exploration of its origins, characteristics, and potential. *The Journal of Transpersonal Psychology, 47*(1), 44–63.

68. Heitzman, The plateau experience in context.

69. Krippner, *The plateau experience*, p. 113.

70. Maslow, A. H. (1970). *Religions, values, and peak experiences.* New York: Viking, p. xiv. (Paperback reissue of 1964 edition; preface added in 1970).

71. Krippner, *The plateau experience*, p. 114.

72. In writing about the life of Karen Horney and her struggles—including her intense need for the affection of men and her conflicted self-image—the psychoanalyst Harold Kel-

man (who was personally acquainted with Horney's struggles) writes: "She created in spite of her problems, because of her problems, and through her problems." The same can be said of Maslow, and I would add, the same can be said for all of us. See: Kelman, H. (1977). *Helping people: Karen Horney's psychoanalytic approach*. Lanham, MD: Rowman & Littlefield.

73. Heitzman, The plateau experience in context, p. 296.
74. *Psychology Today* (August 1970); International Study Project. (1972). Abraham H. Maslow: A memorial volume. Brooks/Cole, p. 29.

LIVE MORE IN THE B-REALM

1. Adapted from "Living in the World of Higher Values" and "Regaining Our Sense of Gratitude" in Hoffman, *Future visions*.

AFTERWORD: "WONDERFUL POSSIBILITIES AND INSCRUTABLE DEPTHS," REPRISED

1. I know because Don Blohowiak was kind enough to help guide me to the proper location of the document.
2. Maslow, A. H. (1969–1970). Chapter 2—*The possibilities for human nature*. Maslow Papers, Folder: Mostly Tapes "Rough"—Prop, Box M 4483, Archives of the History of American Psychology, Cummings Center for the History of Psychology, University of Akron, Akron, OH.
3. International Study Project, Abraham H. Maslow, p. 21.
4. Maslow, Chapter 2—*The possibilities for human nature*.

APPENDIX I. SEVEN PRINCIPLES FOR BECOMING A WHOLE PERSON

1. Buhler, C. (1971). Basic theoretical concepts of humanistic psychology. *American Psychologist, 26*(4), 378–386.
2. Portions of this section were adapted from this blog post: Kaufman, S. B. (2019). Authenticity under fire. *Scientific American Blogs*. Retrieved from https://blogs.scientific american.com/beautiful-minds/authenticity-under-fire.
3. Rogers C. R., *On becoming a person*, p. 108.
4. Jongman-Sereno, K. P., & Leary, M. R. (2018). The enigma of being yourself: A critical examination of the concept of authenticity. *Review of General Psychology*, http://dx .doi.org/10.1037/gpr0000157; Kaufman, *Authenticity under fire*; Kenrick, D. T., & Griskevicius, V. (2013). *The rational animal: How evolution made us smarter than we think*. New York: Basic Books; Kurzban, R. (2012). *Why everyone (else) is a hypocrite: Evolution and the modular mind*. Princeton, NJ: Princeton University Press.
5. Strohminger, N., Knobe, J., & Newman, G. (2017). The true self: A psychological concept distinct from the self. *Perspectives on Psychological Science, 12*(4), 551–560.
6. Jongman-Sereno, K., & Leary, M. R. (2016). Self-perceived authenticity is contaminated by the valence of one's behavior. *Self and Identity, 15*(3), 283–301.
7. Strohminger, Knobe, & Newman, The true self.

8. Debats, D. L., Drost, J., & Hansen, P. (1995). Experiences of meaning in life: A combined qualitative and quantitative approach. *British Journal of Psychology, 86*(part 3), 359–375; Fleeson, W., & Wilt, J. (2010). The relevance of Big Five trait content in behavior to subjective authenticity: Do high levels of within-person behavioral variability undermine or enable authenticity achievement? *Journal of Personality, 78*(4), 1353–1382; Garcia, D., Nima, A. A., & Kjell, O. N. E. (2014). The affective profiles, psychological well-being, and harmony: environmental mastery and self-acceptance predict the sense of a harmonious life. *PeerJ,* doi: 10.7717/peerj.259; Lenton, A. P., Bruder, M., Slabu, L., & Sedikides, C. (2013). How does "being real" feel? The experience of state authenticity. *Journal of Personality, 81*(3), 276–289; Rivera, G. N., et al. (2019). Understanding the relationship between perceived authenticity and well-being. *Review of General Psychology, 23*(1), 113–126; Ryan & Deci, Self-determination theory and the facilitation of intrinsic motivation, social development, and well-being; Sedikides, C., Lenton, A. P., Slabu, L., & Thomaes, S. (2019). Sketching the contours of state authenticity. *Review of General Psychology, 23*(1), 73–88; Vess, M. (2019). Varieties of conscious experience and the subjective awareness of one's "true" self. *Review of General Psychology, 23*(1), 89–98.

9. McAdams, D. P. (1996). Personality, modernity, and the storied self: A contemporary framework for studying persons. *Psychological Inquiry, 7*(4), 295–321; Ryan & Deci, Self-determination theory and the facilitation of intrinsic motivation, social development, and well-being; Vess, Varieties of conscious experience and the subjective awareness of one's "true" self; Sheldon, K. M., Ryan, R. M., Rawsthorne, L. J., & Ilardi, B. (1997). Trait self and true self: Cross-role variation in the big-five personality traits and its relation with psychological authenticity and subjective well-being. *Journal of Personality and Social Psychology, 73*(6), 1380–1393.

10. Baumeister, R. F., Ainsworth, S. E., & Vohs, K. D. (2016). Are groups more or less than the sum of their members? The moderating role of individual identification. *Behavioral and Brain Sciences, 39,* e137.

11. Baker, Z. G., Tou, R. Y. W., Bryan, J. L., & Knee, C. R. (2017). Authenticity and well-being: Exploring positivity and negativity in interactions as a mediator. *Personality and Individual Differences, 113,* 235–39; Baumeister, R. F. (2019). Stalking the truth self through the jungles of authenticity: Problems, contradictions, inconsistencies, disturbing findings—and a possible way forward. *Review of General Psychology, 23*(1), 143–154; Jongman-Sereno & Leary, Self-perceived authenticity is contaminated by the valence of one's behavior; Rivera et al., Understanding the relationship between perceived authenticity and well-being; Ryan & Deci, Self-determination theory and the facilitation of intrinsic motivation, social development, and well-being; Schmader, T., & Sedikides, C. (2018). State authenticity as fit to environment: The implications of social identity for fit, authenticity, and self-segregation. *Personality and Social Psychology Review, 22*(3), 228–259.

12. Baker, Tou, Bryan, & Knee, Authenticity and well-being; Kernis, M. H., & Goldman, B. M. (2006). A multicomponent conceptualization of authenticity: Research and theory. *Advances in Experimental Psychology, 38,* 284–357; Sedikides, Lenton, Slabu, & Thomaes, Sketching the contours of state authenticity.

13. Baumeister, Stalking the truth self through the jungles of authenticity.

14. Baumeister, R. F. (1982). A self-presentational view of social phenomena. *Psychological Bulletin, 91*(1), 3–26.

15. Baumeister, Stalking the truth self through the jungles of authenticity, p. 150.

16. Christy, A. G., Seto, E., Schlegel, R. J., Vess, M., & Hicks, J. A. (2016). Straying from the righteous path and from ourselves: The interplay between perceptions of morality and self-knowledge. *Personality and Social Psychology Bulletin, 42*(11), 1538–1550; Jongman-Sereno & Leary, The enigma of being yourself; Strohminger, Knobe, & Newman, The true self.

17. Jongman-Sereno & Leary, The enigma of being yourself.

18. Goldman, B. M., & Kernis, M. H. (2002). The role of authenticity in healthy psychological functioning and subjective well-being. *Annals of the American Psychotherapy Association, 5*(6), 18–20; Heppner, W. L., et al. (2008). Within-person relationships among daily self-esteem, need satisfaction, and authenticity. *Psychological Science, 19*(11), 1140–1145; Kernis & Goldman, A multicomponent conceptualization of authenticity; Liu, Y., & Perrewe, P. L. (2006). Are they for real? The interpersonal and intrapersonal outcomes of perceived authenticity. *International Journal of Work Organisation and Emotion, 1*(3), 204–214, doi:10.1504/IJWOE.2006.010788; Wood, Linley, Maltby, Baliousis, & Joseph, The authentic personality.

19. Rivera et al., Understanding the relationship between perceived authenticity and well-being.

20. Tiberius, V. (2015). Well-being, values, and improving lives. In S. Rangan (Ed.), *Performance and progress: Essays on capitalism, business, and society* (pp. 339–357). New York: Oxford University Press.

21. Yalom, I. (2005). *The theory and practice of group psychotherapy* (5th ed., pp. 77–98). New York: Basic Books; Yalom, *Existential psychotherapy*, pp. 265, 354.

22. Morgan, M. (2015). A glazed donut stack topped with melted cheese, a triple-meat combo and fried chicken hot dogs: The 10 most calorific burgers from around the world revealed. *Daily Mail.* Retrieved from https://www.dailymail.co.uk/femail/article-2998330/The-10-calorific-burgers-world-revealed.html.

23. Rogers, *On becoming a person.*

24. Vess, Varieties of conscious experience and the subjective awareness of one's "true" self.

25. Rogers, *On becoming a person*; Rogers, C. R. (1980). *A way of being.* New York: Houghton Mifflin Company.

26. Kierkegaard, S. (2013). *The sickness unto death.* Belmont, NC: Wiseblood Books, p. 19.

27. Rogers, *On becoming a person.*

28. Rogers, C. R. (1964). Toward a modern approach to values: The valuing process in the mature person. *The Journal of Abnormal and Social Psychology, 68*(2), 160–167.

29. Govindji, R., & Linley, P. A. (2007). Strengths use, self-concordance and well-being: Implications for strengths coaching and coaching psychologists. *International Coaching Psychology Review, 2*(2), 143–153.

30. Sheldon, K. M., Arnt, J., & Houser-Marko, L. (2003). In search of the organismic valuing process: The tendency to move towards beneficial goal choices. *Journal of Personality, 71*(5), 835–869.

31. Sheldon, Arnt, & Houser-Marko, In search of the organismic valuing process.

32. Kaufman, *Ungifted*; Kaufman, S. B. (2018). *Twice exceptional: Supporting and educating bright and creative students with learning difficulties.* New York: Oxford University Press; Ryan, W. S., & Ryan, R. M. (2019). Toward a social psychology of authenticity: Exploring within-person variation in autonomy, congruence, and genuineness using self-determination theory. *Review of General Psychology, 23*(1), 99–112; Schmader & Sedikides, State authenticity as fit to environment.

33. Schmader & Sedikides, State authenticity as fit to environment.

34. Sheldon, K. M., & Krieger, L. S. (2004). Does legal education have undermining effects on law students?: Evaluating changes in motivation, values, and well-being. *Behavioral Sciences and the Law, 22*(2), 261–286.

35. Jongman-Sereno & Leary, The enigma of being yourself.

36. Kenrick & Griskevicius, The rational animal; Kurzban, Why everyone (else) is a hypocrite.

37. Carver & Scheier, On the self-regulation of behavior; DeYoung, C. G. (2015). Cybernetic Big Five Theory. *Journal of Research in Personality, 56*, 33–58; DeYoung, C. G., & Weisberg, Y. J. (2018). Cybernetic approaches to personality and social behavior. In K. Deaux & M. Snyder (Eds.), *The Oxford handbook of personality and social psychology* (2nd ed.) (pp. 387–413). New York: Oxford University Press; Weiner, N. (1961). *Cybernetics or control and communication in the animal and the machine* (Vol. 25). Cambridge, MA: MIT Press.

38. Maslow, A. H. (1943). A theory of human motivation. *Psychological Review, 50*(4), 370–396.

39. Kenrick & Griskevicius, The rational animal; Kurzban, Why everyone (else) is a hypocrite.

40. Griffiths, J. (2018). Swede dreams: Model, 25, wants world's biggest bum after having three Brazilian butt lifts in four years. *The Sun.* Retrieved from https://www.thesun.co.uk/fabulous/7978425/model-three-brazilian-butt-lifts-worlds-biggest-bum.

41. Reuben, A. (2017). Mental illness is far more common than we knew. *Scientific American Blogs.* Retrieved from https://blogs.scientificamerican.com/observations/mental-illness-is-far-more-common-than-we-knew.

42. Sheldon, K. M., & King, L. (2001). Why positive psychology is necessary. *American Psychologist, 56*(3), 216–217.

43. Walsh, F. (2016). *Strengthening family resilience* (3rd ed.). New York: Guilford Press, p. 5.

44. Sternberg, R. J., & Weiss, K. (Eds.). (2008). *The new psychology of love* (1st ed.). New York: Cambridge University Press.

45. Fisher, H. The drive to love: The neural mechanism for mate selection. In Sternberg & Weiss, *The new psychology of love* (pp. 87–115). New York: Cambridge University Press, p. 106.

46. Fisher, The drive to love. In Sternberg & Weiss, *The new psychology of love,* p. 106.

47. Diamond, What does sexual orientation orient? A biobehavioral model distinguishing romantic love and sexual desire. *Psychological Review, 110*(1): 173–192.

48. This notion is echoed in the writings of Plato, when he noted that "everything arises in this way, opposites from their opposites."

49. Horney, K. (1945). *Our inner conflicts: A constructive theory of neurosis.* New York: W. W. Norton.

50. Horney, K. (1942). *Self-analysis.* New York: W. W. Norton, p. 57.

51. Horney, *Self-analysis.*

52. Vaillant, G. E. (1993). *The wisdom of the ego.* Cambridge, MA: Harvard University Press, pp. 1, 7.

53. Horney, *Our inner conflicts,* p. 242.

54. Note the similarity to Brené Brown's modern writings about wholeheartedness: Brown, B. (2010). *The gifts of imperfection: Let go of who you think you're supposed to be and embrace who you are.* Center City, MN: Hazelden Publishing.

55. Horney, *Self-analysis.*

56. Maslow, *Toward a psychology of being,* p. 65.

57. Aaron Beck, personal communication.

58. Beck, A. Schizophrenia and depression. Aaron T. Beck Center for Recovery-Oriented Cognitive Therapy Research and Practice. Retrieved from https://aaronbeckcenter .org/projects/schizophrenia.

59. Pinker, S. (2002). *The blank slate: The modern denial of human nature.* New York: Penguin Books.

60. Kaufman, *Ungifted*; Zimmer, C. (2018). *She has her mother's laugh: The powers, perversions, and potential of heredity.* New York: Dutton.

61. The founding humanistic psychologists were deeply influenced by the European existential philosophers, including Albert Camus, Simone de Beauvoir, Martin Heidegger, Karl Jaspers, Søren Kierkegaard, Gabriel Marcel, Maurice Merleau-Ponty, Friedrich Nietzsche, Jean-Paul Sartre, and Paul Tillich. Indeed, a number of practitioners of humanistic psychology refer to themselves as "existential-humanistic" psychologists, acknowledging the incorporation of existential philosophy and existential issues such as meaning and self-construction into their clinical work.

 While the founding humanistic psychologists agreed that personal growth involves an active process of self-construction, and that we are often much freer to self-create ourselves than we generally assume, many of them disagreed with Sartre's strong stance that "existence precedes essence." Humanistic psychologists such as Maslow and Rollo May recognized that other forms of "destiny"—such as one's culture, language, circumstance, and biology—restrict the range within which we are free to determine our existence; see: May, R. (1981). *Freedom and destiny.* New York: W. W. Norton. Explicitly rejecting "Sartre-type existentialism," Maslow wrote the following in an unpublished manuscript toward the end of his life: "Aristotle, Spinoza, Aquina[s] and others have stressed as a basic law of all being that everything has a tendency and a right to persist in its own nature. The human species has a 'species-specific character' the peculiarity that 'persisting in its own nature' is a long slow process of *growing* into one's own nature. It takes a lifetime to become fully-human, i.e., it takes a lifetime for a baby to persist and [become] its own nature . . . essence is potential and therefore has to be actualized, made." See: van Deurzen et al., *The Wiley world handbook of existential therapy*; Maslow, A. H. (1969–1970). Axioms. Maslow Papers, Folder 6, Publications-Drafts, Box M 4431, Archives of the History of

American Psychology, Cummings Center for the History of Psychology, University of Akron, Akron, OH; Schneider & Krug, Existential-humanistic therapy.

62. Hounkpatin, H. O., Wood, A. M., Boyce, C. J., & Dunn, G. (2015). An existential-humanistic view of personality change: Co-occurring changes with psychological well-being in a 10 year cohort study, *Social Indicators Research, 121*(2), 455–470; Kaufman, S. B. (2016). Can personality be changed? *The Atlantic.* Retrieved from https://www.theatlan tic.com/health/archive/2016/07/can-personality-be-changed/492956; Kaufman, S. B. (2016). Would you be happier with a different personality? *The Atlantic.* Retrieved from https://www.theatlantic.com/health/archive/2016/08/would-you-be-happier -with-a-different-personality/494720; Roberts, B. W., et al. (2017). A systematic review of personality trait change through intervention. *Psychological Bulletin, 143*(2), 117–141.

63. Kaufman, Can personality be changed?

64. Fleeson, W. (2001). Toward a structure- and process-integrated view of personality: Traits as density distributions of states. *Journal of Personality and Social Psychology, 80*(6), 1011–1027; Kaufman, *Ungifted;* Kaufman, S. B. (2019). Toward a new frontier in human intelligence: The person-centered approach. *Scientific American Blogs.* Retrieved from https://blogs.scientificamerican.com/beautiful-minds/toward-a-new-frontier -in-human-intelligence-the-person-centered-approach.

65. Little, B. R. (2014). *Me, myself, and us: The science of personality and the art of well-being.* New York: PublicAffairs.

66. Meindl, P., Jayawickreme, E., Furr, R. M. & Fleeson, W. (2015). A foundation beam for studying morality from a personological point of view: Are individual differences in moral behaviors and thoughts consistent? *Journal of Research in Personality, 59,* 81–92; Berger, D. M., & McGrath, R. E. (2018). Are there virtuous types? Finite mixture modeling of the VIA Inventory of Strengths. *The Journal of Positive Psychology, 14*(1), 77–85; Helzer, E. G., Fleeson, W., Furr, R. M., Meindl, P., & Barranti, M. (2016). Once a utilitarian, consistently a utilitarian? Examining principleness in moral judgment via the robustness of individual differences, *Journal of Personality, 85*(4), 505–517; Jayawickreme, E. & Fleeson, W. (2017). Does whole trait theory work for the virtues? In W. Sinnott-Armstrong & C. B. Miller (Eds.), *Moral psychology: Virtue and character* (5th ed.). (pp. 75–104). Cambridge, MA: MIT Press.

67. Berger & McGrath, Are there virtuous types?

68. Fleeson, W. (2004). Moving personality beyond the person-situation debate: The challenge and the opportunity of within-person variability. *Current Directions in Psychological Science, 13*(2), 83–87; Fleeson, W. (2017). The production mechanisms of traits: Reflections on two amazing decades. *Journal of Research in Personality, 69,* 4–12; Baumert, A., et al. (2017). Integrating personality structure, personality process, and personality development. *European Journal of Personality, 31*(5), 503–528.

69. Roberts, B. W., & Jackson, J. J. (2009). Sociogenomic personality psychology. *Journal of Personality, 76*(6), 1523–1544; Little, *Me, myself, and us.*

70. Kaufman, S. B. (2018). What happens when people are intentionally more open to new experiences? *Scientific American Blogs.* Retrieved from https://blogs.scientificamerican .com/beautiful-minds/what-happens-when-people-are-instructed-to-be-more-open

-to-new-experiences; Kaufman, S. B. (2018). Can introverts be happy in a world that can't stop talking? *Scientific American Blogs.* Retrived from https://blogs.scientific american.com/beautiful-minds/can-introverts-be-happy-in-a-world-that-cant-stop-talking.

71. Cain, S. (2013). *Quiet: The power of introverts in a world that can't stop talking.* New York: Broadway Books.

72. Lawn, R. B., Slemp, G. R., Vella-Brodrick, D. A. (2018). Quiet flourishing: The authenticity and well-being of trait introverts living in the West depend on extroversion-deficit beliefs. *Journal of Happiness Studies, 20,* 2055–2075.

73. Hudson, N. W., Briley, D. A., Chopik, W. J., & Derringer, J. (2018). You have to follow through: Attaining behavioral change goals predicts volitional personality change. *Journal of Personality and Social Psychology,* http://dx.doi.org/10.1037/pspp0000221; Kaufman, Can personality be changed?

74. McCabe, K. O., & Fleeson, W. (2012). What is extroversion for? Integrating trait and motivational perspectives and identifying the purpose of extroversion. *Psychological Science, 23*(12), 1498–1505; McCabe, K. O., & Fleeson, W. (2016). Are traits useful? Explaining trait manifestations as tools in the pursuit of goals. *Journal of Personality and Social Psychology, 110*(2), 287–301.

75. David, S. (2016). *Emotional agility: Get unstuck, embrace change, and thrive in work and life.* New York: Avery; Ivtzan, I., Lomas, T., Hefferon, K., & Worth, P. (2016). *Second wave positive psychology: Embracing the dark side of life.* New York: Routledge; Kashdan, T., & Biswas-Diener, R. (2014). *The upside of your dark side: Why being your whole self—not just your "good" self—drives success and fulfillment.* New York: Plume; Wong, What is existential positive psychology?; Wong, Positive psychology 2.0.

76. McNulty, J. K., & Fincham, F. D. (2011). Beyond positive psychology? Toward a contextual view of psychological processes and well-being. *American Psychologist, 67*(2), 101–110; Shiota, M. N., et al. (2017). Beyond happiness: Building a science of discrete positive emotions. *American Psychologist, 72*(7), 617–643.

77. Rogers, C. R. (1962). Toward becoming a fully functioning person. In A. W. Combs (Ed.), *Perceiving, behaving, becoming: A new focus for education.* Washington, DC: National Education Association.

78. Goodman, F. R., Disabato, D. J., Kashdan, T. B., & Kaufman, S. B. (2018). Measuring well-being: A comparison of subjective well-being and PERMA. *The Journal of Positive Psychology, 13*(4), 321–332.

79. The dark horse project. Laboratory for the Science of Individuality. Retrieved from https://lsi.gse.harvard.edu/dark-horse.

80. Rose, T., & Ogas, O. (2018). *Dark horse: Achieving success through the pursuit of fulfillment.* New York: HarperOne; Stulberg, B. (2018). The dark horse path to happiness. Outside Online. Retrieved from https://www.outsideonline.com/2373876/three-steps-happiness.

81. Rogers, *On becoming a person,* p. 105.

82. Rogers, *On becoming a person,* p. 106.

83. Bohart, A. C., Held, B. S., Mendelowitz, E., & Schneider, K. J. (Eds.). (2013). *Humanity's dark side: Evil, destructive experience, and psychotherapy.* Washington, DC: American

Psychological Association; May, R. (1982). The problem of evil: An open letter to Carl Rogers. *Journal of Humanistic Psychology, 22*(3), 10–21, p. 15.

84. May, The problem of evil, p. 15.

85. May, *Love & will*, p. 123.

86. May, *Love & will*, p. 123.

87. As May wrote in *Love & Will*, "The concept of the daimonic seems so unacceptable not for intrinsic reasons, but because of our own struggle to deny what it stands for. It constitutes a profound blow to our narcissism. We are the 'nice' people and, like the cultivated citizens of Athens in Socrates' time, we don't like to be publicly reminded, whether we secretly admit it to ourselves or not, that we are motivated even in our love by lust for power, anger, and revenge. While the daimonic cannot be said to be evil in itself, it confronts us with the troublesome dilemma of whether it is to be used with awareness, a sense of responsibility and the significance of life, or blindly and rashly. When the daimonic is repressed, it tends to *erupt* in some form—its extreme forms being assassination, the psychopathological tortures of the murderers on the moors and other horrors we know only too well in this century. 'Although we may recoil in horror,' writes the British psychiatrist Anthony Storr, when we read in newspapers or history books of the atrocities committed by man upon man, we know in our hearts that each one of us harbors within himself those same savage impulses which lead to murder, to torture and to war." See: May, Love & will, pp. 129–130.

88. Maslow, *Toward a psychology of being.*

89. Vaillant, *The wisdom of the ego.*

90. Vaillant, *The wisdom of the ego,* p. 11.

91. Maslow, A. H. Yea and nay: On being an optimistic realist. In Hoffman, *Future visions* (pp. 61–63).

APPENDIX II. GROWTH CHALLENGES

1. Maslow, *The psychology of science: A reconnaissance*, p. 22.

2. Several of these growth challenges are original interventions designed to accompany the content discussed throughout the book. Some are positive interventions that have been previously published in other works. Portions of this appendix were adapted from Feingold, J. H. (2016). *Toward a Positive Medicine: Healing Our Healers, from Burnout to Flourishing.* Master of Applied Positive Psychology (MAPP) Capstone Projects. 107. http://respository.upenn.edu/mapp_capstone/107.

3. Bland, A. M., & DeRobertis, E. M. (2017). Maslow's unacknowledged contributions to developmental psychology. *Journal of Humanistic Psychology,* doi: 10.1177/0022167817739732.

4. These statements were adapted from the Horney-Coolidge Type Inventory (HCTI): Coolidge, F. L., Moor, C. J., Yamazaki, T. G., Stewart, S. E., Segal, D. L. (2001). On the relationship between Karen Horney's tripartite neurotic type theory and personality disorder features. *Personality and Individual Differences,* 30, 7–1400.

5. Horney, K. (1945). *Our inner conflicts: A constructive theory of neurosis.* New York: W. W. Norton.

6. David, S. (2016). *Emotional agility: Get unstuck, embrace change, and thrive in work and life.* New York: Avery; Ivtzan, I., Lomas, T., Hefferon, K., & Worth, P. (2016). *Second wave positive psychology: Embracing the dark side of life.* New York: Routledge; Kashdan, T., & Biswas-Diener, R. (2014). *The upside of your dark side: Why being your whole self—not just your "good" self—drives success and fulfillment.* New York: Plume.

7. Schönbrodt, F. D., & Gerstenberg, F. X. R. (2012). An IRT analysis of motive questionnaires: The unified motive scales. *Journal of Research in Personality, 46*(6), 725–742.

8. Dutton, J. E. (2003). *Energize your workplace: How to create and sustain high-quality connections at work.* San Francisco: Jossey-Bass.

9. Rogers, C. R., & Farson, R. E. (2015). *Active listening.* Mansfield Center, CT: Martino Publishing.

10. Gable, S. L., Reis, H. T., Impett, E. A., & Asher, E. R. (2004). What do you do when things go right? The intrapersonal and interpersonal benefits of sharing positive events. *Journal of Personality and Social Psychology, 87*(2), 228–245; Gable, S. L., & Gosnell, C. L. (2011). The positive side of close relationships. In K. M. Sheldon, T. B. Kashdan, & M. F. Steger (Eds.), *Designing positive psychology: Taking stock and moving forward* (pp. 266–279). New York: Oxford University Press.

11. Patterson, R. J. (2000). *The assertiveness workbook: How to express your ideas and stand up for yourself at work and in relationships.* Oakland, CA: New Harbinger Publications.

12. Barker, E. (2016). This is how to be more assertive: 3 powerful secrets from research. Retrieved from https://www.bakadesuyo.com/2016/09/how-to-be-more-assertive.

13. Ratey, J. J., & Manning, R. (2014). *Go wild: Free your body and mind from the afflictions of civilization.* New York: Little, Brown.

14. Beck, A. T., Davis, D. D., & Freeman, A. (Eds.)(2015). *Cognitive therapy of personality disorders* (3rd ed.). New York: Guilford Press; Gillihan, S. J. (2018). *Cognitive behavioral therapy made simple: 10 strategies for managing anxiety, depression, anger, panic, and worry.* Emeryville, CA: Althea Press; Gillihan, S. J. (2016). *Retrain your brain: Cognitive behavioral therapy in 7 weeks: A workbook for managing depression and anxiety.* Emeryville, CA: Althea Press.

15. Gillihan, S. J., *Cognitive behavioral therapy made simple.*

16. Burns, D. (1989). *The feeling good handbook.* New York: Morrow; Gillihan, S. J., *Cognitive behavioral therapy made simple.*

17. Gillihan, S. J., *Cognitive behavioral therapy made simple.*

18. Gillihan, S. J., *Cognitive behavioral therapy made simple.*

19. Fredrickson, B. L. (2013). *Love 2.0: Finding happiness and health in moments of connection.* New York: Plume.

20. At http://self-compassion.com, see Guided Meditations, Exercise 1: How would you treat a friend?

21. Seligman, M. E. P. (2015). Chris Peterson's unfinished masterwork: The real mental illnesses. *The Journal of Positive Psychology, 10,* 3–6.

22. Biswas-Diener, R., Kashdan, T. B., & Minhas, G. (2011). A dynamic approach to psychological strength development and intervention. *Journal of Positive Psychology, 6*(2), 106–118.

23. Maslow, A. H. (1964). *Religions, values, and peak experiences.* London: Penguin Books.

24. Csikszentmihalyi, M. (1990). *Flow: The psychology of optimal experience.* New York: Harper & Row; Kotler, S. (2014). *The rise of superman: Decoding the science of ultimate human performance.* New York: Houghton Mifflin Harcourt. Lyubomirsky, S. (2008). *The how of happiness: A scientific approach to getting the life you want.* New York: Penguin Press.

25. Lyubomirsky, *The how of happiness.*

26. Kaufman, S. B. (2018). Can you quantify awe? *Scientific American Blogs.* Retrieved from https://blogs.scientificamerican.com/beautiful-minds/can-you-quantify-awe.

27. Bryant, F. B., & Veroff, J. (2007). *Savoring: A new model of positive experience.* Mahwah, NJ: Lawrence Erlbaum Associates, Publishers.

28. Bryant, F. B., Smart, C. M., & King, S. P. (2005). Using the past to enhance the present: Boosting happiness through positive reminiscence. *Journal of Happiness Studies, 6,* 227–260.

Index

Page numbers in *italics* indicate figures; those followed by "n" indicate notes.

abnormal psychology textbook, 84–85
"Absolute Unitary Being," 202
abuse, 10, 13, 23, 24, 25–27, 67–68
    emotional, 24, 26, 67–68
    physical, 13, 27, 67
    sexual, 24, 25–26, 67
    verbal, 25, 67
acceptance, xxxiv, 38, 39, 42, 46, 51, 61, 69,
    89, 119, 123, 126, 134, 166, 196, 217, 221,
    225, 237, 240–41
    See also self-acceptance
acceptance and commitment therapy (ACT),
    70, 105
achievable (quality of SMART goals), 171–72
"achievers," 168
"acute richness of subjective experience," 111
addiction to self-esteem, 75–78
"additional callings," 182
Adler, Alfred, xviii, xxiv, 22–23, 54, 55,
    56–57, 58, 78, 83, 156
adult attachment, 16–22, *18*
adventure seeking, 94, 97–102
aesthetic sensitivity, *108*, 109
affection, xxx, 6, 8, 34, 35, 36, 37, 63, 84, 86,
    142, 146, 221
affective empathy, 127–28
agency, 32, 61, 72, 126–27, 147, 169, 170, 206
aggressive instinct, 54, 54n
Ainsworth, Mary, 16
Algoe, Sara, 42
altruism, 19, 48, 103, 128, 130, 132, 203,
    211, 228
ambitions, suppression of, 70–71
American Anthropological Association, 4
American Psychological Association, xiii, 36,
    56, 195
American Psychologist (scientific journal), 195

amygdala, 25, 26–27, 44, 99
animals vs. humans, xxxv–xxxvi
antagonistic social strategies, 122–23
anterior cingulate cortex, 25
anthropology, 3–6, 83, 152, 197, 234
anticipation, 129
anxiety, xviii, xxv, xxxi, 246
    growth, 91, 92, 93, 95, 98, 99, 104, 105,
      129, 130, 132, 145, 176, 177, 182
    healthy transcendence, 196, 202, 209, 211,
      212, 213, 223, 233, 235, 240
    security, 9, 10, 12, 13, 14–15, *15*, 16, 18, *18*,
      18n, 19, 22, 24, 25, 26–27, 36, 48, 61
anxious-attachment dimension (adult),
    17–22, *18*
"anxious-resistant attachment" (infants), 16
"appetitive" rewards, 94
"Approaching Awe, a Moral, Spiritual,
    and Aesthetic Emotion" (Keltner and
    Haidt), 206
Aron, Arthur and Elaine, 138–39
Art of Loving, The (Fromm), 120
Asrani, U. A., 242
assertiveness, 57, 72, 76, 126, 147
Association for Humanistic Psychology, 185
attachment security, 13, 14–23, *15*, *18*, 40, 94,
    144–45
attention-deficit/hyperactive disorder
    (ADHD), 31
attention-switching, 31
authenticity, xviii, xxiv, 68, 79n, 89, 121,
    135–37, 147, 155, 174, 205
authentic self, 211
"authentic voice," 32
autonomy, xxvi, 68, 90, 93, 139, 153, 165, 174,
    205, 214
autonomy-supportive environments, 180–82

avoidant attachment, 16, *18*, 18–19, 21–22, 144
awe, xx, xxvi, xxxix, 89, 141, 142, 196, 203,
   203, 205–8, 213, 222, 223, 225, 228n,
   229, 230, 246
Awe Experience Scale, 208
"awe induction" techniques, 213, 214

Bakan, David, 126
Barra, Herminia, 136
Baumeister, Roy, 77, 96
Beaty, Roger, 115–16
beautifying all things, 222
Becker, Ernest, 114, 233, 234, 236, 239
behavior and hierarchy of needs, xxvii–xxviii
Being Abraham Maslow (documentary), 216
Being-Psychology, xxiv, 151
   See also positive psychology
Being-Realm. See B-realm
belonging, x, xiii, *xiv*, xxvii, xxx, 9, 34,
   38–41, 46, 48, 51, 52, 61, 67, 69, 71, 74,
   86, 94–95, 119, 138, 167, 231, 232, 236
Benedict, Ruth, 4, 83–84, 152–53
Bennis, Warren, 216, 251
Berg, Justin, 181
Bhutan, 237
black-and-white view of others, 75
Blackfoot Indians, 4–5, 153, 233
Bloom, Paul, 127, 198
B-love, 128–30
"Bodhisattva path" to enlightenment, 220
Bowlby, John, 14, 15, 16, 24
brain, 9–12, 24, 25–28, 29, 39, 40, 43–45, 86,
   99, 110, 112, 113, 116, 200, 202, 214
Braudy, Leo, 46
brave (quality of moral exemplar), 168
B-realm, xvi, xx, xxiii–xxiv, xxx–xxxi,
   245–48
   growth, 120–31, 134, 135–37, 138, 140,
      143–48, 175
   healthy transcendence, 219, 220–25, 228,
      229–30, 232, 238, 243
Bridgman, Todd, xxix
Brown, Brené, 71
Brown, Kirk, 59
Buddhism, xxxi, 120, 132, 133, 140–41, 142,
   174, 205, 237
Buettner, Dan, 51–52
Bugental, James, xxiv, 155
Bühler, Charlotte, xviii, xxiv
"Building a New Politics Based on
   Humanistic Psychology" (Maslow),
   227, 232
Buss, David, 143

Cacioppo, John, 39, 39n, 46
Calcutta, India, study, 48
Calhoun, Lawrence, 102–3
calling and purpose, 156–57, 157–58
"calm-and-connect" system, 43, 44
Campbell, W. Keith, 68
cancer and psychedelics, 211, 212
career and purpose, 157
"cathexis of the self," 65
Cave of Forgotten Dreams (documentary), 154
celebrity suicides, 46–47
chaos, 7–9, 125, 231, 240
character strengths, 166, 177
charity donations and income, 49
Chauvet Cave, 154–55
childbirth and awe, 193, 207
childhood and trauma, 24–30, 30–31,
   67–68, 68n
childhood attachment, 22–23, 40
   See also infant attachment
Chirico, Alice, 214
civilization and Theory Z, 232–33
clinical psychology, xx, 102, 106, 143, 146,
   226, 240
"Cognition of Being in the Peak Experiences"
   (Maslow), 195–97
cognitive-behavioral therapy (CBT), 70
cognitive empathy, 127–28
cognitive exploration, 94, 104, 106, 107–8,
   108, 116, 116n, 117
"cognitive needs," 94
cognitive neuroscience, 25, 115–16, 115–16n
coherence, 8–9, 11, 34, 161, 174–75, 231
coin flip and cohesion study, 39
Colby, Anne, 167–68
collective narcissism, 77
Collins, Nancy, 19
Commentary magazine, 46
communal narcissism, 73–74, 74n
communion, 126–27, 147, 169, 170
compassion, 127–28
"compassion fatigue," 128–29
"compensatory dominance," 57, 58
"conflicting" desires, 84
Connectedness (Awe Experience Scale), 208
connection, xx, xxi, xxiii, xxviii, xxx, xxxii,
   xxxiii, *xxxv*, 245
   growth, *81*, 98, 119, 120, 123, 136, 148,
      160, 167, 174, 181
   healthy transcendence, 203, 204, 211, 212,
      228, 236, 243
   security, *1*, 34, 35–53, 54, 59, 63, 69, 74
consistent (quality of moral exemplar), 167,
   168, 173, 174

constructive developmental theory, 226
context, 27, 29, 30, 31, 44, 84
continued freshness of appreciation, 89, 111
control systems theory (if/then), 14–15, *15*
Cook-Greuter, Susanne, 226
coping mechanisms, healthy, 128–30
corpus callosum, 25
Cosimano, Mary, 211–12
cosmos, 202, 222, 246
Council Grove conference (1970), 242
coworker support, 181
creativity, *xiv*, xviii, xx, xxiv, xxix
    growth, 89, 100, 106, 107, 108, *108*, 111,
        152, 160, 162, *165*, 174, 176, 178, 179, 180
    healthy transcendence, 194, 210, 238
    security, 6, 33, 42, 65, 79, 80
creativity paradox (exploration), 114–17
"Critique of Self-Actualization Theory"
    (Maslow), xiv
"Crooked-A's," 33–34
cross-cultural variation, xxix–xxx
"crystallizing experience," 3
Csikszentmihalyi, Mihaly, 160, 203
"culture of overprotection," 92
curiosity, xxxiv, 14, 22, 90, 94, 95–97, 98,
    104, 107, *108*, 112, 113, 126, 204, 208,
    235, 238
cybernetics, xx, xxxi, 14

Dabrowski, Kazimierz, 104
Damon, William, 158, 167–68
dark triad, 101n, 121–25, 127–28, 136, 147
dating websites, 51
Daukantaite, Daiva, 174
"deadly sins," 122
death, xvi, 45, 150, 203, 209–10, 233–39, 244
    fear of, xvi, 150, 203, 210, 236, 237, 244
    as given of existence, xxxvii
    ultimate unknown, xvi, xxxvii, 45, 150,
        203, 210, 233–39, 244
De Botton, Alain, 138
Debrot, Anik, 146
default mode network, 110, 116
deficiency needs. *See* D-realm
"deficit model," 30–31
deficit-reduction orientation, belonging,
    94, 95
Denial of Death, The (Becker), 233, 234
De Pree, Max, 158
depression, 13, 19, 27, 33, 39, 47, 48, 59, 65,
    72, 76, 104, 129, 130, 132, 159, 160, 177,
    178, 211, 214, 215, 229–30, 246
deprivation sensitivity, *108*, 112–13

"desacralizing" of science, 228n
detached awareness, 134
developmental psychology, xx, xxvii, 3, 14,
    16, 127, 238
development as two-steps-forward,
    one-step-back dynamic, xxviii
DeYoung, Colin, xxxvi
dialectical behavioral therapy (DBT), 70
dichotomy-transcendence, 222, 225–26
Diebels, Kate, 60–61
disabled people and social media, 50
disadvantage and creativity, 106
dismissing/avoidant attachment, 17, *18*, 18n
diversity vs. inconsistency of interests, 173–74
"Dominance-Feeling, Behavior, and Status"
    (Maslow), 57–58
dopamine, 93–94, 98, 110
D-realm, xx, xxx–xxxi, 245
    growth, 119–20, 125, 135, 144, 167
    healthy transcendence, 220, 223, 225, 228,
        232, 238
"drowning in possibility," 110
Drucker, Peter, 151
"Drugs—Critique" (Maslow), 215
Duality of Human Existence, The (Bakan), 126
Duckworth, Angela, 173
Dutton, Jane, 42, 181

education, 29–30, 32, 33, 152, 227, 228–29
"ego integrity," 226
Ellis, Bruce, 30, 31
Emerson, Ralph Waldo, 189–91, 191n
Emmons, Robert, 160
Emotionally Focused Therapy (EFT), 21
emotion-focused coping strategy, 101
empathic accuracy study, 31
empathy, 19, 65, 72, 110, 122, 127–28,
    134, 242
"empathy burnout," 128–29
End, The (game), 234–36
end-experiences/values/cognitions/goals,
    xxiii–xxiv
    See also Being-Psychology
energizing aspect of purpose, 156
engagement in life, xxvi
Engler, Jack, 205
enlightened culture, 179, 180–83
enlightened leadership, 152, 179–80
"enlightened self-interest," 169
entitlement, 64, 68n
environmental mastery, xxv, 10, 90, 174
equanimity and grit, 89, 171, 172–75, 178, 183
Erickson, Erik, 226

eros (romantic passion), 145, 146–47
Esalen Institute, xviii, 184, 185
ethology, 14
Eupsychian Management (Maslow), 152, 152n, 159, 164
"evil, reconciled with," 223–24
evolutionary psychology, xx, xxxi, xxxiv, xxxvi, xxxvii–xxxviii, 26, 38, 43, 51, 67, 69–70, 93, 96–97, 112, 143, 191n, 196, 228, 236
executive attention brain network, 112, 113, 116
existential-humanistic psychotherapy, xxiv, 155
"existential paradox," 234
existential positive psychology, 238
existential psychotherapy, xvii, xxxvii, 121
experiential avoidance, 74, 105–6
"experiential sampling," 160
experiential self, 166
experimental psychology, xxiv, 150, 200, 206
exploration, xx, xxxiv, *xxxv*
  growth, *81*, 90, 91–117, *108*, 136, 141, 143, 144–46, 148, 167, 173–74, 176, 177, 183
  healthy transcendence, 195, 208, 225
  See also self-actualization

Facebook, xiii, 50–51
face-to-face interactions, 51–53
fact and value, 196, 196n
Faith in Humanity, 123, *123*
fame, 45, 46, 49, 77
"Farther Reaches of Human Nature, The" (Maslow), xv–xvi, 149, 170, 217, 227, 228
fear, xxv, xxvii, xxix, xxxi, 6, 10, 14, 21, 22, 24, 25, 26–27, 44, 66, 67, 69, 70–71, 75, 92, 93, 98–99, 100, 105, 107, 139, 168, 196, 202, 204, 206, 208, 212–13, 215, 232, 238
fearful/fearful-avoidant attachment, 17, *18*, 18n
fear of death, xvi, 150, 203, 210, 236, 237, 244
Feigenbaum, Ken, 150
Feng, Gia-Fu, 184
fewer negative emotions, xxv
Figueredo, Aurelio, 122
First and Last Freedom (Krishnamurti), 194
First Nations perspective, 5
flow, xx, xxvi, 107, *108*, 109, 110, 140, 145, 160, 203, 208
Folkways (Sumner), 3
food preferences, 35
food security, xxvii, xxx, 9, 12–13, 24, 36
Forgeard, Marie, 106

Fowler, Susan, xxix
Fox, Nathan, 24, 27
Fraley, R. Chris, 17, 19–20, 23
Frank, Anne, 121, 124
Frankl, Viktor, xviii, xxiv, 102, 104, 154, 156
Fredrickson, Barbara, 43, 213
freedom (given of existence), xxxvii
free-soloing, 97, 98, 101, 101n
free will, 161
Freudians/Freud, Sigmund, xxiv, 14, 36, 54, 54n, 55, 56, 57, 65, 129–30, 156, 194n
Frick, Willard, 220
Friedan, Betty, 56
friendships, xv, xviii, 38, 51, 139, 164, 225, 228
Frimer, Jeremy, 167, 168, 169
Fromm, Erich, xviii, xxi, xxiv, xxxvi–xxxvii, 83, 120–21, 130, 131, 138, 159
"fruits, not the roots," 199
Fry, Stephen, 46–47
fully human, xxvi, xxxiii, 87, 251
future selves studies, 33

Gaggioli, Andrea, 207
gambling casino royalties, 29
Gandhi, Mohandas, 168, 169
Gardner, Howard, 3
generativity, 226, 238
"generosity burnout," 128–29
genes, xxxi, 9, 10, 11, 25, 26, 40, 67, 98, 143, 198, 213
Geography of Bliss, The (Weiner), 237
Gesselman, Amanda, 144
Gestalt psychology, 83, 86
"givens of existence," xxxvii
goals, xv, xxiv, xxv, xxviii, xxxi, xxxv–xxxvi
  growth, 84, 103, 105, 110, 116, 122, 133, 139, 147, 155–56, 159–66, *161*, *162*, *163*, *164*, *165*, 168, 170, 171–72, 173, 177–78, 180, 182–84
  healthy transcendence, 228
  security, 8, 9, 11, 13, 30, 49, 60, 61, 62, 72, 73, 74, 78, 80
  See also purpose
Goldstein, Kurt, 83, 85–86
Goldstein, Rebecca, 155
"Good Human Being [GHB] Notebook" (Maslow), 87, 88
good life, vision of, xxxv, xxxviii–xxxix, 166, 238
good moral intuition, 89
"good" vs. "evil," 240–41
gossip, 43, 96–97

"gradient of autonomy," 165
grandiose narcissism, 64, 71–76, 77, 78, 80, 122
Grant, Adam, 33, 166
Graves, Clare, 226
greed, 4, 131, 244
Greenberg, Jeff, 59
Griffiths, Roland, 209
grit and equanimity, 89, 171, 172–75, 178, 183
Grogan, Jessica, 185
Gross National Happiness, 237
group cohesion, 39–40, 44
growth, xviii, xix, xx, xxi, xxiv, xxv, xxvi, xxvii, xxviii, xxx–xxxi, xxxii, xxxiii–xxxiv, *xxxv*, xxxix, 29, 69–71, 72, *81*, 81–185, 238
growth challenges, 279–309
growth-driven life motivations, 79, 80
growth-mindedness, 135
growth purchases vs. material purchases, 49–50

Haidt, Jonathan, 92, 201, 204, 206
"hangry" (from "hungry" and "angry"), 12
happiness, xx, xxi, xxv, xxvi, xxxiv, xxxvii
    growth, 84, 93, 100, 131, 132, 146–47, 153–54, 155–56, 170
    healthy transcendence, 197, 208, 213, 214, 219, 223, 229, 237
    security, 11, 26, 41, 43, 48–50, 51, 70, 79
Harari, Yuval, 213
Harlow, Harry, 35, 36, 54, 55
harmonious passion, 145, 171, 175–76
Hatt, Beth, 32
Hayes, Steven, 70
"health-fostering" victory, 215
health insurance, Americans', 7
"healthy childishness," 225
healthy transcendence, xxxi, 187–244
    See also transcendence
Heaphy, Emily, 42
heart disease and loneliness, 45
Heavy Head, Martin, 4
"hedonic treadmill," 49
hedonism, 100, 229–30
Heitzman, A. Lynn, 240, 241, 243
"helicopter parenting," 92
Herman Miller, 158
Herzog, Werner, 154
hierarchy of needs, xiii, *xiv*, xvi, xvii, xxi, xxiii–xxxix, *xxxv*, 7, 44, 148, 163, 167, 175, 185, 191, 219
"higher needs," xv, xxviii

high-quality connections, 42–45, 52
hippocampus, 25, 26–27
Hirsh, Jacob, 10
Hitler, Adolf, 167, 168
Hoffman, Edward, 150, 194
holistic perceiving, 222
Honnold, Alex ("No Big Deal"), 97–98, 99, 101
hope, 28, 30–34, 126, 129, 171, 177–78, 179, 228, 229, 237
Hope Scale, 178
Horney, Karen, xviii, xxiv, 83, 136
horticulturists (teachers, therapists, parents), xxiii
hubristic pride, 79
human existence. *See* agency; communion
Humanism, 123, *123*
humanistic psychology, xviii–xxi, xxiv–xxvi, xxviii, xxxii, xxxviii, 54, 59, 79, 106, 107, 110, 117, 133, 155, 184, 185, 220, 227, 228–29, 231, 232, 239, 243, 250–51
"Humanistic Revolution," xv–xvi, xviii
humanitarianism, xxiv, 89
humanity formula, 123
human nature and society, 216
Human Side of Enterprise (McGregor), 151
humans vs. animals, xxxv–xxxvi
humble (quality of moral exemplar), 168
humor, 65, 126, 129–30, 221, 240, 247
hunger, 12–13
"hunger" vs. "appetites," 35
Hyde, Elizabeth, 121, 123, 207
hypoegoic state of consciousness, 203–4

ideal personality, 84–85
Ikarians, 52
ikigai, 52
Ikiru (movie), 153
imagination, xxxvi, 107, *108*, 109, 114, 115, 143, 146, 147, 214, 236
"imagination network" (default), 110, 116
"Importance of Falling in Love with 'Something,' The" (Torrance), 162
imposter syndrome, 68, 74
inclusive identity, 134
incomes, Americans', 7
individual differences, xxix–xxx
individualism/altruism dichotomy, 205
individuality and love, 141
industrial (managerial) psychology, 151
infant attachment, 16
    See also childhood attachment
influential moral figures, 167–69

in-group positivity, 77–78
"inner core," xxvii
inner/outer dichotomy, 153
insanity/being sane in insane society, 159
insecurity, xxxiii, 10, 13, 94, 100, 144–45,
    159, 160, 165, 175, 194, 204, 236–37, 238
    See also security
"insecurity cycle," 5–6
inspiring (quality of moral exemplar), 168
instrumental agency, 169
instrumental social value, 61, 62, 64, 73
integral theory, 226
integrated hierarchy of needs, xix, xxiv, xxv,
    xxviii, xxxi, xxxiv, 44, 148, 163, 167,
    175, 245
integrity, 89, 136, 137, 174, 183
intellect, 94, 108, *108*, 111–14, 116
intellectual curiosity, 107, *108*, 112, 113
intelligence, xx, 30–34, 116–17, 126
intensity seeking, 101, 101n
"internal working models" of others/self,
    15–16
Interpretation of Dreams, The (Freud), 54
intimacy, 21, 34, 37, 38, 41–43, 46, 53, 125,
    146, 222, 238
"intrinsic conscience," 159
intuition, 89, *108*, 109–10, 115, 240, 242
Inzlicht, Michael, 10
IQ, 63, *108*, 112, 113, 116, 222, 223
isolation (given of existence), xxxvii

Jacobs, W. Jake, 122
James, William, xviii, 88, 172, 194, 194n, 195,
    199, 200, 202, 203, 206, 233
Jauk, Emanuel, 76
Jim's story, 71–72
job and purpose, 157, 158
job-crafting, 181–82, 183
job performance and self-actualization, 90
Johns Hopkins, 209, 210, 211
"Jonah Complex," 71
Jongman-Sereno, Katrina, 60–61
Journal of Humanistic Psychology, The, xxiv
Journal of Transpersonal Psychology, 220
joy and Theory Z, 229–30
Jung, Carl, 172, 194, 268

Kane, Jennifer, 105
Kant, Immanuel, 114, 123
Kantianism, 123, *123*
Kashdan, Todd, 93, 95, 99, 100, 105, 146
Kasser, Tim, 163–64

Kaufman, Scott Barry, xiii–xxxix, 249–52
    See also self-actualization; transcendence
Kay, Andrew, 150, 151, 152
Kegan, Robert, 226
Keltner, Dacher, 77, 80, 206, 207, 213
Kenrick, Douglas, xxxiv
Kierkegaard, Søren, 110
knowing when to move on, 171, 182–84
Kramer, Deirdre, 226
Krishnamurti, J., 194
Kushner, Rabbi Harold, 103
Kuszewski, Andrea, 168

latent inhibition, 110–11, 116
Laughlin, Bill, 216
Lavigne, L. Geneviève, 94
learned helplessness, 27–28
Leary, Mark, 60, 203
Leriadis, Ilias, 52
Let Grow, 92
libidinal drive, 54, 55
life motivations clusters, 79, 80
life satisfaction, xxv, 41, 42, 48, 49, 50, 51, 59,
    65, 68, 74, 90, 101, 132, 146, 157, 158,
    160, 164, 174, 206, 211
light triad (Kaufman), 101n, 121–25, *123*,
    132, 206
Loevinger, Jane, 226
logotherapy, 156
loneliness, 19, 37, 39n, 41, 45–48, 50, 95, 121,
    146, 219
*Loneliness: Human Nature and the Need for Social
    Connection* (Cacioppo), 45
Lopez, Shane, 177, 178
love, *xiv,* xv, xviii, xx, xxiv, xxv, xxvii, xxx,
    xxxiv, *xxxv,* 248
    growth, *81,* 84, 90, 102, 104–5, 117, 118–48,
        123, 162, 167, 174, 175–76, 177, 182, 183
    healthy transcendence, 193, 194, 198, 201,
        203, 208, 210, 225, 228, 230, 232, 233,
        236, 237, 238, 243, 244
    immature vs. mature, 120–21
    needing vs. unneeding, 120
    romantic, 138, 139, 141, 142, 194, 228
    security, 8, 14, 15, *15,* 36, 37, 41, 42, 44, 46,
        55–56, 74, 77–78, 80
    unconditional, 44, 127
    whole, 137, 138–48
    See also self-actualization
"Love and Power" (Morgenthau), 46
Love & Will (May), 146
"Love in Self-Actualizing People"
    (Maslow), 139

"Love: The Nature of Our True Self" (Cosimano), 211–12
Lowry, Richard, 88, 190, 239
Luisa's story, 118, 119

MacGregor, Douglas, 220
Machiavellianism, 101n, 122, 123
MacLean, Katherine, 209–10, 211, 215
Maier, Steven, 27–28
"manifestations of normality," 84
Manson, Mark, 143
Man's Search for Meaning (Frankl), 154, 156
Manuel, Frank, 71
Martela, Frank, 8–9
Mary's story, 65
"masculine protest," 55
Maslow, Abraham, xiii–xvii, *xiv*, xvii, xx, xxiii–xxiv, xxvi
anthropology impact, 3–6
B-realm exercises, 245–48
exploration, 91–92, 93, 94, 107, 111–12, 113
love, 119–20, 123, 124–25, 131, 138, 139–40, 141, 142, 143, 143n, 146
"Over-Soul, The" (Emerson), 189–91, 191n
peak experiences, 193–97, 194n, 196n, 201, 205, 206, 207, 208, 214–15, 216
purpose, 149–52, 150n, 152n, 153–54, 156–57, 159, 164, 169, 170, 175, 179, 183, 184–85
security, 7, 8, 11, 12, 23, 29, 35, 37, 54–58, 59, 60, 64, 70–71
Theory Z, 218–25, 227–28, 229, 230, 231, 232, 233, 239, 240–44, 243n
"wonderful possibilities and inscrutable depths," 249–52, *250*
See also self-actualization; transcendence
Maslow, Bertha, xiii, xvii, 4, 83, 184, 216, 249, *250*
mass shootings, 39
mastery, *xiv*, xxv, xxxvi, 52, 57, 58, 59, 60, 61–62, 68, 78, 93, 119, 135, 160, 163, 176
materialism and money, 48–50
Mating in Captivity (Perel), 141–42
mattering, form of meaning, 8
"mattering instinct," 155
May, Rollo, xviii, xxiv, xxxv, 117, 146, 147, 185
McGregor, Douglas, 151, 153
MDMA-assisted psychotherapy, 211
Mead, Margaret, 4, 83, 152
meals in schools, reduced-price, 8

meaning, xviii, xxv, xxvi, xxxii, xxxv
growth, 93, 94, 102, 104, 105–6, 110, 119, 146–47, 152n, 154, 155, 156, 161, 167, 180, 184
healthy transcendence, 211, 212, 213, 214, 226, 238–39, 243
security, 6, 8–9, 79
meaningfulness and creativity, 114, 115, 116
meaninglessness (given of existence), xxxvii
measurable (quality of SMART goals), 171
medial prefrontal cortex, 25, 28
meditation, xxviii, 131, 200, 203, 208, 209, 213, 215, 228, 235, 245
Meston, Cindy, 143
metamotivations, 220–21
"metaneeds," 221
"metapathologies," 221
"metapay" and "metareward," 225
"micro-awakening," 39
"micro-moments of connection," 43
Miller, Joshua, 68
mind-altering interventions, 208–16
mindfulness, xix, 134, 174, *203*, 237, 238
"miserable privileges," 156
Mittelmann, Bela, 83, 84
money, xx, xxxviii, 45–46, 48–50, 52, 73, 77, 79, 80, 122, 160, 169, 221, 225, 233, 238, 244
monkey studies, 35, 36–37, 55, 56
moods, xxv, 146, 160, 164, 172, 202n, 211
Moors, Amy, 144
moral exemplars, 167–68, 169
moral purpose, 167–70
more positive emotions, xxv
Morgenthau, Hans, 46
mortality, xvi, xxxvii, 45, 150, 203, 210, 233–39, 244
mortality risk controllability study, 28
motivation, xxv
growth, 85–86, 87, 93–94, 108, 127, 131, 132, 138–39, 143, 151, 152, 164–66, *165*, 171, 181
healthy transcendence, 191n, 196, 203, 219, 220–21, 225, 226, 231–32, 243
security, 8, 12, 13, 59, 79–80
motivational quality (MQ), 165, *165*
Motivation and Personality (Maslow), 7, 12, 37, 58, 64, 118, 125, 139, 143, 151, 193, 217
Mudde, Cas, 232
multiple needs, simultaneous, xxix–xxx
Murphy, Michael, 185
Murray, Henry, 219

mutuality, high-quality connections, 38, 42, 46
mystical experiences, 193, 194n, 195, 197, 199, 201, 202, 202n, 203, *203*, 210, 213, 225–26, 228, 230

Nakkula, Michael, 32, 33
narcissism, xix, 39, 62–78, 79, 80, 101n, 122, 130, 132, 135, 194n, 236
Nasby, William, 170
"natural" dominance, 57
natural scenery and awe, 207
Nazis, 55, 156, 159
Need for Accommodation (Awe Experience Scale), 208
Neff, Kristin, 132
negative emotions, xxv, 106, 282
neglect, xxvii, 10, 24, 25, 26
Nelson, Barnaby, 111
Nettle, Daniel, 13, 28, 29
"neural coupling," 43
neural plasticity, 25
neurology, 26, 85, 86
neuropsychiatry, 83
neuroscience, xx, xxxvi, 25, 44, 115, 200
neurotheology, 200
neuroticism, 10, 19, 68n, 131, 155, 194n, 197
Newberg, Andrew, 200, 201, 202, 215
Nietzsche, Friedrich, xxxviii, 55, 156
Nobel Prize winners, 115, 194n
"noetic" quality of mystic experience, 204
nonattachment, 140–41
"normal personality," 84–85
novel events, xxxiv, 91, 93, 95, 97, 98, 99, 100, 101, 101n, 111, 114, 115, 142
Nuer, Claire, 119

obsessive-compulsive disorder, 10, 19
obsessive passion, 139, 145, 175–76
opening your sail, xxxii–xxxiv, xxxix, 34, 53, 80, 129, 136
openness to experience, 94, 106, 107–11, *108*, 112, 114, 116, 208, 210, 211, 238
opioid system and connection, 43–44
orbital prefrontal cortex, 25
Organism, The (Goldstein), 86
organizational psychology, xx, 136, 153, 158
"orthopsychology." *See* Being-Psychology
Osborne, Arthur, 242
Otto, Max, 189–90
overarching purpose/possible self, 155, 159, *161*, 162, *162*, 163, *163*, *164*, 170, 172

overcompensation, 6, 57–58
overconfidence, 72, 74
overevaluation, parental, 63, 63n
"Over-Soul, The" (Emerson), 189–91, 191n
oxytocin, 44

painters and physical illnesses, 106
Pankhurst, Emmeline, 168, 169
"paradoxical self-esteem," 62
"paradox of choice," 49
parenting, xix, xxiii, xxxiv, 15, 16, 22–23, 24, 25, 63, 63n, 67–68, 92, 166
Park, Asaka, 50
passion, 117, 139, 141, 142–43, 145, 146–47, 171, 172–73, 175–76, 182
pathways (Hope Scale), 177, 178
Paulhus, Delroy, 122
Pauling, Linus, 115
Paulos, John Allen, 10
peak experiences, xxxiii, 89, 185, 193–216, 219, 221, 223, 225, 228, 228n, 230, 242, 243
"Peak Experiences as Acute Identity Experiences" (Maslow), 205
Pearl Harbor, World War II, 85
Pepper, Gillian, 28, 29
Perel, Esther, 141–42
perfectionism, 19, 55, 58, 69, 72, 75, 222, 240, 252
personality psychology, xx, xxxi, 107
Personal Mastery, 119
personal values research, 33
personology, 219
perspective-taking (quiet ego), 127, 134–35
Phillippe, Frederick, 145
Philosophy of Civilization course, 3
Physical Sensations (Awe Experience Scale), 208
physiological needs, *xiv*, 11–12, 14, 37, 78, 143n
plateau experience (Theory Z), 221, 239–44
"pleasure system," 43
Poe, Edgar Allan, 111
politics and Theory Z, 231–32
"pooling of needs," 146
"positive disintegration," 104
positive emotions, xxv, 93, 101, 146
"positive interpersonal processes," 42
positive psychology, xx, xxiv, xxv, 103, 133, 151, 200, 238
positive relationships, xxv, 90, 174–75, 176
positivity resonance, 43, 120
Possibilities for Human Nature (Maslow), 251
possibility development, 32

"postambivalence," 225
posttraumatic growth, 94, 102–6
post-traumatic stress disorder (PTSD), 19, 102, 211
poverty, 7, 24, 28, 29, 33
power, xviii, xix, xx, xxxviii, 35, 45–46, 55, 56, 58, 65, 73, 75–76, 77, 78, 79, 80, 115, 122, 127, 143, 156, 160, 169, 179, 221, 231, 232
Practice of Management, The (Drucker), 151
praise, 61, 63, 63n, 72, *165*
prayer, 208, 213
predictive-adaptive-response theory (PAR), 25
prefrontal cortex, 25, 27, 28
preoccupied attachment (adult), 17, *18*, 18n
Price, Richard, 184
pride, xix, 57, 76, 78–80, 79n, 132, 151, 180, 246
primate psychology, 35
principled/virtuous (quality of moral exemplar), 167, 168
problem-focused coping strategy, 101–2
projection, 74–75, 130
proximity-seeking behaviors, 14–15, *15*, 16
psilocybin, 202n, 208, 209, 210, 211, 212, 213
psychedelics, 208–16
Psychiatry (scientific journal), 195
psychoanalysis, xxiv, 5–6, 54, 56, 65, 83, 84, 136, 234
psychological defensiveness, 107
psychological entropy, 9–12, 13
psychological flexibility, 105–6, 174
Psychological Review (scientific journal), 195
Psychology and the Human Dilemma (May), 117
"Psychology of Happiness, The" (Maslow), 155–56
Psychology Today, 85, 244
psychopathology, xx, 10, 26, 101, 101n, 102, 122
psychopharmacology, 209
"psychopolitics," 231
psychosocial development, 226
psychotherapy, xxiv, xxviii, xxxvii, 50, 70, 117, 121, 141, 155, 156, 185, 205, 211, 237
public and historical figures, 88
pure Being. *See* B-realm
purpose, xx, xxiv, xxvi, xxviii, xxxiv, *xxxv*, xxxvii
   growth, *81*, 89, 90, 103, 148, 149–85, *161*, *162*, *163*, *164*, *165*
   healthy transcendence, 203, 210, 212, 213, 233, 237, 238
   security, 8, 9, 11, 68, 80
   See also goals; self-actualization

pursuing wisely, 170–84
pyramid hierarchy, xiii, *xiv*, xxviii–xxix, xxxi–xxxii, 7, 8

quiet ego, 133–35, 204–5, 238

Rank, Otto, 234
rational vs. experiential self, 166
Ravert, Russell, 101
Rawlings, David, 111
Read, Nancy, 170
"realer than real," 204
"real love," 120
Real Love (Salzberg), 142
Rebele, Reb, 79, 173
refeeding and hunger behaviors, 13
reflection, 14, 110, 114, 116, 133, 238
Reker, Gary, 238
relational social value, 60–61, 62, 73
relationships and Theory Z, 228
relevant (quality of SMART goals), 171, 172
religion and Theory Z, 230–31
Religions, Values, and Peak Experiences (Maslow), 197, 208, 239, 242
religiousness, 193–94, 194n, 199–200, 201, 205, 206, 208, 224, 230–31
resilience, 21, 95, 101, 102, 132, 178, 181
responsibility, xviii, xxv, xxxvii, 69, 71, 89, 126, 133, 136, 149, 151, 158, 164, 180, 233, 239
Review of General Psychology (scientific journal), 201
Rholes, W. Steven, 22
right to shine, 71
"rising tide," high-quality connections, 43
Robbers Cave study, 39
Rogers, Carl, xviii, xxiv, 42, 59, 78, 107, 165, 185
"role abandonment"/role engulfment, 139
romantic love, 138, 139, 141, 142, 194, 228
romantic passion, 145, 146–47
Roosevelt, Eleanor, 88, 168, 169, 180
Rowan, John, xxviii
"rumble of panic," 234, 235, 236
rumination, 10, 104–5, 106, 176, 214
Russian nesting dolls analogy, xxviii
Ryan, Richard, 59

Sacks, Oliver, 85
sacredness in all things, xxiii, 222, 223

safety, xiii, *xiv*, xxviii, xxx, xxxi, xxxii, xxxiii, xxxiv, *xxxv*, *1*, 6, 7–34, 37, 39, 48, 71, *81*, 86, 91, 92, 98, 119, 136, 148, 167, 221, 231, 245
sailboat, xxxi–xxxix, *xxxii*, *xxxv*, *1*, 34, 53, 80, *81*, 129, 136, 183, *187*
salience network, 116
Salzberg, Sharon, 120, 142
samadhi, 194
Sam's story, 37
Sandelands, Lance, 42
Sane Society, The (Fromm), xxxvi
Saroglou, Vassilis, 213
Schachtel, Rabbi Hyman, 50
Schnell, Tatjana, 238–39
scientific/intuitive, 240
scientific investigation and Theory Z, 228, 228n
Seale, Colin, 33–34
Search for Authenticity, The (Bugental), 155
"second naivete," 225
"second tier" spiral dynamic, 226
"sectarians," 168
secure attachment, 17, *18*, 42, 140–41, 144
security, *xiv*, xviii, xxix, xxx, xxxi, xxxii, xxxiii, xxxiv, *xxxv*, *1*, 1–80, 84, 86, 93, 98, 100, 119, 141, 146, 147, 167, 225, 227, 231, 233, 238
    See also insecurity
seismic earthquake metaphor for trauma, 103–4
self-acceptance, xxv, 68, 90, 174, 238
    See also acceptance
self-actualization, xiii–xv, *xiv*, xxi, xxiii, xxix, xxx, xxxi, xxxiii–xxxiv, xxxvi, 83–90
    peak experiences, 193, 195, 196, 197, 205, 215
    security, 7, 70, 79, 80
    Theory Z, xiii, 217–44
    See also exploration; Kaufman, Scott Barry; love; Maslow, Abraham; purpose; transcendence
"Self-Actualization: A Study of Psychological Health" (Maslow), 88
selfactualizationtests.com, xxi, 89, 123, 131, 208
self-awareness, xxv, xxxvi, 17, 26, 117, 133–34, 136, 141, 236
self-compassion, 132–33, 238
self-concordant goals, 166
self-control, 100, 133
self-determination, 164–65, 170, 180
Self-Diminishment (Awe Experience Scale), 208

self-esteem, xiii, *xiv*, xxviii, xxx, xxxiii, *xxxv*, xxxvi, 245
    growth, *81*, 84, 86, 98, 132, 134, 135, 136, 143, 148, 152, 160, 167
    healthy transcendence, 219, 236, 238
    security, *1*, 5, 6, 19, 35, 43, 53, 54–80
self-expansion theory of love, 138–39, 142
self-honesty, 136–37
"Selfishness and Self-Love" (Fromm), 130
selfish/unselfish dichotomy, 153
self-loss, 203–6
self-love, 130–33, 139, 147, 174
    pathological, 132
self-presentation strategy, 68, 69, 78
self-preservation, 6, 39, 54, 86
self-regulation, 25, 59, 105, 161
self-respect, xv, 23, 57, 84, 131, 139
self-transcendence, xxiv, 126–27, 181, 200, 201, 227
Seligman, Martin, xxv, 27–28, 115, 200, 201
sensation seeking, 99, 101
sense of self (self-worth), xv, xxv, xxviii, 52, 59, 60–61, 62, 65, 66, 68, 69, 74, 75, 110, 135, 139, 140, 205, 208, 226
Seppälä, Emma, 47–48, 51, 52
sex, 6, 28, 36, 37, 77, 84, 94, 100, 122, 137, 138, 142, 143n, 143–47, 193, 194, 225, 228, 230
sex and dominance research, 54, 55–56, 83
sexploration, 144–46
sexual assault, 102, 214
Sheldon, Kennon, 160, 163–64, 165, 166, 170
Shonkoff, Jack, 24, 27
"sickness-fostering" victory, 215
signature strengths, 166, 171, 176–77
silent vs. quiet ego, 135
Simpson, Jeffry, 21–22
60 Minutes (TV show), 97
Skee-Ball, xxxvi
Skenazy, Lenore, 92
SMART goals, 171–72
Snyder, Charles, 177, 178
social anxiety, 95, 145, 211
social curiosity, 95–97
social environment, 95, 96, 202
"social evasion," 39
social exploration, 94–97
social intelligence, 126
"social interest," xviii, 54, 55, 58, 78
social isolation, 45, 48
social media, 50–51, 52, 163, 166
social protection system, 38, 39, 41, 61, 67, 69–70
social psychology, xx, xxi, 19, 39, 42–43, 45, 60, 77, 133, 144, 152

social value, 60–61, 62, 64, 66, 67, 73
society and human nature, 216
society and Theory Z, 232–33
Society for Personality and Social
     Psychology, 195
Some Do Care (Colby and Damon), 167
specific (quality of SMART goals), 171
Spiritual Evolution (Vaillant), 119
"splitting," 26
"staleness of experience," 111
states of mind and hierarchy of needs,
     xxvii–xxviii
status-driven life motivations, 79, 80
Steger, Michael, 8–9
Sternberg, Robert, 30
"strange situation procedure," 16
stress, 9–10, 11, 15, *15*, 18–19, 21–22, 24, 25,
     26, 38, 43, 45, 49, 69, 91, 101, 102, 106,
     113, 132, 143, 174, 182, 208, 230
stress-adapted children, 30, 31–32
stress tolerance, 93, 98–99
striving for power, 55, 58, 78
striving wisely, 159–66, *161, 162, 163, 164,
     165*, 170, 173, 175
sublimation, 130, 154
suicide, 39, 46–47, 237
"Summer Notes on Social Psychology
     of Industry and Management"
     (Maslow), 152
Sumner, William Graham, 3–4, 5
supportive environment, 171, 178–83
suppression, xxvii, 5, 69, 70, 78, 101, 112, 129,
     130, 140
Swann, William B., Jr., 61
synergy, xxxiv, 152–53, 169, 222, 225, 233

Tafarodi, Romin, 61, 62
Tedeschi, Richard, 102–3
Teicher, Martin, 25, 26
temporo-parietal junction, 202
Terror Management Theory (TMT), 236
"Theory of Human Motivation" (Maslow),
     59, 86
"theory-of-mind" ability, 127–28
Theory of Successful Intelligence, 30
Theory X, 151
Theory Y, 151, 153, 220
Theory Z, xiii, 217–44
thinkLaw, 33
Third Force psychologists, xxiv
Thorndike, Edward, 56, 83
Time (Awe Experience Scale), 208
"timelessness," 194

time-saving vs. material purchases, 49
time-specific (quality of SMART goals),
     171, 172
Torrance, E. Paul, 162
"total personality," 84
Toward a Psychology of Being (Maslow), xv,
     xxiii, 107, 111, 112, 138, 184, 193, 206
Tracy, Jessica, 78, 79, 79n
transcendence, xix, xx, xxi, xxvi, xxviii, xxix,
     xxxiii, *xxxv*, xxxvii–xxxviii, 148
     healthy transcendence, xxxi, 187–244
     peak experiences, xxxiii, 89, 185,
          193–216, 219, 221, 223, 225, 228,
          228n, 230, 242, 243
     self-transcendence, xxiv, 126–27, 181, 200,
          201, 227
     Theory Z, xiii, 217–44
     See also Kaufman, Scott Barry; Maslow,
          Abraham; self-actualization
transcenders, 218–27
transcranial direct current stimulation, 214
transcranial magnetic stimulation, 214
transhumanism, 239, 251
trauma, xix, 9, 23, 24–30, 64, 67, 86, 94,
     101–6, 178
tribal impulses, 40
true self, 211–12, 257–77
trust study, 28
trustworthiness and dependability for close
     loved ones, 126
truth seeking, xx, 89, 112
Tsukayama, Eli, 123
"tyrants," 168

ultimate concern, xxiv, 161
ultimate responsibility, 158
ultimate unknown (death), xvi, xxxvii, 45,
     150, 203, 210, 233–39, 244
unconditional love, 44, 127
unconditional positive regard, x, 42, 123
unitary continuum, 202–3, *203*
"unitive consciousness," 242
universal concern, 126, 127
universal tolerance, 126
unpredictability, 7, 8, 9, 10, 11, 25, 26–27, 28,
     29, 31, 32, 125, 142
upward spirals, 43, 45, 166
"us" vs. "me" place, 52

vagus nerve, 44–45
Vaillant, George, 119, 129
Vainio, Mia, 174

Vallerand, Robert, 175
valuing money, 49
Van Cappellen, Patty, 213
Varieties of Religious Experience, The (James), 194, 199, 200, 233
"Varieties of Self-Transcendent Experience, The" (Yaden et al.), 201, 203, *203*
"Various Meanings of Transcendence" (Maslow), 217
Vastness (Awe Experience Scale), 207–8
Vicary, Amanda, 19–20
violence, xix, 4, 10, 23, 24, 25, 28, 77, 102, 105, 122, 145, 167, 214
virtual reality, 213–14
"virtue pays," 153, 233
Vohs, Kathleen, 77
vulnerable narcissism, 64, 65–71, 72, 73–74, 74n, 75, 76, 78, 132

wanting vs. liking, 142
Watson, John, 36
Watts, Alan, 10, 194
Wayment, Heidi, 133, 135
Weiner, Eric, 237
Weiss, Brandon, 68
well-being, xx, xxv–xxvi
    growth, 90, 93, 94, 101, 113, 125, 126, 134, 146, 151, 160, 166, 170, 171, 174, 175, 176, 177, 178, 180, 181, 183
    healthy transcendence, 197, 201, 210, 211, 214, 234, 235, 237
    security, 43, 49, 50, 59
Wertheimer, Max, 83–84
what of purpose, 160–66, *161, 162, 163, 164*
When Walls Become Doorways: Creativity and the Transforming Illness (Zausner), 106
"Where Were We While the Pyramid Was Collapsing? At a Yoga Class" (Whippman), 7
Whippman, Ruth, 7
whole love, 137, 138–48

wholeness, xx, xxiv, xxx, xxxi, xxxiv, 22, 51, 119, 126, 148, 170, 174, 176, 191n, 221, 245
whole organism, xxviii, 86
whole person, xviii, xxviii, xxxi, xxxiv, 257–77
    growth, 92, 94, 100, 119, 136, 140, 144, 147, 159, 161, 163, 170, 175, 176, 183
    healthy transcendence, 215, 227, 249
    security, 10, 22, 37, 39, 58, 59, 69, 73, 78
wholesome transformation, 65
whole truth and peak experiences, 196
Why Buddhism Is True (Wright), xxxi
Why God Won't Go Away (Newberg), 200
why of purpose, 164–66, *165*
Wilber, Ken, 226
Wilde, Oscar, 142
Williams, Kevin, 122
"will to meaning," 156
"will to pleasure," 156
"will to power," 55, 156
wisdom and Theory Z, 226
Wisdom of Insecurity, The (Watts), 194
Wong, Paul, 238
worldview, xxxi, 97, 104, 210, 225, 226, 228, 229, 230
World War II, 85
"worthwhile pain," 156
Wright, Robert, xxxi
Wrosch, Carsten, 183
Wrzesniewski, Amy, 158, 181

X-Altruists, 168

Yaden, David, 121, 123, 198–201, 202, 203, 205–6, 206–7, 214
Yalom, Irvin D., xxxvii, 121, 236–37
Young, Kimball, 54

Zausner, Tobi, 106
Zhang, Jua Wei, 207

About the Author

Scott Barry Kaufman, Ph.D., is a humanistic psychologist who has taught at Columbia University, the University of Pennsylvania, New York University, and elsewhere. He received a Ph.D. in cognitive psychology from Yale University, and an M.Phil. in experimental psychology from the University of Cambridge under a Gates Cambridge Scholarship. He writes the column Beautiful Minds for *Scientific American* and hosts *The Psychology Podcast*, which has received more than ten million downloads. His writing has appeared in *The Atlantic* and *Harvard Business Review,* and his books include *Ungifted, Wired to Create* (with Carolyn Gregoire), *Twice Exceptional* (as editor), and *The Cambridge Handbook of Intelligence* (as coeditor). In 2015, he was named one of "Fifty Groundbreaking Scientists Who Are Changing the Way We See the World" by *Business Insider.*